A TREASURE-TROVE
OF
AMERICAN JEWISH HUMOR

A
Treasure-Trove
of
AMERICAN JEWISH
HUMOR

Edited by

HENRY D. SPALDING

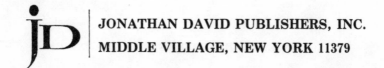

JONATHAN DAVID PUBLISHERS, INC.
MIDDLE VILLAGE, NEW YORK 11379

A TREASURE-TROVE
OF
AMERICAN JEWISH HUMOR

Copyright © 1976

by

Henry D. Spalding

Jonathan David Publishers
68-22 Eliot Avenue
Middle Village, New York 11379

Library of Congress Cataloging in Publication Data

Main entry under title:

A Treasure-trove of American Jewish humor

  1. Jewish wit and humor. 2. American wit and humor. I. Spalding, Henry D.
PN6231.J5T7   817'.008'0352   75-40192
ISBN 0-8246-0204-8

PRINTED IN THE UNITED STATES OF AMERICA

ACKNOWLEDGMENTS

My sincere thanks go to Dorothy H. Rochmis, editor of *Israel Today*, Los Angeles, for her gracious permission to again use the many Yiddish, Hebrew and Russian words and phrases which appear in the glossary of this book, many of which were originally prepared for the *Encyclopedia of Jewish Humor* (1969). I have added a number of new items to the glossary and, of course, if there are any errors in interpretation they are mine, not Dorothy's.

My deep thanks are also conveyed to a considerate and dedicated gentleman, Leopold Fechtner, author and Curator of the Museum of Humor, Kew Gardens, New York, for his kind permission to quote from his book, *American Wit and Gags*, and for his continued interest in this work.

Literally, scores of other people—far too many to mention here—gave unstintingly of their knowledge, time and effort, and their contributions will be found on many of these pages. In fact, all parts of this book which do not meet with your approval may be attributed to them.

Finally, as a writer who believes in pursuing his craft without heed to the obstacles in his path, I humbly acknowledge my debt of inspiration to the publishers of *Uncle Tom's Cabin*, a book written under the most trying circumstances by Harriet Beecher's toe.

HENRY D. SPALDING

PREFACE

What with all the introductions and background data which preceed each of the following chapters, I see no compelling reason to make a big hoo-hah of this preface. In any event, it has been my long-held opinion that a preface is like parsley—it looks good but, really, who needs it?

Nowadays, it seems to be the fashion for writers to tell a little something about themselves. According to the professors at such prestigious Ivy-League centers of higher learning as Harvard and CCNY, this is called author-reader identity. It is no longer enough that I wrote a book and for which you paid out good money—we are now exhorted to "communicate" with each other or else accept the scorn of the academic community.

Well, as my dad used to say, "a little rappaport never hurt anybody," so, if I must, I must . . . Perhaps my autobiography may help while away the lonely hours should you ever get trapped at the bottom of a mine shaft, or stuck in a subway car between stations under the East River.

Here, then, is my life story—unexpurgated, uncensored and uninvited:

As a boy on New York's East Side, back in the early 1920's, I was considered an intellectual because of my high forehead. Nobody loved me in that *Galitzianer* neighborhood because my people came from Russia, but I looked like a *Litvak*. My playmates would tease me because I said *azay* for *azoi*, *pittehr* for *pootehr* and *gornisht* for *gornit*. Talk about *tsuris!* Everyone else knew from what's what and who's who, but I didn't even know what's *dus* and where's *dorten*. This was a life?

I began to give serious thought to romance shortly after my *Bar Mitzvah* when I met Goldie. At first I thought she was just another boy with bee-stings on her chest, but when she explained to me the difference, I knew in my heart that if I ever stopped hating girls she'd be the first I stopped hating. When we started going steady she was so sweet I could've eaten her up—later I was sorry I didn't. As she grew older, Goldie became a Women's Libber who went to the joan instead of the john, and we gradually parted company in several directions. When she ran off with Louie the Lox King, I was inconsolable, and, in desperation, almost ran for Congress, but my pride stopped me. So, there I was, so young, so handsome, but with no girl or job—a failure.

Then I got mad! I asserted myself! What was I?—some kind of

Moishe Pippik to be such a failure? Me, with my high forehead? Who needs bee-stings? I'll go on to bigger things! Right then and there I vowed to keep my shoulder to the wheel, my hand to the plow my nose to the grindstone, my ear to the ground, my eye on the rainbow, and pray I shouldn't, God forbid, get a sacroiliac. So I got a job with the CIA (*Chassidic Information Association*) extracting venom from editors, and teaching typesetters how to read. But I quit when I found out they, too, didn't know what's *dus* and where's *dorten*, either.

"Nu" I thought, "I'll strike out on my own. Maybe I can be a famous inventor. Let's see, how about a stepladder without steps for washing basement windows; or a sprinkling can without holes for people who prefer artificial flowers? Aha, maybe I could go on the stage and tell a few jokes. Another Jack Benny, yet! Hmmm, how does that one go about the crook who got inside the house by climbing *intruder* window? *Feh!* That joke is for the Polish navy. Well, how about the *shnook* who wanted to buy his girl a lipstick, but didn't know the size of her mouth? Nah, I can't be a comedian—I can never remember jokes. But—wait a minute!— maybe I could write them down! Write? Who, *me?*

"*Eureka! Bonzai! A mazel auf Columbus!* That's it! I'll write down the jokes for a book! I'll be a big author! I'll show them what's *dus* and where's *dorten!* I'll get so rich, I'll have a double-decker bathtub so I can sing duets with my guests! I'll have monogrammed money! I'll have wall-to-wall carpets in the garage, and a five-room kitchen!"

You should excuse me, but finally I'm so laughing. I never did get rich, but I wrote a few books and I lived happily ever after. And you know something?—every once in a while, when I hear the tinkling of ice cubes in a glass, or the gurgling of a brook, or the splashing of a waterfall, I get kind of misty-eyed, and I think of Goldie—and her joan.

TABLE OF CONTENTS

INTRODUCTION

Just as man has always devised new schemes on the graves of a thousand disappointments, many Old World Jewish jokes emitted their sparks of wit on the flintstone of tragedy. In America, however, with past agonies receding from racial memory, the people's humor assumed a new and vibrant quality that mirrored the pulsating energy of what was to them, quite literally, the Land of Liberty that had for so long filled their dreams. This humor cannot yet be termed a uniquely American art form, carrying, as it does, the still-fertile seeds of its European origins— seeds which were brought to our shores by hundreds of thousands of bright-eyed immigrants in the present and past centuries. However, it is clearly in the process of evolution and there will come a time when it will be recognized as distinctly native to the United States.

American Jewish humor began with the early colonial settlers, the Sephardic Jews who first arrived in New Amsterdam (now New York) from Brazil in 1654, aboard the *St. Charles*, otherwise known as the Jewish *Mayflower*. Not generally realized, their descendants, multiplied by later-arriving Sephardim, constituted a majority of the Jewish citizenry in the Northern Continent of this hemisphere for more than 200 years. To them we attribute the Oriental mystique, the subtle artistry of expression, the continuity of the ancient exempla and even the Moorish influence of the fables which are still evident in American Jewish humor.

The influx of German Jewish newcomers was next to exert its influence upon the people's humor in the United States. This tide began as early as 1815, but it was not until 1848, when the liberal rebellion in Germany was crushed and the oppression of Jews in that country was resumed, that they joined in a concerted flight to the New World. That human flow did not abate until thirty years later, in 1880. The German Jewish contribution to the humor of their coreligionists in America was an urbanity and worldliness that differed markedly from the more traditional type that existed here. Yet, in time, the sophistication of the German Jews and the gentle wisdom of the earlier Sephardim coalesced into a rare form of humor that was at once intellectual, progressive and reverent—a far cry from the caricatures of Jewish humor carried in the press of that day.

But the most durable and certainly the most pervasive influence upon American Jewish humor began with the immense wave of immigration from Russia during the last third of the 19th century. There, the familiar pattern of persecution rose to new and vicious heights under the reign of Tsar Alexander III, who promulgated the infamous "May Laws" and encouraged widespread terrorism against the Jews. The frequent *pogroms* and the anti-Jewish riots of 1881 resulted in a mass exodus of Russian Jews to America. Between 1881 and 1900, some 600,000 Jews of Eastern Europe, including the oppressed of Poland, Rumania, Hungary, Lithuania and other countries in that region, found a haven of refuge in the United States. But the persecutions did not cease. In Russia, especially, violent *pogroms* followed one upon the other, taking their heavy toll in Jewish lives and added misery for the survivors. Then followed the massacres by the "Black Hundreds,"* and the Russian Revolution, precipitating the flight of nearly a million more Jews to the hospitable shores of the United States.

The 200,000 Jews of Sephardic and German origins who had arrived earlier were now completely inundated by the two million of their brethren from Eastern Europe. This was the era of "melting pot" America, symbolized by the Statue of Liberty and which was inscribed with the immortal sonnet by Emma Lazarus:

> Give me your tired, your poor,
> Your huddled masses yearning to breathe free,
> The wretched refuse of your teeming shore,
> Send these, the homeless, tempest-tost to me.
> I lift my lamp beside the golden door!

Why have I delved into this seemingly irrelevant background of agony suffered by the Russian and other Jews of Eastern Europe? Because therein lies the paradox! Those harried, persecuted and plundered people, whose beginnings in this country were marked by the direst poverty, gave to American Jewish humor its warmth, its deep compassion and its joyful optimism. And these lovely and loving qualities, added to and diffused with those of the Sephardic and German Jews, formed the bedrock of the robust humor we know today.

American Jewish humor is a social documentation of the people's history in the United States, characterized by its playful observation of past events as well as a comic view of the present. Most history, however, is autopsy. But Jewish humor is vivesection, its razor-sharp edges honed on the whetstone of stark reality. Yet, it is not all sardonic and trenchant. As we shall see, most Jews do not spend their lives in somber thought, using their wit as a cloak to hide a "message" or "moral." They also know how to laugh for the sake of good, earthy laughter itself. It is that lighthearted, sunny nature which is the essence of this book.

In these pages you will be introduced to a host of very pleasant people—to say nothing of an assortment of Jewish ghosts and such denizens of the animal world as Zelda the Hebrew zebra, a fox named Kluger and a skunk named Schmock—humorous Sephardic fables that

---

* Bands of ruffians organized by the Tsarist government to perpetrate new *pogroms* upon the Jews.

brought laughter to the tiny Jewish community in the Revolutionary War period. Most of the tales which revolve around such figures as Two-Gun Tannenbaum, the fastest bum in the West, sprang from the imagination of a creative, fun-loving people, but others are true anecdotes by and about specific Jewish Americans, sparkling with the gems of wit and drollery that have made Jewish humor ring out through the centuries.

You will meet here such diverse characters as Bret Harte, Henrietta Szold, Rabbi Stephen M. Wise, Otto Guggenheim, David Sarnoff, Bernard Baruch, Felix Frankfurter, Louis Brandeis, Gertrude Stein, Albert Einstein and many others, some of whom are not usually associated with humor. Most of these older, true anecdotes are published here for the first time, and I must again thank the families and descendants of these historical personalities for their painstaking and time-consuming research of names, locales and dates, all of which immeasurably strengthened and speeded the preparation of my original manuscript.

There is yet another mirthful surprise in store for the reader who believes that slapstick comedy was invented in Hollywood or that zany antics are the exclusive property of modern youth. In these pages you will find a number of uproarious adventures by such stalwart figures as Hayman Levy, the largest fur trader in all the American colonies; Mrs. Rebecca Hayes and her son, Lt. David Hayes, who served under General Washington, and which may well be the first *Yiddishe* mama joke in the United States; Haym Salomon, the beloved Revolutionary War patriot whose financial support of the infant American government resulted in his own impoverishment; Mordecai Manuel (Major) Noah, the writer-statesman who attempted to establish a City of Refuge in the United States for the world's oppressed Jews. And here too are such famous families of early Judaica Americana as the Seixas, the Mendozas, the Franks of Philadelphia and the Sheftalls of Georgia. These and many other Jews played an important role in the shaping of America's destiny, and they now reach out across the centuries in a symbolic clasping of hands, bridging the past with the present, a merry twinkle in their eyes and a smile upon their lips.

A word about the preparation of this volume:

No one knows precisely when the first Jewish book of humor came into being. The *Book of Delight,* issued in the year 1200 by Joseph Zabara, believed to have been a physician of Barcelona, and the *Ma'aseh Book,* a 16th century collection of fables, legends and myths, are early examples of the people's fun-loving nature. In recent times, a number of works devoted to Jewish humor of all nations appeared, including my own *Encyclopedia of Jewish Humor* (1969). However, for reasons which I cannot fathom, no single volume devoted solely to the humor of *American* Jews had ever been published until the issuance of this present book. Consequently, as with any pioneering effort, I had no guidelines to indicate the content or direction that would be most entertaining to the reader and still fulfill the requirements of serious authorship.

For example, what do we mean by authentic *American* Jewish

humor? Is it enough to say that it comprises those humorous anecdotes and witticisms which are told by Jews to other Jews and which revolve around Jewish subject matter? But what is meant by Jewish subject matter? And what of the use of accented English? Should dialect jokes be deleted altogether? These and other perplexing questions are discussed in the introductions to each of the following chapters, but it is only fair to confess that any author's opinion is subjective—no matter what he may say publicly. In my case, this book represents the offspring of a not-too-clandestine love affair with my people, and like any father, I hope to be forgiven for all lapses of objectivity.

The original manuscript of this volume contained 71 categories and 119 sub-classifications—far too unwieldy for a single work. Subsequently, these were consolidated into the present 36 chapters, each bearing up on a distinctive facet of Jewish life or upon qualities of character or personality. The jokes and quips which were translated from the *Yiddish* are so indicated, but the reader will note that I have included the *Yiddish* terms and expressions in many of the stories exactly as they were related to me in the first place—some when I was a boy, and just beginning to collect examples of Jewish folklore and humor. The adults who attended evening classes at Cooper Union, Workmen's Circle or citizen education groups did not speak like Harvard professors, and, if for nothing else than authenticity and the preservation of its *Yiddishkeit*, I thought it best to write as closely to their original telling as possible. For those not familiar with the language employed, I have appended a glossary of the *Yiddish*, Hebrew, Russian, Polish and other words and phrases used throughout this book, prepared, let me hasten to add, by the knowledgable Dorothy Rochmis. The glossary is an expanded version of the one she compiled for the *Encyclopedia of Jewish Humor*.

This volume, obviously, is by no means confined to the turn-of-the-century inhabitants of New York's East Side. As to the *krechtz*, or groan, which permeated much of Old World wit, American Jewish humor may be delivered in a minor key but it has long since discarded its hair-shirt and is anything but a lamentation. I do not deny, of course, that many of the newcomers were bottled up in their tenement-prisons—as effectively pickled in their ghetto environment as a cucumber in brine. Nevertheless, there were times when the ghetto-dweller stood on the tiptoe of expectation as he dreamed and planned of entering that "other" America which he knew existed "out there." The jokes they told echoed those yearnings and ambitions, and many of their mirthful stories remain as cheerful remembrances that have not lost their appeal to this day.

Not all humor evokes laughter; sometimes it produces a wry and occasionally a bitter smile. Through their lore, the Jewish people reveal themselves in a sort of musical pattern adorned with the secret pangs and passions of their innermost selves. But there are times when the music is a cacophony formed by dark memories of their past. These thoughts are the dogs that bark within their Jewish hearts. And it is these which they have siezed by their tails and made to dance to the tune of an old Italian's hurdy-gurdy on Orchard Street. Sometimes the music cannot be gentled because the barking chaos of racial remembrance will not be crushed into silence and yelps its agony like a gutter mongrel hit by a speeding taxi. A few of these momentary gasps are presented here, but on the whole, the music is joyous, lilting and filled with bubbling delight. The reason is clear enough: Down through history the Jew has always managed to find the medicine of humor within the mist and swirl of pain and become the merriest hypochondriac who ever danced the charleston on Parnassus. It was that ability which helped to prevent him from becoming a jacketed and trousered neurosis.

To its credit, Jewish jokes and witticisms are usually told or written in simple language, without the abstruse stories or intellectual crossword puzzles that are unintelligible to those who do their thinking in plain English. And this is where the author parts company with the academic folklorists, the professional joke-analyzers and the psychologists who are bound hand and foot, tongue and mind, to the mumbo-jumbo of motifs, leitmotifs, patterns and other esoteric jargon which they have inherited from past generations of dryasdusts. What they fail to see is that humor is a social *history* of a people, not a social *problem* that calls for the psychiatrist's couch. Humor which is studied under a Freudian micro-scope is humor without laughter.

In this rather extensive collection I have tried to include only those jokes and flashes of wit which I believed to be genuinely funny, which do not insult your intelligence, and which are truly representative of America's Jewish people. But whether the attempt merits a *kaddish* or a *mazel tov* is your decision to make.

Shalom!

HENRY D. SPALDING

January 15, 1976
Hollywood, California

1

Hearts and Flowers and Fiddle Music

INTRODUCTION

Someone once said, quite correctly, that humor is no laughing matter. The same might also be said for love.

What brooding secrets are hidden in the hearts and minds of lovers—and in our case, Jewish lovers? What secret yearnings haunt their dreams and drive their primitive passions?

No matter how one turns and twists his words or thoughts, one conclusion is inevitable: Love is love; and Jewish love is the same as gentile love—only more so. When a man finally decides to take that fateful step into matrimony, it is not always at a time of romantic fervor under a bower of roses.

The Jewish man or woman sees love from its practical as well as its esoteric side. A Yiddish maxim tells us, "Love tastes sweet, but only with bread." Another solemnly declares, "A heart without love is like a pocket without money." And, in 1831, Disraeli said, "Where we do not respect, we do not love." Sometimes, the sayings get a little out of hand. One enthusiastic biblical sage made the rather startling declaration, "Love covers all transgressions." Bluebeard might have taken that passage literally, but, then, look what it got him. And he wasn't even Jewish.

But, if Jewish love can be practical, it can also soar on the wings of gossamer beauty. It tells the world that the magic of first love lies in believing that it will never end. "Every goose is a swan in the eyes of a lover," states the Talmud. "You are not loved when you are lovely, but when you are loved, you are found to be lovely," wrote the romantic Boern in 1824. Today, it seems, many of us appear more anxious to hide our love than our hate.

The gifted poet, Louis Ginsberg, understood the need for tender expression. In his poem, "Song," published in *The Liberator* (1930), Ginsberg cautioned the undemonstrative lover with this quatrain:

Love that is hoarded, moulds at last,
Until we know, someday,
The only thing we ever have,
Is what we gave away.

1

The most enduring love is the love that laughs, as George Jean Nathan once pointed out. Had I been one of the early settlers in the New World, I would not have chronicled the experiences of the long voyage across the uncharted ocean or even the later privation of the colonists. Instead, I would have written a romantic novel, *The Shenandoah Shammes and his Shayneh Shikseleh*, the story of how pious Pincus the Pilgrim pursued and proposed to pretty Pocahantas between Purim and Passover and proudly produced the first *parve* papoose on Pitkin Avenue.

Or, as Samson murmured ecstatically to Delilah while she gave him a non-union haircut, "Love-shmove—as long as you really care!"

H.D.S.

While we're on the subject, let us bear in mind that true love can come to us no matter what our age might be. For example, eighty-five-year-old Mr. Becker fell in love with a grandmotherly lady of seventy-five. They decided to marry.

"Do you take this woman for your bride?" the rabbi asked the faltering groom.

Replied Mr. Becker: "I should only live so long."

*   *   *

The Greenbergs were one of a handful of Jewish families in Sumter, South Carolina. The nearest community with a sizable Jewish population was in Columbia, about 65 miles away.

Sally, their 17-year-old daughter (and only child) was very attractive, and she had no trouble getting dates. In fact she was the most popular girl in her senior class at Sumter High. But, Mr. and Mrs. Greenberg were not pleased. Not one of Sally's boyfriends was Jewish, and her parents were terribly worried. The thought of their daughter marrying a *goy* was extremely disturbing, and it kept them up nights, talking and talking about their problem.

They finally decided to try to interest their daughter in going to the Hebrew University in Israel. They broached the subject.

"I will not!" she cried. "All my friends are here!"

They begged Sally. They pleaded. And, finally, they arrived at a compromise.

She would go for her freshman year—on condition that they would promise not to make a fuss if she wanted to come back to the States after the year was up.

All agreed, and all were happy.

At the end of August, the Greenbergs drove to New York and put Sally on an El Al flight to Israel.

Sally settled down in a comfortable dormitory room at the Hebrew University and the term began.

Everything seemed lovely. Her letters to the family were pleasant, although uneventful. The letters Sally received, likewise, carried a happy tone.

The first term drew to a close, and a very upsetting letter was received by the Greenbergs from Sally. They started to read the letter and could hardly believe their eyes.

> Dear Mother and Dad,
> I'm sorry I haven't been writing too frequently, but what with exams just over, and everything else, I haven't had much time. I hope you haven't worried. I've been very busy, but I have been very happy too—except for one thing. I just got my grades, and I haven't been doing too well. I flunked Math and Biology and Hebrew. I got a D in History and Social Studies, and a C in Music Appreciation. I hope this won't upset you too much. I'll try better next term. Don't worry. I promise.
>
> Mom—I never told you this before, but I met a wonderful, handsome boy in my class, and we're planning to get married soon. I know you'll like him. So will you, Dad.
>
> He is really good-looking, and rather dark-skinned, but not as dark as most Arabs. I met his parents, and they are very nice. You'll like them. They are not Moslems like most other Arabs; they're Catholics.

Mr. Greenberg gasped as he read these words, and clutched at his left breast. Mrs. Greenberg almost fainted.

"There's more to the letter on the other side of the page," said Mr. Greenberg. "What does she say there," he added angrily.

Mrs. Greenberg composed herself and read on.

> Everything I wrote on the other side of the page isn't true. I made it all up. The only part that *is* true is that I failed Math and Biology and Hebrew; and I did get a D in History and Social Studies.

* * *

For those loving hearts who prefer all their music integrated in one "swell foop," we are pleased to pass along a new trend in Reform Jewish marriage ceremonies, as reported in the *Zion Chronicle:*

"Cantor Shamir Baumgarten's wedding was absolutely beautiful and quite traditional, except for the fact that the cantor himself sang 'I Love You Truly' to his blushing bride, while the organ played some Strauss waltzes."

* * *

We're not thoroughly convinced that this was merely a writing error and not a peculiar papa, but here's another news item from *Zion Chronicle:*

"The bride was given away by her father wearing a white satin gown with a long train."

* * *

Poetry time again, dear young lovers:
A romantic Jewish young Mr.
Had a girl and he often Kr.
But he asked her to wed,
And she solemnly said:
"I can never be more than a Sr."

* * *

"My boyfriend's name is Dorfman, but I call him Draftsman," explained the girl with a trace of annoyance in her voice. "Every time I mention marriage he draws the line."

* * *

He was debonnaire, he was handsome, he was rich. He approached the lady's table and bowed.

"Madam," he said in a cultured voice, "may I join you?"

"*Join* me!" she screeched in maidenly horror. "Am I coming apart?"

* * *

Talk about marital compatibility! One of those proverbial marriages that are made in heaven occurred when Tillie and Willie said "I do."

Tillie happens to be a hairdresser and Willie a sculptor. She curls and dyes; he makes faces and busts.

* * *

Worldshaking Events Department: This is to advise our readers that there is no substance to the gossip concerning Moshe Dayan and Zza Zza Gabor.

But, as the man said when the boarding house blew up, "Roomers are flying."

* * *

He was a persistent suitor and very anxious to marry the girl. For the tenth time he proposed to her, but, to be painfully frank about it, she couldn't stand the man.

"Sweetheart," he said ardently, "I would go to the ends of the earth for you."

"That's what you say now," snapped the girl, "but what guarantee do I have that you'd stay there?"

* * *

When Gimpel the grocer arrived at his lodge meeting on Saturday evening, his best buddy quickly noticed his sad expression.

"How come you're looking so downhearted, Gimp?" asked the friend.

"I lost my girl," said Gimpel.

"I'm sorry to hear that," said the friend sympathetically. "And I'm surprised, too. I thought she was interested in you."

"So did I," answered Gimpel sorrowfully. "But, last night, I told her I'd lost my capital, and right off she lost her interest."

* * *

After repeatedly warding off her date's amorous advances throughout the evening, the pretty young thing decided to put her foot down.

"See here," she demanded, "this is positively the last time I'm going to tell you 'no.' "

"Fine!" enthused her date. "Now, maybe we can start making a little progress."

* * *

The Orchard Street Gezenge, Marshe and Tentze Dramatic Society

Presents

GENZINEH GRIBBENES
—A One-Act Play—

The Distinguished Cast

Stella . . . . Constant Bleeding
Sam . . . . Borscht Karloff

Stella: Did anyone ever tell you what a handsome, brilliant remarkable man you are?

Sam (eagerly): No.

Stella: So tell me, where in the world did you ever get the idea?

* * *

Baruch Beeman, the bagel baker of Bedford Avenue, received a letter from his son in far-off California stating that he had fallen in love and was planning to marry.

Baruch and his wife were understandably concerned. Their son was studying medicine at the University of California at Los Angeles, and he still had a year to go before graduation. How, they asked, could he support a wife on an intern's wages? And wouldn't marriage at this time interfere with his studies?

"Maybe she's so beautiful our boy was carried away," suggested Mrs. Beeman.

"Could be," her husband agreed, remembering the passions of his own youth. "I'll bet she's gorgeous!"

At his wife's worried insistence, Baruch flew to Los Angeles to see his son and future daughter-in-law, but, when he returned to New York, Mrs. Beeman took one look at his downcast face and her heart sank.

"What's the matter?" she cried. "The girl's a *shikse*?"

"No, she's Jewish all right," he moaned. "But that face—*oy vay!*"

"What does she look like?"

"That girl would be a perfect model for Picasso," he said almost sobbing. "The only thing she has in her favor are her bright red lips. The trouble is, she has a nose to match. Did you ever see a girl who parts her teeth in the middle? Believe me, even when she looks good, she looks terrible."

"*Gevald!* Why would our son want to marry such a girl?"

"By me there's only one answer," said Baruch, a tiny note of encouragement in his voice. "With a face like hers, it's a million to one she's rich."

A thought occurred to Mrs. Beeman, and she actually smiled.

"With so much money she could afford a face-lift."

He shook his head. "Listen, you haven't seen that girl. Her face looks like it was done up in curlers. No doctor could lift it—he'd have to lower her body."

"What are we going to do about it?" wailed Mrs. Beeman.

"Nothing. They say they have much in common."

"What's in common?"

"I'm not sure," replied Baruch uncertainly, "but the way it was explained to me, "she has a bad kidney and, as a medical man, our boy is fascinated with it." He sighed and added, "I'm also afraid they're both in love with the same girl!"

* * *

" . . . and as far as I'm concerned, *Mister* Oscar Kaplan, you won't be needing a fan this summer—I'm giving you the air."

* * *

Clara was simply ecstatic as her suitor, on his knees, proposed marriage. Never had he or anyone else spoken so beautifully to her. His voice was like a tender caress, his words as delicate as rose petals.

"Oh darling," she breathed, "I wish this would never end. But I'm still not sure. Let me hear that part again where you realize you're not half good enough for me."

* * *

Julius: How many Cammandments are there?
Julia: Ten.
Julius: What would happen if you—er—well—you know—if you broke one of them?
Julia (encouragingly): So, there'd be nine.

* * *

It was Saturday evening, and Joe was without a date. He was a good looking enough young fellow but he had just returned from military service overseas, and had lost his earlier contacts. He phoned his older brother who agreed to supply him with a girlfriend for the evening. Joe met his blind date, took her to a dark restaurant for dinner, then to a dark movie, and finally returned home in a dark mood. He immediately reached for the telephone and dialed his brother's number.

"Hey, what's the idea of setting me up with that girl?" protested Joe indignantly. "Talk about monsters!"

"What was the matter with her?"

"Are you kidding? One eye two inches higher than the other, the left ear way up to here, the other way down there, the chin crooked, the neck . . ."

"Now wait a minute," interrupted the brother. "It's just a matter of taste. Either you *like* Picasso or you don't!"

* * *

Raleigh Rosenbloom, the romantic young bachelor of Palm Beach, who was also a big spender, telephoned the girl he had just met the night before. She was not only gorgeous, but had also proved to be a real swinger. He wanted another date. To his surprise, however, she turned him down.

"How come you're refusing to go out with me tonight?" he demanded. "Only yesterday you said there was something about me you adored."

"There was, baby," she crooned in her husky voice, "but you spent it!"

* * *

Barney the Bagel King had trouble spending the interest on his money. Among his treasures were a palatial home in Palm Springs, California, a townhouse in New York, a yacht and—his most cherished possession—the famous and beautiful actress, Bubbles Bernstein of Beverly Hills. He was really in love with her.

Then, the bottom dropped out of the stock market, and overnight all of Barney's wealth disappeared. The ex-millionaire was broke.

Sadly, he called at her apartment to break the depressing news.

"I lost everything," he told her mournfully. No bank account, no stocks, no yacht, no house—nothing! I haven't got a dime left."

She kissed him sweetly and murmured, "You may have lost everything else, darling, but not my love."

"You really mean that?" he exclaimed in an ecstacy of joy.

"Of course, dear. And I want you to know I'll always remember you with affection."

* * *

It was Selma's birthday and she was watching the six o'clock news on television while her room-mate, Maxine, was thumbing through a magazine. Suddenly, it occurred to Maxine that Selma had not been invited out for this gala occasion.

"Don't you have a date this evening?" she asked.

"No," answered Selma sadly. "I'm afraid I lost my boyfriend."

"What happened?"

"Someone told him that I had an affair with another man before I met him. He just stopped calling me."

"Don't let that worry you," counseled Maxine. "You just go to him in a perfectly straightforward, honest way, and lie about the whole thing!"

* * *

There are very few humorous stories about promiscuity among Jewish girls of past generations. Here is one of those rarities, circa 1930:

Rabbi Isaacs was quite fond of the Shapiro family whose members were longtime congregants of his Temple. So it was understandable that he would react sympathetically when they asked him to have a serious talk with their daughter, Rachel, who was unmarried, but pregnant again for the third time.

He confronted the young lady on the following evening.

"I can't understand how a nice Jewish girl could allow such a disgraceful thing to happen," he began severely. "Three times yet! I suppose the babies all have different fathers?".

"Oh, no!" said Rachel. "It's the same fellow."

"He's single, this man?"

"Certainly. You think I'd go with a married man?"

"Then why don't you marry him?" demanded the rabbi.

"Well, frankly," Rachel answered with complete candor, "he doesn't appeal to me."

* * *

Last line heard on a bus:
" . . . so I said goodbye to him with a permanent wave."

* * *

The book critics whose stuff appears in the *New York Times*, the *New York Review of Books* and other influential papers seldom give favorable reviews to books which do not include a little poetry. To satisfy those gentlemen, and assure ourselves a favorable write-up, we herewith quote some high-class prose, penned by Theodore M. Bernstein, Columbia University, in 1929, and aimed at the intelligentsia, to wit:

> Is oo mama's umsey-wumsey?
> Does oo love her lipsy-ipsies?
> Creepy-eepy closey-osey,
> Hugsy-wugsy tightsy-wightsy.
> Honey, bunny, little sweetie,
> Darling-arling, sugar-ugar,
> Willsie always lovesie-ovesie?
> Pettsey-ettsey, holdsey-oldsey.
> When I hearie-earie suchie
> Talksie-alksie in my earsie,
> Then you bet I knowsie-owsie
> Thatsie-atsie spring is heresie.

* * *

After one year of marital bliss:

She: Whenever I talk to you, it's like a dog barking. You never answer me.

He: It's not true! When's the last time you barked and I didn't answer?

* * *

It had been three years since Morris left for the battlefields of Europe during World War II. Most of the time, he had been stationed in France. And now that he had returned home, he could hardly wait to display his newly-acquired French vocabulary to Jennie, his best girl.

The autumn evening had turned chilly, but inside the apartment the lights were low and the hi-fi was playing soft music. If the room was a bit drafty, neither of them noticed. Morris turned to Jennie.

"Djhonveeyev," he murmured caressingly, coming as near to the French pronunciation of "Genevieve" as he was able. *"Je t'adore."*

"Why, you lazy thing," snapped Jenny. "Shut it yourself!"

* * *

Velvel was aghast to learn that his sister, Odelia, had decided to marry Al Scharf, a nightclub comic.

"You call that guy a comic?" Velvel demanded. "Believe me, you can get more laughs watching a guy fix a flat tire. He's an arrogant, pushy slob—the type who gets into a revolving door behind you and comes out first on the other side. He's not for you, Sis. That character couldn't cheer up a laughing hyena."

"You're just jealous because he's a self-made man," Odelia retorted.

"Well, if that's what he told you, I gotta hand it to him," acknowledged Velvel grudgingly. "At least he's taking all the blame!"

* * *

Karl the Knaidel King of Kansas City had everything in life that a man could ask for, except for one thing—he wanted a grandson to carry on the family name, to say nothing of the family business. So, he was understandably happy when his bachelor son told him, one evening, that he had fallen in love and was planning to marry.

"It's a smart thing you're doing," advised Karl. "Until a man marries he's incomplete."

He pondered the wisdom of his own statement for a moment or two and then added solemnly, "He's not only complete—he's finished!"

* * *

Murray and Judith both liked the same things, but the problem was that she didn't like him. For a whole year he pestered her to marry him, but was always met with the same rebuttal: "Who needs you?"

"Why do you keep asking that silly question?" he finally demanded.

"It's not a question, it's a statement," she snapped. "I need you like Rembrandt needed number paintings!"

* * *

If the powers-that-be ever decide to grant an Academy Award for diplomacy, the Oscar will—or should—be given to Mannie Margolies, a salesman with a company headquartered in Cincinnati. Hearken to this titillating tale of triumphant tact.

Mannie was out on his first date with a woman he had met only a few days earlier. Seeing her in the daytime he had imagined her to be in her mid-thirties, but now, by candle-light, and after a few drinks, he was having second thoughts. Perhaps it was her carefully-applied make-up, or it might have been her girlish giggles. Whatever the reason, he admitted he might have been mistaken. Right now she looked younger than he had figured.

As though reading his mind, the lady batted her newly-purchased eyelashes, threw back her shoulders so that her falsies might make a good impression, and peeked at him over her glass of wine.

"I'll bet you could never guess my age," she said, her voice oozing with coyness. "How old do you think I am?"

"I don't know," said Mannie, gallantly rising to the occasion, "but whatever your age, you certainly don't look it!"

* * *

"Now see here, young lady," bellowed the outraged father, "I demand to know who that fellow was that you were kissing last night on the front porch."

"It all depends, papa," replied the girl calmly, "what time?"

* * *

The young man finally summoned up enough courage to ask the girl's father for his daughter's hand in marriage.

"I'll have to think about it for a while," said the stern old father. "And I'm sure I needn't remind you that whoever marries my daughter gets a rare and beautiful prize.

"Oh, really?" exclaimed the fellow, brightening up. "How's chances of seeing it now!"

* * *

"That was some blind date you fixed for me last night," fumed Tobias. "Was she homely!"

"Aw, she wasn't all that bad," protested the fixer-upper.

"Listen," grated Tobias, "she should hire a pickpocket to lift her face, and someone should steal her dog-food! Tell me, who does her nails —a gardener? And with a mustache yet! I've seen girls like her before, but I always had to pay admission."

"Sorry I introduced you," muttered the friend.

"You oughtta be sorry! And what's the idea of telling me she was a model?"

"But she was!" declared the friend. "For five years she modeled for Preparation-H."

* * *

"And now," said the father, raising a glass of *schnapps* aloft, "I propose a toast to this, the happiest day of your life."

"But, Pop, I'm not getting married until tomorrow," protested the son.

"Yeah," said the father, "I know!"

* * *

It was a happy morning for Bernice the bookkeeper. Only the night before, her fiance had given her a beautiful diamond engagement ring and, now, as she seated herself at her desk, she was sure that the other girls in the office would comment on her new sparkler. To her chagrin, however, no one noticed it. She gestured with her left hand every time she spoke; she tried every subtle trick to call attention to the lovely adornment; but without success.

At lunchtime, Bernice and the other girls spread their sandwiches on their desks, removed the tops of their paper cups of coffee brought to them by the office-boy, and started to chat—as was their custom. But still, no one mentioned the diamond on her finger.

Finally, Bernice was siezed with an inspiration.

"Oh, my!" she exclaimed, waving her hand languidly in the air. "It's so hot in here! I think I'll take off my ring."

* * *

The girl regarded him with ill-concealed distaste.

"I'm sorry, Raymond," she said, "but I can't marry you."

"Why not?" demanded the lovesick swain. "Is there someone else?"

"Oh, Raymond," she sighed, "there *must* be!"

* * *

Extremes are drawn to extremes, and true love will push us to the outer dimensions of our human capacity. These are well known facts, and I cannot claim the honor of being the first to direct attention to them. But, at least they help introduce this story about the great Charles Steinmetz who, although a dwarf, was also the genius who helped fashion the General Electric Company into the kind, compassionate and humane conglomerate it is today. But, this tale has nothing to do with business or electrical wizardry. It is a love story.

Steinmetz, born in Germany in 1865, emigrated to the United States in 1889, with only ten dollars in his pocket. In 1893, he joined the engineering staff of General Electric in Schenectady, New York, where he carried out experiments that brought him great fame.

One afternoon, Steinmetz attended a circus performance, and while viewing the sideshow, he met and fell madly in love with the giantess, as athletic a person as any Olympic star ever was.

However, the lady was coy; she had been properly raised. Once, when he climbed a ladder, she wouldn't even let him hold her hand.

One Sunday morning in the spring, when the circus train was

preparing to leave, and with it the giantess, little Steinmetz realized he would have to act fast if he was ever going to keep her at his side. So, he invited her for a walk. Soon, they were strolling across rolling green fields. As they meandered in the soft, deep grass Steinmetz begged the lofty object of his affections for just one kiss. Finally, she yielded to his importunities, but in order for his eager lips to reach hers it would be necessary for her to kneel down. Merely bending over wouldn't do it for there still remained a hiatus of at least a foot between her face and his upturned lips.

She absolutely declined to kneel. In the first place, the posture was not dignified; in the second place the grass was damp, and she had on her smartest walking-skirt, made to order for her by the designers at Hirschberg's Tent and Awing Company. And there was no fence or large rock in sight upon which he might climb.

Desperation made the tiny man resourceful. As they approached a roadside blacksmith shop, he spied a huge, 300-pound anvil. At the sight of it, an inspiration entered his agile mind. He induced the fair one to back up against the side of the shop. He ascended the anvil and stood on tiptoe on its flat top. Then, as she bent forward, he was able to plant a chaste salute of affection upon her maidenly lips.

They continued their stroll; she, stepping along with her splendid strides; he, trotting alongside, his Lilliputian figure half hidden behind her swishing draperies. A mile or two further on, he begged for another kiss—just to seal the bargain their hearts had agreed upon.

"No, Charles," she said firmly. "One's enough for today."

"Only one more," he pleaded.

"No."

"You mean it?"

"I do."

"Absolutely? Positively? Your decision is final!"

"It is."

He gave vent to a deep sigh.

"Well then," Steinmetz said resignedly, "if that's the way you feel, there's no use my carrying this damn anvil around any longer!"

2

Martial Relations

INTRODUCTION

Marriage, in the traditional Jewish view, is a better prescription for what ails a person than chicken soup—and chicken soup has a time-tasted reputation. It might not be a real cure, but chances are pretty good that it will help. This analysis is especially applicable to the *nahr*—the foolish one—when it comes to setting his life straight. ("What! That *shlemiel*? Better he should marry!")

If a man is already married, it is pro-forma evidence of his wisdom. After all, look how many times Solomon stood under the *chuppeh*. This faith of the Jew in the curative powers of the marriage canopy is international, and has persisted since the earliest times, even though no one has ever discovered a simpleton who became a sage after the knot was tied.

This way of life—this attitude—is ingrained in the Jew. It is expressed at the strangest times. You may recall the historic visit of United Nations mediator Dag Hammarskjold to Israel at the time of the Suez blockade. The UN, as usual, was marching to the drumbeat of Egypt rather than that of Israel. Hammarskjold flew to Israel and went to see Prime Minister David Ben-Gurion and there he met B.G.'s wife, a woman who was more frank than diplomatic. "Listen, you are a nice man," said Paula to Hammarskjold, "so why don't you get married and leave Israel alone?"

Jewish wit being what it is, marriage was an easy solution, and Jewish literature abounds in cynical proverbs and caustic commentaries about wedlock. The Talmud ruefully states, "When love was strong, we could have made our bed on a sword's blade; now, when it has become weak, a bed of 60 cubits is not large enough for us." The sages were not above mixing a little humor with their declamations. Wrote one Talmudist: "A great man should not disdain to serve as best man to one of minor position. The Holy One, Blessed-be-He, was best man at Adam's wedding."

It is no secret that humor serves as a cloak for anger and indignation. We express our hostility indirectly—often with a derisive quip or a funny anecdote. And the smile or the laughter it evokes gives us a sense of vengeance fulfilled. We have gotten even! We have struck back! The feeling gives us more relief than Alka Seltzer.

If we are to believe the psychologists, and I suppose we should—as long as we don't make a habit of it—they tell us that even Sholem Aleichem reflected a degree of hostility in his humor: He once said: "I ask you, my friend: Who started all this business of marriage and wives?" This was his way of striking back. It also explains why Disraeli made the wry comment, "I have always thought that every woman should marry— and no man." He voiced his resentment with a smile, but Gloria Steinem would never have voted for him.

Considering all the marriages that were made in heaven and that culminated in the other place, they must be doing a big export business up there. We have entered the age of the gay divorcee and the unshackled, uninhibited ex-hubby. It is also the era of the liberated housewife. This means that her loving spouse is now entitled to change the baby's diapers and wash the dishes, but it does not necessarily mean that she need ever take out the garbage. As a liberated woman, she can now hang her stockings, pantyhose and other frillies on the shower-curtain rod, with the cold drip-drip tattooing hubby's bare bottom when he tries to sneak into the tub. But, if *he* is so thoughtless as to hang his underwear on the bedroom door-knob so he can find it in the morning, he is a male chauvinist (you-should-pardon-the-expression) "pig." He is just like *his* family. He is not *neat*! He is a *slob*! That's what happens when a decent, well-brought-up *Litvak* girl marries one of those *Galitzianers*! Sound familiar? Go make a joke and get it out of your system. Then kiss your wife—if she'll let you.

But, is all this really hostility, or is it simply good-natured *kibitzing*? Don't ask your friendly neighborhood marriage counselor. There are more divorced marriage counselors than there are divorced actors. Whatever the marital expert happens to know about connubial bliss, he learned from reading this chapter.

All this hostility hoopla has gone too far. There are undoubtedly times when we are hostile, but as a rule we are simply and innocently amused.

As an example, the New Testament tells us, "It is better to marry than to burn." In response, Jewish wit slides off at a tangent and retorts, "So what else is new?" But, the Jew is just as quick to read a funny meaning into his own literature. Take the "Palestine Bridal Song" as an illustration: "The bride: no powder, no rouge, no hair-do, yet a graceful gazelle." It is really a lovely phrase, but that impish sense of humor flashes a question in our mind: "If all brides are so beautiful, then why do they always wind up looking like Mrs. Khrushchev?"

H.D.S.

Hymie, the henpecked hubby of Houston Street, hoisted a hefty hooker of holiday happiness at "Herbie's Hangout," and tearfully told a tippler of his trials and tribulations with his spouse, Tillie.

"My wife doesn't understand me," moaned Hymie, who happened to be a linguistic innovator.

"Why don't you just assert yourself?" suggested the drinking companion curtly. "What are you, a man or a mouse?"

"I must be a man," sighed Hymie. "Tillie's afraid of mice."

*   *   *

The newspapers carried a number of stories about the nation's most beautiful actresses and the insignificant men they sometimes choose as husbands.

"I'll never be able to understand why the biggest *shnooks* always get the prettiest women," sighed the very-much-married Moishe.

"Why, darling," exclaimed the pleased and surprised wife, "what a very sweet compliment!"

*   *   *

"Rose, explain me something," said the girl's sister. "Your husband's name is Gedalia. So why do you always call him 'Abie'?"

"Because it fits him," sighed Rose. "He's everything I used to dream about—from A to B."

*   *   *

A TIFFANY TEEYATER PRESENTATION

The Distinguished Cast

Eve.................Pat Hand
Adam..............Paris Franz

Scene

The Garden of Eden

(Adam is speaking while Eve knits
baby-booties)

Adam: We had plums, we had oranges, we had pineapples, bananas, figs, pomegranates, nectarines, watermelons, cantaloupes, peaches—but no, *you* wanted an apple!

*   *   *

Joan and Jake were having another of their interminable arguments. This time it was about Jake's annoying habit of criticizing her family, and at the same time praising his own. The accusations grew so barbed that Joan burst into tears. Jake knew he had gone too far, and was immediately contrite.

"I'm sorry, honey," he said abjectly, "I really didn't mean all those nasty things I said about your family. In fact, if you want to know the honest truth, I like your mother-in-law much better than I do mine."

*   *   *

"What is a wife?" asks Oren, the oracle of Orchard Street, who likes to answer his own questions.

"A wife is a woman who stands by her husband through all the *tsuris* he wouldn't have had if he'd stayed single in the first place.

"Generally speaking, she's generally speaking," observes Oren. "She spends more time mending your ways than your socks. She's a dish-jockey who never has anything to wear, and has four closets to keep it in. She can dish it out, but she can't cook it.

"Still and all, she's never still at all, but make no mistake about it—a wife is a thing of beauty and a jaw forever!"

* * *

Feivel the furrier was talking to his partner over a cup of coffee.

"Tomorrow my wife leaves for two weeks to visit her mother on the West Coast."

"How about your own vacation?" queried the partner. "When does that start?"

"I just told you," explained Feivel. "Tomorrow!"

* * *

Schoenberg, the silk manufacturer, who had been married for twenty-five years, took council with one of his bachelor friends.

"It seems to me," he complained, "that my domestic affairs are slipping into a rut. I'm afraid my wife is getting bored with me. There doesn't seem to be any of the old romance left that we had in our early married life. I wish I knew what the problem could be."

"I can make a guess," said his confidant. "Do you still pay your wife those little attentions that you once did when you were courting her?"

'Well, no," confessed Schoenberg. "I can't say that I do."

"I thought as much," replied the friend. "Now this is my advice to you: Turn over a new leaf. Start this very day. Begin paying your wife some attention. Fuss over her just like you used to do when you first got engaged. Try to be a sweetheart to her instead of just a husband."

"Say, that's pretty good advice!" exclaimed Schoenberg. "Take my word, I'll do it!"

That evening, when he burst into the house, his arms laden with parcels, he planted a warm kiss upon the cheek of the astonished Mrs. Schoenberg and, in tones of well worked-up enthusiasm, he cried out: "This is going to be a big night for us, baby! Here's a five-pound box of candy for you and here's a dozen American Beauty roses. Now, I want you to slip into your best gown. I reserved a table at the Ritz-Carlton for dinner, and I ordered two seats for the concert at Carnegie Hall."

He stopped short and stared at his wife. Her face was pale and her lips were beginning to tremble. "What's the matter?" he asked.

"Well, to start with," she answered, "our daughter told me today she's interested in a *shaigetz.* Your aunt Clara arrived unexpectedly this morning for a visit. Our little Sammy was sent home from school with a bad cold. I lost an earring someplace while I was shopping, and now—now—" she burst into tears—"and now you have to come home drunk!"

* * *

Miriam was a good housekeeper, but this evening she had an early appointment with her dentist. The apartment was a mess so she interrupted her gambler-husband who was studying a race-track sheet.

"Do me a favor, Larry," she asked. "Straighten out the house while I'm gone."

Her hubby looked up in surprise. "Sure," he agreed. "Did somebody tilt it?"

* * *

We've heard of many optimists in our time, but Hollywood's Oren Opatashu is the mostest with the bestest. He went down to City Hall to find out when his marriage license expires.

* * *

"I love you truly."

"Only me?"

"Baby, I said *truly*, not *only*!"

* * *

Mrs. Silver and Mrs. Gold were gossiping over the back fence as they hung out the wash.

"My husband—ahh, such a faithful man," boasted Mrs. Silver. "He never even looks at another woman."

"The same with my husband," said Mrs. Gold. "He never chases after women either. He's too fine, too decent—too old!"

* * *

Phil Bernstein, the Bronx furniture retailer, was walking along Fordham Road when he encountered a woman who appeared vaguely familiar to him. He nodded his head in greeting.

"You're Mrs. Kovacs, aren't you?" he asked.

"That's me, in person," she replied.

"Aren't you a member of Hadassah?"

"For a good twenty years."

"Were you at the executive meeting today?"

"Certainly. Why are you asking?"

'Well, my wife was there also. She'll tell me all about it when I get home this evening, but I'd like to know now if she was one of the speakers."

"Hmm, I don't know your wife, but there was one short, stout lady who got up . . ."

"Yes-yes, that must have been my wife. Go on."

"She got up and said she couldn't find the words to express her feelings."

"No," said Bernstein, shaking his head, "that couldn't have been my wife!"

* * *

Wifey: I'm wearing my new dresses shorter this year.

Hubby: I'd like it better if you wore the old ones a little longer.

* * *

"Well, I finally did it—I tied the knot!" cried the brand new husband as he entered his office. He handed a photograph of his bride to his partner, Saperstein. "Here's a picture of my wife."

Saperstein studied the photo in silence for a few moments, then commented tersely:

"I guess she's very rich."

* * *

The butcher and the milkman were discussing the pros and cons of married life. "Do you really believe it's better than being single?" demanded Weiss, the butcher.

"In a way," said the milkman, who was fond of philosophizing. "After all, if it weren't for marriage, we'd have to do all our fighting with strangers."

* * *

"My wife deserted me," moaned the unhappy husband. "She took the car and ran off with a traveling salesman."

"Why, that's terrible!" exclaimed his friend, aghast. "Your brand new car!"

* * *

"You ungrateful loafer! I gave you the best years of my life," screamed the wife.

"Now just a minute!" retorted the husband. "In the first place, who made them the best years of your life? And in the second place, what do you want—a receipt?"

* * *

"My husband, he's a mean man," Mrs. Schechter complained to the rabbi. "From Harry I'm suffering multiple neurosis."

"What has he done?" asked the rabbi.

"He's taking me too much for granite, that's what. And always it's on Friday."

The rabbi sighed. "You'd better explain," he said wearily.

"It's like this: Every Friday night I'm cooking the *shabbes* meal like a good Jewish wife is supposed. So, first I'm roasting a chicken. Then, I'm chopping the liver. Next, I'm stuffing the *helzel*. After that, I'm making a nice *tsimmis*. Then, I'm standing over a hot stove everything should cook. And then, I'm setting the table so Harry he should have a nice place to eat. Then, I'm lighting the candles. And then, I'm calling Harry he should sit down . . .

"And then," she concluded, weeping, "he's thanking *the Lord* for the wonderful meal!"

* * *

"Happy birthday, darling," gushed the young wife. "Have I got a surprise for you!"

"Why, thank you, sweetie-pie," said the pleased husband. "I can hardly wait to see it."

"Wait just a minute," she cried enthusiastically, "and I'll try it on for you."

*   *   *

". . . and so Myron and Sybil were married and they lived happily forever after for several months.

*   *   *

Weeping plaintiff: "Believe me, your honor, when she ran her fingers through my hair, she was after my scalp!"

*   *   *

Frieda was listening to some music on the stereo system while Freddie was reading a newspaper article concerning the population explosion.

"It says here," remarked Freddie, "that nine out of ten people were caused by accidents."

"Terrible, terrible," responded Frieda. "But such a big accident rate wouldn't happen if people didn't drive so fast."

*   *   *

"What annoys me most about my mother-in-law," observed Herman the hair stylist, "is that she thinks I'm effeminate. And yet, compared to her," he added after a moment of reflection, "I guess I am."

*   *   *

"I'm convinced that there would be more happy marriages if couples would go out at least once a week for dining, dancing or a movie," said Barney, the Beau Brummel of Broadway. "My wife and I always make it a point to doll up and paint the town red. She goes on Fridays and I go on Saturdays."

*   *   *

A book without at least one shaggy dog story—an involved *megillah* —is like coffee without danish. So, here's our modest contribution to culture:

Mary and Joseph were having serious marital difficulties, so they decided to consult a highly recommended marriage counselor. The advisor's office happened to be next door to a mental institution, and the squabbling couple accidentally entered the wrong door. They were greeted by an impressive-looking, elderly gentleman with a trim black beard and gold-rimmed glasses. He looked more like a doctor than a doctor looks like a doctor and so they were sure he was a doctor— although, sometimes, who can tell a doctor from a patient?

"Are you Dr. Avekgetrugen, the big psychiatrist?" asked Mary.

He nodded genially. "Who else?"

"We're always fighting, and we thought you might help us save our marriage."

"What's your problem?"

"Well, it's all Joseph's fault," Mary began, launching into a ten-minute tirade of her troubles and woes while Dr. Avekgetrugen listened patiently.

The doctor now turned to Joseph. "And what's your side of the story?"

"Where there's smoke there's Mary's cooking, that's my side of it," grumbled Joseph. "She not only dresses to kill, she cooks the same way."

"Oh, is that so!" snapped Mary. "Maybe if he took me out to dinner once in a while, I'd be more interested in cooking. The only thing he ever takes out is the garbage."

"Say, that's pretty good!" chortled the doctor. "Wait till I write that down." He finished a quick scribble, and then asked the surprised couple, "Do you still love each other as you canter along the bridal path of life?"

"If he really loved me, he'd have married somebody else," Mary sniffed. "Before we were married, he told me he was pulling down 12,000 a year at the Manhattan Window Shade Company. How was I to know he meant shades, not dollars?"

"So what?" yelled Joseph. "She lied too. She knew I loved dancing, so she told me that dancers ran in her family. But, she didn't tell me they *really* ran, not danced."

The doctor extended his hand, palm out, as though stopping traffic. "Hold on a minute," he ordered. "Curiosity killed nine lives. How did you happen to meet in the first place?"

"We lived in the same building," explained Joseph. "I had an apartment in front, and she had a flat behind. But, actually, we didn't really get to know each other until we met at a baseball game. And right away I knew the ballpark was haunted when the old bat spoke to me."

Mary's eyes blazed. "All right, I've had it!" she screeched. "Living with that man is like trying to unlock a door with a wet movie ticket—impossible! I want a divorce!"

"Now-now," interposed the doctor, "let's not get overemotional about this. You must understand that the main cause of all divorce is marriage."

"Wh-what?" they gasped.

"A rolling stone makes strange bedfellows," said Avekgetrugen, "and furthermore a married couple should never change horses while Rome burns. In that context, my dear lady, I would put a question to you: Has your husband ever abused you physically?"

Mary laughed spitefully. "He *amused* me physically."

"Be careful," Joseph warned. "You're breaking our marriage vowels in front of a witness."

"Yes," the good doctor agreed sternly. "A fool and his money flock together. And, I might add, parenthetically, beware of Greeks as you would have others do unto you. Many are called, but after the horse is stolen."

"Joseph," Mary whispered, "do you have any idea what he's talking about?"

"No," Joseph also whispered. "Let's pay him off and get the hell out of here." He reached for his wallet.

"Oh, I wouldn't dream of accepting money for my advice," protested Dr. Avekgetrugen. "People should sleep like a wooden nickel is the best policy, and I never put all my eggs where my mouth is. Go, my children, and remember that millions for defense is a penny earned."

Outside, Mary and Joseph discussed the doctor's strange behavior.

"I think all that *meshuggeneh* talk was for a reason," said Joseph thoughtfully. "He was making with the silly talk just to demonstrate how silly *we* are to fight over nonsense."

Mary took his arm and gave it a loving squeeze. "You're right, Joey darling. We were being just as ridiculous as he. No wonder he's such a famous psychiatrist.

"People who live in glass houses gather no moss," grinned Joseph.

"A stitch in time is a girl's best friend," laughed Mary.

* * *

Down at the shop, Izzy had just finished talking to his wife on the telephone. When he finally hung up, his partner remarked, "You certainly must love your wife very much to call her 'Angel' all the time."

"It isn't that," explained Izzy. "I call her 'Angel' because she's always up in the air and harping about something or other."

* * *

Morris and Millie were taking a Sunday walk along Wilshire Boulevard when a gorgeous woman crossed their path.

"Boy," exclaimed Morris rapturously, "she looks like a million!"

"Well, I don't think she's quite that old," responded Millie coldly, "but you're close."

* * *

"For the whole ten years of our married life I always trusted my wife," moaned the unhappy husband. "And then, we moved from New York to Los Angeles and I discovered we still had the same milkman!"

* * *

For a period of some forty years, from the mid-1890s until about 1925, there flourished on New York's upper and lower East Side a unique, itinerant dealer in *alteh shmattehs* (old rags) and used clothing. His cry, "I-kesh-cloze," as he weaved his way through the tenemented streets, was a familiar sound in those now almost-forgotten days. The haggling, by dealer and customer alike, was done in Yiddish, and few if any of the wandering businessmen knew that the words "I-kesh-cloze" meant "I cash clothes."

The merchandise, which was bought for resale to larger dealers, was carried on the left arm (always the left one), and when the load grew too heavy to carry they would lighten the burden by wearing the clothing, one jacket or coat upon the other, sometimes in 100° weather. Old hats which they bought for a few pennies were often worn one atop the other, adding to their ludicrous and demeaning appearance. In retrospect, they were a comical sight, but we children did not laugh—the comedy was too close to pathos.

This nostalgic bit of repartee was popular in the early 1920s.

The *alteh shmatteh*-man knocked on the door of a likely-looking prospect. "I-kesh-cloze," he announced as usual when a man opened the door.

"Not today," said the householder curtly.

Undaunted, the rag-man tried another approach. Speaking in Yiddish, of course, he asked, "Don't you have anything old and worn out that you won't be needing any more?"

"Yeah, that I have," sighed the man, "but right now she's out shopping."

* * *

Chanukah was approaching—the time for gift-giving and happy memories. Berel and Barney were having a few beers at the corner tavern and exchanging little confidences.

"I'll tell you a secret," confided Berel. "I got a poodle for my wife."

"Say," exclaimed Barney admiringly, "I'd like to make an exchange like that myself!"

* * *

"It's true that your wife ran off with your best friend?"

"Yeah, I'm gonna miss him!"

* * *

Sam the salesman walked into the office with a dour expression on his face. He scowled at the typist; he glowered at the bookkeeper; he frowned at the shop foreman.

"What's the matter?" asked the shipping clerk. "You get up with a grouch this morning?"

"No," grumbled Sam. "She got up first."

3

Yiddishe Mamas

INTRODUCTION

One of the distinctive characteristics of Jewish humor is the tendency to satirize whatever is most dear and closest to one's heart. The narrator or writer will employ irony, sarcasm, travesty and ridicule—to deride or expose what he considers to be vice or folly. Nothing is sacrosanct. But the difference—and this is what makes Jewish humor unique—is that the "derision" is aimed at the *quality* of weakness, seldom at the weak *person;* it denounces human frailty, not the human being. There are obvious exceptions, of course. Hitler may be cast as a buffoon in a Jewish joke, but the expression of hostility towards him and his likes is quite understandable.

The "Jewish mother" joke may burlesque, jibe and scoff, but, at its core, there is profound compassion and deep affection. She may be the subject of the story, and is not always presented in an admirable light, but she is still *mamenyu*—dear mother. The conclusion or punch line of the joke arouses a feeling of compassionate understanding, a desire to implant a kiss upon the cheek of the hapless Yiddishe mama.

Turn-of-the-century European Jews told very few Yiddishe Mama jokes. The Yiddishe Mama joke is a strictly *American*-Jewish phenomenon.

Many Jewish comedians excel in the Jewish mother type story. These include George Jessel, Joey Bishop, Zero Mostel and Buddy Hackett, to name a few. Their humorous tales often mirror their own life experiences—tragic as well as pleasant. Thus, from the treasure trove of personal remembrances, they are able to weave their funny, fanciful jokes, mostly fiction, to be sure, but with just enough sprinkling of fact to nudge our own memories.

And, now, before we get to the meat of the matter, let us resolve never to forget the ancient Yiddish saying, "God could not be everywhere, so he created mothers."

H.D.S.

For several months, Esther the hairdresser had urged her mother to have her hair styled, but each time she was met with a firm refusal.

"But, mama, how does it look for a successful hair stylist to have a mother who needs her hair done? It's a shame and a disgrace!"

The daughter's persistence finally wore her mother down. "All right. Just don't make me I should look like a heepie."

"Listen, mama, you'll look perfectly marvelous," Esther gushed. "When I get through with your hair-do, your best friends won't recognize you. Even your own family won't know you."

It took almost two hours, but finally mama's new hair-style was finished. "Now go look in the mirror over there," said the daughter, "while I wait on this other customer."

In a few minutes, Esther returned to the same spot where she had left her mother.

"Yes, madam," she said courteously to the old lady, "can I help you?"

* * *

Zero Mostel is fond of telling the story about his mother's worried insistence that he start a savings account. "Show me a bankbook with $10,000 and I'll be satisfied," she would constantly tell him. The day finally came when he proudly displayed his bankbook showing a total deposit of $10,000. She shrugged, and murmured, "You call that a lot of money?"

* * *

Sadie Greenspan was running for the office of secretary of the local PTA. But, although the other parents and teachers liked her and recognized her good qualities, she was making little progress against Sally Blum, her rival candidate. The reason was obvious: Sadie was a shy, soft-spoken Yiddishe mama type, while Sally Blum was a fast-talking, quick-thinking, glib young woman.

One of the teachers drew Sadie aside.

"Look, Mrs. Greenspan, it's all right to be reserved and to display such commendable humility but, if you expect to win the election, you'll have to be more outspoken. Let the members know how smart you really are. Do a little bragging about yourself the way Mrs. Blum does."

Sadie shook her head. "That I won't do," she said firmly. "By me it's a question of principles. I'm very proud to be so humble."

* * *

Joey Bishop's quip: "Back in 1942, I said, 'Mama, I'm going into the Army.' And she told me, 'All right, but don't come home late.'"

* * *

The young man had just landed a job as a census taker, but he returned home quite despondent after making his first day's rounds.

"I thought you liked your new job," said his mother. "What's the matter you're so sad?"

"I just can't get any cooperation," answered her son. "The women simply refuse to give me their right age."

"That's not the way to learn a woman's age," said the mother reprovingly. "You have to do what I do."

"What do you do?"

"When I want to find out how old a woman is, I just ask her sister-in-law."

* * *

A rabbi said to six-year-old Bobby: "So your mother says your prayers for you each night. Very commendable. What does she say?" And Bobby replied: "Thank God he's in bed!"

* * *

Two ladies were in the beauty parlor, sitting under the hairdryers, and with obvious difficulty, were discussing their families.

"Do you mean to tell me that your son and daughter-in-law were married six months ago, and you haven't visited them yet?" exclaimed the first lady. "I'm shocked!"

"What's to be shocked?" demanded the second lady. "I'm waiting until they have their first baby. Everybody knows that a grandma is always more welcome than a mother-in-law."

* * *

"Mama," asked the young bride, "is it true that the way to a man's heart is through his stomach?"

"Well," replied mama thoughtfully, "that depends on what he's hungry for."

* * *

Thirteen-year-old Tessie came home in tears.

"What's the matter, dear?" asked her mother.

"Oh, mama, my best boyfriend left me for another girl," she sobbed, throwing herself full-length on the bed as she had seen Barbara Stanwyck do in a late-late TV movie. "Oh, the agony of it all! Why must we women suffer like this!"

"Tessie, you really want to forget all that agony and suffering?" asked her mother calmly. "Try wearing tight shoes for a few days."

* * *

A "sushel" worker was making a visit to a poor widow on the East Side. The woman's four little boys all wore glasses.

"What a pity!" exclaimed the visitor sympathetically. "I'm sorry that all your children have eye trouble."

"Trouble? What trouble?" demanded the mother. "Their eyes are perfect, *Gott sie dank!*"

"Then, why in the world do you make them wear glasses?"

The mother stared at the social worker in amazement. "Tell me the truth," she said carefully, as though speaking to a retarded child, "You ever in your life saw a doctor or a lawyer *without* glasses?"

* * *

"Mama, is there anything at all that will keep my lipstick from smearing?" asked the daughter.

"Well, you can always do what I do when your papa comes home all *shikkered* up and in a romantic mood," suggested the mother. "Chew a little garlic!"

* * *

It was an embarrassing moment for both mother and daughter, but there was no putting it off.

"Now that you're getting married, it's time I should give you a little advice," said mama, trying hard to sound casual.

"Oh, mother, *please*, it really isn't necessary," protested the sophisticated daughter. "That's so old-fashioned!"

"Old-fashioned, new-fashioned, it makes no difference. A good Jewish mother gives her daughter advice when she marries, and that's all there is to it," declared the older woman flatly.

The daughter gave a resigned shrug. "All right, I'm listening."

"The first thing I have to warn you about," said mama, choosing her words carefully, "is that you should never line the closet shelves with newspapers. If you do, everybody will know when you last gave the house a good cleaning!"

* * *

Marvin went to Boy Scout camp for the first time. During the required inspection, the scoutmaster found an umbrella neatly placed inside Marvin's bedroll.

"Now look here," reproved the scoutmaster, "you know perfectly well that an umbrella is not listed as a necessary item."

Marvin, echoing the sentiments of untold millions of other Jewish boys, replied wearily, "Sir, did you ever have a mother?"

* * *

"*Oy*, doctor, have I got *tsuris* with my son," wept the lady. "All day long he's doing nothing but blowing bubbles. From soap suds he's making the bubbles and he's blowing them out from a clay pipe."

"Really, madam, there's no reason for you to be concerned," said the psychiatrist, smiling indulgently. "Lots of sons blow bubbles."

"Well, I think it looks funny," insisted the woman, "and so does his wife."

* * *

"I wish Miriam would stop wearing those tight sweaters," complained the father.

"Stop picking on her," protested the mother. "Those sweaters bring out her best points."

* * *

The young mother, not long in the United States, and still unaccustomed to American ways, diffidently entered a photographer's studio.

"How much it costs, please, for children's pictures?" she asked.

"Ten dollars for six," replied the photographer.

The mother's face fell. "Oh, I'm sorry, but I'll have to wait," she cried, her voice full of disappointment. "So far, I only got two."

* * *

"*Oy, iz dos a shandeh!*—such a shame!" groaned elderly Mrs. Vinter-hoyzen, looking up from the newspaper she had been laboriously reading.

"What's so shameful?" asked her daughter, Sharon, a sociology major in college.

"It says here in black and white, five *goyim* got arrested for smuggling in from Mexico, Mary's Jewish hyena. But what happened to poor Mary, the paper doesn't say."

"Let me see that story," demanded Sharon, leaning over her mother's shoulder. In a moment her face lit up. "Oh, mama, you misunderstood. What they smuggled in was marijuana! It's a Spanish word."

"*Aha! Spanishe Yidden!* Like I always told your papa—he should rest in peace—even back in Russia I told him, those *Sephardim* should either be forced to act like respectable Jews or they should go start their own religion!"

* * *

"Do you think our son will be happy?" asked the groom's anxious mother as the newly married couple left on their honeymoon.

"Why not?" said her husband cheerfully. "He was still smiling when they left the synagogue."

* * *

A mother and her little boy were making the grand tour of the Metropolitan Museum of Art in New York. They came to a halt before the beautiful painting, "Madonna and Child."

"Look at that!" snorted the lady. "They say she was Jewish. But, I ask you, would a Jewish mother who couldn't even afford a hotel room pay out good money to have her picture taken?"

* * *

The young woman, her children in tow, was visiting her mother.

"You look tired," said the elderly grandmother to her daughter.

"I am," said the daughter. "Mama, isn't there any way at all for a housewife to get a few precious minutes to herself?"

"Yes," said the old lady sadly, "just start doing the dishes."

* * *

From our bulging file on modern-day androgyny, we are pleased to report the following encounter.

A visitor to the University of California at Berkeley stopped in amazement at the sight of a wild-looking student with long, straggly hair, tight jeans, cowboy boots and wearing a necklace of large wooden beads.

"Boy, talk about weird-looking girls!" he remarked to a person standing beside him.

"I beg *your* pardon," replied the stranger, "but that happens to be my son."

"Oh, I beg your pardon," apologized the embarrassed visitor. "I didn't know you were his father."

"I'm not," snapped the offended one, "I'm his mother!"

* * *

There is an amusing folk tale which illustrates the fact that the traditional Yiddishe mama was much in evidence during colonial times and the Revolutionary War period. The story revolves around the real-life David Hays, his younger brother, Michael, and their strong-willed mother.

David Hays was the Jewish patriot in the War of Independence who accomplished the singular feat of driving cattle from his Westchester farm, through the British lines, to the hungry Colonial troops. In reprisal, British forces visited his farm while he was away serving in Washington's army and burned his house down. Defiantly, he returned to the farm under the very noses of the enemy and, with his brother, Michael, rebuilt the house. Again, David left home to fight under Washington's command.

Back at the farm, David's mother was at the water-well in the front yard when a Colonial officer approached her. He pointed to a plow team in the adjacent field and asked:

"Are those your horses?"

"Yes," she replied, thinking of all the cattle they had furnished the army, "and that big strong man at the plow is my son Michael. So don't make trouble."

"I'm sorry, madam," the officer said politely, "but the army is badly in need of horses. I'm afraid I'll have to confiscate them in the name of the government. You'll be reimbursed after the war, of course."

"Who is your commanding officer?" demanded Mrs. Hays.

"Captain David Hays," replied the army man.

"Oh, it's Captain David Hays, is it?" she exclaimed, a smile softening her hitherto stern features. "Well, you go right back and tell him his mama said he can't have her horses!"

* * *

The ultimate joy of motherhood: That beautiful, exquisite moment, when the kids are finally in bed and mama can take off her shoes and stockings, settle back on the sofa, put her *feeselach* up on the coffee table, wiggle her cramped toes, and murmur, "Ahhh!"

4

Yiddishe Papas

INTRODUCTION

The Bible and the Talmud are replete with references to fathers—some humorous, but mostly philosophical. Aside from the sage guidance found in the Book of Proverbs, the Talmud contains many passages of this type: "He who brings up, not he who begets, is the father"—which might be interpreted as meaning that many mothers are fathers. Dear old dad seems to have gotten the worst of it in a number of Talmudic sayings! As for example this one: "A father's love is for his children; the children's love is for *their* children." One would think that having given all that love, the law of compensation would take effect, and the weary father might expect a little something in return for his efforts. But here we are confronted with another proverb: "One father willingly maintains ten children, but ten children are unwilling to maintain one father." Such ingratitude!

Franz Kafka, the Austrian novelist, gave the needle another gratuitous push when he observed, "Parents who expect gratitude from their children (there are even some who insist on it) are like usurers who gladly risk their capital if only they receive interest." With that statement, Kafka aroused the anger of his Jewish brethren everywhere. All *Litvak* parents castigated him as "that *Galitzianer*." All *Galitzianers* scorned him as "that *Litvak*." The Russian Jews, from their lofty perch on the Judaic totem pole, coldly accused him of being both—and of being improperly potty-trained as well. Retorted Kafka: "*Bopkes!*" Damn clever, these Austrians.

The modern male parent is no longer called a "Yiddishe papa." We now refer to him as a Jewish father—and often even the "Jewish" is omitted. Yet, like the Yiddishe mama, he displays many of the traditional responses of the older generations, modified in the context of today's culture. He may be humming his favorite tune from *Fiddler on the Roof*, but listen more closely and you will hear the faint echo of *Eli, Eli.*" Moreover, the people's bond with the past also extends to each other as individuals. That is why a Jew finds it easy to identify with the concerned father who sighs, "Young man, you can't afford my daughter—but then, neither can

29

I." And he understands the acidity with which a suspicious father addresses his daughter's suitor: "My Goldie tells me you have that certain something, but I wish you had that something certain."

Still, could not these wry jokes be gentile just as well? Here, we run into that intangible Jewish sense of humor. *Schmaltz* on "wry" is the appetizer in nearly all Jewish jokes. Without the *schmaltz* they would lack the innate sentimentality that makes them distinctively Jewish, and without the wryness they would be devoid of that sharp Jewish tongue that can clip a hedge. Honey and acid—a strange combination for humor! Attribute it to all the "begats."

The bond between father and son has evoked countless expressions of admiration in ancient and modern literature. This continuity of the father-son relationship was well expressed by Abraham Mendelssohn, son of Moses Mendelssohn and father of Felix. He observed: "Formerly I was my father's son, now I am my son's father." That close tie exists today, vibrant as ever, although the rhetoric may be in breezy, contemporary language. An embarrassed father will shrug off your sentimental and flattering reference to the subject with the quip: "Whenever you hear it said that there is a beautiful tie between father and son, the son is probably wearing it." It may take several minutes to realize that he is saying "thank you" for a nice comment, but that is precisely what he is doing.

Yes, but is the quip *Jewish*? You will be interested to know that, aside from the obvious Hebraic origins of the ancient sayings, every joke used in this introduction was first heard some forty years ago on New York's East Side, and *all* have been translated from the Yiddish! There is one that I especially remember hearing around 1927 or so—a sweet little story, also translated from Yiddish to English—about the boy who proudly said to his mother, "Daddy never went past the sixth grade in school, but I think he's just as smart as if he went to the seventh."

In this chapter, we fondly offer that grand old man of ours his honorary diploma. He earned it!

H.D.S.

Among the first things that a Jewish boy learns is the Biblical injunction, "Honor thy father and mother"—or else! Herschel, age six, was reminded of the admonition the day his father came home and announced that he had decided to buy a car—the first his family had ever owned.

The father was in high spirits. "Imagine! We're in this country only a few years and soon we'll own a new car," he said proudly. "I can just see us riding around in Central Park. In the front I'm steering, and sitting next to me is mama. And in the back is our little Herschel."

Mama nodded, smiling her approval. "So when you're planning to buy the car?" she asked.

"In two weeks, a month maybe. No later."

The pleasant interlude was suddenly shattered by Herschel's mournful cry: "I don't wanna sit in the back. I wanna sit in the front and help steer."

"Only one steerer we need in this family," the father reminded his son. "In the front sits mama. In the back sits you."

"If I hafta sit in the back I'll bang my head on the wall, you'll see," wailed Herschel. He ran to the wall and assumed a threatening pose, ready to give action to his words. "Mama is sitting in the back. *I'm* sitting in the front!"

"No, Herschel, you're in the back," said the father sternly.

"In the front!"

"In the back!"

Herschel's voice rose to a shrill screech. "I ain't gonna sit in the back."

Father, his manner grim, extended his arm and pointed a commanding finger.

"Herschel," he said coldly, "get out of my car!"

* * *

Goldberg was reminiscing about his boyhood in Russia.

"I was born in Minsk," he said, "but actually I went to school right here in Brooklyn."

"Wow!" exclaimed his son. "That's what I call *busing!*"

* * *

It was getting on toward the close of business hours and Sanford Siegel was in an expansive mood. He lit a cigar, leaned back in his chair and reflected on his good fortune. The Siegel Clothing Company was flourishing, he had a loving wife, and his infant son was handsome and alert. Yes, some day that boy would be a partner. Sanford could visualize the new sign over the display window: *Siegel and Son.*

The telephone rang suddenly, jarring him from his pleasant contemplations. It was his wife, breathless with excitement.

"Oh, have I got news for you!" she cried. "The baby just spoke his first words. Plain as day, and *three* words, at that!"

"Wonderful!" enthused Sanford. "What did he say?"

"Mama, papa and gabardine!"

* * *

"Pop, when does old age start?" asked the youth as he viewed his image in the mirror and inspected a few imaginery lines at the corner of his eyes.

"It can start at any age, depending on the individual," said the father, smiling. "But actually, old age is the time when you find yourself giving good advice instead of setting a bad example."

* * *

Danny came home from school with some exciting news.

"Y'know somethin', pop," he began, "half of the kids in my class said their fathers have false teeth. Are yours false too?"

"No, Danny," said the father good-humoredly. "They're all mine."

"How come?"

"Well, for one thing I'm only thirty-five and my teeth are in good shape."

"Yeah," persisted Danny with all the determination of any six-year-old, "but how do you keep them in such good shape?"

"Very simple," said the young father, "I mind my own business."

* * *

Keenly aware of the old man's penchant for biting sarcasm, the young suitor was understandably nervous about asking him for his daughter's hand in marriage. Summoning up the necessary courage, he approached the girl's father and, in trembling tones, asked:

"May I have your daughter for my wife?"

"I don't know," came the reply. "Bring your wife around and let me have a look at her."

* * *

Edna's father was in a dither of outrage.

"I forbid you to marry this sailor!" he stormed. "Anyway, what respectable Jewish girl would marry a man, still in his twenties, who's been divorced three times?"

"Four!" Edna corrected.

"*What?!* screamed her dad. "My God, that guy isn't a sailor, he's a *whole*saler!"

* * *

Walter had only been married two years but already his absentmindedness was causing friction at home. So, he decided to seek the advice of his elderly father.

"Pop," he began, "is there anything I can do to help me remember my wife's birthday?"

"Sure," said the father promptly. "From my own long experience as a married man, my advice to you is that you should just try forgetting it once. Believe me, you'll never do it again!"

* * *

The young man looked up from the editorial page of the newspaper he had been reading.

"Dad, you're a man of the world," he said. "Tell me, what exactly is diplomacy?"

"Well, son," began the father, clearing his throat, "if you were to say to an ugly girl, 'Your face would stop a clock,' that would not only be undiplomatic but very unkind as well. However, if you said to that same ugly girl, 'When I look into your eyes, time stands still,' you'd be saying the same thing, but *that*, my boy, would be diplomacy!"

*   *   *

Marty Tilberg, the Meatball King of Detroit, had been highly successful in the food business. It was his cherished wish that Reuben, his son, would outgrow his laziness and occupy himself with the responsibilities that attend the running of a profitable enterprise. But, as the saying goes, some people grow up and other people just grow older. Reuben was growing older—and lazier. It was now high-time that the young man was told the who's who and what's what about working for a living.

"Sit down, Ruby, I want us to have a serious talk," the older man began. "You're now twenty-three and it's time you stopped chasing around with loafers and attend a little to business. From now on, I'll expect you on the job early every morning."

"But, pop, there's really nothing for me to do here." protested Reuben. "We have enough employees to handle everything."

"That's not the point. Some day, when I'm gone, you'll have to take over. Then what?"

"In that case I'd be the boss and I'd be paying others to do all the work. Isn't that the whole idea of being on top?"

Old man Tilberg shook his head.

"No," he replied wearily. "Some day maybe you'll learn an important fact of life: It doesn't matter how high up a man's throne may be—he still has to sit on his own bottom!"

*   *   *

The ambitious daughter was growing increasingly irritated with her father's snorts of derision whenever she mentioned her favorite subject—the Women's Liberation movement.

"Daddy," she fumed, "do you really have any notion at all about the meaning of 'career woman'?"

"Sure," he replied cheerily. "A career woman is a gal who goes out and earns a man's salary—instead of staying home and *shlepping* it away from him!"

*   *   *

The boy's father was appalled at his son's liberal use of slang.

"Now see here," he demanded sternly, "there are three words I never want to hear you use again. One is *swell*, the other is *lousy* and the third is *screwy*."

"Okay, pop," the boy agreed. "What are they?"

*   *   *

"Whoever would have thought that our own son would turn out to be a hippie?" sighed the unhappy father.

"You mustn't judge Harold by his clothes," the mother protested. "Lots of boys are wearing toeless galoshes this year."

"Well, at least he could be a little neater. The last time that boy washed his face was when he cried."

"Harold explained it all to me," said the mother protectively. "He says a young person in today's world has to be a little crazy or he'll go nuts."

"That's what I like about our son—a vast mind with half-vast notions," sighed the father. "His I.Q. finally caught up with his eyesight—20-20. Did I tell you what happened when he came home from the beach yesterday? He went right to the medicine cabinet. And when I asked him what he was looking for, he said he needed something for sunburn on top of poison ivy on top of acne."

"You shouldn't be so hard on our Harold," reproved the mother. "He's only trying to make a life for himself."

The father shook his head. "The only thing that boy makes around here are mistakes and cigarette ashes."

"You know, it could be a medical problem," suggested the mother after some thought. "The doctor advised that Harold should have a change."

"I already took his advice," said the father wearily. "I changed doctors!"

* * *

The kid looked up from the book on ancient history he was reading and asked his father, "Pop, what's a millennium?"

The father scratched his head and thought deeply.

"I think," he finally answered, "it's something like a centennial, only it has more legs!"

* * *

The father and his five-year-old son were in Wanamaker's Department Store. They were making the grand tour of the mezzanine when they were confronted by a formidable-looking woman—the type that would make Bella Abzug look like Miss Goodie-Goodie-Two-Shoes.

"Sir," she said in a steely voice, "don't you think you are walking too fast for that child?"

Without a word, the father slowed down.

On the second floor, whom should he meet again, but the old battle-axe.

"Sir," she grated once more, "isn't that boy a little thirsty?"

He bought the boy a Coke.

On the third floor: "Sir, don't you think the child might want to visit the bathroom?"

He took his son to the bathroom.

On the fourth floor, having seen all they cared to see for the day, they got on the "Down" elevator. It was quite crowded but they found a space.

"Sir," called a familiar voice in the back of the elevator, "don't you think he'll be crushed?"

"No, lady!" the father yelled at the top of his lungs. "The little stinker bites!"

* * *

It says here," remarked ten-year-old David, his nose buried in a book, "Benjamin Franklin tied a key on his kite and discovered that lightning comes from 'lectricity."

"It's nice he found out," grunted the boy's father, engrossed in his newspaper.

"I don't get it," said the boy, puzzled. "Ain't lightning and 'lectricity the same thing?"

Annoyed with the interruptions, the father replied brusquely:

"No, Davey, they're not the same. Lightning we get free!"

* * *

The uneasy father confronted his daughter as she was leaving for the evening.

"Young lady, I'll expect you home by eleven, not a minute later," he said sternly.

"But, daddy," the daughter protested, "I'm not a child any more."

"Exactly," he snapped. "That's why I want you home by eleven!"

* * *

Little Jesse had found a cheap paperback book and was now plying his father with some pointed questions.

"It says here in the book that a guy was fired for kissing the boss's daughter," said Jesse. "But, I wonder why he got fired for that."

"They're not supposed to kiss," explained the father vaguely.

"Why not? You and mama kiss all the time."

"That's different. We're married."

"What's the difference?" persisted Jesse.

"Well, son," the father began with a scarcely-concealed grin, "the difference between kissing your wife and kissing your sweetheart is about sixty seconds."

* * *

"I think," said the expectant mother, "we should name the baby Leonard."

"No, absolutely not!" shouted the papa-to-be. "Every Tom, Dick and Harry is named Leonard!"

* * *

"Pop, can I ask you a very personal question?" queried teenaged Bertram.

"Sure," came the obliging answer. "That's what fathers are for."

"Well, if I take a girl out for the evening and show her a good time at the movies and, on the way home, I buy her an ice-cream sundae, do you think it will be okay if I kiss her goodnight?"

The father gave his son's question some intensive study.

"No, Bertram," he said at length, "don't kiss her. You did enough for her in just one evening."

* * *

In the waiting room of the maternity wing at Mt. Sinai Hospital, an expectant father paced the floor nervously while another calmly read his newspaper. Finally, a nurse appeared and greeted the calm one with a cheery smile. "Congratulations," she chirped. "you have a beautiful new daughter."

"Hey, what's the big idea?" demanded the nervous pacer. "I was here first!"

* * *

The little boy's hands were none too clean.

"Georgie," demanded the father, "I want you to leave the table this instant and go wash your hands."

"Ya mean both of 'em?" asked the youngster.

"No," retorted the father, "I mean one of them. I'd be most interested to see how you do it!"

* * *

"When I first emigrated to America," reminisced Sam the radish exporter, "I was forced to settle in the Bronx instead of Schenectady. After all, who can spell a *meshuggeneh* name like that?"

* * *

Little Ruthie swallowed a penny.

"*Aii-yi-yi!*" screeched the child's mother. "Call the doctor!"

"Doctor, nothing!" yelled the father. "Send for the rabbi. That guy can get money out of anybody!"

* * *

The day before *Chanukah* found daddy in Bloomingdale's, shopping for a gift for his tiny daughter.

"I can recommend this pretty doll," said the saleslady. "It's just like a real little girl. When you lay her down she immediately closes her eyes and goes right to sleep."

"Madam," said daddy, looking a little more than skeptical, "with all due respect to your sales ability, it is clear that you never had a baby girl."

* * *

Bill Isaacson and Andy Kuhn, the furniture moguls of Grand Rapids, were concerned about the future of their respective daughters.

"I just can't make up my mind about sending my daughter to college or not," said Bill. "It isn't the cost, though God knows it's high enough. But, it takes her out of the marriage market for four years. Who needs an educated old maid for a daughter?"

"It isn't all that much of a problem," replied Andy with an airy wave of hand. "I solved the situation, and now both of my older daughters are happily married."

"You solved it? How?"

"I spent $3,000 a year to send my oldest daughter, Edith, to college and it took her four years to capture a husband. But for my other daughter, Velma, it cost me only $300 to send her to the mountains for two weeks, and she came home married.

* * *

The little girl was watching a heavy romance on television. Nearly all of the dialogue was too mature for her, especially a phrase used by one of the actors.

"Daddy," she asked, "what's a love bug?"

Grinning, he gave her the perfect answer:

"A love bug, honey, is a desirous virus!"

* * *

"It was a bitter cold day, and we shivered in the dingy tenement flat on the East Side where we lived," reminisced Rachel Weintraub, now the proprietress of Raquel's Boutique on Fifth Avenue. "My father was seething with rage because the janitor, or 'super' as they are now called, would not, or could not, give us more heat. It seemed to us kids that it was as cold inside our flat as it was outdoors.

"In his anger, my father started to bang on the steampipe, and made such noise with his hammering that the 'super' came up to stop the racket.

"'Mister Weintraub,' pleaded the man, 'we got just so much coal. Am I the landlord, you're making such a to-do for me? Later I'll start the furnace and you'll feel better.'

"'You'll do it right now!" shouted papa. 'I don't want to set the world on fire—I just want a little heat in my rooms!'"

* * *

Expletive Deleted Department:

"Mommy, can Lisa and I go out to the garage and hear Daddy fix the flat tire?"

* * *

For the era in which this tale is laid, we must hark back to those days when the ukelele was the national instrument of joy—or torture, depending on your sensibilities—and young people were doing the Charleston and singing "The Sheik of Araby." The specific locale was the Pennsylvania Station in New York, and the raconteur of the following story was the late Belle Baker.

A whiskered gentleman, evidently hailing from the East Side, was administering physical punishment to a small boy. A stranger of humane instincts pushed his way through the interested crowd of onlookers and placed a firm hand upon the arm of the bearded one.

"Here, hold on!" he ordered. "Why are you slapping this child?"

"He's mine own son," explained the East Sider. "Who got a better right?"

"I don't care whose son he is," stated the interrupting citizen. "You have no business to be slapping and shaking him this way. You stop it immediately or I'll make trouble for you!"

"Mister, listen to me," said the parent. "Two years ago mine wife runs away with mine best friend. One year ago mine partner cheats me in business and I go broke. Three months ago I get rheumatism and the doctors they pulled out all mine teeth. Six weeks ago mine daughter got married to a *shaigetz* who it also happens is a loafer, and I got to support them both. The day before yesterday mine old mother dies in Philadelphia and I'm spending my last penny for tickets so me and mine boy here we should go to the funeral. I give the tickets to him and he puts them in his mouth and just when we're ready to get on the train he's breathing the wrong way and he swallows them."

The father gave a short, hard, bitter, metallic laugh.

"And *you'll* make trouble for me?"

5

Foxy Grandmas and Feisty Grandpas

INTRODUCTION

Isaac Leibush Peretz was an illustrious Yiddish novelist who wrote beautifully and succinctly. But his view of old age, as a person gray and forlorn, did not represent the mainstream of Jewish thought then, nor does it now. True, there are a number of ancient sayings that seem to support his contention. The Talmud, for example, offers us the gratuitous diagnosis, "Old age is a bad sickness." But the Bible takes a more cheerful and traditional stand: "The hoary head is a crown of glory." Actually, the most practical approach is found in the old Jewish expression, "A man is as old as his wife looks." When you think about it, it makes sense.

Why is a grandparent's reaction to children different from that of a parent? Let us go back to beginnings. According to the rabbis, the unborn baby possesses the accumulated knowledge of all the past generations. But, when the infant is born, so goes the Talmudic legend, an angel touches its forehead, and it forgets everything. As a result, the child is much sweeter, friendlier and less inhibited because it has no memories. Dwelling in the past—living with old memories—represents a kind of regression, a going backward when we should be going forward.

Young parents have not yet reached the point where they can selectively blot out unhappy memories. They are still actively engaged in the busy process of living life's joys and sorrows: their memories have yet to be earned. But, lucky indeed are the grandparents—those fortunate ones who have attained the age where they can afford the gentle art of forgetting. In that context, they are closer to their grandchildren than they are to their own sons and daughters.

The small child, of course, has not lived long enough to store up a variety of experiences; the grandparent draws from his treasure-chest and dwells upon those memories which give him most pleasure. And if, in his nostalgia, he embellishes his recollections to the point of childlike naivete, and conveniently forgets the unpleasantries he has known, who shall blame him? It has taken him most of his lifetime to learn the difference between forgetting and forgetfulness. Awareness of that difference is a sign of wisdom.

The Jewish maxim, "Wine and wisdom improve with age," is no less valid today than it was centuries ago. Only the dates are changed. Men and women do not grow old because they have lived a certain number of years. They grow old only when they desert their ideals, when they no longer laugh at the foibles of humanity—and their own frailties as well. Are they living in a make-believe world? Perhaps, to a degree. But that is why they can enjoy such intimate rapport with their grandchildren. To grow old in years, but not in spirit; to attain a modicum of wisdom, but not vanity; to understand love, but not to use it as a lever; to accept mortality, but not to dread it; to understand that man is the only creature on earth to have knowledge of his grandchildren and grandparents, but to respect all other living things; and to savor one's anecdotage without becoming a bore or a burden—these make for the golden years and constitute the essence of a fruitful Jewish family life.

Some Jewish grandfathers in America would shock their shrouded ancestors if they could but hear some of the modern anecdotes. In 1974, at the Queen Esther Retirement Home in Chicago, a venerable old man in his early nineties was asked the customary question by a young reporter: "Sir, to what do you attribute your good health and longevity?" The oldtimer grinned and replied, "Drinking a fifth of *schnapps* every day and chasing girls." Like many another grandfather, he was not only adept at selective remembering, but he recalled things that probably never happened. Nevertheless, it is inconceivable that a grandfather in yesteryear's Europe would have made any such assertion. But these are "fun" rather than "wisdom" jokes. They have evolved quite naturally as a result of the freer climate in the United States.

Much the same may be said of Israel, although there are subtle differences between Israeli humor and ours. As an example, who would have thought that the sedate Golda Meir, at age 75, would refer to herself as a militant grandmother who not only believed in women but in fighting for Lib as well? "I am no chicken libber," she said, chuckling over her use of the Jewish-Americanism. But why not? She spent her young years in the United States.

It has been said that one of the primary differences between the Jewish people of old Europe and those of the United States is that European Jews belonged to a patriarchal society, while modern America is matriarchal. Perhaps Portnoy did have something to complain about, at that. The American Jewish male is influenced by women from the time of his birth to the time of his death. As a child, he is ruled by his mother. During his school years, he is governed by a series of female teachers. When he marries, he is dominated by his wife. From the day his daughters learn to say Da-da, he comes under their jurisdiction. And, when they have little girls of their own, he is ruled by his granddaughters. Poor grandpa cannot remember a day when some female was not tugging at his heartstrings or purse-strings—or both. Needless to say, he does not want to remember! To him and to the doting grandmother, it is a constant source of amazement that their mediocre children managed to produce such geniuses of their own. Sam Levenson, probably the finest exponent of authentic Jewish humor in America, aptly defined a genius as ". . . .a stupid kid with very happy grandparents."

To put it another way—and this is really what this chapter is intended to convey—we are truly grandparents when we realize that grandchildren are God's way of compensating us for old age.

H.D.S.

"Well, what did you learn today?" asked the grandfather as 12-year-old Izzy returned home from Hebrew school.

"All about the Exodus. Wow, what an adventure! The teacher told us how the Hebrews got chased all the way to the Red Sea, and how ten big boats in just two hours sailed them across to the other side. But when the Egyptian soldiers got to the Red Sea a big wave rolled up. It must've been a mile high—and it drowned all of them, and the Jews were saved!"

"What!" shouted the grandfather. "Your teacher told you that?"

"Well, not exactly, grandpapa," explained Izzy. "But if I told you the story he told us, you'd never believe it in a million years!"

* * *

The old couple was sitting at the kitchen table, sipping tea and listening to some vintage music on their ancient Victrola. The silver-haired lady grew misty-eyed.

"Hymie," she began nostalgically, "remember how romantical it was when we were young? Every minute you wanted to *shmoos*."

"Yeah, I used to get pretty *schmaltzy*," Hymie agreed with a chuckle.

"So why don't you ever nibble on my ears or bite me on my neck anymore? You're not too old for that."

He rose abruptly from his chair and started out of the room.

"Oh, Hymie, Hymie, I didn't mean to hurt your feelings," the old lady cried in dismay.

"What do you mean, hurt my feelings?" said Hymie cheerfully. "I'm going to get my teeth!"

* * *

Grumpy grandpa was his usual self this morning.

"Why is it," he growled as he struggled with a newly-washed shirt, "that a wife who can see right through her husband of forty years can't notice a missing button?"

* * *

A couple of old-timers were sunning themselves on a bench in Seward Park—when it was safe to do so.

"There's one thing I can say in defense of children and grandchildren," remarked the first graybeard. "They're such a comfort in our old age."

"True," agreed the other oldster, "and they also help us get there faster!"

* * *

"Grandma, how long have you and grandpa been married?" asked the romantic young granddaughter.

"Forty-nine years," replied the old lady.

"Oh, what a beautiful life you must have had," sighed the girl. "And I'll bet you never even thought of a divorce."

"Well," said grandma, "divorce, no—murder, yes!"

* * *

Daniella was in a quandary. Her new boyfriend's birthday was approaching and she could not think of a suitable gift. Her grandmother noticed her worried expression.

"What's the matter?" she asked.

"You know how rich my new guy is, grandma. He drives a Rolls Royce from his town house to his country estate and uses a Lincoln Continental just for shopping. He already has diamond rings for each day of the week, platinum watches, mink-lined shoes, jewelled cigarette cases, eight electric shavers, 500 pairs of socks and 1,000 neckties. Tell me, what can a girl give to a man who has everything?"

"Encouragement" said the wise old grandma.

* * *

Plaintive voice from the fourth floor, rear:

"I wish you'd stay away from that electric fan, grandma; you're too old to be blowing your top!"

* * *

"My grandmother didn't understand English too well," explained the young fellow, "but what she heard she heard good.

"I recall the time I went to meet her at the bus stop. To my surprise I saw her get off the bus backwards. So I asked her the reason.

"'I get off backwards,' she explained, 'because your grandpa once told me that on New York buses everybody wants to grab your seat!'"

* * *

For almost fifty years Mr. and Mrs. Klein had lived on the East Side, but now that her husband had passed away Mrs. Klein accepted an invitation to live with her wealthy son and his family.

She loved the opulent but strange neighborhood, and spent the first few days wandering around and familiarizing herself with the local landmarks so that she would not get lost if she went too far from the house. In her explorations, she found the neighborhood temple, one of those imposing modern structures where new arrivals are never sure whether to pray, make a bank deposit or order a pizza.

On the very next Sabbath, old Mrs. Klein timidly entered the synagogue. Inside the ornate portal she hesitated and peered about uncertainly, overwhelmed by the splendor of the fashionable house of worship. She was quickly noticed by an usher, a bowlegged man who swayed from side to side as he approached her. He smiled a warm welcome and pointed to a seat.

"Just walk this way, *bobeh*," he said.

"All right," said the old lady, anxious to please but somewhat dubious, as she observed his shambling gait, "My knees are a *bissel* stiff but I'll try!"

* * *

"I don't know what this world is coming to," sighed grandpa. "When grandma was a girl she didn't do the things girls do today. However," he added after a few reflective thoughts, "grandmas didn't do the things that grandmas do today, either."

* * *

Just prior to the turn of the century, Mrs. Rabinovitch, the *alteh bobeh,* and her beautiful young granddaughter, were among the fortunate ones who emigrated from Russia to the United States, thereby escaping the recurrent *pogroms* in their remote little *shtetl.* Acting on the advice of their friends, they settled in Peoria, but the memory of the persecutions was not easily erased from their troubled minds.

They had only been settled in their new home for a few days, and were just getting ready to light the *shabbes* candles, when a delegation from the Men's Club of Temple Beth Israel, arms laden with gifts for the newcomers, burst in upon them with shouts of "Surprise! Surprise!"

Neither the girl nor the old woman understood a word of English, and in their minds they entertained the worst of fears. An American pogrom! The granddaughter threw herself in front of her *bobeh* and cried:

"Take me instead! Rape me, if you must! But please, I implore you, spare my old grandmother!"

Sizing up the situation quickly, and seeing how respectable the visitors were, the old lady stepped around her granddaughter, protectively, and shrugged resignedly.

"My child," she said, her words slow and deliberate, "who are we to interfere with fate? After all, a *pogrom* is a *pogrom!*"

* * *

"I knew my husband was getting old," averred the silver-haired lady, "when he started making excuses to stay home instead of to get out!"

* * *

Grandma was feeble of limb but still able to hobble around. She looked forward to Saturday nights when she could always count on an interesting speech at the community civic hall around the corner from where she lived.

Came this Saturday night and grandma reached the lecture hall.

"Mister," she said to a young fellow who was also about to enter, "would you be so kind to help me up the steps?"

"Sure," he agreed pleasantly.

"Tell me," she asked as they mounted the stairs, "who is speaking tonight?"

"Muhammad Ali. He'll be talking about the Black Muslims."

"Mister," said grandma, "would you be so kind to help me *down* the steps?"

* * *

"Grandpa, my new boyfriend will be twenty-one years old next week," confided the teenage girl. "I'd like to give him something nice for his birthday. What do you think he'd like?"

"Never mind what he'd like," snapped grandpa. "Give him a tie!"

* * *

The two *alteh bobehs* were discussing their husbands as they sipped tea and lemon.

"I wish mine Leo would stop biting his fingernails," complained *bobeh aleph*. "It's making me *azoi* noivous."

"You should do like me," advised *bobeh baiz*. "I broke mine Sol from biting his nails real quick."

"How?"

"I hid his teeth!"

* * *

"How's your arthritis today?" asked the sympathetic granddaughter.

"*Oy*, dollink, much worser!" groaned the old lady. She lifted her arm high above her head. "Yesterday I could get my hand way up there. But today," she said tearfully, lifting her hand only as high as her shoulder, "I can only lift it up to here!"

* * *

A little old lady decided to return to Europe for a short visit to see her sister before she died. So she went downtown to the Federal Building to apply for a passport.

"You'll have to take the oath first," said the passport clerk. "Raise your right hand."

The old lady raised her hand.

"Do you," he intoned, "swear to defend the Constitution of the United States against all its enemies, domestic or foreign?"

The old lady's face paled. "Who, me?" she asked in a quavering voice.

"Yes, lady, you. Just answer 'I do' if you want a passport."

"Mister, to tell you the truth, what with house cleaning, laundry, cooking and taking care on my grandchildren, who knows when I'd have time?"

"Look here," barked the exasperated clerk, "can't you do us both a favor and simply say 'I do?' That's all there is to it."

"B-b-but . . ."

"All right," he interrupted, "let me ask you this: Do you or don't you want a passport?"

"I do."

"Well," he smiled, handing her the document, "that wasn't so hard to say, was it?"

* * *

Sadie was engrossed in doing her homework when her grandfather's raucous voice, raised in song, shattered her trend of thought.

"Grandpa," she complained later, "you have a horrible voice. Why do you insist on singing in the shower?"

"Because," said grandpa with sweet reason, "there's no lock on the bathroom door."

* * *

Some men grow more mellow with age despite the vaunted generation gap. Take middle-aged Marvin and his aged father, Morris. Marvin was grousing about his teenage daughter's frequent dates.

"Her name's Sophie," he grumbled, "but I might as well call her Appendix—everybody takes her out."

"Don't be such a shtik in the mudpie," chided old Morris. "How else will she find a husband? And while we're on the subject, what kind of a name is Appendix for my granddaughter? Better you should call her *Blintzes*—she's such a popular dish!"

* * *

Si and Dottie had never been to a fancy nightclub before. Now, on their 35th wedding anniversary, they were celebrating the occasion with a visit to a Las Vegas night spot.

The lights were dimmed and then the ageless Marlene Dietrich appeared on stage, her famous legs encased in sheer tights.

"Oh," gushed Dottie, "how marvelous for a grandmother!"

"You mean," corrected Si, enthralled, "how marvelous for a grandfather!"

* * *

The boy and his grandpa were discussing the youngster's future one evening, just after the Nixon expletive-deleted transcripts were made public. The grandson, it seemed, was interested in a political career.

"Watergate or no Watergate, I'd like to do something big—but clean," said the youth.

"The only political job left in that category," sighed the grandfather, "is to get a position in the White House and then wash everybody's mouth out with soap."

* * *

Grandpa Kalman was grumbling through his beard as he read the evening paper.

"What's the matter? Why are you so mad?" asked grandma.

"It says here that a gang of loafers painted a swastika on a synagogue in Brooklyn and beat up the *shammes*," grandpa fumed, stabbing the paper with his forefinger. "And all the judge gave them was six months in jail."

Grandma clucked disapprovingly. "That wasn't enough," she agreed. "A year would have been better."

"*What?*" grandpa shouted. "A year they will spend in a nice warm jail with television and a radio? And with visitors yet, who will bring cakes with files in them like in the movies? Listen, if it was me, I'd give them 25 years in the electric chair!"

* * *

There was a loud knocking on the door and when grandpa opened it, there stood a distraught woman wringing her hands.

"Sir," she faltered in a choking voice, "do you own a calico cat with a red collar and a silver bell attached to it?"

"Yes, that's my cat," said grandpa.

"Well, I just ran over it," explained the woman, her face a picture of anguish. "I'm terribly, terribly sorry. Will you let me replace it?"

Grandpa shrugged. "It's all right with me if it's all right with you," he replied. "How are you at catching mice?"

* * *

The little girl asked her grandfather to mend her broken doll.

"Tomorrow," he promised.

"Grandpa," admonished the precocious youngster, "you must never put off until tomorrow what you can do today."

"You're right, little pigeon," he sighed. "Tomorrow there may be a law against it."

* * *

The venerable old man was celebrating his one-hundredth birthday and was asked by a reporter: "To what do you attribute your advanced age and remarkable physical condition?"

"I'll tell you," replied the centenarian. "When my wife and I were first married, the rabbi who performed the ceremony suggested that whenever I saw an argument coming I should take a walk around the block. I took the rabbi's advice and I want you to know that for seventy years the constant exercise did wonders for my health."

* * *

The grandfather had been leafing through a magazine.

"Talk about compatible marriages," he said to his wife, "it says right here in black and white that an old guy my age with a wooden leg just married a young girl with a cedar chest. Boy, will they have a problem with splinters!"

* * *

"Grandfather struck it rich almost as soon as he came to this country," explained the proud grandson and heir to the family's millions. "He invented a pen with a matzoh-ball point. It writes under chicken soup."

* * *

Julius, the genius of CCNY, was giving his grandfather the benefit of his 18-year-old wisdom. Cliche after tired cliche flowed from the youth's mouth with all the effervescence of cold vaseline, and with each new banality the old man's irritation mounted.

"And another thing," pontificated Julius, "behind every successful man you'll find a woman."

"Yes, and usually one with a big mouth," observed the grandfather, oozing spite and malice.

Julius smiled. "Grandpa, you just don't believe in romance," he said indulgently. "You should go to the movies a little more."

"*Yingatsh!*" snapped the old man, "at my age, when a girl smiles at me in a movie she's probably after my popcorn!"

The old man's irate reaction startled the youth.

"I don't know what's gotten into you lately," he observed. "Maybe it's your diet. You should be like me, grandpa—a light eater."

"You're a dietician all of a sudden?" demanded the oldster. "I know exactly what kind of a light eater you are. As soon as it gets light you start eating."

"B-b-but . . ."

"Don't but me no buts," rasped the grandfather, thoroughly aroused. "You are nothing but a long-distance talker. It's a wonder your tongue doesn't get sunburned. I get hoarse just listening to you. You are also disrespectful, arrogant . . ." The old man abruptly halted his tirade, seeing the offended look on his grandson's face.

"However," he concluded in a kinder voice, "nobody's perfect!"

* * *

When the Horowitz family moved from bustling Manhattan to a little village on the far end of Long Island, grandfather Horowitz was supremely happy. A lazy man all of his life, he now devoted himself to science.

For his first project, he devised a five-year plan calling for concentration and controlled study. He would sit in his rocking chair on the porch to see whether it was easier to rock north and south with the wind, or east and west with the grain on the floor.

* * *

The social science major at Columbia University was on an "observation" tour of the lower East Side. She noticed a white-bearded, gnarled patriarch sitting on a bench.

"Sir," asked the student, "have you lived here in this neighborhood all your life?"

"No," he replied coldly, "not yet."

* * *

Old man Epstein had never strayed more than ten or fifteen blocks from his flat on Second Avenue since he emigrated to America fifty years earlier. So he was understandably taken aback when his little grandson broached a subject that was far beyond his area of knowledge.

"Today we learned in school that sailors can tell time by the sun," announced the boy. "Tell me, grandpa, how do they do that?"

Old Epstein, who hadn't even noticed the sun since the eclipse of 1925, pondered the question for several long moments before he answered.

"It's nothing new those sailors are doing," he declared. "Back in Minsk when I was a boy we used to do the same thing. First you shade your eyes so the sun shouldn't hurt them, then you look at your watch."

* * *

Pre-teenager Gertrude had been thumbing through a copy of *Mademoiselle*. An article caught her eye and, a few moments later, she turned to her grandfather.

"I was just reading about models," she began, "but I don't understand something. What's the difference between a model woman and a woman model?"

"There's really no difference," he finally explained after much thought. "I don't believe there ever was a woman who didn't think of herself as both."

* * *

"Grandpa, wouldn't you rather be dead than Red?" asked Shlomo the chauvinist.

"What kind of a question is that for a nice Jewish boy to ask?" demanded the old-timer. "I don't know what's happening to America. Some people would rather be dead than Red. Others would rather be Red than dead. But by me a man's color should make no difference."

* * *

The following hoary classic can be traced back to the 1870s, and may well be far older than that. In this version, circa 1920, we see a perfect example of the dire consequences that can result from asking foolish questions.

The family had just finished dinner and aged Joseph Sachs settled back to read his favorite newspaper when his little grandson, sweet-faced Bernard, approached him.

"Grandpa," said the boy, "may I ask you a question?"

"Certainly," replied the old man in a benevolent tone, at the same time stroking his splended white beard which foamed from his chin and cascaded down past his chest.

"It's about your whiskers."

"Well, what about them?"

"When you go to bed at night do you sleep with your whiskers under the covers or do you let them spread out on top of the covers?"

Mr. Sachs gave a start.

"Why, bless my soul," he exclaimed, "I don't believe I know. I've been wearing this beard for a great many years and until this moment it never occurred to me to remember just what I did with my whiskers at bedtime. I'll tell you what I'll do, Bernard. Tonight I'll take note and let you know tomorrow. Hmmm—over or under the covers, eh? Peculiar thing," concluded the venerable one, shaking his head in perplexity.

That evening when he retired he pulled the top sheet and blanket quite up to his chin, hiding all the whiskers except their beginnings.

"Now, there," he said to himself, "that's undoubtedly the way I've been doing it all these years. See how the force of habit asserted itself so that I automatically put them under the covers? Ahh—now I'm comfortable."

But, a few moments later, he realized that he wasn't as comfortable as he had thought. His whiskers tickled his bare throat. He felt self-conscious, ill at ease. So he heaved his whiskers out and spread them in a broad fan shape upon the blanket.

"Now, that's better," he sighed. "This must have been the way I was doing it all along."

But he couldn't sleep. His beard, stretching out before him in plain view, was, for the first time in his life, an encumbrance and an annoyance.

So he drew them back in again. Then he hauled them out. Then he put them in again. Then in, out, in and out again. All night long he shifted his whiskers and got not a wink of sleep. And the next night it was the same maddening thing all over again: no rest for the poor, harassed, half-frantic old gentleman. And the third night was a hideous repetition of the two preceeding ones.

So, on the fourth night, in stark desperation, he cut his throat, blew out his brains, took poison, leaped from the top of the Flatiron Building, hanged himself and drowned in the East River.

And the moral to this tragic tale is that curious little boys should never ask nice old grandpas what they do with their whiskers at night.

* * *

"Grandpa, I just saw the most wonderful movie!" cried Ruthie.

"What was so wonderful?" asked her grouchy grandpa.

"It was called *Tour d'Amour*, and its all about Gustav Eiffel who created the Eiffel Tower, and the two women in his life."

"*Two* women?" exclaimed grandpa. "No wonder he didn't have time to stucco the tower!"

6

Those Cockamamie Kids

INTRODUCTION

Scientists have for years attributed a sense of humor to porpoises, dogs and the great apes. Yet, for reasons never clearly defined, some psychologists will not concede a sense of humor to human children. Sigmund Freud, himself, not only denied that a child possesses wit and humor, but declared that it "lacks all feeling for the comic."

Freud, to be sure, adduced no facts to prove his stark assertion. It was an inference from his own theory that humor is all a matter of release from adult inhibition. If we may be forgiven an iconoclastic observation, the good doctor may have known his adult psychology, but he didn't know *beblach* about kids. Even an infant will squeal with laughter when his father playfully throws him into the air and safely catches him—fully aware that the smile on his father's face means it is all in fun. Or the mother will pretend to offer a tasty tidbit to her baby, and then, teasingly, pull back the spoon from the infant's waiting mouth. Again the baby joins in the merriment because the smile on his mother's face tells him it is only a joke. But, the very fact that the child participates in the little game indicates that he understands that he has only been teased. It is the ability to *take* a joke, not only to *make* one, that proves you have a sense of humor.

The comic sense in children is quicker and more active than in grown-ups, and less discriminating. They laugh at nothing, and that is precisely how we reprove them when we say, "Oh, stop laughing at nothing!" The older child will remain undaunted. "Mama, here's a riddle," he will persist: "What's long and green, has warts, is shaped something like a banana, and flies through the air like a bullet?" Mama gives up, and with whoops of delight, the child provides the answer: "Super pickle!" He has responded to his own question with the equivalent of nothing—but to him, a *funny* nothing!

The pious and mature philosopher, Immanuel Kant, maintained that adults also laugh at nothing (". . .the sudden transformation of a strained expectation into nothing"). Small wonder, then, that grown-ups can enjoy the statement, "As to capital punishment, if it was good enough for my father, it's good enough for me!" Here we have a plausible movement of the mind that has come to nothing. It is childish, perhaps, but not childlike. The point is that while children are the greatest laughers, in later years their free and boisterous humor becomes refined and intellectualized. But until then, they laugh upon a less exquisite provocation than we do: they do not require that comic things mask a serious thought or tap the deeper reservoirs of feeling in order to give sanction to a hearty laugh.

Juvenile humor falls into two primary categories: Jokes told *by* children and those told by adults *about* children. A number of Yiddish proverbs illustrate the latter. "Small children disturb your sleep, big children your life" is one illustration. Another: "Small children, small joys; big children, big annoys." But those negative sayings are overwhelmed by the more tender expressions in Jewish literature which portray love and understanding. The compassionate Mendele, the Hebrew-Yiddish-Russian satirist (1837-1917), wrote: "Children without childhood are a frightful sight." This was written in a serious vein, of course, but Jewish humorists have used the tragedy of unhappy childhood to make the same statement. Consider the following from Jewish history of the last century.

In the 1880s and 1890s, Russian Jewish boys were often snatched off the streets and sent to the Czarist army. If they were unmarried, they would be conscripted at any age. As the story goes, "Jews being Jews, they found a way out." Children were married at age six and seven, and husbands could be seen playing marbles in short pants. One day, a Jew happened to see such a child and asked him why he wasn't in school. The little boy replied, "I don't go to school. I was married yesterday." So the Jew asked again: "If you got married yesterday, and are now the head of the family, why aren't you wearing long pants?" The child answered, "Yesterday I got married so I wore the long pants; today my little brother is getting married, so he's wearing the pants."

American humor, especially as it applies to jokes about children, is not nearly as grim as that of the past. Here, the *leitmotif* of the accumulated Jewish tragedy has given way to the carefree approach that more nearly coincides with the Jewish experience in the United States. This is not to say that the Jew has forgotten his heritage; nor is he any less concerned with his destiny. His humor is the barometer of the change from the past to the present.

We can laugh about that change. Historically, Jews have studied Torah in one form or another: the philosophy of Maimonides, Spinoza, Gabirol and other scholars of old. But today, Jewish adults acquire their wisdom from television: Kung Fu at one extreme and Archie Bunker at the other. Jewish youngsters in America derive most of their philosophical wisdom from Pogo the Oppossum, Smokey the Bear, Snoopy the Dog and a seagull named Jonathan, all of whom appear to be *goyim*. Where else but in America would a nice Jewish boy name his four goldfish Matthew, Mark, Luke and John—and then feed them crumbled matzos for their evening *nosh*?

The Americanization of the Jewish joke has evolved so far that it is often difficult to distinguish it from its gentile counterpart. Even those jokes which originated in the first and second decades of this century in New York's teeming ghetto cannot always be labeled as uniquely Jewish, as the following anecdote suggests:

Miltie's mother had just bought him a new suit of clothes and sternly warned him to keep it clean. A half-hour later, he returned home from play, covered from head to foot with sticky, clinging mud. Grimly, the mother seized his arm and marched him into the basement, with Miltie screaming bloody murder all the way. "Oh, be quiet," snapped the mother, "you've been spanked before!" The boy stopped shrieking instantly. "Spanked?" he exclaimed with obvious relief. "Gosh, mom, I thought you wuz gonna *wash* me!"

A similar so-called "Yiddish joke" which knows no ethnic boundaries, but which was current in the 1930s on New York's East Side, is given here in translation: A father presented himself at the offices of the telephone company and requested a 50-foot extension cord for his phone. When asked the reason, he explained: "I want my teenaged daughter to spend a little more time outdoors now that it's summer."

Obviously, the above jokes are not Jewish, even though originally told in the Yiddish tongue. Jewish humor, it is clear, has nothing to do with the employment of the Yiddish language, the use of Jewish names, or even the liberal use of ethnic words and phrases. It is the *circumstances* inherent in the joke that gives it its sense of Jewishness—the flavor of *schmaltz* on pumpernickel.

So here's some humor about Jewish kids in America. America!—*a mazel auf Columbus!*—America where Jewish children run everything but the vacuum cleaner; where parents teach children who hit not to hit, and children who do not hit to hit back.

H.D.S.

Most of us are familiar with the reason given by mountain-climbers for their activities:—they climbed the highest peak because "it was there." One little boy recently brought the expression down to basics.

The five-year-old kindergarten pupil was made to stand in the corner for putting mud in a girl's mouth during recess.

When the boy's mother heard of his misconduct she was aghast.

"Mud in a little girl's mouth? Why did you do such a thing?"

"Because," said the kid sullenly, "it was open."

*   *   *

It was two o'clock in the morning and Gedalia the *goniff* was trying to break into a house. He tried all the doors and windows but he could not pry any of them open. Cautiously, he climbed up to the second floor balcony. Peering through a locked window, he saw a baby in its crib. By this time he was quite desperate so he decided to enlist the aid of the infant.

"Hoo-hoo, bay-bee," he called softly. "Itsy-bitsy boo-boo, is oo gonna open window for nice mansie-wansie, hmmm?"

"*Open the window?*" yelled the baby. "Why, ya dumb *shnook*, I can't even *walk* yet!"

* * *

Two small children were discussing the latest addition to their family.

"I heard daddy say that a new baby costs almost a thousand dollars," said the little sister in a hushed voice.

"So what?" retorted her brother. "Look how long they last!"

* * *

It was a scene of tranquility as mama watched television, grandma knitted and little Johanan played on the floor. All at once there was a loud crash as the child knocked over the coffee table.

"Oh, Joey, what am I going to do with you?" wailed mama. "Every time you do something naughty I get another gray hair."

Johanan glanced at silver-thatched grandma and then turned to his mother.

"Wow," he cried, "you musta been horrible when you wuz my age!"

* * *

(If your IQ is over 75, do yourself a favor and skip this one.)

It was the Fourth of July and the Independence Day celebrations were being observed with the usual displays and noisemakers.

Little Shirley, the six-year-old patriot, rushed breathlessly into the house crying, "Mama, can you cut my hair real short on my forehead?"

"Why in the world should I do that?" asked the mother.

"It's for the holiday," explained Shirley excitedly. "My teacher said it would grow out in bangs!"

* * *

Danny's mother received a stern complaint that he had been throwing snowballs at the little girls in the neighborhood.

"Is this true?" she demanded.

"Yeah, but they threw 'em at me first," Danny protested, though not very convincingly.

"I don't care who started it," the boy's mother retorted. "The next time they throw snowballs at you, come and tell me."

"Aw, ma, what good would that do?" he asked plaintively. "You couldn't hit the side of a barn!"

* * *

The sweet old lady in tennis shoes stopped to chat with a new little boy in the neighborhood.

"What is your name, sonny?" she asked.

"Abe," he replied.

"Oh my, that's a famous name. Our greatest president was named Abe. Tell me, would you like to grow up to be like Lincoln?"

"What!" gasped the kid. "And be a tunnel?"

* * *

The lady who taught the "Small Fry" class on Fridays was on maternity leave, so a delegation from the synagogue called at Mrs. Abrams' home to ask if she would take over until the regular teacher returned to her duties. The rabbi, the *rebbetzn* and the *shammes* who comprised the delegation were greeted at the door by Mrs. Abrams' little daughter.

"Mommy is upstairs," said the child. "I'll go get her."

On the second floor, Mrs. Abrams was in the midst of spring cleaning. Boxes were strewn about, clothes were heaped on the bed, the draperies were down and she was busily engaged in washing the windows.

"Oh, my goodness," she groaned when her daughter told her that "company" was waiting for her in the living room. "Honey, you go back downstairs and tell them to wait a few minutes. I'm loaded down with work."

Dutifully, the girl returned to the august delegation and conveyed the message:

"Mama can't come right now—she's loaded!"

* * *

Second-grade schoolperson (male) to third-grade schoolperson (female):

"Are you the opposite sex or am I?"

* * *

Irving and Marva, both in the same class in grade school, had little liking for each other. One day during recess, Marva came up to the teacher on the playground and tattled: "Irving said a four-letter word!"

The teacher called him over at once.

"Marva tells me you used a four-letter word," she said severely. "Is that true?"

"No, it ain't," said Irving, his face flushed with resentment. "I don't even know my three-letter words yet!"

* * *

A baby, according to Peeksville pediatrician Max Vogel, is an alimentary canal with a loud voice at one end and no responsibiliity at the other.

* * *

Hello," came the voice at the other end of the line, "is this Sammy's mother?"

"Yes, it is."

"This is Miss Broyges, at the Hebrew School. I'm afraid you'll have to reprimand your son for upsetting class routine."

"What did he do that's so bad?"

"He made a tasteless joke, that's what he did. We were discussing the lesson for today—how Lot's wife, who looked back, turned into a pillar of salt. And your Sammy stood up and told the class that you once looked back while driving your car and turned into a telephone pole."

* * *

Little Ralphie came to visit his friend Arthur who happened to be in the tub.

"Wow," exclaimed Ralphie, "do you always take a bath in muddy water?"

"Aw, don't be such a wise guy," grumbled Arthur defensively. "It wasn't muddy when I got in!"

* * *

"Sidney, be a good boy and eat your spinach," urged the boy's mother. "It will put color in your cheeks."

"But, ma," Sidney whined, "who needs green cheeks?"

* * *

Joanie walked into the corner drugstore and, standing on tiptoe, just managed to peer over the counter. The pharmacist smiled down at her.

"Yes, little girl, what can I do for you?"

"My mama sent me for two rolls of toilet paper," said Joanie.

"All right, here y'are. That'll be sixty cents."

"Charge it, please."

"Okay," the pharmacist agreed pleasantly. "Who are they for?"

"They're for all of us," explained the blushing Joanie.

* * *

Voices in the night:

"Herbie, stop poking your baby sister!"

"I ain't pokin' her, ma. I'm countin' her measles."

* * *

Kenny the Kindergarten Komic has a riddle to present to the world:
What's the most popular gardening magazine?
Answer: Weeder's Digest.

* * *

The new little girl in the neighborhood had just made "best friends" with another little girl. They got around to discussing the new girl's poodle.

"Does your dog have fleas?" asked the best friend.

"Dogs don't have fleas, silly," giggled the other girl. "They have puppies."

* * *

Sylvia wondered whether her boyfriend was sophisticated enough to provide her with a corsage for the prom dance that night.

Her fears, however, were groundless. A messenger from the local florist delivered a lovely orchid, and with it was a note from her beau:

"With all my love and half of my allowance."

* * *

The late Irvin S. Cobb stands sponsor for this one, popular around 1918 or so.

Sounds betokening intense juvenile grief caused a passing lady to halt in front of a tenement. On the front stoop of the house sat a small boy. Tears coursed down his cheeks and from him issued a series of heartbroken laments.

"*Ai*, poor little boy," said the lady. "What's the matter you're crying like that?"

"Oh-h-h" the youngster howled. He brought his long-drawn wail to an abrupt end, sniffled deeply and checked his sobbing.

"Daddy and mommy won't take me to the movies tonight. And I wanna go to the movies with them. Oh-h-h! Wow-w-w!"

"But don't cry so," advised the sympathetic woman. "Are they ever taking you when you cry like that?"

"Sometimes they do and sometimes they don't," admitted the boy. "But what does it hurt to holler?"

* * *

"Bobby," exclaimed the shocked mother, "you mustn't pull the cat's tail!"

"I'm just holdin' it, ma," protested Bobby. "The cat's doin' all the pullin'!"

* * *

"And do you pray every night?" asked the new rabbi.

"No," answered the little boy. "Some nights I don't need nothin'!"

* * *

"Shirley, drink your milk like a good girl," ordered the child's mother. "It will make your teeth strong."

Shirley took an unwilling sip. "Mama, if it's so good for the teeth," she commented crossly, "why don't you give my share to grandma?"

* * *

Two little sisters were watching a British documentary about the royal family on television. Miriam, age seven, was perplexed by one of the scenes.

"I wonder how Queen Elizabeth knew she was gonna have a baby," she asked.

Her eight-year-old sister was disgusted with such a display of juvenile ignorance.

"Anybody knows that," said the child loftily. "She read it in the papers."

* * *

"Some people's voices," opined ten-year-old Thelma with unconscious wisdom, "are very hard to extinguish over the telephone."

* * *

Mother heaved a sigh of relief as she tucked the children into bed and went into the living room for a little peace and quiet. But in a moment there came the sounds of uproar in the bedroom. Wearily, she returned to the scene of battle where her two little boys were fighting.

"All right, enough is enough!" she snapped. "Who started this?"

"Harry did," yelled the younger of the two, pointing a finger at his brother. "He started it by hitting me back!"

* * *

If you have ever been the parent of an inquisitive child, this brief anecdote should help recall some nostalgic memories.

The young mother could not find a baby-sitter so she took her little boy with her on a shopping trip. But from the moment they left the house, the youngster began to ply her with questions. They came in a steady stream: questions about birds, questions about animals, questions about the stork, questions about God, questions about the sky, earth, the oceans—questions, questions, questions. The mother's patience finally snapped.

"Now you listen to me," she hissed through clenched teeth. "If you ask me just one more question I'll give you a good spanking right here in the street!"

"But, mama," said the boy, "where would you sit?"

* * *

"Last year I caught the Hong Kong flu," bragged seven-year-old Raymond. "I couldn't even go to school. I had it so bad it almost kept me from building a snowman."

* * *

"Sylvia!" exclaimed the indignant mother. "Why did you kick your brother in the stomach?"

"It was an accident, mama," said the little girl defensively. "He turned around."

* * *

Kenny the Kindergarten Komic has another one for us:

Teacher: Stanley, will you please tell the class what happened on July 4th?

Stanley: Grandpa losted his glasses, an' now he hasta drink from the bottle.

* * *

The late Rose Stein (no one ever knew whether she was Mrs. or Miss) went to her reward at the ripe old age of 87, after more than half a century of teaching in New York's public school system. Judge Leon Gwersky, at a testimonial dinner to the grand grammarian of the Grand Street school, recalled an incident which accurately portrayed her precise use of the English language.

"I was in the third grade," grinned Judge Gwersky, "and Miss Stein (we called her 'Miss' in the absence of 'Miz'—a title not yet coined), found good and sufficient reason to send me home with a note to my mother. Let me read it to you:

> My dear Mrs. Gwersky:
> I am a strong advocate of the admonition, "Children should be seen and not heard."
>
> But Leon I can smell!
>
> Yours for more fragrance,
> Rose Stein
> Teacher, P.S. 40

"In my own defense," concluded his honor, "my mother had given me a good scrubbing before I set out for school, but en route to class I had gotten into a garbage-throwing contest with a school chum. However, my mother never forgave Miss Stein."

* * *

Mama: Get into your pajamas, Davey, and I'll tell you a nice story before you go to bed: The Three Bears.

Davey: Aw, ma, Idawanna hear about no bears. Tell me the one Daddy tells—about the Chicago hood. His name was Robin and he had a kid sister named Little Red Riding.

* * *

It was the first time that little Benny of the East Side had ever been in the country. Now, thanks to the Hebrew Summer Camp Fund, he was spending two glorious weeks in this different world.

On the second day, Bennie solemnly watched as one of the counselors buried a dead bird to demonstrate camp hygiene.

"Do you know what I am doing?" asked the counselor.

"Yeah," said the little East Sider, "but how much ya wanna bet it don't grow?"

* * *

It was necessary that dad work later than usual, and tonight he returned home after his wife and three children had had their dinner.

"Did you help mama today?" he asked the kids.

"Yes, papa," said Margaret. "I washed the dishes."

"I dried," announced Mannie.

The father smiled. "And what did *you* do?" he asked, giving his youngest child, Carla, an affectionate pat.

"I helped the betht," she cried, clapping her little hands. "I picked up all the pietheth!"

* * *

The kids were watching a shoot-'em-up western on television. Just as the hero, Hopalong Schwartz, was downing a quart of whiskey in a saloon, the mother of the boys entered the room.

"What kind of picture is this for children to watch?" she clucked disapprovingly. "Such drinking!"

"It ain't like that at all, mama," protested the older boy. "He didn't go into the saloon to get drunk. He just wanted to kill somebody!"

* * *

Over their strenuous objections, two eleven-year old twins were taken by their mother to see the tender motion picture, *Love Story*. The boys had pleaded that they be taken to see a detective or western film, but they had lost out.

"Wow, all that kissin' an' stuff," groaned one of the boys after the show. "It was an awful picture!"

"I didn't mind it so much," said the other boy cheerfully. "Whenever they started kissin' I just closed my eyes and imagined he was chokin' her!"

* * *

Father was scolding his teenage daughter for her slovenly appearance.

"You should be ashamed to be seen in public with those filthy blue jeans and torn sneakers," he carped. "And why can't you do something with your hair? It looks like a mop."

The girl's eyes widened. "Daddy," she asked, puzzled, "what's a mop?"

* * *

Marvin was banging away on his amplified electric guitar and singing his own lusty accompaniment.

"Will you stop that infernal yammering!" shouted his father, scarcely making himself heard above the din. "You call that music?"

"Sure it's music," Marvin revealed. "It's called sock-rock. Garfinkel and his Groovie Ghoulies got a big hit with it. Nice, huh?"

"Who can tell if it's nice or not?" snapped the boy's father. "Nobody can understand the words . . . What's the name of that so-called song?"

"'Lulu Sniffed Glu-lu But Found Nirvana in Marijuana.'"

The father's face turned every shade of purple.

"How dare you sing a song like that in this house—and in front of your own mother! You should be ashamed of yourself! When I was your age we at least kept it clean—and we were grammatical, too."

"What songs did you sing?"

"We kids sang *'Jeepers Creepers, Where'ja Get Those Peepers?'* *'Dirty Gertie From Bizerte,' 'The Virgin Sturgeon'* and *'Mairzy Doats.'* And we didn't scream the songs at the top of our lungs, either. We *crooned*, soft and quiet."

"I don't blame ya, pop," said Marvin coolly. "With titles like that I'da kept it quiet too!"

* * *

Even as a boy, Felix Warburg, the financial tycoon of the last century, displayed the kind of caution he was later to exhibit as an adult in his various banking enterprises.

Warburg was about twelve when he ambled into the kitchen of his parents' home and asked the elderly housekeeper:

"Do you know where the nutcracker is?"

"No, Felix, I'm afraid not," she said. "It's been misplaced somewhere."

"Can you crack nuts with your teeth?" he persisted.

"Good heavens, no!" she laughed. "I lost my teeth ages ago."

"Then," requested Master Warburg, extending two hands full of nuts, "would you mind holding these for me while I go and get some more?"

* * *

In Macy's, one afternoon, a woman was shopping for a suitable toy for her six-year-old son. The sales clerk brought her a large box, colorfully lettered "Today's World." At first she was delighted, but when she opened it and saw the assortment of cogs, cams and wheels inside she gasped in dismay.

"Don't you think this is far too complicated for a small boy?" she asked.

"Not at all," replied the clerk. "This is an educational toy, especially designed to help children adjust to the modern world. No matter how your little boy puts it together it'll be wrong!"

* * *

The family was just sitting down at the dinner table when their teenage son rambled into the dining room, tossed his baseball cap and glove aside, and slouched into a chair next to his father.

"Pass the potatoes, pop," he began.

"I'll pass you nothing!" retorted the father. "You go right into the bathroom and wash your hands."

"Aw, c'mon, pop," groaned the youth. "I'm just gonna eat, not do a heart transplant!"

* * *

"When I first came to Brandeis University as a raw freshman," observed the stately senior, "I was terribly conceited. But it didn't take long for that to get knocked out of me. Now I'm one of the nicest fellows in the whole school!"

* * *

A few years ago, the chancellor of Brandeis was accused of excessive permissiveness during the student protest movements that were sweeping the nation's campuses.

"It's not a question of being permissive at all," the chancellor retorted in his defense. "I just happen to be an ardent supporter of giving young people adult responsibilities."

When the student disorders finally abated, he decided to take a vacation deep in the north woods of Maine. One night, while resting in a clearing, a mile or two from a tiny village, he suffered a heart attack.

"And that was when I changed my mind about giving youngsters too many adult responsibilities," he said. "I found out that the local doctor was eighteen, and the pilot who was to fly me back to New York for an operation was only twelve!"

* * *

A young mother was about to light the Sabbath candles.

"Do you know what's happening?" she asked her six-year-old little girl, as she made ready to say the prayers.

"Yes," said the youngster. "Liberace's coming."

* * *

God's destruction of the wicked cities of Sodom and Gomorrah is another story that makes a vivid impression. A teacher, relating the story to her class, explained: "Lot was warned to take his wife and flee out of the city which was about to be destroyed. They got away safely. Then, Lot's wife looked back, and was turned into a pillar of salt.

Now, children, do you have any questions to ask about this story?"

"Yeah, I have a question," announced one boy, raising his hand. "Could you please tell us what happened to the flea?"

* * *

At the Henry Street Hebrew School, Goldblatt, the new teacher, finished the day's lesson. It was now time for the usual question period.

"Mr. Goldblatt," announced little Joey, "there's somethin' I can't figger out."

"What's that, Joey?" asked Goldblatt.

"Well, accordin' to the Bible, the Children of Israel crossed the Red Sea, right?"

"Right."

"An' the Children of Israel beat up the Phillistines, right?"

"Er—right."

"An' the Children of Israel built the Temple, right?"

"Again you're right."

"An' the Children of Israel fought the 'gyptians, an' the Children of

Israel fought the Romans, an' the Children of Israel wuz always doin' somethin' important, right?"

"All that is right, too," agreed Goldblatt. "So what's your question?"

"What I wanna know is this," demanded Joey. "What wuz all the grown-ups doin' all that time?"

* * *

Six-year-old Thelma rushed into the house and tearfully told her mother that her brother, Stanley, had hit her.

Stanley, two years older than his sister, was immediately summoned into the living room and asked to explain.

"We wuz playin' Adam 'n Eve," said Stanley defensively, "but instead of temptin' me with the apple-she ate it herself!"

7

Dialect Stories

INTRODUCTION

The use of dialect in the telling of a Jewish or Jewish-oriented joke has all but passed into history. Modern Americans consider it to be in poor taste—and sometimes it is. The gifted author, Nathan Ausubel, in *A Treasury of Jewish Folklore*, states: "A large body of Jewish dialect jokes are not Jewish at all, but the confections of anti-Semites who delight in ridiculing and slandering the Jews."

There is truth in Ausubel's assertion, of course. Accented jokes have, indeed, often been used as a cloak to obscure anti-Semitism. However, we must also remember that humorous anecdotes which are about Jews or about Jewish customs and mannerisms, and which are told by Jews to other Jews, are often told in dialect for a variety of valid reasons. One of them is simply that the denouement, or "punch line," might *require* an accent. Without it, the very point of the joke is lost.

Another point: Many of the stories are premised on a misunderstanding of the English language. For example: Mrs. Goldberg, who has been suffering from insomnia, is being questioned by a psychiatrist. "Tell me," he asks the grandmotherly woman, "what is your attitude toward sex?" And Mrs. Goldberg responds pertly, "I love it! It's the finest sturr on Fift' Evnoo."

But there is a more compelling reason for the proper use of dialect. The humorist, if he is true to himself and to his readers, understands that folk humor is not propaganda to be rewritten to accomodate the psychological and political views of each generation. As a social historian, he must record the experiences of each, maintaining intact those of previous generations. This is essential if there is to be a reliable history that embodies authenticity and continuity. And there is no doubt that humor does reflect a people's history! Boiled down to its essence, the use of dialect, coupled with the authentic portrayal of a people, enables the humorist not only to "tell it like it is," but to "tell it like it was." He is a people's folklorist with a smile.

The properly accented anecdote should be recognized as a major component of Jewish-American lore because it accurately mimics (though often exaggerating) the Yiddish inflection and pronunciation of literally millions of immigrants for whom English always remained a second (and usually a third) language.

The telling of dialect stories in the United States began with the second generation of fun-loving American-born youngsters who delighted in exchanging among themselves the linguistic mistakes of their foreign-born parents and neighbors. From these inchoate beginnings, the dialect stories gained in popularity among the children, grandchildren and great-grandchildren of the immigrants who were discerning enough to acknowledge that their antecedents represented a slice of America.

Americanized Yiddish expressions have invaded every facet of life. Sometimes dialect is not used, but is implicit. One popular example, which probably never happened, is the delightfully warm invitation from an El Al Airlines stewardess at dinner time: "Ladies and gentlemen, please fasten your seat belts, you should eat a little something." And then there is the malediction: "All his teeth should fall out except one—and in that one he should have a toothache!" But these are Yiddish inflections and transpositions of words rather than actual dialect.

The exclamation, "*oy*" (the definition of which will be found in the glossary of this book), has a perfectly legitimate function and has been used for generations. When properly employed, it is marvelously expressive. Here is an example:

During the time of the French Revolution, when the guillotine was employed almost around the clock, a Jew who lived in a village outside of Paris met a friend who had just returned from the city.

"What's happening there in Paris?" asked the Jewish man nervously.

"Conditions are absolutely horrible," replied the friend. "They're cutting off heads by the thousands."

"*Oy*," moaned the villager, "and me in the hat business!"

But enough is enough! The author is reminded of the botanist who found a beautiful flower by the wayside. He sat down to analyze it. He pulled it apart and examined every part under a microscope. When he had finished he could tell the color of the flower, its classification, and the number of stamens and pistils and petals and bracts, but its beauty and fragrance and life were gone.

So let us be done with analyzing and enjoy a little reading. And, incidentally, should a Yiddish word appear here and there that you don't understand, don't be lazy, but turn to the Glossary in the back of the book.

H.D.S.

Three doting mothers met for the first time in the dining room of the "Founting Blue" hotel at Miami Beach. As good *Yiddishe* mamas will, they soon got around to discussing their sons.

"Tell me," said Mrs. Goldfarb, "vot is your son doing for a living?"

"Mine son Oiving, he should live *biz a hundert un tsvantsik*, he's treveling for a silk house," replied Mrs. Levy.

"Vere your Oiving is treveling?"

"In de Vest."

"Dot's nice," said Mrs. Goldfarb. "Mine son, Harry, he also is a salesman. He's treveling in de Vest too."

Mrs. Goldfarb and Mrs. Levy turned to the third lady. "And your son, Mrs. Silverstein—vot he does?"

"Mine Joey, he trevels also."

"Vere he trevels?"

"In de South, mine Joey trevels."

Mrs. Goldfarb and Mrs. Levy looked at each other in utter bewilderment, and then at Mrs. Silverstein.

"In de *South?* Vere is de South?"

"Vell, I'm not sure," said Mrs. Silverstein uncertainly, "but I tink it's also in de Vest."

* * *

Mrs. Rosenberg, whose features were as unmistakably Jewish as her accent, became stranded one evening in a very "exclusive" resort section of Cape Cod—"exclusive" meaning that Jews were excluded. She needed accomodations for the night so she entered the town's only good hotel, a posh establishment, and approached the desk.

"I vould like, please, a room for the night," said Mrs. Rosenberg.

The desk clerk made a quick appraisal of his visitor and shook his head.

"Sorry," he said curtly.

"Vy you're sorry?"

"The hotel is full, madam."

"So vy the sign says 'rooms available'?"

The desk clerk stammered, hesitated, made a few feeble attempts to dissuade her, and then confessed:

"We don't admit Jews. Now if you'll try the other side of town . . ."

Mrs. Rosenberg drew herself up to her full height of five feet and addressed him heatedly:

"Jewish? By you I'm Jewish all of a sudden? From vere you got such a crazy idea, from vere? It so heppens I'm a convoitable."

"You're a *what?*"

"A convoitable. For a long time I'm vatching on the telewision this Fulton Schine and finally he's making me a Kedillac."

"Ah, I see," the desk clerk said. "You're a Cadillac convertible."

"Execkly," Mrs. Rosenberg answered huffily.

"Well, I happen to be a Catholic myself," said the keeper of the hotel. "Do you mind if I test you with the catechism?"

"Test! Test!"

"How was Jesus born?"

"By a himmeculit contraption from Heaven. The mama's name vas Mary and the papa's name vas Yussel."

"Very good. Now tell me, where was Jesus born?"

"In a menager, he vas *gevayn ge-borned.*"

"That's right. And why was he born in a manger?"

"Because," Mrs. Rosenberg snapped, "some *paskudnyak* like you vouldn't give to a Jewish lady a room for the night!"

* * *

"Hello, is this the Levy residence?"
"Ahah. Mit whom you vish to speak?"
"Is Mr. Levy there?"
"Dis time of day Mr. Levy he's voikink."
"Is Thelma at home?"
"In school is Thelma."
"Then how about Harry? Can I speak to him?"
"Harry? In collitch is Harry, he should be a doctor."
"I see. Is this Mrs. Levy?"
"Mrs. Levy she's shoppink in de supermokkit."
"Well, who is this?"
"Dis? Dis is Daisy, de *schvartze*!"

* * *

"*Oy*," moaned the lady as she and her neighbor sipped tea in the kitchen, "did I have *tsuris* and a pleasure dis veek."
"So vat vas de *tsuris*?" asked the neighbor.
"De *tsuris* vas mit mine daughter. She married already a *shaigetz*."
"And de pleasure?"
"De pleasure is, denks to Gott, he's a doctor!"

* * *

An immigrant, who is also an aspiring author, spills out his feelings:
    Mine duble-spased tiping is svell,
    Mine storys and pomes is strong,
    Yet notting I'm riting don't sell—nu, tell me—what can be rong?

* * *

Old Mrs. Bender was called into court as a witness in a civil suit. It seems that her friend, Mrs. Gold, had been cheated by Mr. Gross, owner of a furniture store.
    The judge entered the courtroom and took his seat at the bar of justice. The bailiff called Mrs. Bender as the opening witness.
    "First," instructed the bailiff, "you'll have to swear in."
    "Vell, if I must I must," agreed Mrs. Bender. "Dot Mr. Gross is a crook und a bestid!"

* * *

The following may be the only Martian joke to employ an accent:
    A flying saucer landed in Miami Beach, and out stepped a Martian visitor to earth. He strode across the street to a filling station and tipped his hat to a gaudily painted gas pump.
    "Hollo, dollink, hoz by you this evenink? You'll take me please to your leader like a nize girl?"

There was no reply, so the Martian tried again.

"Swittie-pie, it's good you're not talkink with strange men, but all I'm eskink is you should take me to your leader. Yes?"

His, polite request was again met with silence, and the Martian's patience came to an abrupt end.

"Lady," he snapped, "take your finger out from your ear when I'm spikkink, and pay a little attention!"

* * *

Are you acquainted with Theresa Van Gogh of Park Avenue? No? Then perhaps you will remember her when she was Tessie Vogel of Henry Street. She arrived in this country in 1902 where she met and married young Lazar, a recent immigrant from Galicia. Tessie's hubby sold notions from a pushcart, but as a result of his wife's ambitious planning, he soon opened a dry goods store on lower East Broadway. He proved to be a good businessman and, with the passage of time, he became a prosperous merchant with stores in New York, Philadelphia and Baltimore. Yes, *that's* the Lazar Vogel—I knew you'd remember!

Anyway, Tessie's social-climbing ambitions started right away. First she promoted Lazar from *Galitzianer* to *Litvak*. Then she graduated from orthodox to conservative and finally to the reform branch of Judaism. But it wasn't until Lazar died and went to reform heaven that she decided to get closer to God by praying to His son and other members of His personal family. Besides, what does it hurt to be an Episcopalian when you're rich?

So Tessie moved from her middle-class apartment on Mosholu Parkway to a fancy-shmancy condominium on Park Avenue, and metamorphosed from Tessie Vogel to Theresa Van Gogh. After completing her studies in the new Christian faith, Tessie (as we shall continue to call her) presented herself at the altar of the exclusive Christ Episcopal Church in the heart of New York's "Silk Stocking" district, ready for conversion.

"Have you prayed to our Lord and Saviour?" asked the minister.

"Who else?"

"And what did you ask of the Lamb of God?"

"I did just like it says in the *goyishe* Bible—I esked he should save me."

"Very good. And what did our Saviour say?"

"Vot he said? He said 'hokey-dokey!'"

* * *

A Chassidic rabbi in Brooklyn, during World War II, received a telegram from his grandson who had been drafted into the army and was now stationed at Camp Vernon, near Leesville, Louisiana. It seems that the young man had fallen in love with the only Jewish girl in Leesville—a Miss Rae Weill—and they had decided to marry before he was shipped overseas. Of course, nothing else would do but for the grandfather to perform the wedding ceremony.

What choice did the old man have? A grandson is a grandson and that's all there is to it! So he packed a few personal items in a cardboard box, fastened it securely with twine, boarded a train and rode for three days and nights until he arrived at the little town whose population at that time numbered about 3,000. An attendant at the depot pointed out the street where Miss Weill lived, and, with a slip of paper containing the address of his future grand-daughter-in-law clutched in one hand and his carton gripped in the other, he slowly set off in search of the girl's house.

As he trudged along, glancing down at the paper, children stared in astonishment at the weird figure. He was dressed in typical *Chassidic* garb; a long, black kaftan that reached almost down to his ankles; on his head was a black, broad-brimmed *shtreimel;* and to complete the picture, he displayed a pair of white woollen socks that were clearly visible over his black, highbutton shoes. Pepper-and-salt *peyess,* or side-curls, engulfed his ears and were lost in a bushy beard that hid his chest.

To the children of that little southern town he might have been a visitor from outer space. Soon a bevy of other youngsters joined their playmates and proceeded to follow the apparition down the street, but kept a sizable distance behind him.

From time to time the rabbi glanced around him, noting with growing irritation that the line of curious followers was becoming longer with every minute. When he stopped, they stopped. When he started, they started. And not a word did they dare utter.

The old man could stand it no longer. He halted, put his carton down on the sidewalk, turned around and glared at them. But the children, instead of fleeing before his fierce gaze, were frozen to the spot.

"Vot's de metter mit you kids?" the exasperated rabbi finally shouted. "You never before saw a Yenkeh?"

* * *

Teacher: And now, Isidor, can you name a delicious drink that begins with a *G?*
Isidor: G'malted.

* * *

This *klayneh tsimmes,* from Dr. Jerry Segal's delightful *God Bless Mine Patients,* was published by the dentist-writer in 1926, almost entirely in Yiddish. In order that it may also be enjoyed by those with a limited knowledge of that language we have taken the liberty of anglicizing part of the anecdote.

Faigele, a *griener*—or "greenhorn" in English—found it necessary to visit Dr. Seligman's dental office. From the moment she entered, it was evident that she was new at this sort of thing, and terribly nervous. She scrutinized the equipment with wide and apprehensive eyes. Reluctantly she seated herself in the chair, and it was only after much hesitation that she obeyed the dentist's request to open her mouth so that he might examine the tooth which had been misbehaving. Her nervousness perceptibly increased as he jabbed a sharp little instrument at the offending molar.

"I guess we can do something for it," he said in a tone meant to be soothing.

But Faigele was not to be thus soothed by mere words. Her rigid fingers gripped the arm-rests of the chair until her knuckles showed white through the skin.

The dentist filled an automizer with an antiseptic fluid and treated the gum. As he withdrew the spray, she clamped her mouth shut tightly.

"You may expectorate now," said Dr. Seligman.

She turned her frightened eyes up to him, her face terror-stricken. Trembling, her voice strained with fear, her jaws still clenched, she gasped:

"I should expect *vot*?"

* * *

A muffled gong sounded as the little old lady opened the carved and gilded door and walked into the exotically furnished reception room. A silk-draped young woman appeared in a cloud of incense as if from nowhere and bowed.

"Do you wish to consult with the all-seeing, all-wise guru, Maharishi Mah-jongg?"

"Yes," said the visitor. "Tell mine Seymour his *mamaleh* is here."

* * *

An *alteh bobeh*, in this country for half a century, never could get used to the American way of doing things, and had neither the intention nor the slightest desire to learn. But it was the last straw when she showed up at her granddaughter's wedding ceremony wearing curlers in her hair.

"Grandma, how could you!" stormed the humiliated bride.

"Dollink," explained *Bobeh*, "I only vanted I should look nice for the reception!"

* * *

Now that he had retired, old man Koenig was determined to spend the remainder of his life where he could enjoy peace and tranquility in the warm sunshine.

"I tink maybe I'll settle in Pollim Beach, Kelifoornia," he announced.

"Oh, papa," cried his daughter, "how many times have I told you not to say Pollim Beach!"

"*Oy, shayneh,* I forgot!" he exclaimed, smacking his forehead with the heel of his hand. "It's my *goyishe kop*. Pollim Beach is in Florida. In Kelifoornia is Pollim *Springs*!"

* * *

An elderly couple, only a few weeks removed from Ellis Island, took their first tour of New York and wound up at Macy's Department Store.

They had not taken a dozen steps inside the building when the wife stopped dead in her tracks, clutched her husband's arm and pointed wordlessly to the escalators laden with people riding up and down.

He was as thunderstruck as she, but as he watched the passengers moving and at the same time standing in one place, his amazement gave way to awe.

"*Ach, America goniff!*" he breathed admiringly. "*M'shtait, m'gait!*"*

* * *

It was graduation day at the Adult Citizenship Class, and Mrs. Pomerantz smiled with pleasure as the teacher announced that she was the winner of a prize for having the highest marks in the class.

"And here is your reward," said the teacher, handing her student a replica of the Liberty Bell.

"Denk you," said Mrs. Pomerantz. "Dis prize I'm graciously accapting, even if it *is* crecked!"

* * *

In days gone by, before the Catskills became a popular summer haven for Jewish vacationers, Grossinger's famous resort in the Borscht Belt was little more than a rural farmhouse. Inside plumbing had yet to be installed, so the newly-arrived Grossinger family constructed a three-hole privy at the rear of the place.

One day, the cry of "fire!" rang out. Family and guests rushed through the front door and gazed wildly about, but could see neither fire nor smoke.

Once again came the anguished yell: "Fire! Fire!"

Old man Grossinger ran to the back yard and this time the screaming seemed to emanate from the outhouse. He bolted inside, but the place was empty and not a sign of a blaze anywhere.

"Fire! Fire!" yelled the voice again.

Grossinger whirled about and suddenly realized that the screaming apparently came from below the seats. He peered down into the unpleasant depths and—behold!—there was a man at the bottom of the hole —up to his armpits.

"What are you hollering *fire* for?" demanded Grossinger. "I don't see any fire down there."

And the trapped man snarled back:

"*Shlemiel!* Mit all de ladies present, vot did you expect I should yell?"

* * *

Two young brothers, Maurice and Sammy, age eleven and twelve, were returning from a visit to their grandmother's house. As they sat on the crowded bus, a woman, laden with heavy packages, entered and

---

*The Yiddish word *goniff*, used in this context, does not mean "thief," but rather "clever one" or "rascal." The translation, loosely, reads: "Ah, clever America! People stand, people go."

clutched a straphanger in front of the two boys.

Maurice, always a perfect little gentleman, rose to give the lady his seat.

"Much obliged," said the grateful woman.

But Maurice promptly sat down again. Sammy, amazed at this impolite act, then arose and gave the woman his own seat.

When she finally got off the bus, Sammy confronted his brother.

"What's the big idea of getting up and then sitting down again, Maurice? Especially after she was nice enough to say 'much obliged'."

"*Much obliged!*" Maurice gasped in astonishment. "Holy mackerel— I thought she said '*Moishe, bleib!'* "*

* * *

"The British are coming! The British are coming!" screamed Paul Revere.

"*Nu*, let them come," said Mrs. Revere. "We got chicken soup, lox, bagel, chopped liver, schmaltz herring . . ."

* * *

Jascha Heifetz, the eminent concert violinist, had just finished a recital and was surrounded by a group of admirers. Among them was Mrs. Bloom, to whom he had just been introduced.

"Do you like Chopin?" asked Mr. Heifetz.

"Vell, frenkleh," replied Mrs. Bloom, "it hoits mine feet, valking around from vun stur to de next. Better dey should deliver!"

* * *

"Mine American-born daughter she's telling me: 'Yeah, Popsi-wopsi, I gotcha, but you'll hafta lay some heavy bread on me so's I kin strut new threads at the establishment bust-out, ya dig?'

"So I'm digging for maybe a half-hour to learn she needs money she should have a new dress for the school dance—

"And she is criticizing *mine* dialect!"

* * *

Grandpa, as a boy some fifty-five years ago, began his working life as a presser in a cloak-and-suit sweatshop in a cramped loft on Greene Street, in the heart of the lower East Side. It wasn't much of a start for an ambitious young immigrant, but that was a long, long time ago, and he had made a fair success of his life in the intervening half-century.

But despite his many years in the United States, grandpa still retained a number of his old beliefs, customs and grammatical expressions. For one thing, he could never quite grasp the distinction between such words as "on," "of" and "by." He would claim, for example, that he had once lived *by* Montgomery Street, not *on* it. These innocuous trans-

---

*Bleib: "Stay." As used here, it means, "Maurice, remain seated."

gressions annoyed his granddaughter, Sybil (whom grandpa, with a twinkle in his eye, would call *Tsibileh*, or *klayneh Tsibileh*—little onion—much to her indignation).

On this particular evening they were having their after-supper *nosh* —a glass of tea with lemon and *lekach*—when grandpa innocently remarked:

"You got things easy these days. When I was young I was a presser by cloaks."

"Oh, grandfather!" (Sybil had stopped calling him "grandpa" two years earlier because it sounded so "plebeian.") "*Must* you say 'by' when you mean 'of'? A presser *by* cloaks indeed! You should say *of*!"

"All right, *Tsibileh*, have it your way," agreed the old man pleasantly. "When I was young I was a presser by cloaks of!"

8

Beauty and Fashion

INTRODUCTION

Since ancient Biblical times, when the Mosaic commandments were formulated, personal hygiene and general cleanliness have been an integral part of Judaism—poverty notwithstanding. Many references that prescribe the necessity for good grooming are found in the various books which comprise the Talmud. The bedrock, therefore, was firmly established when the American-Jewish community moved into the vanguard of style, fashion and cosmetic beauty less than 100 years ago.

One reason for this assumption of leadership can be attributed to the early preponderence of Jews in the needle trades; a second, was the influence of the infant motion picture industry which was, in the main, founded by Jewish entrepreneurs. In both spheres of American enterprise the consideration was financial: a profit for the employer; a decent living wage for the employee—(see Introduction to chapter on "Yiddishe Blarney in the Workaday World"). Both industries had one philosophy in common: the garment and film had to be *sold*, and like most consumer goods in this country they required ingenious styling to attract customers and keep abreast of competition.

As public acceptance of changing fashions advanced each year—to the delight of the manufacturing, wholesale and retail trades—so too did the burgeoning fashions in cosmetics. Men baptized themselves daily in oceans of lotions. Women emerged from their bathrooms and boudoirs smelling like chrysanthemums, roses, gardenias, lilacs, honeysuckle, jasmine and orange blossoms. What with the styles they were wearing, the ladies not only didn't look Jewish, they didn't even *smell* Jewish. Thus, the age of the beautician and the designer arrived. And with it came the inevitable humor, the barbed wit frequently aimed at the creator of such apparel as the corset, the bustle, the muu-muu, the sack dress, the peek-a-boo blouse and the bra-less bra. Males especially enjoyed the jokes. Somehow it is easier to forgive an enemy after you've gotten even with him.

Now the girls were fashionable. If you were not fashionable, you were quaint. The Empress Eugenie hat converted a million shopgirls into queens; the pillbox hat made every housewife a walking Jackie Kennedy; pantyhose gave every female a chance to swathe herself in clinging nylon from toe to pelvis.

And then came the Facial Facade for Un-quaint Fashionables, promulgated by a man named Gertrude, the darlingest designer in Greenwich Village. To achieve the Facade, the American woman tweezed her eyebrows into a high arch that almost reached her hairline, giving her, as one sage put it, "a look of perpetual surprise." She used white nail polish and white lipstick, so that when a man took her to dinner he never knew whether to order her a steak or a bowl of vitamin-fortified wheat germ. Her eyes took on added importance, too. She framed them with half-inch lashes purchased at the corner drugstore, encircled them with magenta shadow, and was always careful to keep them averted downward to suggest that they had witnessed indescribable suffering. Now she was satisfied. She had that Haunted Look, just like Sylvia Sidney on the late-late show. Her expression now contained that fine balance between hidden sorrow and smouldering fury, as though she had just received her monthly bill and realized she had again been swindled by the gas company.

According to female psychologists—who are seldom female, and whose psychology is suspect—every woman, at one time or another, views herself with a deep appreciation of her own beauty. This, even though she might be so unprepossessing that she could pass unnoticed in a mirror. Yet, there is a kernel of truth in the assertion—the psychologists can't be wrong *all* the time. Take the case of the Contessa Lavonna de Rothschild who, at the age of 87, commissioned Picasso to paint her portrait. The matriarch of the famous banking family declared that she expected the artist to bring out all her "inner beauty" and to enhance what remained of her external charms. Well, you know Picasso!

Surprisingly enough, when the painting was completed, she was immensely pleased with it. Picasso, however, was terribly disappointed.

"I made the nose too short," he complained.

The contessa, whose proboscis was one of majestic proportions, adored the idea of being portrayed with a tiny nose, but after much argumentation she reluctantly yielded. "Go ahead and change it," she sighed. Picasso emitted a low moan, and from the depths of his misery he confessed, "I would, but I can't find it."

Many of the beauty and fashion jokes revolve around the husband's expenses to maintain his one-and-only's feminine mystique. "My wife made me a millionaire," grumped the late showman, Billy Rose. "So why are you complaining?" asked his unsympathetic friend. "Because," said Billy, "before we were married I was a *multi*-millionaire."

Some Jewish-oriented stories cannot always be definitely classified into a specific category because of their intra-connecting components. Here is one that combines fashion, dialect and medical humor:

A young model was overwhelmed to learn that she was assigned to pose for the front cover of *Vogue*. On her way home that evening, she purchased a bottle of champagne to celebrate the occasion. After dinner, her mother, who happened to be in the kitchen, heard the unfamiliar popping of a cork and went into the living room where her daughter was pouring a festive glass of the bubbly spirits. She took one look at the label on the bottle and frantically rushed to the telephone. "*Oy*, doctor, come quick," she gasped. "Mine Miriam is drinking shempoo!"

Beauty and Fashion cover a wide range of humor. Most of the following anecdotes and quips were popular in yesteryear's Jewish enclaves from New York to Los Angeles. Some are still being told and re-told, albeit dressed up in stylish new expressions. And that is as it should be: Folk humor should never be left to the professional comedians. It belongs to the masses, and it is they who shape and refine it, making of it something quite different from the so-called "Jewish humor" of Las Vegas.

H.D.S.

At the exclusive Uptown Bon-Ton in downtown Upton, Mass. one of the new salesladies was summoned to the front office by the sales manager. She was a new American who had been given a job despite her strong accent.

"Miss Pechter," he began coldly, "I was informed by Madam Van Groysafeese, who is one of our best customers, that you were discourteous to her this morning. Now, you know perfectly well that we do not countenance rudeness to our customers. What have you to say for yourself?"

"First of all, Mr. Saperstein, nobody needs you should holler on me," snapped Miss Pechter. "Second of all, that person—that Groysafeese woman—she starts out by asking for a simple formal, so I showed her our best line. But nothing suited her fancy-shmancy taste. I showed her all kinds of others: strapless, form-fitting, floor-length, mini, just about everything in stock. Then with boxes all over the place and samples covering the whole table, she asked me if she wouldn't look better in something flowing. . .

"So I suggested the river!"

* * *

Theodore and Roz planned to go out for the evening in celebration of their first wedding anniversary. Hubby was already dressed and waiting for his wife who was about to surprise him with her new gown.

Suddenly, she appeared before him, posturing in the doorway like a model. His eyes widened in shock.

"Roz, for God's sake, you aren't going out in *that*!" he gasped. "Your neckline! It's—well—it's indecent! It's cut way too low!"

"But this is the latest style," insisted Roz. "Next year the neckline will plunge even lower."

"Listen," stormed Theodore, "if that neckline goes any lower you'll be barefoot!"

* * *

Elsie had only recently moved into the neighborhood and this was her first trip to the local beauty salon. There, the cosmetician introduced her to Judith, her new neighbor.

"Oh, I've heard so much about you, dear," cried Judith. "Now I'd like to hear your side of the story."

* * *

The good people in Israel were amazed when American girls showed up in mini-skirts. They didn't believe that anything could be shorter than that Six Day War.

* * *

Dorothy was scanning the advertisements, seeking a formal gown for the high school prom, when her eyes fell on a full page ad: *Original Paris Copies—This Week Only!* She talked her reluctant father into accompanying her to the store, and, after trying on a half dozen gowns, each showing more cleavage than the preceeding dress, she finally found one that suited her.

"How do you like this one, daddy?" she asked brightly. "I think it will be adorable for the school dance."

"Honey, I got news for you," said her father, his voice cold. "If I catch any boy dancing with you in that dress he's gonna have to marry you!"

* * *

The local Hadassah club decided to hold a benefit concert to raise funds for an old age home. Fortunately, they were able to engage Madame Faigel la Traifa from Haifa, the famous coloratura.

As the expensively-costumed singer began an aria from *Carmen,* Mrs. Bloom, who was sitting in the first row, leaned over and whispered to Mrs. Levine, "That entertainer has a very big repertoire."

"You said it!" whispered back Mrs. Levine. "And in that gown it looks even bigger."

* * *

The gorgeous, seductive French model, Madamoiselle Beatrix Soigné, formerly Becky Pincus of the Bronx, was displaying the latest Paris fashions. As she turned this way and that way, modeling a sheer negligee (like they taught her in Skolnik's Gay Paree School for Models, Ballet Dancers and Cocktail Waitresses), the buyer for Macy's uttered an appreciative sigh.

"And to think," he murmured, "she started out as a telephone operator."

"A telephone *switchboard,*" you mean, contradicted the buyer from Gimbel's. "When that girl walks, all her lines are busy!"

* * *

Sid Rose, of the John Robert Powers schools, offers this advice to people who are overweight: "If you want to look slim—have fat friends."

* * *

"Do you have a perfume that is especially appealing to men?" asked the lady customer.

"We certainly do," replied the clerk at the cosmetics counter. "May I recommend *Moon Over Hoboken?* This perfume is so sexy it was banned in our Boston store."

* * *

Deborah was celebrating her 14th birthday and felt that she was now old enough to have a permanent wave.

"Well, I suppose so," sighed her father. "How much is this going to cost me?"

"I'll need 15 dollars."

"Fifteen dollars!" exclaimed the outraged father. "Listen, Debbie, you go on over to the same beauty parlor your mother goes to—the gossip alone will curl your hair; and for free!"

* * *

Mrs. Montmorency Gotgelt had just bought some silk underwear, an expensive dress and some high-priced accessories, but the salesgirl was determined to increase the purchase.

"Let me show you our new line of imported hosiery," urged the girl. "You'll like them ever so much better than those wrinkled, old stockings you're wearing now."

"Madam," spat Mrs. Gotgelt, "I am not wearing any stockings!"

* * *

The late Edward G. Robinson contributed this observation on Hollywood fashion mores.

"Film stars today," said Eddie, "look forward to getting their divorce in the same dress their mothers got divorced in."

* * *

Another Robinson quip: "These days you just can't judge a girl by the clothes she wears. There's not enough evidence."

* * *

Two *yentas* were making *meeows* in the beauty parlor.

"I heard that you saw Millie again after all these years. . . So tell me, has she been able to keep her girlish figure?"

"Keep it? Listen, she *doubled* it!"

* * *

It was his wife's birthday and Mr. Shulman was in Sak's Fifth Avenue to buy her a dress.

"What is your wife's size?" asked the saleslady after Mr. Shulman had explained his mission.

"I don't know," he confessed. "But look, you know how thin you are, right? And you can see how thin I am, right? Well, she's thinner than both of us put together."

* * *

At the *Skinny Dipper Reducing Acres* (otherwise known as the "Fat Farm" to uncouth and insensitive persons), Mrs. Schmaltzkopf spent her first day getting acquainted with her fellow fatties. She was introduced to a gentleman whose girth was twice as large as her own. He eyed her speculatively.

"How much do you weigh?" he asked.

"A hundred and ninety," Mrs. Schmaltzkopf confessed.

"Heck, you got nothing to worry about," snorted the rotund one. "I *eat* more than that for breakfast!"

* * *

Rosie was about to take her annual summer vacation, and this time she decided on the seashore. There, she hoped, she might meet a suitable, marriage-minded young man. For that kind of fishing, she needed the proper bait, so she went to a smart shoppe to buy a bikini swim suit.

After Rosie rejected a number of styles, the salesgirl had an inspiration. Reaching under the counter, she brought forth a slinky, brief little number and confided: "This is an exact copy of the bikini worn by Jacqueline Onassis. I myself sold it to her only last week."

"How do you know she liked it?" asked Rosie.

"She tried it on," said the salesgirl, and you should have seen her beam!"

* * *

At Woodward and Lothrop's Department Store in Washington, D.C., the fashionably dressed lady bounced into the elevator and asked the operator: "Where can I find silk covering for my settee?"

"Third floor," directed the young fellow, "lingerie department."

* * *

Mrs. Zelda Zucker fancied herself as both a gourmet and a raving beauty. Unfortunately, these two areas do not usually enhance each other. The more she partook of exotic foods, the fatter she became. But her triple chin, hippo hips and rounded avoirdupois did not seem to affect her vanity. She still regarded herself as a slinky siren. So it was no occasion for surprise when she decided to give her husband a 30th wedding anniversary present of a photograph of herself in a swim suit.

She waddled into the most fashionable studio in New York to have her picture taken. But no matter what angle the photographer used he could not avoid the awful truth. Nothing he tried helped to achieve the flattering effect Zelda demanded. As he continued to change positions, lights and stances she became increasingly irritated with what she considered to be totally unnecessary delays.

"The only trouble with you," she snapped, "is that you're not photographing my good side."

"I can't, lady," he replied coldly, "you're sitting on it."

* * *

It was Gertrude's turn to recite and the English teacher scanned the classroom, but the girl had disappeared. Yet, she had been present only a moment or two ago.

"Can anyone tell me where Gertrude is?" he asked the class.

"Yes, sir," ventured Gertrude's little friend, Miriam. "I think she's round in back."

"Young lady," said the teacher severely, "I asked for her whereabouts, not her physical description!"

* * *

Signposts and guideposts for milady:

The Park Avenue Pedal Adornment Shoppe ("shoe store" to the likes of the Great Unwashed) displayed this neat little sign in its window: *Size four shoes made especially for size five feet.*

And right around the block, on 72nd Street, in the entrance of an outfitter to the kindergarten set, we find this imperious demand: *Be sure to get your cowboy suits at Hopalong's (Formerly Shapiro's).*

In Bucks County, the proprietors of two lingerie shops are right up there with their New York counterparts. One sign reads: *Destiny may shape your ends, but if not, our girdles will.* Across the street is this charming notice of a sale on maternity gowns: *The Ladies' Ready-to-Bear Department offers nine full months of satisfaction.*

The beauty shops and reducing salons in Beverly Hills must be conducted by frustrated or retired comedians. Observe these bits of evidence:

> *Please do not whistle at the girls leaving this establishment—they may be your mother and grandmother.*
>
> *Sam Spiegel—the Master of Your Fat.*
>
> *We make young colts out of old 45's.*

And then there's that sprightly sign in Bertha Brecht's Bra Shoppe in Hollywood: WE FIX FLATS.

But the most elegant sign to be found anywhere in the United States must surely be the announcement posted on Nate's Shoe Shine Stand at Western Avenue and Wilshire Boulevard in Los Angeles:

Your pedal habiliments artistically illuminated with ambidextrous facility for the infinitesmal remuneration of thirty-five cents per operation. For persons of the feminine gender requiring such services for footwear of suede or patent leather, an additional emolument of fifteen cents will be required. The establishment thanks you.

* * *

Ever since that memorable day when she first viewed herself in a training bra, Fifi Chartreuse, formerly Fanny Chernikoff of Far Rockaway, dreamed of becoming a high fashion model. Now that she had blossomed into a perfect 36-22-36 she was ready to launch her career. First, however, she decided to do something about her markedly Semitic features which, rightly or wrongly, she felt would be a hindrance to her success. So, determined to cut off her nose to spite her race, she consulted a famous plastic surgeon. The doctor, an imposing fellow, listened patiently as she explained her problem.

"Yes, I can change your features," he assured her when she had finished. "In fact, I can make you quite beautiful."

"Macy boocoop, mon cherry," Fifi murmured, just to let this fancy surgeon know she was no slouch when it came to continental niceties. "I would like to be swave and oo-la-la, like those girls in the Follies Bejeerie—ya know what I mean?"

"I understand. Now tell me, what kind of face would you prefer? I can make you look like Marilyn Monroe, Zsa Zsa Gabor, Helen of Troy, Cleopatra, Snow White—you name it."

"Listen, Doctor," replied Fifi in a firm voice and forgetting her French accents, "I'm not asking I should imitate anybody. Just make from me a thing of beauty and a *goy* forever!"

9

Communication Capers

INTRODUCTION

The need for communication, both through the spoken and the written word is deeply rooted in the history, folklore, literature and religion of the Jewish people. Admittedly, communication got off to a bad start in the Garden of Eden, with serpents, streakers and Republicans getting the worst of it ever since. The Israelites learned at the outset that you not only can't fight City Hall, but you can't win an argument when the other party has access to all the miracles. Despite this, the Jews became proficient at arguing among themselves—and with everybody else, including the Arabs: *Especially* the Arabs! But the Arabs didn't succeed in outmaneuvering the Jews. The secret: superior communication among the rank and file of the Jewish masses.

In the dawn of Judaic history, the elders of Israel realized that the traditions and laws of their kinsmen could not be adequately transmitted from one generation to the next by word of mouth or through the use of hieroglyphics. The Hebrews needed a written language through which their spiritual philosophy and thought could be expressed. They needed a written language that would convey *ideas*. And so, they created the *Aleph-Bais*—the Hebrew alphabet based on phonetics rather than pictures; a system of writing that had occurred to no other people—one that employed consonants and (implicitly understood) vowel sounds to form root words, prefixes, suffixes and connecting phrases; in other terms, a disciplined structure of grammar. In more recent centuries, Yiddish, rather than Hebrew, became the common language of East European Jews in particular.

The written and spoken language of the ancients, with some modifications, has survived to this day. In the United States, however, the number of Yiddish readers has declined in recent years, as noted by the demise of the *Tag-Morgen Journal*, which passed into history in January, 1972, leaving the *Jewish Daily Forward* as the only important Yiddish daily newspaper in the field. Regrettably, there is not much left of the once lively Yiddish press in America. Jews have always liked newspapers. "When the *Mosheeach* (Messiah) comes," it is said, "they will expect

81

the papers to get out an Extra." The late David Ben-Gurion added: "And why not? When the Jews were in the wilderness, did they not have their Daily Manna?"

The Yiddish press was a link that united the mass of Jews who came to America during one of the great exoduses of history. The Jews going out of Egypt had no need to learn a new language, but those coming here from Europe did, and the Yiddish press served as a vehicle of indoctrination to the ways of a new world. The papers were held in very high esteem by a variety of Jews: immigrants from Bialystok and Grodno, Vilna and Cracow, Minsk, Pinsk and Yekaterinoslav, representing many types and local cultures—but brothers and sisters all, under the Star of David.

Among those who made the strongest journalistic impression in the Yiddish press was Abraham Cahan, editor of the *Forward*, or *Forvertz*, as it was and still is called by many of its readers. Cahan was a *Litvak* from a town near Vilna. When he liked a *Galitzianer*, he converted him into a *Litvak*. A case in point is the noted humorist, B. Kovner, a *Galitzianer*. His real name was Adler, but Cahan was so impressed with the man's humorous writings that he pursuaded him to change his name to that of a Lithuanian city, Kovno. Thus, he became B. Kovner.

Cahan had worked for a time on several English-language papers in America, and was no doubt influenced by them. Today, editors are usually polite—or about as polite as an editor can be—but in those days they were often somewhat rough. Abe Cahan learned to be just as rough as his gentile counterparts—and often tougher. To illustrate: A man came to the *Forvertz* office one day and asked for a job. Cahan asked him what he could do.

"I can write poetry," explained the applicant.

"Poetry doesn't sell papers," snapped Cahan. "Can you make *pogroms? Pogroms* sell papers!"

Bayarsky of the *Tag-Morgen Journal* was just as bellicose as Cahan. He would hire some radicals for his religious-oriented paper, and then mutter: "It gives me pleasure to see these athiests praising Jewish religious institutions for a pittance."

But it wasn't all irony and sarcasm. There was the "Bintel Brief" of the *Forvertz*, for example. English dailies have since appropriated the same idea with columns like "Dear Abby." In the *Morning Journal*, Abraham Shomer wrote novelettes which gave the Jewish mother a nice cry as she prepared *gefilte* fish. After the cry, she would use the paper to wrap herring in. And let us not forget Zevin, the interesting little hunchback who worked for the *Tageblatt*. We recall the likes of him with deep nostalgia. In order to reach his desk, he would sit on a big copy of *Webster's Unabridged Dictionary*, which inspired his colleagues to declare that he had the most educated *tuchus* on the staff.

Some people are less communicative than others, of course. Leo Aikman, in the *Atlanta Constitution*, told of seeing a Bell Telephone truck in New York which carried the message on its side panel: "Ask Me About Better Telephone Service." Underneath, in the dust, someone had scrawled, "I don't talk to no truck." In yet another sphere, that of television, communication can be anything but explicit. Consider the case of Herb Newman, the weather forecaster, who gloomily predicted, "There's a 100% chance of possible rain."

Many Jewish writers are engaged in the business of public relations. Somewhere in my earlier jottings, I mentioned the imaginative publicist who was handling the press notices for vocalist Eydie Gorme. He phoned her one morning with a "terrific, stupendous" idea for a photo that would "surely make page one in the dailies." It seems that the battleship *Missouri*—the famous "Mighty Mo"—had arrived in port and he wanted Eydie at the dock that very day so her picture could be taken alongside the ship. "Can't you just see the caption under that picture?" he rhapsodized: "Eydie Meetie Mighty Mo!"

I did not think that any other flack could top that one—at least not until I was informed otherwise by Dave Kellerman, the Hollywood press agent whose father, also a publicist, was responsible for the following press wizardry:

Down in Florida, papa Kellerman had been retained to publicize the Roney Plaza in Miami, one of a string of hotels owned by tycoon J. Myer Schine. Kellerman knew that Schine doted on personal publicity (and never mind the hotel), so he sat up all one night cudgeling his brain for an idea. Then, like the electric bulb in the oldtime cartoons, the solution burst upon him with brilliant illumination. He drove out to the Gulfstream racetrack and, after some shopping around in the boneyard of the stables, found an old horse whose owner was happy to unload for only ten dollars. Kellerman promptly changed the horse's name from "Footloose Filly" to "Harvest Moon." Then he got J. Myer Schine to climb into the saddle while a photographer snapped his picture. A day or two later, press agent Kellerman released the photo to the newspapers with the inspired caption: "Schine on Harvest Moon."

Speech is actually the means by which the currency of mental wealth is passed from mind to mind. While this is basically true, it is also true that much of our speech is not all that rich in meaning—and the less said about some of the minds the better. Specifically, this applies to direct communication, or one-to-one speech with which individuals make their thoughts known to each other. When our thoughts are awry, so must be our speech. And, of all the transmitters of one-to-one speech, none can surpass the woman who worships at the feet of the Jewish goddess of communication, Yenteh Tellabendeh.

The *Yenteh* is purely mythical, of course, and is no more addicted to idle gossip than her gentile sisters—it's just that she does it better. But no other group of people has ever succeeded in individualizing and humanizing her as have the Jews. The most striking aspect of the *Yenteh's* proclivity for spreading rumors, or for minding everyone else's business but her own, is that her gossip and interference is seldom vicious. Usually she is quite perceptive. For example, a daughter reads a love letter aloud—one of many such tender missives from her beau. Mother says suspiciously: "If he loves you so much why doesn't he compromise himself a little?" Or take the neighbor who glances around furtively so no one else can overhear her, and then whispers: "About Mrs.

Levy, you'll never in a million years believe this, but. . . ." And madame *yenteh* eagerly interrupts with: "I believe, I believe!" Small wonder, then, that a *yenteh's* idea of hell is a place where all are required to mind their own business.

And now, let's communicate.

H.D.S.

A few days before *Chanukah*, back in the 1920's, two well-known citizens of New York met on Broadway. One was Otto Kahn, the distinguished financier; the other was equally famous in certain circles as the most persistent borrower of money—without security—on the entire Eastern seaboard. This notorious *schnorrer*, on one pretext or another, was forever getting sums, great and small, from friends or comparative strangers, and never paying anybody back. He made a fairly comfortable living at it, too.

Mr. Kahn was no intimate of the *schnorrer*; their acquaintance was of the sketchiest sort. But each knew the other by reputation. They exchanged cool greetings as they encountered each other and, after a few casual remarks, they separated.

That evening, at his residence, the financier received a letter sent by special delivery. It was from the champion borrower, and it read as follows:

My dear Brother Kahn:

Meeting you today so pleasantly revived memories of our former meetings. It stirred in my heart certain thoughts of the approaching Chanukah season when, with joy and gladness, we commemorate the miracle of the cruse.

Now, as it happens, the coming of this most festive holiday finds me financially a bit embarrassed. This condition is only temporary, I assure you, but I need funds—in short, a loan to be repaid of course at the earliest opportunity.

So, in order that I and some who have a sentimental claim upon me may enjoy a happy Chanukah, I am asking you to send me, by return mail, your check for one thousand dollars.

Thanking you for this modest favor, I am, as ever,

Yours in friendship,
John J. Epworth

The financier sat right down, wrote a reply, and mailed it that same night. He said:

My dear Mr. Epworth:

I have read your communication of this date and I am wondering what has become of Jacob Epstein—"Epworth" does not seem to have a familiar ring about it. But no matter. Here is my answer, and I fear you will search these contents in vain for any check bearing my signature.

With you I share the delight of the holiday. Like you I look forward to enjoying it. But, if I sent you a thousand dollars of my money, you might have a happy Chanukah, but I'm damned if I would.

> Yours cordially
> Otto Kahn

* * *

In New Jersey, recently, the directors of a bank in Long Branch were deliberating about the possibility of absorbing the one in Red Bank.

"I'm against it," announced one of the board members emphatically. "A bank's name should reflect dignity. How would it sound if people started calling it the Long Branch branch of the Red Bank bank?"

* * *

Who said that when a married woman begins misbehaving, her husband is the last person to hear the news? Whoever it was, he appears to have uttered a universal truism.

Take the case of Michael Helfman, recently of Hunters Point. It was a long time—so it seemed to the watchful and gossiping neighbors— before Mr. Helfman's jealous suspicions became aroused. However, once he was convinced that his wife's love of admiration had carried her beyond the bounds of discretion, he proceeded to act.

He sat down and wrote this note to the good-looking Mr. Dash, who lived just across the street, and sent it over by messenger:

> Sir:
> I shall expect you to appear at my office this afternoon at three o'clock to explain why you have been carrying on with my wife.
>
> Yours truly,
> Michael Helfman

Promptly the messenger returned with an answer, which read:

> Dear Mr. Helfman:
> Your circular letter of even date received and comments duly noted. Thanks for the invitation. I shall be very glad to attend the caucus.
>
> Sincerely,
> Morris H. Dash

* * *

A *palindrome* is a word, phrase or sentence which reads the same forwards or backwards. Considering the frequency with which these brain-twisters appear in the Jewish press, one might think that the Jews invented it. Perhaps they did, at that. According to this author's secret files, the first palindrome was created by that eminently respected

Jewish boy, Adam. He introduced himself to Eve with the welcoming speech:

"Madam, I'm Adam."

"Eve," she responded with one of her own.

Here are a few others, some retaining the unmistakable flavor of *Yiddishkeit:*

Evade me, Dave.

No, Miss, it is Simon.

Able was I ere I saw Elba.

Lew, Otto has a hot towel.

Did Hannah see bees? Hannah did.

A man, a plan, a canal: Panama.

Semite Moses orders madam's red rose sometimes.

* * *

Nominated for the Bravest Letter of the Year Award:
  Dear Teechr
  Mannie Weil was lait for skool yestidy coze it wasint his folt.
                                                    My farver

* * *

Hubby: If there's anyone I can't stand, it's the person who interrupts a conversa . . .

Wifey: And takes the words right out of your mouth.

* * *

"Dear Papa," wrote little Shirley to her father who was out of town on business, "we're having a speling b in school and I'm in the finnals."

* * *

Computers have a habit of going haywire, as thousands of hapless householders will attest—especially when bills are normally due at the first of the month. But no computer ever went so completely and vengefully mad as the one that singled out old Lou Lieberman as its legitimate prey.

Lieberman was minding his own business, tending his little dry cleaning agency, when the mailman came in one morning and dumped 143 letters on the counter—all of them identical requests that he renew his subscription to the *Catholic Digest*. It so happens that Lieberman had never heard of the magazine and would not have subscribed if he had. He threw the entire lot into the wastebasket.

But on the following day he received 153 more, on the next 278, and on the third day over 400. For the remainder of the week, he received the requests for renewal at the rate of a thousand or more a day.

Finally, he could stand it no longer. He closed the shop, went to the Western Union office and wired the *Catholic Digest* his payment, along with a cryptic telegram:

ALLRIGHT ALREADY, I GIVE UP. RENEW!

* * *

Motorists driving along Drexel Boulevard in Chicago were recently greeted with a bold new sign on Mendel's Modern Car Wash. It read:
—KEEP AMERICA CLEAN—
Run a Hippie Through Our Car Wash

* * *

"My third grade pupils were darlings. Especially Henrietta Szold, a serious little girl with an alert mind, but a child who smiled brightly enough when praised. I recall hugging her as a result of an incident that occurred just prior to George Washington's birthday, in 1867.

"During our history period I spent much time emphasizing the fine qualities of the Father of Our Country, telling the children of his bravery, his resourcefulness, his honesty, sincerity, kindness and faith in God. When the time for questions and answers arrived, I said to the class:

"And now, children, for what great position would such a man as this be most suited?"

"Henrietta raised her hand and I gave her permission to speak.

"'Miss Wickwire,' said the girl, 'I think he would make a very nice husband.'"

Another remembrance: this time by one of America's great orators of yesteryear—William Jennings Bryan:*

"In 1892, as a freshman Congressman, I was introduced to a Miss Henrietta Szold, a lady whom I should not have wanted as an opponent in debate. That meeting is memorable for it was the first time in my life that I was left absolutely speechless—which, for me at any rate, was and is an event of cataclysmic proportions. That it was occasioned by a member of the gentler sex has, ever since, caused me to wonder if women are, in fact, as gentle as has been claimed.

"I had been declaiming at some length on the hardships endured by the Pilgrim Fathers when it gradually dawned on me that Miss Szold did not seem as impressed as the others of my audience. When I paused briefly for a glass of water, Miss Szold asked:

"'Mr. Bryan, have you nothing to say about the Pilgrim *Mothers*?'

"'Why, what about them?' I replied.

"'It would appear to me,' she said with an aplomb I admired on the instant, 'they endured all that the Pilgrim Fathers did, and the Pilgrim Fathers as well!'"

* * *

In the old days, before the invention of the air-brake simplified the dangerous job of coupling the steam cars that were then in use, and bringing to an end the many cases of accidental amputations that resulted from hand-coupling the cars, Arnold Bogen, the Chicago writer and lecturer, went to Peoria to make an address during a trainmen's convention.

---

*From *The Commoner*, William Jennings Bryan, ed., 1901.

Upon his return home, he wrote an account of his visit in his newspaper column:

"It was one of the most remarkable experiences in my entire career on the lecture platform. The guests of honor were all retired switchmen, and they attended in a body. They seemed to like my comments immensely but there were so many one-armed men down front that they had to do their applauding in pairs."

* * *

Bret Harte, the noted writer of short stories and humorous verse of Western local color, was a contemporary of Mark Twain. Both men detested each other. Harte was only part Jewish so we shall tell only part of the story—but the best part.

During a trip back East in 1871, Harte chanced to meet Twain while strolling on Fifth Avenue, adjacent to Central Park. It was a balmy day in early June, exactly suited for a pleasant walk in the sunshine. Both men would have preferred not to address the other at all, but some sort of comment at this face-to-face encounter could not be avoided.

"Nice day," said Twain, his voice cool.

"Yes," replied Harte drily, "I've heard it very highly spoken of."

* * *

The late David Sarnoff, the radio and television pioneer who rose to the presidency of RCA, came to America from Russia in 1900 as a boy of nine. Securing a job with the Marconi Wireless Company, he won national recognition for his reporting of the news of the Titanic disaster. Marconi Wireless was later absorbed by Radio Corporation of America, and Sarnoff became a legend as well as an historical figure. We can thank the folklorists for the following tidbit.

As a telegrapher, young David received his share of complaints from subscribing newspapers to the wire service for which he worked. One telegraph editor of a Long Island paper complained because names were being omitted from the cabled stories. He wrote to the company that if it neglected this essential detail in the next wired yarn, he would cancel the paper's subscription. The telegraph company passed the ultimatum on to Sarnoff with the added postscript that if the offense were repeated, he would be discharged.

The young man was quickly converted to the idea of including names in his stories wherever possible. A few days later, the complaining editor received this dispatch:

VALLEY STREAM, L.I., N.Y. JUNE 6—A SEVERE STORM PASSED OVER THIS SECTION THIS AFTERNOON AND LIGHTNING STRUCK A BARBED-WIRE FENCE ON THE FARM OF HENRY WILSON, KILLING THREE COWS— THEIR NAMES BEING FLOSSIE, BOSSIE AND BUTTER- CUP.

* * *

In Hebrew School, little Sarah was asked if she could repeat a verse from the Bible that they had studied last week. She replied, "Not only can I quote the verse, but I can also give you the zip code: Exodus 19:20."

* * *

For you English language buffs: The future of "courting" is "caught."

* * *

"In Russia," enthused a returned tourist, "the phones are really marvelous. In fact, the street-corner telephones are free. The only problem is that you can't hear anything."

* * *

"Kuhn, Kahn, Kohn and Grossmacher, good mo-o-orning."
"Is Mr. Grossmacher there?"
"Who's calling pleee-uz?"
"This is Shlessinger, Shlossinger and Shlepperman: Mr. Shlessinger calling."
"Just a mo-o-ment, I'll connect youuu."
"Mr. Grossmacher's office."
"Mr. Grossmacher, please. Mr. Shlessinger wishes to talk to him."
"Would you put Mr. Shlessinger on the line, please?"
"Mr. Shlessinger? Ready with Mr. Grossmacher."
"Hi, Jake? Mannie. OK for lunch? Atta boy—see ya!"

* * *

Stan and Sid, both on the road with non-competing merchandise, usually traveled together, sharing the same car and hotel rooms to save money. One evening, the two friends registered at a small hotel in Schenectady and Stan immediately sat down to write his wife a letter. Sid happened to notice his buddy's unusual salutation.

"Tell me something, Stan," he said curiously, "how come you always address your wife as 'Dear AT&T'? Is she a big investor?"

"No, nothing like that," answered Stan. "AT&T doesn't stand for American Telephone and Telegraph. It means 'Always Talking and Talking!'"

* * *

Sign in the window of Pechter's Bakery on Fairfax Avenue, Los Angeles: UPSIDE/DOWN CAKES 99¢

* * *

Paul Berger, owner of the LaSalle Furniture Store in Chicago, after a series of futile attempts to collect payment from a delinquent customer, sat down and wrote a personal letter. His command of English, however, was somewhat deficient, so he asked his college-educated son to read it and give his opinion.

"This isn't bad at all, dad," avowed the offspring. "You presented your case in a thoughtful, orderly and concise manner. In fact, you only made two little errors: *Momzer* is spelled with a *z*, not an *s*, and there is no *w* in 'louse'!"

* * *

Josh Berman, who later became the Seattle representative for Paramount Pictures in the old days, had only been in America for six months and was attending night classes in citizenship.

"I'll never understand this crazy English language," he sighed to his wife as he labored over his homework for the next evening. "On page five of my textbook it says that a radio draws waves. And only yesterday I read in the papers that a clothesline waves drawers."

* * *

Communique to our Similar Standards Dep't.:
From Israel comes a report with an international flavor. It seems that Zurith, of kibbutz Hakhoshlim, won the title of "Beauty Queen of Northern District Cows."

The judges' criteria: "A cow must be well built, have a straight back, a deep body and good legs, with wide ribs which enable her to breathe deeply. But above all she must have good udders, well formed, productive and nicely fitted to her body."

* * *

"Young people today have absolutely no respect for their betters," fumed Al Rosen, Los Angeles co-ordinator of the Bonds for Israel drive. "Last night at the rally, there was an Israeli poster with a big picture of Moshe Dayan on the wall and, underneath, some resident genius had scrawled, *Hire the Handicapped.*"

* * *

Dear Grandpa,

I really loved the book you sent me for my birthday. I am reading it night and day and am now on page 6.

Love, Gloria

* * *

Whether the Decalogue was inscribed in Hebrew characters when it was handed to Moses on Mt. Sinai, or whether it was written in archaic English as per the King James version, is not a subject for discussion in this book. It is mentioned only to illustrate that biblical language remains a popular form of expression. For example:

A sign in the lobby of a Beverly Hills synagogue warns: *Thou Shalt Not Smoke*! And in the recreation room of the same opulent temple, an out-of-order coffee machine was adorned with this announcement: *This machine taketh. It giveth not.* And a block away, in the Stein and Katz Medical Building was this no-nonsense command: *Goliath down, thou looketh weary!*

* * *

"Sorry, my wife's not here," said the husband to the phone caller. "Would you care to leave a rumor?"

* * *

Sol, the New York *mohel*, moved to New Orleans where he hoped to find new horizons in that southern atmosphere. Settling in a quaint little house in a Jewish neighborhood, he put up a big sign on his front lawn: *Sol the Circumciser.*

Soon, however, the local rabbi called on Sol and explained that the sign was in poor taste.

"Surely you can find another way to advertise your profession," the rabbi said. "Just word it differently—a little more respectably. Use some of that New York ingenuity you brought down here with you."

"All right," Sol agreed. Within an hour he removed the offending sign.

A week later the good people of that Dixie neighborhood were greeted with a huge, brand new neon sign, proudly emblazoning the northern *mohel's* occupation:

Sol, the Yankee Clipper.

* * *

Out of latter-day Jewish-American folk humor—the "Tin Lizzie" era of the mid-1920's—comes this Ferocious Ford Fable. In that period which marked the birth of assembly line production, Henry Ford was winning acclaim for his success in the mass production of cars, but he was also drawing scathing denunciation from Jews and informed gentiles for his support of the bogus *Protocols of the Learned Elders of Zion.*

The Protocols were purported to be the minutes of a secret international committee or congress of prominent Jewish leaders. According to this canard, these "Elders of Zion" devised a conspiracy whereby the Jewish people would dominate and control the world. Despite their indisputable falsity, the *Protocols* were taken seriously by millions of people throughout the world and, even today, Arab factions are still distributing copies of this literary garbage.

The most widespread dissemination in the United States occurred between 1920 and 1927, when the *Dearborn Independent,* which was controlled by Henry Ford, published excerpts periodically. Ford later apologized in order to "make amends for the wrong done to the Jews as fellow-men and brothers by asking their forgiveness."

It became well-known that Ford could shrug off the angry responses that resulted from his publishing of the *Protocols,* but he would go into a towering rage at the slightest criticism of his auto production techniques. Jewish wit rose to the occasion when this chink in his armor became apparent. If they could not needle him into anger with references to his gullibility, they could and did get to him with jokes about his cars—jokes that were created and gleefully repeated until Henry would turn purple with rage. A few of the humorous stories earned a niche in the annals of Jewish-American folk humor. Let us revive one of them.

The telephone rang in the inner sanctum of auto magnate Henry Ford. His secretary answered the ring:

"Mr. Ford's office. Who is calling?"

"This is Mr. Morris Luftmensch," said the voice at the other end of the line. "I would like to speak with Mr. Ford."

"Mr. Ford is very busy," explained the functionary. "May I take the message?"

"No, you can't," was the firm reply. "I must speak direct with your boss. I happen to be an important customer of your company, and what I have to say, only the head man should hear."

"Well, in that case, sir, kindly hold the wire," said the secretary in a respectful manner. Mr. Ford was quickly summoned to the phone.

"Well, what is it?" snapped the auto mogul.

"Mr. Ford," stated Luftmensch without preamble, "you advertised recently that your company is making a complete car in six minutes. Is that right? Yes or no!"

"Yes, in a test we did turn out a car in six minutes. What about it?"

"Well, I'm the guy who bought it!"

* * *

Announcement chalked on the blackboard in the San Francisco office of the Restaurant Employees Union:

Man Wanted to Wash Dishes and Two Waitresses

* * *

A.M.

8:00 - "Hello, Mr. Goldfogel, please."
"Sorry, he hasn't come in yet."
9:00 - "Did Goldfogel show up?"
"He should be here any minute."
10:00 - "Me again. Goldfogel there?"
"He just phoned that he'd be a little late."
11:00 - "Hi! Goldfogel around yet?"
"He came in but he had to leave."
12:00 - "Well, is Goldfogel back?"
"He's gone to lunch."

P.M.

1:00 - "Goldfogel back from lunch?"
"He should be back any minute."
2:00 - "How about Goldfogel?"
"He's in the building someplace. Can I take a message?"

3:00 - "Goldfogel?"

"He must be around somewhere. His hat's still here."

4:00 - "How about Goldfogel?"

"Frankly, I don't know where he is, but I'll keep you posted."

5:00 - "*Nu*, did you find Goldfogel?"

"Sorry, he's gone for the day."

* * *

From the secret archives of the Government of Israel:

Dear Comrade Brezhnev:

You ask that I give you my reaction with reference to your publicly stated desire to permit all Jews who so desire to emigrate to Israel.

My secretary, being a gentleman, cannot type what I think of your promises; and I, being a lady, won't dictate it. But you, being neither, will understand me fully.

Golda Meir

* * *

Conversation between two girls, overheard on the 7th Avenue Express at the Bronx Park Station:

" . . . so I told him we were through, because all he cared about was my body. Then I heard this loud noise on the other end of the line."

"My goodness, you mean a pistol shot?"

"Well, n-no—it sounded more like a champagne cork."

* * *

The late Edward G. Robinson enjoyed telling the story of the hard-of-hearing man who was presented to a beautiful and charming young lady.

"Mr. Rubin," said the mutual friend, "I want you to meet Miss Heffelfinger."

Mr. Rubin's eyes widened in admiration of this gorgeous creature smiling at him. "I'm awfully glad to meet you, Miss—Miss—Miss . . ."

"Heffelfinger," prompted the mutual friend, raising his voice a decible or two.

"I'm terribly sorry to be such a nuisance," said poor Rubin, "but, as the young lady can see for herself, I'm a little deaf." He cupped his hand behind his ear. "Now I think I can hear you. Would you mind repeating the name just once more?"

"HEFFELFINGER!" shouted the friend.

"It's no use," lamented Rubin. "I can't make it out at all. It still sounds to me like you're saying—please don't laugh—*Heffelfinger!*"

* * *

Henrietta Szold (1860-1945), probably the most beloved and respected woman in American-Jewish history, was a founder of *Hadassah*. Born in Baltimore, she started her career as a teacher and, in 1893, she became an editor for the Jewish Publication Society. She is, however, best remembered for her long career in Zionist work and leadership. In 1916, she organized the American Zionist Medical Unit for Palestine and, in 1920, she became director of the School for Nursing in Jerusalem. She was chosen to be a member of the Zionist Executive in 1927 and served in many other high positions of Jewish interest in the United States and Palestine.

Of the several volumes written about this remarkable woman, only two humorous anecdotes about her have been found by this editor. Both are very brief; one from her early childhood, and the other, from the period before she left for the Holy Land, when she was still a young woman.

First, the anecdote told by her grade school teacher, Gladys Wickwire.*

* * *

Back in the old days, language and citizenship classes were held during the afternoon and evening hours for the benefit of the many new immigrants seeking a better life in the *Goldeneh Medina*. These free classes were conducted at Cooper Union, the Henry Street Settlement, Workmen's Circle *(Arbeiter Ring)*, and at a number of public schools in the various boroughs of New York, but mostly in downtown Manhattan. The late Henry Eisenholtz, founder of the East Broadway Bon Ton Store, which later grew into the nationwide chain of retail outlets of today, told of a personal incident that occurred at Cooper Union which he himself attended as a newcomer to the United States.

The instructor, a woman with the very soul of patience, was working mightily to help build a larger vocabulary among her adult pupils—teaching them how to pronounce the various parts of the human body in English. She would point to each place and then carefully enunciate, "Fingers—wrist—elbow—shoulder."

But it seemed that the more she labored, the more confused the students became. Not one could name the parts when called upon—that is, until she came to Henry Eisenholtz.

In a clear voice, and without the slightest hesitation, he pointed to each of the parts of his arm and correctly identified them: "Fingers—wrist—elbow—shoulder."

"Why, Mr. Eisenholtz, that was just fine!" gushed the happy teacher. "How in the world did you remember?"

"Easy," said Eisenholtz proudly, pointing to his head. "I used mine kidneys!"

* * *

---

*From *All My Little Girls*, Gladys Wickwire, Baltimore Press, 1878.

Intriguing sign in the window of Harelick & Roth, booksellers of Los Angeles: BACK IN 15 MINUTES—ALREADY GONE 10.

* * *

The following classified ad appeared in the *San Fernando Valley (California) Jewish-American*, July 20, 1971:

My motorboat and supplies were stolen from its mooring at Marina del Rey two weeks ago. I send my best wishes that the boat breaks in half while it is five miles out, in a storm, and that the thief's mother is unsuccessful in attracting help as she runs barking along the shore.

10

Ask a Foolish Question

INTRODUCTION

> "One fool can ask what
> a thousand sages cannot answer."
> —*Yiddish Proverb*

"Ask a foolish question and you get a foolish answer" is a Jewish maxim which has been repeated in one form or another for many centuries. The Talmud itself contains a full measure of peevish complaints about foolish questions, including the querulous utterance: "There are lions before you, and you ask about foxes?!"

Jews, it is said, would not be Jews if they did not contradict one another, so it should come as no surprise that the people's literature is replete with opposing viewpoints. An old Yiddish proverb states: "Each wherefore has its therefore." Mendele, however, in 1873, wrote his own cautious opinion: "Not all questions may be asked, nor is there an answer for every question." Perhaps he was right.

Someone once asked the late Rabbi Montague Isaacs, Los Angeles spiritual leader of Congregation Tifereth Jacob: "Rabbi, what would you do if the *Mosheeach* were to appear tomorrow?" The old rabbi, a witty man in and out of the pulpit, replied evenly, "I would first ask the Messiah what took him so long."

Clearly, then, the quality of the answer depends on the substance of the question. As Ibn Gabirol pointed out in the eleventh century: "A wise man's question is half the answer." In the modern context of humor, it is evident that the "foolish question" joke is incomplete without the so-called "foolish answer." But here we run into a paradox: the question may be foolish, but the reply can be (and usually is) astute, sardonic or downright insulting—anything but foolish. The answer may be stated in allegorical or hyperbolic terms so as to *sound* nonsensical at first hearing, but it might well be informative or convey a serious message or truth, despite its sarcasm.

Probably the best illustration of the withering reply is found in the classic story of the supposed meeting between King Faisal and David

Ben-Gurion in Saudi Arabia. "Just look at all those gushing oil wells," boasted Faisal. "Isn't this a marvelous country?" Ben-Gurion regarded him with a cold eye. "Your Highness," he finally answered, "if it weren't for those wells, all you'd have is a million square miles of kitty-litter."

Allowing for the usual exceptions, the main difference between the old European "foolish question" joke and its American counterpart is that in the former both the questioner and the respondent are serious, while in the latter it is only the *questioner* who is serious. In old Europe, the *shnook* answered the question: in this country he *asks* it! Moreover, in the European version of yesteryear, it was the foolish respondent who enjoyed the "punch line," rather than the reverse, as is customary here today. One such old-time story tells about the son of a rich merchant of Bialystok who returns home from the university, proud that he has now acquired wisdom. His father tests him to determine if the youth is as wise as now claimed. He hides a small wooden disc in his fist and begins his interrogation: "The object I am holding in my hand is round and made of wood. Tell me, what is it?" Beaming, the son replies: "A wagon wheel." The moral, obviously, is that education can be equated with learning, but not necessarily with wisdom or even with common sense. In the United States, however, very few jokes in this category provide a moral; either implicit or explicit. Here, they are told "for the fun of it."

Many of these little anecdotes should properly be termed "foolish answer" rather than "foolish question" jokes. Often, they are based on misunderstanding. For example, a real estate broker asks: "Would you like to see our model home?" And the prospective customer eagerly responds: "I sure would! What time does she quit work?" But in the majority of such stories in the United States, the humor lies not so much in the foolish question but in the "squelch"—the "put-down"—the reply that satisfies. It serves notice that the question is as meaningless as a Russian election. Thus, we have the query: "Do you believe that the average Negro is really born with a banjo on his knee?" And the answer: "Yes, but when the child reaches the age of three his parents usually have it surgically removed."

"A fool says what he knows, a sage knows what he says," declares the Talmud. Having complied with the first half of the proverb, I ring down the curtain on this Introduction with an admonition of my own:

Beware of the man who asks you a question, answers it for you, and then says you're wrong. Verily, he is worse than the woman whose feminine questions at least give you a choice between two wrong answers.

H.D.S.

The Genealogy of Jack Waters is probably the longest of the "foolish question" anecdotes; it also ranks as one of the funniest *megillahs*, or complicated stories, in this genre. Now a classic, it has attained the venerable age of about half a century and will no doubt be around for decades to come, not only because of its humor and devastating "punch line" (in Yiddish) but also for its all-too-recognizable reality in this age of Anglicized names which have been adopted by many Jewish Americans. We might add that the denouement, or final word in this joke, would lose its verve, its hilarious connotation were it translated into English; therefore it has been left in the original. And now the story.

Two men happened to meet on a train and as they opened a discussion they soon learned that they were both Jewish.

"What is your name?" asked one.

"My name is Jack Waters."

"Jack Waters! How does it happen that a Jew should have the name Jack Waters? Are you an American-born Jew?"

"Well, no," replied the other. "As a matter of fact, before I came to this country I lived in England, and in England my name was Fountain."

"Oh, then you're an English Jew!"

"Not really. Before I lived in England I lived in France, and in France my name was LaFontaine. I came to England, so from LaFontaine it became Fountain. When I came to the United States, from Fountain, Jack Waters."

"Aha, I see! You're a French Jew."

"Well, not exactly. Before I lived in France I lived in Germany. And there my name was Spritzwasser."

"Oh-h-h, now I got it!"

"Yes, and when I went to France, from Spritzwasser it became LaFontaine; from LaFontaine, Fountain; from Fountain, Jack Waters."

"Actually, then, you're a German Jew?"

"Well," the man concluded, "I was really born in *Gubernja*, and there they used to call me Bevelterpisher."

* * *

For weeks he had been calling regularly on the young lady, spending the evenings at her house and discussing a variety of subjects, but not once did he ever get around to the subject she was waiting to hear—marriage. One evening she decided to put the question to him in a forthright manner.

"Look," she began rather tersely, "a man has honorable intentions or he doesn't, he's serious or he's not serious, and that's all there is to it. There's something wrong with me you're not popping the question?"

He knew, of course, that sooner or later she would bring up the subject, and he answered slowly but emphatically.

"*Shayneh*, I'm here in this country for five years now and I learned a little about American women. That's why I'm not talking on you about marriage. You ask me if something is wrong with you, and as long as you're asking, I got to confess I'm wondering. After all, what kind of a girl are you that every evening you're sitting down with a man like me who is forever sitting down to talk on a girl like you and we're doing nothing but sitting?"

* * *

Stewardesses employed by Israel's airline, *El Al,* are instructed in the technique for handling predatory males. Here are two of the standard questions and the girls' answers.

"What's your phone number, baby?"

"You'll find it in the directory, sir."

"Okay, what's your name?"

"You'll find that in the directory, too."

* * *

"Do you believe in love and marriage?"

"Yes, but not necessarily with the same person."

* * *

Steve and Stella were among the tourists in Washington, D.C., visiting the Lincoln Memorial on the occasion of the Great Emancipator's birthday.

"There will never be another like him," murmured Steve reverently as he gazed upon the noble statue. "Good old Honest Abe!"

A puzzled look crossed Stella's face. "Tell me something, Steve," she said hesitantly. "If Abraham Lincoln was so honest, why do they close all the banks on his birthday?"

* * *

Social Worker: Is the high cost of living a problem in your family?

Welfare Applicant: No, just the *taste* for high living!

* * *

Shimkus the chemise manufacturer had been having an illicit affair with his head model, but lately his ardor had been cooling—or perhaps it was her soup that no longer simmered. Anyway, he turned a deaf ear to her repeated demands for expensive gifts. The showdown came one evening when she made her final imperious request.

"I demand an explanation," she snapped. "Why won't you buy me a mink coat? You know I'm terribly cold."

"Look, kid," he retorted, "if you already knew the answer why'd you ask the question?"

* * *

"This airplane looks awfully old," said the nervous lady. "You're sure it's safe?"

"Of course it's safe," assured the pilot. "How else did the plane get so old?"

* * *

The rabbi was being considered for a position in a large synagogue.

"Do you have any difficulty making decisions?" asked a member of the congregation.

"Wel-l-ll," replied the rabbi, "sometimes yes, sometimes no."

*   *   *

It is said that this story is true, but don't bet your month's rent on it. At any rate, back in the 1930s, there used to be a permanent resident of "The Retreat," a private Jewish home for the mentally disturbed on the outskirts of Los Angeles. It seems that all at once he fancied himself a painter. Up until that time he had leaned to the theory that he was the biblical Isaiah, and before that he was of the opinion that he was Disraeli. But now, quite suddenly, he decided that he was intended to depict important historical episodes with pigment and brush.

In such privacy as the management afforded, he fitted himself up with a studio. The management also provided him with supplies. After some weeks he announced that he was prepared to hold a private unveiling of his first masterpiece. He invited the superintendent of the institution to be his chief guest on that occasion.

At the appointed moment, he brought forth a large frame shrouded in cloth. Having placed it where the light would bring out the best values of the composition, he removed the cover with a flourish. There was revealed a stretch of canvas untouched by so much as a single brush stroke. It was as free of paint as the day he purchased it.

"Now," said the artist with pride in his voice, "what do you think of that for a beginning?"

"Very fine," said the tactful superintendent. "But, pardon me for asking, what does it represent?"

"Why, don't you see? That represents the passage of the Children of Israel through the Red Sea."

"But where is the sea?"

"It has been driven back."

"And where are the Israelites?"

"They have crossed over."

"But the Egyptians—how about them?"

"What kind of a silly question is that? They've all drowned, naturally."

*   .*   *

Flo: I hate to mention this, but did you know that your hair is thinning on top?

Moe: So let it get thin! Who needs fat hair?

*   *   *

Willy Brandt, at the time he was Mayor of West Berlin, visited the great new Mann Auditorium in Tel Aviv. "I am moved to commend Israel on this forgiving gesture," he said. "I think it's wonderful of you to name a concert hall after the late German writer, Thomas Mann."

But he was quickly corrected: The hall was not named after the German writer but after Frederic R. Mann of Philadelphia.

"What did he ever write?" demanded Mayor Brandt.

"A check," was the reply.

*   *   *

It would seem that a regrettable occurrence—what is known in educational circles as a "hazing"—had taken place at Brandeis. A freshman was the victim and he complained to the faculty. The fact that he was the son of a wealthy donor to the university may have had something to do with the furor engendered by the complaint, but whatever the reason, the dean himself undertook an investigation.

One of the first to be summoned before him was a youth who owned up to the fact that he had participated in the festivities.

"Ah-*ha*!" erupted the dean. "You confess, then, that you, a supposedly decent Jewish boy, helped carry off this inoffensive young man by force, and took him to the campus fountain and there immersed him?"

"Yes, sir," said the culprit meekly.

"And what part did you take in this disgraceful affair?"

"The right leg, sir."

* * *

This one's for the birds.

Barbara Streisand, taking time off from her Hollywood chores, went shopping for a gift to present to her nephew. Visiting Farmer's Market in Los Angeles, she spied a handsome, talkative parrot and immediately took a fancy to it.

"Does he fly?" Barbara asked the pet shop owner.

"Usually," replied the owner. "But sometimes he takes the train."

* * *

A lonely traveling salesman struck up a conversation with another at a rural hotel.

"Does your wife miss you much?" asked one.

"No," said the other, "not with her aim!"

* * *

When her weight went over 200 pounds, the housewife thought it best to consult a doctor. In his office, he gave her a thorough examination.

"There is nothing wrong with your metabolism," said the physician. "In fact there is nothing organically wrong with you at all."

"That's nice," said the housewife. "But why am I so fat?"

"You are clearly eating too much. Tell me, what do you do all day?"

"Like you said, doctor. I eat, that's all."

"Don't you do any housework?"

"My three daughters do it for me," she said, becoming annoyed with the persistent questioning.

"Well, how about exercise?"

"Doctor," snapped the woman, now visibly irritated, "I'm over 200 pounds and I'm five feet tall. And you're asking me what exercise I do? Well, as long as you're asking I'll tell you: I read murder mysteries and let my flesh creep!"

* * *

Mendel: What's the difference between gossip and news?
Marvin: That depends on whether you're hearing or telling.

* * *

He had left Russia forty years earlier and arrived in the United States as a poor but ambitious youngster, not unlike the tens of thousands of other emigrants to these shores. By dint of hard work and downright pluck, he managed to put himself through medical school. Now, so many years later, the man was recognized as one of the most prestigious doctors in America. He felt he had earned a long vacation, so he decided to visit the little *shtetl* where he was born. He was somewhat concerned that the humble peasants might be a little fearful of so eminent a medical man, but he promised himself that he would exercise modesty when talking with these simple people.

When he arrived in the far-off village, he was welcomed by the little community's only rabbi.

"Tell me, rabbi," the great doctor began conversationally, trying hard not to appear too learned before this untutored man of the cloth, "what is the death rate here?"

"The same as it is in America, I'm sure," replied the good rabbi after a thoughtful pause: "One per person."

* * *

Blumstein the electrician was working in an elevator shaft when his safety belt broke and he fell two floors to the very bottom. He was unhurt but somewhat bruised.

An elderly lady on the second floor heard him yell and then heard the crash. She rushed over to the open elevator door and peered down into the murky recess below.

"My dear man," she cried, "did you fall down the shaft?"

"No," Blumstein called back, "I was born here and they built the shaft around me!"

* * *

"Doctor," asked the pretty girl after an operation, "will the scar show?"

"I don't know," said the medic. "It's up to you."

* * *

"I just don't understand that wife of mine," grumbled the old skinflint. "Last month I gave her a whole dollar to spend on a few luxuries for our home. And when she had that awful cold last week I bought her a whole box of aspirin. And then, to show what kind of gratitude she has, she kicked me out of the house this morning. How do you account for that?"

"Maybe," suggested his friend, "you clashed with the decor!"

* * *

Some questions, foolish or wise, can be answered only with great difficulty or not at all. For example, there is the question posed by elderly Mrs. Samuels, a resident of the Hebrew Home for the Aged in Chicago. The lady was reading the book, *The Nixon Nobody Knows*, a favorable biography of the President. Gradually, a look of perplexity crossed her features.

"You look puzzled," remarked another lady resident.

"I am," responded Mrs. Samuels. "It says right here that Mr. Nixon is just as nice and as honest as the Republicans claim. But let me ask you a civil question: Why is it that such a fine gentleman needed five preachers and two Bibles when he was sworn in?"

* * *

Grandma absorbed every rumor and bit of gossip like a sponge. This particular evening she had been reading a Hollywood gossip column about an aging movie star who had married a girl in her early twenties. Grandma turned to her granddaughter.

"Tsailt mir eppes," she asked, her voice brimming with curiosity, "it's true that Cary Grant's son was born with gray hair?"

* * *

The worldwide population explosion has resulted in numerous associations and organizations whose primary concern is the balancing of births and deaths. Among these groups is one called "Population Zero."

One evening in November, 1973, Rabbi Steven Roth of Adat Shalom Synagogue, in Chicago, attended a forum presented by Population Zero advocates. The speaker, an unsmiling Protestant churchman who stood high in the hierarchy, immediately launched an attack against modern sexual mores. For the first few minutes, Rabbi Roth was inclined to agree with the cleric, but when the speaker directed his fire against marital intimacies with equal vituperation and stated some fanciful opinions which, to the rabbi, were completely unfounded, he lost all respect for the minister's argument.

After the meeting, Rabbi Roth approached the churchman.

"Sir," he began, "you stated without any equivocation that most wives actually prefer celibate husbands. Tell me, Reverend, where did you get that information?"

"From an unimpeachable source," said the clergyman. "My wife told me!"

* * *

The Israeli stewardess aboard the *El Al* airliner had just returned to Tel Aviv after her first flight to the United States. Her romantic roommate, another new stewardess, was eager to learn about the American male preferences and attitudes toward women.

"Is it true," she inquired, "that they prefer beauty over brains?"

"I'm afraid so," replied the other girl. "That's because the average American male can see better than he can think."

* * *

The visitor to New York rushed from the airport into a waiting taxi, trying to keep dry in the heavy downpour.

"Can you think of anything worse," grumbled the visitor, "than raining cats and dogs in New York?"

"Sure," said the cab driver cheerfully. "Hailing taxis!"

* * *

As a concerned citizen of Beverly Hills, Groucho Marx once agreed to teach a first-aid class. It was a pleasant enough assignment but he grew increasingly annoyed by some of the utterly foolish questions that were asked. He endured them patiently until one woman made the inquiry to end all inquiries.

"Mr. Marx," she began, "speaking of suicide cases, suppose you happened to come home and found your wife with her head in the oven. What would you do?"

Groucho gave the questioner his most ferocious Marxian glare.

"That's easy," he barked. "I'd baste her every half hour!"

* * *

Baby stork to mama stork: "Well, at least give me a hint. Who *did* bring me?"

* * *

"Hey, Oiving," jeered the anti-Semite with his caricature of dialect, "how did your nose ever get that big?"

"Simple," replied Irving calmly. "I just kept it out of other people's business!"

* * *

A man was found shot to death in his bedroom. The door had been locked from the inside and there were no windows in the room. No intruder could possibly have gotten inside. A note was found, in the man's handwriting, declaring that he had decided to take his own life.

"I still don't see why the coroner pronounced it suicide, do you?" asked the country cousin.

"He pronounced it suicide," said the dead man's brother acidly, "because that happens to be the way you pronounce it!"

* * *

The old lady in the black babushka was having difficulty selecting a suitable fish at the store. She'd pick one up, sniff, put it down again and then try another.

"Mister," she finally asked the annoyed proprietor in a voice loud enough for the other customers to hear, "don't you have any fish they're not smelling?"

The outraged merchant gritted his teeth.

"*Tanteh*," he said when he had gained control of his temper, "you want a fish that don't smell? All right, just for you I'll cut off its nose!"

* * *

The put-upon husband was complaining about his nagging wife.

"I kept promising my wife a mink stole for her birthday," he sighed, "but when the day arrived, all I could afford was a pair of rabbit-fur earrings. But even then, don't you think she has a lot of nerve to keep on kicking about it?"

"Just between you and me," replied his philosopher-friend, "he who acts by the inch after talking by the yard deserves to be kicked by the foot."

* * *

Seymour the Sheik: When we met on the street last night I had on my new suit. You didn't even know me, did you?

Sheila the Shikse: No, who were you?

* * *

It had been years since the big city manufacturer had had his ego deflated, but, as must happen to all who persist in asking foolish questions, he finally received his comeuppance.

He was driving back to New York from an important conference in Boston when he stopped for gas in a small, out-of-the-way village. He watched the lanky attendant who was filling the tank of his Cadillac and then grinned to himself. 'Why not have a little fun with this country bumpkin?' he thought.

"Hey, Rube," he asked, trying hard not to laugh, "any big men born around here?"

The native straightened up, scrutinized him carefully, and drawled:

"Nope. Best we kin do in these here parts is babies!"

11

Military Matters and Don't Matters

INTRODUCTION

The abhorrence of war and dedication to peace has always been emphasized in Judaic teachings. Over the many centuries, Jews have traditionally bestowed admiration and honors upon their scholars, poets and spiritual leaders, rather than upon their warriors. It is no accident that the biblical David, for instance, is more remembered for his psalms than for his valor in battle. This Hebraic yearning for peace was beautifully expressed by the English political economist, Leone Levi, in his rhetorical question: "Who can reflect on the sacredness of human life, in view of its eternal destinies, without coming to the conclusion that war, with its attendants of hatred, destruction and slaughter, is incompatible with the high dictates of religion?"

But, if Jews are dedicated to peace, they are not now, nor have they ever been pacifists. Had they been unwilling to fight for their existence, they would not have survived the onslaughts of their enemies and remained the unified people they are today. This is no apologia for war, of course. Only a fool would prefer military action to diplomacy. But some wars can be justified despite the idealists who confuse peacefulness with pacifism. "It is simply not true that war never settles anything," observed Felix Frankfurter. Justice Frankfurter might well have been referring to the American Revolution or the Civil War, or Hitler's try at world mastery, or one of a dozen other justified confrontations.

In the United States, Jewish fighting men have participated in every war this nation has ever had. Indeed, their *insistence* on serving in the armed forces began in the earliest colonial times when Jacob Barsimson and Asser Levy, among the first 23 Jews to settle in New Amsterdam in 1654, successfully challenged the anti-Semitic Governor Peter Stuyvesant who attempted to exclude Jews from guard duty (and then had the temerity to tax them as non-combatants). As a direct result of Levy's courageous persistence, the Jews of New Amsterdam (later New York) were finally granted full civil rights. Levy not only won the right to serve in the military establishment, but became the first American of the Jewish faith to be accorded complete citizenship in the New World.

Barsimson, whose battles with Stuyvesant are legendary, earned the well-merited sobriquet, "America's first fighting Jew." And let it be remembered that this occurred more than 120 years *before* the signing of the Declaration of Independence.

This is not to say that Jewish humor connected with the military is devoid of the usual sarcasm, ridicule and natural reluctance to be shot full of holes—a type of humor which was prevalent among the millions of Jewish immigrants who brought their jokes with them from the early 1880's to about 1905. Their jests revolved around the absurdity of fighting in defense of their persecutors, and need no explanation here. These jokes were passed on to their American-born children and, in diminishing numbers, to their grandchildren.

The armed services are uniquely suited to ridicule. The unyielding, sometimes asinine orders; the pomposity of young officers; the necessary harshness during basic training; the very real possibility of death in combat—these and many other aspects of military life find expression in humor. The witticisms are as old as recorded history and as modern as nuclear warfare.

William Chernof, a New Yorker who enlisted in the Israeli army upon the advent of the Six Day War, commented in the *California Jewish Voice:* "I had heard much about the vast arsenal of weapons the Soviets had given to the Arabs, but I found it to be only half-vast."

Among the personalities still being selected as a target for military as well as political jokes is Senator Barry Goldwater, the 1964 Republican candidate for President. As a conservative and an Army Reserve officer, he is something of a distinctive individual. According to the humorists, he sent only half a jet plane to Israel because he happens to be only half Jewish. "We know he's only part Jewish," grinned one observer. "If he was a full Jew, Arizona would be irrigated by now." No one, however, enjoys a joke about his Jewishness or conservatism more than Goldwater himself. Asked what he would do if the Soviet Union were to attack the United States, he laughed and said, "I'd order the wagons to form a circle."

The military humor of Israel and the United States is often as alike as two *knaidlach* in a pot of soup. In fact, a number of jokes have evolved to the point where they are now interrelated. One of them, not too surprisingly, concerns Goldwater's son, Congressman Barry Goldwater, Jr., of California. *Azoi:*

Baruch Goldwasser, Jr., who, like his father, is licensed to fly a plane, heard about the Yom Kippur attack on Israel, and immediately flew to Tel Aviv to offer his services as a fighter pilot. He was closely examined by an Air Force colonel, but, although he easily passed the flying test, he was unable to pass the oral examination. Sadly, he returned home.

"Those questions must have been mighty tough," sympathized the elder Goldwasser.

"The stiffest test you can imagine," agreed young Baruch. "That Israeli colonel asked me what I would do if I was flying a Phantom jet at an altitude of 60,000 feet, at a speed of 1,200 miles an hour, and my oxygen tank was riddled by enemy bullets. Then he asked me what I'd do if one of my engines caught fire and the wing crumpled at the same time. After that, he wanted to know what I'd do if my ejection system failed and I was caught way up there without a parachute."

"What did you answer?" asked papa Goldwasser.

"Answer? Who answered?" demanded Baruch. "From the questions alone I blacked out!"

If the reader will permit a little *haimisheh* philosophy, arguing for peace with the Arabs is like running uphill with your pants down. It seems to me that all this *tsuris* between Jews and Mohammedans could have been avoided if they had tried to settle their differences in a Christianlike manner. But who knows? Maybe that's what started it in the first place!

H.D.S.

A college student, home for the weekend, was reading the papers when a news item caught his eye.

"Say, pop, here's some pleasant news for a change!" exclaimed the youth. "It says here that Russia's intercontinental missiles are so primitive that only half of their rockets would ever hit their targets."

"That's nice," the father replied drily. "Maybe now half of us will be only half dead."

* * *

The infamous Yom Kippur attack on Israel by Egyptian and Syrian military forces had just begun. An Arab pilot and his co-pilot had flown over the Suez Canal and were crossing a desolate area of the Gaza Strip, many miles from the nearest habitation, where they thought they would be safe from detection. But they were quickly spotted by the crew of an Israeli Phantom Jet and a few seconds later the Egyptian invader was shot down from the skies.

As they parachuted to earth in that isolated wasteland, the Arab pilot snarled to his co-pilot:

"Now you can see for yourself how these Jews are. Their rescue trucks are probably miles away at the airbase."

* * *

Sol Silvers, the sage of Syracuse, was arguing that the Secretary of Defense had made a grievous error by cutting the Pentagon's budget for social studies.

"Now," moaned Sol, "we'll never find out why people don't like to be killed."

* * *

Like all other peoples, the Jews have their quota of eternal optimists and infernal pessimists.

Take the case of the two Israeli soldiers, Adir and Adiva, who became lost in the Negev Desert during the last hostilities. Fortunately, they had an ample supply of water in their canteens, but they were totally without food, and quite hungry.

"We'll never make it," wailed Adir, the pessimist. "We'll die of starvation before we reach a settlement.

"Cheer up," said Adiva encouragingly, "we're bound to find something to eat very soon. With all this sand there must be some spinach around here."

* * *

One of the most interesting families of the Revolutionary War period was the Franks clan of Philadelphia. This Jewish family was unique in being predominantly Tory but, as if to atone, it produced several outstanding patriots and rebel officers, among them Colonel David Salisbury Franks, nephew of Tory David Franks. Well known to General Washington and Benjamin Franklin, he was closest to Thomas Jefferson and was a dinner guest at the home of the Sage of Monticello on a number of occasions.

The subject of this story, however, is yet another member of the famous family: Isaac Franks, who was only seventeen when he enlisted in the rebel army shortly after the Battle of Lexington. Young Ike served under Washington in the Battle of Long Island, was wounded several times in battle and at one time was taken prisoner by the British. He continued in active service in various posts until illness forced his retirement in 1782. It was at his home in Germantown that President Washington resided when the capital was located in Philadelphia. Isaac sat for Gilbert Stuart, renowned for his portraits of Washington and other colonial leaders. In 1794, he was appointed a lieutenant-colonel in the Pennsylvania militia.

If all this sounds rather austere, let it be said that Isaac Franks was all too human and committed his fair share of blunders. His most comical misadventure, in fact, earned him a special niche in the humorous folklore of the people. It occurred shortly after the Battle of Long Island, when teenaged Ike was ordered, by General Washington himself, to repair the roof of a building in which arms and ammunition were being stored. The episode, contained in a formal request for sick leave, must surely be the most uproariously funny document in the archives of the United States Government. But let young Ike's request speak for itself:

8 September, 1776

Gen. G. Washington
Respected Sir,
As per my orders to make repairs on the roof of Company Magazine B, I arrived at the building at seven o'clock in the morning, only to find that the storm of the previous night had torn loose some of the cross-beams from the eaves. I therefore

rigged up a beam with a pulley at the top of the building and hoisted up six heavy iron brackets and a hundredweight kegge of nails.

Having effectuated the repairs I saw that I had brought up more brackets than I needed and I had used only a pound or two of the nails. So I hoisted up the empty kegge again and tied the rope at the bottom. Then I went up to the roof and filled the kegge with the iron brackets and nails. After that I returned to the ground to unfasten the rope.

Unhappily, the kegge of brackets and nails were heavier than my own weight, and ere I could say Jack Robinson, the kegge started down and jerked me into the atmosphere. I made a quick decision to hang onto the rope, but halfway up I met the kegge coming down and received a mightly blow on the head and shoulders. I then continued the rest of the way to the top, banging my head against the beam and getting my fingers caught in the pulley.

The kegge hit the ground with such force that the impact bursted the bottom, allowing those heavy brackets and the near-hundred-weight of nails to spill out. I was now heavier than the broken kegge and so I started down again at an uncommonly fast rate of descent. Halfway down I met the kegge coming up and received several painful injuries to my legs.

When I hit the ground I landed on the spilled brackets and sharp nails which resulted in my sustaining a number of grievous cuts from the sharp points. At that moment, I fear I lost presence of mind because I released my hold on the rope. The kegge then came down again, giving me another blow on the head and putting me in the infirmary.

I respectfully request sick leave.

Cpl. Isaac Franks*

* * *

At the height of the unfortunate American involvement in East Asia, an owlish-looking young fellow approached the recruiting officer's desk.

"What must I do to get to Vietnam as soon as possible?" asked the prospective soldier.

"Well, first you have to sign up," explained the officer with a grin.

"Do volunteers have to take a physical?"

"Certainly."

"Darn—that'll slow me up. I want to get to the front lines right away."

---

*Adapted from *The Franks of Philadelphia*, Joseph Mendes, Baltimore, 1871. Also see, *Jews in American Wars*, J. George Friedman and Louis A. Falk, published by the Jewish War Veterans of the U.S., 1942.

"In any case, you'd have to go to boot camp for training," explained the officer. "Nobody goes where the fighting is until he's properly trained."

"Then at least will the army fly me to Vietnam? I'd hate to go by slow boat."

"What are you so all-fired anxious about?" growled the army man. "Don't you realize you could get killed or wounded over there?"

"So I get killed or wounded: What's the difference, as long as I'm getting all the glory?"

"Listen, buddy," snapped the recruiter, "why don't you go home and forget the whole thing? You're crazy!"

The young fellow abruptly reached into his coat pocket, pulled out a paper and thrust it into the army officer's hands.

"Here," he said quickly. "Just sign!"

* * *

It isn't generally known (and remember, you saw the news here first), but after the Six Day War with Israel, Egypt's Nasser slept like a baby. . .

He woke up every four hours and cried.

* * *

A tough career sergeant of the old school was haranguing a squad of new recruits.

"Tell me," he barked, "why shouldn't a private smoke during drill?"

"I agree!" blurted a teenage rookie from the Bronx. "Why shouldn't he?"

* * *

It is stated in the *Encyclopedia of Jewish Humor* that Israel, with a population of two-and-a-half million Jewish citizens, has two-and-a-half million presidents. A military twist has been added to that quip which warns all soldiers to refrain from giving advice to their superior officers.

During the *Yom Kippur* War an Israeli division was about to drive the Syrians out of the Golan Heights, but there seemed to be some dissension as to the best way to accomplish it. The arguments about strategy and tactics grew so intense that General Moshe Dayan issued this stern directive:

"For the time being, all born generals will henceforth take their orders from all *commissioned* generals!"

* * *

Did you ever stop to think that the 1967 conflict between Israel and the Arab states was the only six-day war in history to last for seven years?

* * *

"Them Jews in Israel ain't so tough," sneered the redneck anti-

Semite. "Back in 1967 it took 'em six whole days to defeat only five Arab states!"

* * *

D-Day had finally arrived, and with it the invasion of the European mainland by the American and British armed forces. Grandpa Isaacson was reading an account of the military invasion in the *New York Times*. His command of the English language was fairly good, but he came upon a word that perplexed him.

"Lena," he addressed his granddaughter, "it says here that General Eisenhower's strategy was excellent. *Vos maynt* strategy?"

Fifteen-year-old Lena's knowledge of military terms was somewhat less than that of a West Pointer's. She bit into an apple to help her think, munched for a while, and then gave her studied opinion.

"Strategy," she said carefully, "is when you don't let the other side know you are out of ammunition, but keep right on firing!"

* * *

"The reason we beat those Nazis," averred George the armchair general, "is that our sophisticated communications system was fifty years ahead of theirs. American scientists crossed a carrier pigeon with a woodpecker. It not only delivered messages . . . it even knocked on the door!"

* * *

The young recruit had just finished basic training and was home on leave for a few days.

"They made me take three physical examinations," he grumbled to his mother. "All those doctors thought I was deformed because my uniform was a perfect fit!"

* * *

World War II had just broken out and teenager Phil Feldman was drafted. For six whole weeks his anxious mother waited to learn if her darling little boy was to be shipped overseas. Finally, one day, her telephone rang. It was Phil.

"Mama, I got great news!" the son declared jubilantly. "I'm coming home on a furlough."

"Oh, Phil, I'm so happy!" cried Mrs. Feldman, her voice brimming with joy. "When you're coming . . ." She stopped abruptly in mid-sentence as her son's message registered in her mind.

"You're coming home on a *what*?"

"On a furlough."

She let this information sink in before expressing her maternal concern.

"Listen, Phil," she said nervously, "about furloughs I know from nothing, but what's the matter you can't take a bus like everybody else?"

* * *

"Squads right!" yelled the sergeant.

"So now he admits it!" muttered the weary recruit.

* * *

Henpecked Henry was inducted into the army and, as luck would have it, was assigned to a drill sergeant who had all the sensitivity of Ivan the Terrible.

"Hey, you!" screamed the sergeant, glaring at Henpecked Henry. "Straighten that back! Pull in that chin! Lift that head! Tote that rifle! Throw back those shoulders!"

A vision of his usual domestic life flashed across Henry's weary mind.

"Yes, dear," he murmured.

The sergeant's face turned livid. "Step outta line," he roared.

Henry stepped forward.

"How long you been in this man's army?"

Shoulders drooping, a picture of abject defeat, Henry replied sadly, "All day, sir."

* * *

Jimmy Bortnik of the Bronx confesses that he might have gone farther in life had he not been so cautious.

"Even as a college student I was afraid to burn my draft card like the other fellows did," he admitted. "I boiled it!"

* * *

The new recruit had been in the United States for only a short time but he had already adopted all the pugnacity for which native-born Americans are so well noted.

On his first day at boot camp, the drill sergeant, a sarcastic if not too original man, barked, "You there, Private! You'll be interested to know that the whole Company is out of step but you."

"*Nu*, so tell 'em," shrugged the recruit. "You're the one in charge!"

* * *

The following is dedicated to all delicate, tender-hearted sergeants whose sweet little feelings have been hurt by all the nasty jokes told about them:

Scene: Poverty Pictures Studio, Hollywood. Lights! Cameras! Action!

Bernie Schwartz and Issur Danielovitch, better known as Tony Curtis and Kirk Douglas, were in the midst of their co-starring roles in the film, *Spartacus*, the famous costume picture in which they appeared as slave-gladiators in combat against the mighty Roman legions. At lunch time, the two stalwarts decided to get away from the studio for awhile, so instead of eating at the commissary or in their dressing rooms, they drove out to Pacific Highway for a fish dinner.

Still wearing their glittering tufted helmets, glistening breastplates and flannel knee-length skirts, they entered Sam's Seafood Salon and seated themselves at one of the ocean-view tables. A waiter approached, started to hand them a menu, and then just stood there gaping at them as though they had just landed in a flying saucer. Kirk reached for the bill of fare but the waiter remained as motionless as a statue, just staring at the uncommonly garbed duo.

At last, when it seemed that the waiter would never recover from his rigor mortis, Tony spoke up.

"What's the matter, fella?" he demanded. "Don't you serve members of the Armed Forces?"

* * *

A moment of silent prayer, please, for the submarine sailor who insisted on sleeping with the windows open.

* * *

Anecdotes about ferocious drill sergeants have been told by generations of hapless soldiers. But the toughest one who ever came to our attention was the World War I sergeant who became somewhat annoyed with one of his recruits who had overslept. He lined up his squad and, as they stood at rigid attention, he singled out the offender.

"Private Goldberg, step forward!" he bellowed.

Private Goldberg stepped forward.

"All right, Sleepin' Beauty," the sergeant snarled, "from now on you're gonna *rise* an' *shine* at five ayem if I hafta hand-feed ya a pound of *yeast* an' a bucket of *shoe polish* every night!"

* * *

It was 1967 and Egypt's President Nasser was making threatening gestures against Israel. Young Joe Skolnik, in New York, decided to fly to the Holy Land in defense of his ancestral homeland. He was immediately inducted into the Israeli army and sent to basic training camp.

Skolnik's heart was in the right place but he missed New York's social life—specifically, girls. He knew there would be no chance of socializing until he got out of boot camp. Three months later, just when his training period was over and young Joe was preparing to visit the nearest town for the evening, the Six Day War broke out and he was suddenly shipped to the front lines.

Throughout that first day he fought the Arabs, and when the sun went down he approached his commanding officer.

"Captain, how's chances of letting me go to town this evening?"

The captain looked at him in amazement.

"Private Skolnik," he barked, "it may not have occurred to you but there happens to be a war on. A visit to town is considered a reward in this army, and nobody gets a reward around here unless he earns it. You want a pass to get to town? Then do something heroic. Make a victory of some kind—win a battle—take a few prisoners—capture enemy equipment—be a *mentsch!* Then maybe I'll consider it."

Skolnik shrugged. "That's okay by me," he said.

The next day Private Skolnik showed up at the captain's tent with an Arab tank. "How's this for a start?" he asked.

The captain's eyes bulged. "Marvelous! Wonderful!" he exclaimed. "Do that just once more and I'll give you *two* days off!"

"Fine!" said Skolnik. On the following day he drove up to the captain's camp headquarters with another Arab tank, bigger than the first one.

The captain was ecstatic. "Listen, Skolnik," he enthused, "if you can capture just one more tank I'll give you a weekend pass to town. How would you like that? Three whole days!"

Sure enough, on the third day of the war, Joe Skolnik came rolling in with the biggest tank the Arabs had gotten from the Soviet Union, completely equipped with every modern device the Russians had secretly developed.

The overjoyed captain was as good as his word. He sat down to fill out the promised weekend pass.

"Tell me something, Private Skolnik," said the officer as he was writing, "how in the world did you ever manage to bring back those enemy tanks?"

"Nothing to it," explained Skolnik. "I simply drive up to the border and holler, 'Any of you guys want a pass to town?'" Then we just exchange tanks!"

* * *

Born in Lissa, Poland, in 1740, Haym Salomon, who had been fighting for Polish independence from Russia, escaped the clutches of the Czarists when his native country was conquered and found his way to New York in 1772. It wasn't long before he joined the Sons of Liberty, a patriotic organization fighting to free the colonies from England.

In his new homeland, Salomon, well educated and possessed of a remarkable talent for business, achieved extraordinary success as a commodities broker. And, as is well known, he almost single-handedly maintained the bankrupt Revolutionary government's credit, to say nothing of substantial personal loans to such founding fathers as James Madison, among others. Haym Salomon died in 1785, at the age of 45, completely impoverished. Neither he nor his heirs were ever repaid a copper cent for all the loans made to the United States.

But let us return to his earlier and happier days when he was an active fighting man in the cause of liberty. He was captured twice; on the second occasion he was sentenced to death but, luckily, he managed to escape. Yet, despite the grimness of his ordeal as a prisoner, his wit was never far beneath the surface.

When Salomon was captured by the Hessians, who were mercenaries of the British, he was ordered to take the oath of allegience to King George. Salomon not only refused but kept up a running commentary on the courage of the Americans and their brave defense against the better equipped British. Finally, the Hessian general lost all patience:

"You'll take this oath of allegiance right now or you'll hang!"

"Well, as long as you put it that way . . ." Salomon answered amiably.

"That's the spirit," said the Hessian after the oath had been administered on a *New* Testament. "Now you can come and go as you please. You are one of us."

Grinning, Salomon resumed his boasting, with only a slight modification:

"Say," he enthused, "didn't those Americans give us a hell of a fight?"

* * *

A number of these examples of Jewish-American military jokes indicate that they can be traced back to the earliest of colonial times. But it would be remiss to end this chapter without reference to the almost legendary hero of World War I, Sergeant Sam Dreben, whose exploits inspired Runyon's epic poem about this unassuming but truly heroic little immigrant: *

There's a story in the paper
I just tossed upon the floor,
That speaks of prejudice against the Jews;
There's a photo on the table,
There's a memory of the war
And a man who never figured in the news . . .
He is short and fat and funny,
And the nose upon his face
Is about the size of bugler Dugan's horn;
But the grin that plays behind
Is wide and soft and sunny,
And he wore it from the day that he was born.
There's a cross upon his chest—
That's the D.S.C.
The Croix de Guerre, the Militaire,
These too.
And I think, thank God, Almighty,
We will always have a few,
Like Dreben,
A Jew.

Sergeant Sam Dreben was a fugitive from the Czarist *pogroms* in his native Russia. Failing to adjust to civilian life in America, bored with the humdrum jobs he was offered, he joined the army and found his career. He battled Pancho Villa's troops in Mexico under "Black Jack" Pershing, fought in the Spanish-American War and in the Philippine insurrection, and later in the Boxer rebellion in China. So, life amid the grim sights and sounds of World War I was hardly a novelty to him.

But the squad of new recruits to which he was assigned had not been informed that this helpless-looking little man was the famous "Fighting

---

*Excerpted from *The Fighting Jew*, Damon Runyon, The New York World Press, 1918.

Jew" who had been awarded the French Government's highest honors, or that he had won the Distinguished Service Cross when he single-handedly rushed a German machine gun nest and killed 23 of the 40 Germans, capturing the survivors. To the new group of soldiers, toward the end of the war, Sergeant Dreben was just a quiet fellow who was "short and fat and funny."

As Dreben stood before the new men, many audible comments were made about his small size and apparent ineptness. From the rear of the ranks a voice called out:

"And a little child shall lead them."

Seemingly undisturbed, Sam Dreben finished the business of the day. On the following morning, there appeared a notice on the bulletin board:

> Company A will take a 25-mile hike today with full packs. And a little child shall lead them . . . on a damn big horse!
>
> Sgt. S. Dreben

12

Shnooks and Shnookesses

INTRODUCTION

The only thing some people ever learn from experience is that they've goofed again. Send a *shnook* to find a greenhorn and he'll look for a man with a pistachio nose. He's the *shmo* who can barely peel his own bananas. His left hand never knows what his left hand is doing. He's the *shlemiel* who goes through life *pushing* doors marked "pull." If he's in politics, as many of them seem to be, he proves that the tongue is mightier than the mind by telling his audience, "If elected, I promise to grab the bull by the tail and look the situation squarely in the face."

From whence came this anomaly that sprang from the loins of a people renowned for their spiritual wisdom and earthy sagacity? Before we answer the question, let us first define the descriptive words themselves. "*Shnook*" is a slang expression usually meaning an unimportant or stupid person; a variant of the Yiddish word *shmok*, itself a slang term, denoting a fool or dope. From *shmok* we additionally derive the truncated word *shmo*, and also *shmuck*, meaning an oaf or jerk. The most popular of the expressions in the people's literature and folk humor is the Yiddish word, *shlemiel*, an awkward or unlucky person for whom things never turn out right because of his native stupidity—his lack of what is called *Yiddishe saichel*.

In 1813, Adalbert von Chamisso's Peter Schlemihl gave added currency to the word and it has been popularized by generations of Jewish humorists ever since.

There is one other word, *shlimazl*, which is often confused with *shlemiel*. One is merely a cousin to the latter. The *shlemiel*, as we have seen, is a failure because of his *own* stupidity, but the *shlimazl* fails because his lucklessness is due to conditions beyond himself. *Shlimazl* is a Yiddish word denoting a bungler who suffers from unremitting bad luck. The distinction between the two is expressed in the classic rule of thumb: a *shlemiel* spills the soup, but it falls into the lap of the *shlimazl*. The former's misfortune is his character; the latter's, his position or situation.

Unlike the oral folk humor of the Jewish people—that is, the stories

118

and witticisms handed down by word of mouth from one generation to the next—the written tradition, beginning with the Bible itself, has dealt harshly with the fool. But, that harshness, let it be understood, was born of necessity.

The early Israelites, as a numerically small, agrarian community of people, situated as they were at the strategic crossroads between the merchants and traders of the West and the spice and silk suppliers of the Far East, surrounded by stronger states who coveted their strategic bit of land, simply could not afford to tolerate the fool in their midst. His actions, quite understandably, elicited concern, not humor.

Later, beset on all sides by religious persecutors, confronted by inquisitions and pogroms, faced with genocide by Hitler who added a race rationale to the religious canards, and the spectre of cultural and spiritual extermination in the Soviet Union, the Jew had, literally, as a matter of survival, been forced by circumstances to place a premium on intelligence. Lacking arms, and short on diplomatic muscle in the international halls of power, his strength was in the armory of his mind. It still is.

Nevertheless, frowned upon or not, the fool *did* exist, and while the earliest stories about him may have been told furtively, the decibles have increased with the march of the centuries, reaching full resonance only in the past 150 years or so. The fool, or *shlemiel* or *shnook*—call him what you will—has not only been around for a long time, but has been celebrated in such tales as the *Wise Men of Chelm* and the exploits of that lovable con-man of yesteryear, Hershel Ostropolier, among others. He has also been a subject of humor among the *Chassidim* who found virtue in simplicity over cleverness. The *shlimazl*, too, has been affectionately remembered in Yiddish literature in such stories as the mystically haunting *Bontshe the Silent*, by I. L. Peretz.

In the United States, the growth and popularity of the *shlemiel* joke may be attributed in large part to our democratic institutions. Here, in the freer atmosphere of a society devoid of religious and social repression, the very idea of somehow being "different" than others has waned to a degree where it is now almost non-existent.

The American Jew can laugh unselfconsciously at the *shlemiel* who hoped to reach Europe by stowing away on a ship and found himself on the Staten Island ferry. Our amusement is tolerant because we know we are all prone to errors of judgment, even though the *shnook* makes a career of it. Most importantly, the American of the Jewish faith can enjoy the humor objectively rather than subjectively, because he accepts the fact that some Jews are not *Bar Mitzvah* until they are sixty.

And now that you know what makes your brother-in-law tick, I present to you a collection of familiar characters. As my dear departed papa used to say, "May you find pleasure in shaking hands with so many old faces."

H.D.S.

Dov the dogcatcher was a typical *shlemiel*. He knew he was supposed to catch dogs but he didn't know what he was supposed to catch them at.

* * *

This one is probably as old as Aladdin and his lamp, and a whole lot sillier, but it's worth repeating.

Mordecai, an aged junk dealer, was rummaging through the pile of odds and ends he had accumulated that day when he came upon an old, dirt-encrusted bottle. It looked interesting, so he began to rub off some of the dirt to make the bottle shine.

Suddenly, the cork popped out and from the neck of the bottle there arose a spiral of thick smoke. And when the smoke cleared away, there before him towered a huge figure attired in Arab robes.

Mordecai stepped back. "What are you doing in my store?" he asked nervously.

"I'm a genii," replied the figure.

"What kind of a name is Jeannie for a respectable man?"

"It's a magic Arabic name."

"Arabs I don't need in my store. Out!"

"But you don't understand. I can make your every wish come true. I can do anything and make anything you desire."

"All right, if you're so smart," Mordecai retorted, "make me a malted."

The genii instantly complied:

"Abracadabra, zippity-zoom—you're a malted!"

* * *

The new baby was not expected for another week, but a sudden onslaught of labor pains, spaced five minutes apart, made it clear that the delivery was imminent. Hurriedly, Sadie threw a few necessities into a suitcase and waited at the front door while her husband, Morris, brought the car out of the garage, wheels screeching.

"Hurry, hurry!" she pleaded. "The pains are now coming two minutes apart!"

"All right already, I'm hurrying!" Morris assured her. And indeed he was. The car was soon speeding at an unholy clip, the engine wide open and roaring. An excitable fellow under normal circumstances, he was now so nervous that he lost control and the car careened off the highway, knocking them both unconscious.

When Morris finally awoke in the hospital, only dimly aware of what happened, he was aghast to learn that he had been unconscious for the past ten days. His first thoughts were of his wife.

"Sadie," he called anxiously. "How's my Sadie? Is she okay? Did she have the baby?"

"Take it easy—take it easy," advised the doctor. "Everything is under control. Your wife is fine. In fact, she not only had a baby—she gave birth to twins! A boy and a girl, no less."

"*Twins!*" Morris breathed ecstatically. "How marvelous!"

"But," added the doctor, "you were so sick that for a while we didn't think *you* would make it. We had to call your brother in to name the babies. We needed the names for the *bris* and the birth certificates."

"My brother! That *shlemiel?* He's a know-nothing—an empty-head! So what did he name my little girl?"

"He named your little girl Denise."

"Hey, that's not too bad. I like that. Denise is a pretty name. And what did he name my little boy?"

The doctor shrugged and said: "He named your little boy De Nephew!"

* * *

The story, *Bye-bye Feival*, was probably told by the ancient Israelites when the first travelers and explorers set off on camels across the uncharted deserts. Perhaps another variant was told by the first Jewish settlers to reach the Dutch colony of New Amsterdam in 1654. The following is the 20th century version.

Feival, the first Jewish astronaut, had passed beyond the outermost planet of the solar system, his rocket ship now hurtling into the farthest reaches of deep space. Back on Earth, the world's Jewish community waited breathlessly for his return. Now, at last, the Jews would be able to smile indulgently at the comparatively puny efforts of the *goyishe* astronauts who had not even reached Mars.

Feival, in his space ship, was now speeding high above the crescent of the Big Dipper and had long since lost radio contact with Earth. Far below, trillions of miles away, the outlines of the familiar Little Dipper faded from sight and disappeared. To his left, he could see what appeared to be a bright nova on some star he had never known existed. To his right, he observed whole new systems of strange constellations as he sped past the rim of the Milky Way and completely out of the galaxy. Now he was in a deep black void, his ship approaching the speed of light as all gravity was left far behind in the mysterious nothingness of outer space.

"Now let me think," muttered Feival. "In which direction was I headed?"

* * *

Herman, the famous private-eye, arrived at the scene of the crime. His steel-trap mind evaluated the clues with one sweeping glance.

"Gentlemen," he announced, "this was both an inside and an outside job. The window's broken on both sides."

* * *

For more than a week, Barney had been having difficulties with his vision, so he went to see his family physician.

"Doctor, something's wrong with my eyesight," complained the troubled patient. "For ten days I've been seeing blue and gold spots before my eyes."

"Have you seen an oculist yet?" asked the doctor.

"N-no," said Barney uncertainly. "Just blue and gold spots."

* * *

It was Sunday morning, but instead of sleeping an hour or so later as he usually did, Max sat upright in bed and groaned. The sound awakened his wife.

"Boy, did I have a nightmare," he muttered.

"Everybody gets bad dreams once in a while," said his wife soothingly. "Just forget it."

"I can't, Bertha."

"What was so bad about this nightmare?"

"It was like this: I'm driving along on the Parkway with you and your papa. All of a sudden I'm hearing a siren and when I stop the car a policeman comes up to me and he says 'Congratulations, Max, you just won $500 because you are the millionth driver on this new stretch of road.' "

Bertha stared at him, wide-eyed. "By you that's a bad dream?"

"Wait, I'm not finished. So I'm answering the policeman, 'With the $500 I'll take driving lessons and maybe get a driver's license.' "

"My goodness, what kind of an answer is that?" sympathized Bertha.

"That's nothing," said Max, his voice turning accusatory. "So you had to open your big mouth and say, 'Mr. Policeman, you shouldn't believe a word my Max is saying. He's all *shikkered* up!' "

"I did not!" retorted Bertha defensively.

"Yes, you did," was Max's bitter reply. "But your papa, in the back seat, really fixed me good. He hollers out to the policeman, 'I knew we wouldn't get far in this stolen car!' "

* * *

What happens when a man, raised in primitive surroundings, first comes to grips with the modern machine age? Hark to the tale of one such wandering soul, Ben-Ami Shlepper, newly arrived with his wife and son in the United States from a remote *shtetl* in the Pale of Settlement.

Ben-Ami was lucky enough to find a job in the shipping department of Bertram's Buttons & Bows, on lower Second Avenue. For a few days everything went swimmingly for good-natured Ben-Ami, but then a problem arose. He began to report late for work. After he had failed to arrive on time for several mornings in a row, Bertram, the boss, suggested that Ben-Ami buy an alarm clock. But the poor immigrant had never heard of such a new-fangled contraption, let alone see or use one.

"Come along with me," said Bertram that afternoon at quitting time. He led the greenhorn to a department store, picked out an alarm clock and explained the general plan of its workings to his new employee.

For several days, the clock behaved perfectly. But a week or so later, Ben-Ami's little son, being of an inquiring turn of mind, opened the case to study the device during his father's absence. As small boys will, he removed some important parts which he forgot to put back. Next morning, the bell failed to ring and Ben-Ami overslept.

He couldn't understand why the clock had betrayed him. On his own account he undertook an investigation. He took the back off the clock, and there, mixed up with the machinery, he discovered the mortal remains of a large cockroach.

"Aha!" exclaimed Ben-Ami. "No wonder the clock wouldn't run. The engineer is dead!"

* * *

"*Aii*, my feet are killing me!" lamented unhappy grandpa. "I got up on the wrong side of the bed this morning, and all day I'm walking around in my wife's high-heeled slippers."

* * *

The electric chair was all plugged in and everything was in readiness. The jailer approached the condemned man's cell.

"You have an hour of grace," he said.

"So what are you waiting for?" demanded the prisoner. "Send her in!"

* * *

A man showed up at Dr. Kvetchmir's office. He stopped at the receptionist's desk and politely removed his hat, revealing a chrysanthemum growing from the top of his head.

"I would like to see Dr. Kvetchmir," he said.

"What about?" asked the receptionist.

* * *

They had met only two weeks earlier and their romance was beginning to blossom like a lovely flower. But the girl was troubled. She had a problem with her vision and was fearful of his reaction. Now the time had come for her to face the matter squarely.

"Darling," murmured the sweet young thing hesitantly, "could you love me in spite of myopia?"

"I don't know," he replied, anxiety showing in his face. "What's your opia look like?"

* * *

Olga Yosseloff, co-starring in the Los Angeles production, *My Fair Sadie*, started out for the theatre in plenty of time, but on the way her car developed engine trouble. It took a local garage mechanic a half hour to fix it, and now she was somewhat late. Afraid that she would not reach her destination by curtain time, she took a shortcut and found herself going the wrong way on a one-way street. A siren quickly sounded behind her and, in the rear-view mirror she caught sight of a patrol car. She pulled over to the curb and stopped.

"Lady," the policeman began sarcastically, "do you have any idea where you're going?"

"To the theatre," replied Olga, "but I'm sure it's too late. Everybody else seems to be going home!"

* * *

"I always have trouble remembering three things," commented the absent-minded professor: Names, faces and—hmm—now what was that third thing again?"

Chauncey DePlotkin was suffering from the heartbreak of psoriasis. After vainly trying the usual patent medicines sold over the counter, he finally consulted a doctor and was given a prescription for medicine and told how and when to take it.

That evening, at home, Chauncey's wife was astonished to see her husband swallow a spoonful of the medicine, race out of the house and dash around the block. When he returned, he was so exhausted that he flopped down onto the bed and fought to catch his breath. On the second evening, he repeated the performance, gulping down the medicine, galloping around the block and returning home a few minutes later. On the third evening, he changed his tactics. This time he took his medicine as usual, but instead of racing he began to skip around the room with all the grace of a prancing pachyderm.

The wife could stand it no longer.

"Chauncey," she cried, "what in the world are you doing—racing around the block and jumping about like that? Have you lost your mind?"

"Of course not," replied the weary hubby. "I'm just following the doctor's orders. He told me to take my medicine two nights running and to skip the third night!"

* * *

The sign in the theatre's box-office window read: Service Men—90c.

Anita Nahr went up to the window, laid down a five dollar bill and said, "I'll take two marines, two sailors and a paratrooper."

* * *

Wladimir Kowalski dropped in at the *You Jane, I Ching* Polish Restaurant for a snack. To his surprise he saw an elderly man of unmistakable Jewish features dining at one of the tables.

"Stanislaw," he whispered to his friend, the waiter, "what's that Jew doing here in a Polish eating place?"

"He's eating," replied Stanislaw helpfully.

"Yeah, I can see that, ya flathead. But in this neighborhood? There ain't a Jew lives around here fer miles."

"Nobody needs a residency permit to eat here."

"Yeah, but where does he come from?"

"How do I know? Jews come from Israel, don't they?"

"Where's Israel?" asked Wladimir.

"I ain't sure," replied Stanislaw, "but it can't be very far. That guy's been in this restaurant three times already just this week."

* * *

The judge looked down upon the quaking little man who stood at the bar of justice.

"Is this the first time you've been up before me?" he barked.

"I don't know, your honor," gulped the little guy, almost collapsing with fright. "What time do you get up?"

*   *   *

Al and his brother, Fred, were discussing their sister's new fiancé.

"That guy should walk through a screen door and strain himself," grumbled Al. "He's so dumb he'd stay up all night studying for a blood test. If he drank eight Cokes, he'd burp 7-Up."

"I know what you mean," affirmed Fred. "His own father told me he once took a hammer and a fifth of *schnapps* to bed with him so he could hit the hay and sleep tight. He's the kind of guy who would move to the city because he heard the country was at war."

"Not only that," agreed Al, "but he thinks he was built upside down because his feet smells and his nose runs. What do you do with a man who claims he wants to die with his boots on so he won't bruise his toes when he kicks the bucket?"

"On top of all that," said Fred, shaking his head disparagingly, "the guy is so lazy he'd stick his head out of the window so the wind could blow his nose."

"Oh, it's not laziness," objected Al. "It's just that he doesn't have to work. Didn't you know that he's worth over a million dollars?"

"No! You don't say! Well, he's not such a bad fellow when you get right down to it. He has a lot of fine qualities. I can't recall what they are at the moment, but I'm sure I will, in time."

"I think our sister made a good catch," reflected Al.

"I think our sister made a good catch," reflected Fred.

*   *   *

Shapiro the shipping clerk wandered in to work at ten minutes of nine. He was confronted by the indignant shop foreman.

"You should have been in at eight-thirty," growled the straw boss.

"Why?" asked Shapiro. "What happened at eight-thirty?"

*   *   *

Senator Javits of New York was in England on one of those fact-finding junkets so dearly beloved by congressmen.

A constituent happened to be in Washington, D.C. and decided to stop in and see his senator. After wandering around the cavernous Senate Office Building for a while, he finally located the proper office and introduced himself.

"I'm sorry," said the secretary, "but Senator Javits has gone to the United Kingdom."

"Oh, my goodness!" exclaimed the visitor, clearly taken aback. "Is it too late to send flowers?"

*   *   *

Obadiah, the obese one, was being examined by his doctor.

"If you really are sincere about reducing," advised the doctor, "then I want you to take a daily walk on an empty stomach."

"Okay," said Obadiah cheerfully. "But whose?"

* * *

A timid-looking young lady, the soul of honesty, was in the United Nations Building, applying for a job as UN translator. She was handed an application blank which she proceeded to fill out, thus and likewise:

Name: Nadine Berman
Age: 24
Present Position: Sitting down
Sex: Only once, at Lake Placid

* * *

Myron, a kibbitzer, was strolling down Fairfax Avenue in Los Angeles when he came to the little diner owned by his friend Abe. Thinking to amuse himself, he stepped inside and went into the kitchen where Abe was making preparations for the dinner hour.

"Mind if I look at this?" asked Myron, picking up a slice of pastrami and, with seeming absent-mindedness, popping it into his mouth. His eyes fell on the pickle barrel. He fished around in the brine and picked one out. "Hmm, very nice. Mind if I look at this pickle?" he repeated, popping the pickle into his mouth.

Abe, watching his friend from a corner of his eye, retrieved a pan of baked potatoes from the oven, but said nothing.

Myron made a grab for one of the potatoes. "Mind if I have a look at this?" he asked innocently. But the potato was smoking hot and, with a yelp of pain, he dropped it.

"Burned you, didn't it?" asked Abe, grinning.

"No, it didn't," snapped Myron, ever unwilling to be on the losing end of a joke. "After all, how long does it take to look at a potato?"

* * *

For reasons which only scientists can explain, the sisterhood of shnookesses is far smaller than the corresponding brotherhood of shnooks, so let us approach this rare tale with the proper deference due an endangered species.

A male student at the University of California at Berkeley was about to drive home to Los Angeles for the New Year holidays when he was introduced to a very pretty girl. She, too, was anxious to return home for a visit with her family in L.A., and would he be so kind as to give her a ride.

Our manly young student was the sort of fellow who is able to assess unexpected gratuities without too much mental exertion. Opportunities such as this, he instantly realized, occur only too infrequently during a man's productive years. Cordially, he agreed to provide the asked-for transportation.

Driving south, they engaged in the usual small talk and listened to the car radio. Then he began his insidious campaign.

"Care for a cigarette?" he asked.

"Sorry," she replied rather tartly, "I do not smoke, nor do I approve of people who do."

A few miles further, he produced a pint bottle of Laughing Tiger and offered her a snort and a swallow.

"Absolutely not!" she said sternly. "The use of alcoholic beverages is not only dangerous to one's health, it is disgusting as well."

They continued on for another 20 or 25 miles, with the undaunted student thinking, 'What the hell, nothing ventured, nothing gained; faint heart ne'er won fair lady,' and other original phrases he composed to suit the occasion and the mood.

"I have an idea," he finally said with as much nonchalance as he was able to command. "What do you say we stop at a motel in the next town and spend a couple of hours there?"

"Oh, that sounds like real fun!" exclaimed the girl. "I'd love it! As I always say, it's possible to have a good time without all that smoking and drinking!"

* * *

Cry from the Panic Section:
"Bring the hammer quick, *Zayda*, there's a fly on baby's nose!"

* * *

The surly cop on the corner observed Vogel as he dashed across the street in the face of the oncoming traffic.

"What's the matter with you?" rasped the policeman, pointing to the *Don't Walk* sign. "Can't you read plain English?"

"I'm sorry, officer," replied Vogel, embarrassed. "But I thought it was just propaganda from the bus company."

* * *

After a lifetime of arduous research, Mendel invented a new dentifrice made of shoe polish and toothpaste, for the man who is always putting his foot in his mouth.

"If the user lives," said Mendel proudly, "there are no side effects."

* * *

Should you be one of those sensitive souls who cry at sad movies, consider yourself warned in advance: This one's a real hankie-wringer.

It was a bitter cold day in January. The streets were covered with hard-packed snow, and under the snow was a film of solid ice. Shivering, her lips blue with the cold, Lilith Eisenberg, the Jackson Heights librarian, was hurrying home to her husband and cozy apartment. On the way she passed a pet shop and, there in the window, she saw the sweetest little white rabbit she had ever seen in her life. She couldn't help but stop to look at it. The rabbit, looking out, stood up on its hind legs, pawing at the window as though begging her to take it home.

Lilith's resistance broke down completely. She went inside and bought the little bunny.

With her precious, quivering prize snuggled against her for warmth inside her coat, the young lady hurried on her way. Suddenly she slipped on the icy pavement. Her feet flew out from beneath her and she fell heavily to the sidewalk. Slightly stunned, she opened her coat and, to her horror, she found that she had crushed the poor little rabbit to death. Aghast at the accident, Lilith burst into tears.

At that moment, Herman the mortician rounded the corner and took in the scene with one sweeping glance. He noted the young woman lying on the sidewalk, sobbing her heart out, and the creature lying dead inside her open coat. He felt the need to comfort her somehow.

"Lady, please don't cry," he murmured, his voice full of sympathy. "It wouldn't have been normal anyway. Look at those ears!"

* * *

Here is a gem told by Bernard Baruch, sometime in 1918 or 1919.

In western New York, on the lower edge of the Adirondack region, there used to be a guide over in the mountains who, being reckless by nature, made a specialty of escorting city sportsmen into the wilderness during the hunting season. Any North Woods veteran will tell you this is a hazardous calling. Moreover, the mortality figures prove it. Green sportsmen invade the tall timber carrying high-power rifles and shoot at everything they see moving in the bushes. The result is that a few of them kill one another and the majority destroy their guides, even though the latter, for self-protection, wear red shirts and red hats and white neckerchiefs. It is a true state of affairs these days just as it was when this incident occurred.

This particular guide had several close calls. Finally, when a bullet had ripped his shoulder and another had blown his cap off, he had an inspiration. He made a suit of awning cloth of alternate white and blue stripes. But the first time he wore the costume they brought him home again—bored through and through. As he emerged from a thicket, a city gunner, one Arthur Blumenthal, stationed across a clearing, had plugged him.

At the inquest, the remorseful Mr. Blumenthal was introduced as a witness.

"Now look here," said the coroner, "of course nobody accuses you of killing poor Jim intentionally. But it does seem curious to me—and I imagine it strikes everyone else in this room the same way—that when Jim was in striped clothes which could be seen a mile away, you, standing not a hundred yards distant, should mistake him for a deer."

"I didn't mistake him for a deer," said Blumenthal unhappily. "I thought he was a zebra."

* * *

Turn back the pages of time to the turbulent year of 1910. The

International Ladies Garment Workers Union in New York, and the Amalgamated Clothing Workers Union in Chicago had won the first of their "Great Revolts," ushering in a renaissance of American industry and labor relations. The few dollars of extra pay won by the needle workers helped expand their miniscule social life. In November of that year, at 63 Hester Street, a group of stalwarts organized "The East Side Sick Benefit and Fraternal Society, Lodge No. One." And therein lies a tale, as the authors of yesteryear liked to say.

One day, at the peak of its popularity in 1911, Lodge No. One (the Society never graduated to a "Lodge No. Two") welcomed Eliezer Cherkis to its fraternal bosom. There was an impressive initiation ceremony with hailing signs, secret handclasps and a ritual and all the rest of it. The greenhorn (Cherkis, in later life, became a bank director but he was indubitably a greenhorn in 1911) entered with enthusiasm into the solemnities of the occasion and at spare moments during the following week he strengthened his memory in the secret work so dearly cherished by the Lodge.

On the following Monday, Cherkis received a postcard announcing that the Lodge had moved to the Union Square Building, a three-storied structure where a number of other clubs and associations also maintained meeting halls. Monday also happened to be Lodge-meeting night, so Cherkis went to the new address and rapped three times upon a locked door.

Fifteen minutes later, the new member, looking very disconsolate, encountered one of the officers of the Lodge a few blocks from the building.

"Listen here, what's the big idea you wouldn't let me in tonight?" Cherkis demanded heatedly.

"Wouldn't let you in where?" countered the mystified brother member.

"Into the Lodge, of course. Where else? I tried to get past the Grand Outer *Malach*, but the way he talked to me it was a shame and a disgrace."

The other gave a start of surprise.

"Believe me, Eliezer, I don't even know what you are talking about. What happened?"

"It was like so," began the novice. "I climbed up the stairs and I'm knocking on the door. Then a little slot opens up in the door like from a mailbox, and somebody inside sticks his eye to the Peeping-Tom hole and he's hollering on me, 'What is it?' So I made the Grand Hailing Sign and I say to him like I'm supposed to, 'Next year in Jerusalem,' just like that. And he says 'Who gives a damn?' and slams shut the peeping-hole in the door."

"*Idiot! Shlemiel!*" cried the Lodge officer. "Don't you know that our meeting doesn't start for another hour?"

"No, I didn't know that. So who is meeting there earlier?"

"The Knights of Columbus, that's who. And you had to give those Catholics our secret passwords."

"*Oy vay!*" gasped the penitent blunderer. For a moment the enormity of his mistake stunned him. Then he brightened.

"listen," he added, "it could be worse."

"Worse? How could it be worse?"

"Well, look at it like this. Maybe I gave them our passwords but you got to admit—I got their countersign!"

13

Exaggerators, Distorters and Plain Liars

INTRODUCTION

Humor is truth in an intoxicated condition; a good reason why opera can lie, but seldom a comic opera. It may be attributed to the fact that humor is a gift of the heart, not the mind.

The bearer of false tales wears many hats. There is the teller of tall stories who spins his exuberant yarns for the pure enjoyment it affords. He's the one who will stoutly maintain that he caught a fish that was so big it took two men to carry the photograph.

Then there's the articulator of the white lie, often a compassionate person who adheres to the ancient Jewish maxim: "Better to tell a little lie that hurts no one, than a big truth that breaks someone's heart."

There is also the charming exaggerator or distorter who uses wild flights of allegory and imagery to convey his thoughts. This fellow isn't actually a liar—he's just gifted with a hyper-active imagination. If he happens to be an actor, he'll say, "I starred in a play titled *Oh, Sugar,* a musical spoof of diabetes." He loves the overstatement, and will unabashedly claim that he went to see an adult film where even the popcorn was over 18 years old. And he is often addicted to the understatement, as well. "I left my little home town in Montana," he will solemnly declare, "because it was a hotbed of tranquility." This amusing raconteur gets his message across by means of hyperbole. Ask him if his wife is as pretty as ever, and he'll reply, "Yes, but it takes her a half-hour longer." The statement is not quite as false as it initially sounds.

And not to be ignored is the chronic liar, an individual who is usually a victim of his own sense of inferiority. In order to capture the admiration and applause of others, he embellishes his stories to attract attention to himself, consequently boosting his self-esteem. He often realizes his shortcoming, but he is like a rider on a runaway horse, desperately hanging on because he is afraid to get off. He epitomizes the difference between a liar and a damn liar.

Nevertheless, exaggeration has its supporters—especially in the realm of art. In his *Critic and the Drama,* George Jean Nathan wrote:

131

"Art is a gross exaggeration of natural beauty: there never was a woman so beautiful as the Venus di Milo, or the song of a nightingale so beautiful as Ludwig von Beethoven's . . . or human speech so beautiful as Shakespeare's." However, Nathan himself exaggerates.

It would be nice to say that no hyperbole exists in Jewish literature —nice, but untrue. We find this statement in the Apocrypha, for example: "Each vine shall yield a thousand branches, each branch a thousand clusters, each cluster a thousand grapes, and each grape a barrel of wine." Gentlemen! Gentlemen!

On a somewhat grander scale, we find this enthusiastic description in the hallowed pages of the Talmud: "There were 365 thoroughfares in the great city of Rome, and each had 365 palaces; each palace had 365 stories, and each story had enough food for the whole world." All right already: *enough*!

But there are numerous references in the Bible and in Jewish traditional writings that take a dim view of the liar. "Lying lips are an abomination to the Lord," is one. Or, "The Messiah will come only when the world will realize that to speak an untruth is adultery," is a concept we are reminded of by the sages of old.

Yet, on the whole, the people's literature is surprisingly tolerant of the lie when there seems to be reasonable cause. Mendele, in 1878, for example, made the witty and unarguable assertion, "He who doesn't lie can't be a marriage broker." In the Talmud, we are politely informed: "You may tell an untruth in the interests of peace." And in the 12th century, anticipating Freud by some 700 years, Ibn Izra advanced his own unique theory for posterity: "People tend to lie because of impotence," he asserted. Well, it takes all kinds . . .

The late author, Benjamin Di Casseres, valiantly sprang to the defense of the much-maligned fabricator. "The art of survival," he wrote in his *Fantasia Impromptu*, "is the art of lying to yourself, heroically, continuously, creatively. The senses lie to the mind; the mind lies to the senses. The truth-seeker is a liar; he is hunting for happiness, not truth." But before you accept Casseres' opinion at face value, hark to the admonition of Maimonides who wrote in his book, *Iggeret Teman*, "Do not consider it proof just because it is written in books, for a liar who will deceive with his tongue will not hesitate to do the same with his pen."

There are scores of American-Jewish "liar jokes" which follow the light-hearted banter of Old World Jewry, and which are still told as though the Jews did not have a care in the world. Among those anecdotes which have survived in somewhat altered form is this brief illustration: A Second Avenue dealer in antiques was using all his powers of persuasion to sell a pocket watch to a wealthy customer.

"This marvelous timepiece originally belonged to the great Maimonides himself," enthused the dealer. "He used this very watch to count the pulse-beats of his patients. A servant stole it and brought it to this country."

Obviously, that little story needed no alterations, except for the locale, because of its absurdity. Maimonides lived in the 12th century and there were no pocket watches in his day. The pulse was unknown:

William Harvey discovered the circulation of the blood in the year 1628. And, of course, America was not discovered until some 300 years after Maimonides' death. But the tale of the dealer and the watch is only one of many that have remained virtually unchanged from its original European telling by the immigrants who flocked to these shores at the turn of the century.

The truly clever joke of universal appeal may be adapted and adopted, but seldom is forgotten. In any case, it is rather unseemly to criticize the dealer in a society where parents always demand that their children tell the truth, the whole truth, and nothing but the truth—except when there are visitors present.

And, lest we end this introduction on too frivolous a note, you are reminded of the stern injunction: Thou shalt not bear false witness against thy neighbor—without good reason.

H.D.S.

Little Alma, a pupil in the first grade, arrived home from school all out of breath.

"Daddy, daddy," she cried, her eyes sparkling with excitement, "we had our very first fire drill today!"

"That's good, *shayneh*," he said, smiling. "I believe in fire drills. Why, I once almost died in a fire."

"Ooh, tell me."

"Well, it was like this: I fell into a great big vat of chicken soup. So I climbed on top of the *knaidlach* to keep from drowning and I hollered 'fire' at the top of my lungs."

"*Fire?*" exclaimed Alma. "Was there a fire, too?"

"No," grinned her father, patting her curls, "but who'd have helped me if I yelled 'chicken soup'!?"

* * *

One evening in Schwartz's Deli on Delancey Street (before it was converted from pastrami to pizza), Mannie, Moe and Jack were discussing the difference between Jewish and gentile wives. As they talked, their imaginations soared into the wild blue yonder.

"Why is it that Jewish wives always get so fat after they're married a few years?" asked Mannie plaintively. "Take my wife, for instance. "She's so fat she has to put on a girdle to get into her kimono. No matter where she might be in the house I'm never more than a few feet away. Five more pounds and she won't need any clothes—they'll make her wear license plates."

"You call that fat?" asked Moe. "Now you guys know how much I love to play golf. My wife is always pestering me to take her along for a game. But that woman is just too fat to play. When she places the ball where she can see it, she can't hit it; and when she places the ball where she can hit it, she can't see it."

"You fellas have nothing to complain about," observed Jack. "You should see my wife. All she has to do is turn around in the supermarket and she rearranges the canned goods. She sits on a chair and right away she has a hangover. Even in her high school graduation picture she wasn't just sitting in the front row—she *was* the front row. Now *that's fat!*"

* * *

The Wassermans were watching the six o'clock news on television. A fire had erupted in a downtown hotel and a number of guests had been injured.

"Those people shouldn't have panicked," observed Mr. Wasserman. "I remember the time I was once caught in a bad fire but I kept my head."

"You were in a bad fire?" echoed his wife. "For thirty years we're married but this I'm hearing for the first time. Where did it happen?"

"Back in Vilna, when I was a young fellow, just before I came to this country. I was working in a soap factory when all of a sudden the whole building went up in flames. I was the only one who escaped."

Mrs. Wasserman sighed. 'Trapped again, after all these years.' She should have known that her husband was off on one of his "stories." But she bravely played out the game.

"All right, I give up. So how did you escape from the soap factory?"

"Nothing to it," he grinned. "I climbed up on the roof and just waited for the firemen to come and shpritz water on the flames. When the soap bubbles reached up to where I was I just climbed down on the lather."

* * *

Kitzel, Karp and Kornblum were arguing as to who was the richest man in the world.

"It has to be Rothschild," said Kitzel. "I heard that he has a different dentist for each tooth. And cars—let me tell you: Rothschild has four Rolls Royces—one for each direction. And he has a station wagon that's bigger than the station. That guy doesn't even need to have his cars air conditioned. He just keeps a half-dozen cold ones in his freezer."

"Rothschild is a rich man—no question about it," agreed Karp, "but the Strausses are richer. Old man Strauss gave his six-year-old grandson a cowboy outfit for a birthday present—110,000 acres, 2,000 head of cattle and 500 horses. I tell you, when this guy Strauss cashes a check, the bank bounces. Come to think of it, the finance companies owe *him* money!"

Kornblum dismissed his friends' arguments with an airy wave of his hand.

"Rothschild and Strauss are suffering from poverty compared to Solomon Guggenheim," he said lightly. "He doesn't count his money like those other two—he weighs it. The Chase National Bank has a branch office in his living room. Did you know that Guggenheim owns an unlisted telephone company? Believe me, he keeps Swiss money in an American bank. And you're talking about Rothschild's and Strauss's cars! I don't even know why you mentioned those welfare cases. Guggenheim buys only split-level Cadillacs, and he takes his change in Volkswagens. Even his bicycle is made by Lincoln Continental."

Kitzel and Karp surrendered before the onslaught.

"All right, Guggenheim is the richest," cried Karp, completely overwhelmed. "Just so he remembers that money isn't just for show. It should help others and also buy him some personal comforts, too."

"It does," replied Kornblum, enjoying his conquest. "The Guggenheim Foundation takes care of his philanthropies, and as to his personal comforts, the man has two armchairs—one for each arm. And you should see his bathroom! It has two tubs—one for rinsing. And each tub has three faucets," concluded Kornblum triumphantly, "hot, cold and luke!"

* * *

Mark Shreiber, the Beau Brummel of Bronx Park South, made himself comfortable in his favorite barber chair and ordered his usual mod style haircut.

"Sure," said Sam the barber. "And after I get through, how about a nice singe?"

"A singe? What do I need with a singe, except maybe to pay you an extra dollar?"

"Now, you know I wouldn't recommend anything just for the money," said Sam reproachfully. "Actually, a singe not only improves the growth of your hair but it makes your body stronger, too."

"Convince me!"

"It's like this, Mark: Every hair on your head is nothing more than a hollow tube. When your hair is cut it makes a hole at the end of each hair and the energy in your body kind of leaks out of that hole. But if you get your hair singed, it closes up the hole and seals in all that energy, and that's what keeps you from getting weaker and weaker."

"Now wait a minute!" protested Mark. "That's just plain silly. How about the hair on my face? I shave every day and cut the ends off, and it not only improves the growth of my whiskers but it gets thicker and stronger—and I never feel the least bit weak. What's your answer to that?"

Sam shrugged. "There's a very simple answer," he said resignedly. "You're just not the kind of man that story was meant for."

* * *

Karl Carlinsky, the same young gentleman from New England who won a Distinguished Service Cross in the Spanish-American War, had a peculiarity of character that remained with him until the day he died in 1929: Carlinsky could not stand to be bested in *anything!* No doubt there were psychological reasons for this quirk in his otherwise splendid nature, but that is not our concern. He was, in fact, a remarkably able man and, in his later years, he established the K-T Coal Mining Company and a K-T Railroad spur-line on the border of Kentucky and Tennessee.

There was one time, however, when he came perilously close to living in the shadow of someone else's greatness. It happened when he first migrated to the foothills of the Tennessee mountains from his native city of Newport, Rhode Island.

In a small town some fifty miles from Memphis, there resided a native whose claim to distinction lay in three things—his appetite, his capacity and his digestion. He played no favorites in the food line; he could and did eat anything that was edible, and in incredible quantities. But if he liked one thing a little better than anything else, that thing was the canned oyster—the kind that, 75 or so years ago, was packed in a circular can with a bull's head on the label, and which was customarily anointed with pepper sauce before being consumed.

Carlinsky, during a visit to the general store, was informed that the gluttonous one could do away with twenty cans of the bivalves. Immediately, he sensed a challenge to his sense of superiority. He knew he could not equal that kind of prodigious eating, but he also doubted the story. In the hope of testing the other man's storage facilities and, of course, reasserting his own status—at least to himself—he challenged the man to prove his claims. A group of hangers-on at the store formed a pool, each contributing half a dollar. The entire amount was invested in cove oysters and then the champion was invited to come to the general store on an appointed afternoon and show what he could do. He came before an awe-stricken audience and he showed. Oh, how he showed!

Disdaining all the tools prescribed by civilized etiquette, he swallowed down the provided oysters, juice and all, from the container. Almost before the storekeeper could open a fresh can, he had emptied the one opened a minute earlier. In half an hour the supply on the shelves had vanished and still the marvel showed no evidence of being satiated. He scooped up a few errant oysters which had lodged in his whiskers and in the opening of his waistcoat and sent them on their way to join their brethren. Then he remarked:

"Wal, since thar don't 'pear to be no more eatin' goin' on I better be puttin' out fer home—it's getting' on to'rd supper time."

Carlinsky and one of the other contributors to the purse drifted out on the porch to watch his slouching figure disappear in the dusk. For awhile they stood in silence. Then the local man said:

"Tain't no doubt about it—I reckon Gabe Coombs is shorely the champeen eater of all creation. He's the most important man hereabouts —that's fer shore."

Carlinsky, on the verge of impending ego-deflation, gave him a sour look but could think of nothing to say.

"I wonder how many cove oysters could he of et in one sittin'?" speculated the rural one. He mulled the idea in his mind for awhile and then added: "I'll bet he could eat all the oysters in the world."

It was an interesting theory and they were soon joined by the others who drifted out of the store to join the conversation.

At last! Here was Carl Carlinsky's opportunity to redeem himself in the eyes of his beholders.

"Do you have any idea how many oysters there are in the world?" he demanded.

The locals stared at each other blankly.

"More'n you and us could pay fer," opined one of the group.

"Not necessarily," countered Carlinsky. "If Gabe Coombs can eat all the oysters in the world, I am wealthy enough to pay for them. But if he is unable to finish them—and I mean each and every one—then you will pay me double the cost."

Startled, they shuffled their feet and whispered to each other, but could find little enthusiasm for so gigantic a bet. But to ease the uncertainty, one of them asked:

"How many oysters are there in the world?"

"There are in this world," began Carlinsky, his voice ringing with triumphant authority, "three billion, one hundred and eighteen million, seven hundred and ninety-four thousand, six hundred and eighty-two oysters alive at this very moment."

The hillbillies stared at him, open-mouthed.

"And what's more," added Carlinsky in his hour of glory, "I counted them twice—once last month and again this past Tuesday!"

* * *

The judge on the bench fixed a cold eye upon the defendant at the bar. "Why did you assault the plaintiff?" he asked sternly.

"Because he called me a liar, that's why!" stated the accused.

"Is that true?" inquired the judge, turning to the battered victim.

"Sure it's true," said the plaintiff. "I called him a liar because that's what he is, and I can prove it."

"What have you to say about that?" asked his honor of the defendant.

"That's got nothing to do with the case," came the heated retort. "All right, so I'm a liar, but what's the matter—I don't have a right to be sensitive about it?"

* * *

Once upon a time there were two brothers: Mannie, the truthful one, and Josh, the most incorrigible and persistent liar in the whole state. As a result of Josh's chronic embellishments of simple facts, the entire family was getting a bad reputation.

Mannie took his brother in hand.

"Look here, Josh," he scolded, "you're disgracing the family name. This lying has got to stop. The next time you start in to exaggerate just keep your eye on me. When I shake my head that will be a signal to you to soft-pedal—to quit exaggerating."

The very next day the two brothers were in the company of a group of traveling salesmen. The talk drifted to the subject of big city hotels and their comparative sizes. The conversation was irresistible for Mannie's vivid imagination.

"Speaking of big hotels," he said, "I know one out in California that is 96 stories high, has 5,000 rooms, eight dining rooms and 23 coffee shops, 14 bowling alleys, 28 swimming pools, 30 cocktail bars, 48 . . ."—here he caught a hard look and a shake of the head from his truthful brother Mannie, and he knew it was time to back down—"and is three feet wide!"

* * *

An auctioneer, opines Herman the hermit of Hester Street, is a man who can sell nothing for something to a buyer who is looking for something for nothing.

* * *

George Jessel likes to adorn his chest with the many medals awarded him for his numerous jaunts overseas to entertain our armed forces. His pride is justifiable; he has often brought cheer to the boys during wartime, sometimes in the midst of hostilities.

One day, he was explaining the origins of his medals to a young lady who was forty-eight years his junior and therefore a target for his close attention.

"This medal," he explained, "was given to me by General Eisenhower himself. This one was awarded by none other than General MacArthur. This one was presented by General Wainright and this one by General Patton." He went on, right through his vast collection, until he came to the last medal pinned to his chest. But instead of discussing it, he said, "Now, let's go to dinner."

"But you haven't told me about that last medal," protested the girl.

"Well, if you must know," answered George patiently, "that one was given to me by the Pawnbrokers Association of New York for my special redeeming qualities."

* * *

"There's no use you should keep asking me for details," said the *yenta* with high moral purpose in her tones. "In fact, I already told you more than I heard mineself!"

* * *

Fun from our Folklore Files:

Nearly everyone who went to Yellowstone National Park in the old days remembers—or should remember—Petrified Petrovsky. He was a picturesque man and his language was just as colorful. P.P. was born in New York but was taken to Arizona as a small child and was inordinately proud of the natural beauty of the state where he had grown to manhood . . . prouder even than he was of the beauties of Yellowstone, of which he was very proud indeed.

Petrified Petrovsky acquired his sobriquet because of a comment he made to a woman many long years ago. One day, so the folklorists tell us, he was decanting upon the marvels of Arizona's Petrified Forest.

"Is it really so very remarkable?" asked a lady visitor.

"Madam," said Petrovsky, "in the whole world there's nothing like it. It's the most petrified place there is. Believe me—why should I lie to a perfect stranger?—I once saw a petrified bird sitting on a petrified limb high up on top of a petrified tree. And what was that little petrified bird on that petrified limb in that petrified tree doing? It was singing a petrified song!"

* * *

Hollywood: The free-swinging city where some old-fashioned mothers who can remember their husband's first kiss, now have daughters who can't even remember their first husbands.

* * *

Dr. William Steiner, a professor of comparative religion at New York University in the 1930's, was among the most eminent educators of his day. To his mother, however, he remained "Velveleh"—and she used the Yiddish diminutive until her death, when the good professor was in his fifties. A number of stories about his supposedly domineering mother were circulated at the time, probably none of them containing more than a kernel of truth. This one, reconstructed from the versions told by a dozen different sources, is typical.

According to campus gossip, Dr. Steiner was thirty-four years old when he finally fell in love and decided to marry. His "intended" was a vivacious widow of thirty-eight. But when he told his mother of his marriage plans, all *Gehenna* broke loose. Mama Steiner was inconsolable.

"*Oy*, Velveleh," moaned the distraught mama, "that woman is fifty if she's a day. Her birthday candles are costing more than the cake."

"Aw, mama, you know very well she's not that old," protested her son. "In fact she has a nice, youthful appearance."

"What's so nice? She's so skinny she'd look pregnant if she swallowed an olive. This is a nice figure by you? What kind of a woman has to eat garlic to prove she's breathing?"

"Well, she is somewhat slender," admitted Dr. Steiner, "but I was talking about her face, not her figure."

"That's a face? With a mouth like hers she needs a size 36 lipstick. And that nose! *Gevald!* By me, a big nose is handsome on a man or an anteater, but on a woman . . ."

"Now, mama, you're just jealous, and you know it," he interrupted in a placating voice. "But you'll have no complaints about her looks after next week. She's getting her nose fixed."

"*Hah!* A nose-lift, yet!" snapped mother Steiner. "That's all I need—a daughter-in-law who runs around smelling to high heaven!"

* * *

"People in America don't realize how lucky they are," observed Yussel the *chazzan*. "In my whole life I never heard such complaints about small apartments. They should have seen how we lived back in Vilna. My bedroom was so small I rearranged the furniture every time I sneezed. Our little dog had to wag his tail up and down, and I couldn't even brush my teeth sideways. The kitchen was so tiny we could only fry one egg at a time. I would eat in the kitchen and my elbows would be sticking out of the front door. You Americans don't know what it means to be crowded in such a tiny house. I remember, when I was a child, I got sick and all we had room for was one measle and one mump!"

* * *

Anna's husband was scolded by a policeman for jaywalking, and the matter might have ended there without further incident, but he protested his innocence so vehemently that he was taken into custody. In court, he repeated his hot-tempered performance for the judge and wound up with a ten day jail sentence for contempt.

Anna, however, could not bring herself to tell anyone that she had married such a *shlemiel*, so she concocted a little white lie to explain his absence.

"My husband spent the last ten days in a revolving door," she said. "He was looking for the doorknob."

* * *

Al, Jake and Bill were discussing the merits—or rather the demerits —of their respective girlfriends.

"What can you do with a girl who can't even spell DDT?" groaned Al. "Her own father once told me she was ten before she learned to wave bye-bye."

"You're lucky to have such a genius," commented Jake. "My girl was flattered when the doctor told her she had acute appendicitis. Even as a kid, they had to keep her in summer school all winter. The poor girl needed a tutor just to pass recess."

"Listen, your girlfriends are Einsteins compared to mine," observed Bill. "How would you like to have a sweetheart who goes to the zoo to see Christmas seals? Only last week a fortune teller embarrassed us when he read my girl's mind for half price."

Bill paused reflectively. "I could forgive any of those things," he concluded with a sigh. "But can you imagine being married to someone who runs after a street sprinkler for three blocks to tell the driver his truck is leaking?"

* * *

In the early 1870's, before Joseph Seligman stopped attending the posh Harmonie Club, founded by well-to-do German Jews, and affiliated with the Union League Club instead, he would occasionally swap stories with his fellow members. The financial wizard was good at it, too. But on one memorable occasion he was topped by his own brother, Jesse. Aside from its humor, the anecdote is interesting because it shows a human side of these two austere founders of the banking family which has been rarely mentioned.

Old Joseph, enjoying a glass of fine brandy and a Corona Corona cigar in the sanctum of the Harmonie Club, was telling of his experiences as a mighty hunter.

"When I was in India," he began, "a huge Bengal tiger leaped out of the underbrush just ten feet from where I was standing. I raised my trusty rifle but, to my horror, it was out of ammunition. I had forgotten to load it. With great presence of mind, however, I opened my canteen and splashed water right in his face, and that fierce giant of a beast slunk away."

"Gentlemen," spoke up Jesse in his quiet manner, "I can vouch for the absolute truth of my brother's story. Some minutes after the incident occurred, while following the path that Joseph had taken, I met that same ferocious tiger. As is my usual habit when meeting such jungle beasts, I stroked its whiskers."

Jesse paused with all the native instincts of a born dramatist and concluded: "Gentlemen, those whiskers were wringing wet!"

* * *

"Not that I'm making fun of her baby," declared the jealous *yenta*, "but when she takes it out for an airing, people come up to her and say, "Oh, what a beautiful baby carriage!"

* * *

"My wife has a winning smile," sighed Lawrence of Arabia Avenue, "but the trouble is, she has a losing face. And that figure! Where other women have curves, she has detours. It hurts me to say this, but she's the only woman in the world who can be called both pretty and ugly— pretty ugly!"

* * *

"Grandpa, can I keep pigeons on the roof?" asked little Mike. "The other kids have some, and I'll take real good care of them."

"Why sure, Mikey," grandpa agreed. "I used to fly pigeons myself when I first came to this country as a boy."

"You did? Nobody ever told me about that."

"That's because they're all jealous. I'll never forget old Rosalie, my prize homer."

Mike knew the gray-bearded old man well enough to suspect another of his fascinating yarns. "Tell me about it," he pleaded.

Grandpa needed no second urging. He settled back in his easy chair and began:

"Back in Russia I used to train Siberian tigers and wild wolves for pleasure. Well, after I arrived in America I found there were no tigers or wolves running around loose so I took up raising pigeons. I suppose it was the contrast between the ferocious animals and the cooing birds that attracted me. I always liked extremes, you know—liable to be exploring the Polar regions one year and penetrating the jungles of Borneo the next. That's me!"

"But, grandpa, you . . ."

"Don't interrupt, Mikey; I'm getting to it. Anyway, I developed the champion homing pigeon of the entire world. I called her Rosalie. Rosalie was famous in every country on the face of the earth. Wherever people had pigeons they spoke of Rosalie in awed whispers.

"One day, after she had broken all the records for speed and long distance flying, a fellow came over here from Galicia. It seemed that he owned homing pigeons himself. He was a no-good, first-class *paskudniak* —you should pardon my language—but I didn't find that out until later.

That's what I get for trusting *Galitzianers*. Those people . . ."

"Grandpa, the pigeon!"

"Oh yes, the pigeon—and stop interrupting when your grandfather is talking. Well, this—this—*goniff* made a bet with me. The terms were like so: He'd take Rosalie in a closed cage on the fastest train running between New York and Philadelphia. Just as the train pulled into Philadelphia, he'd release her and if she got back to New York within two hours the purse was mine.

"But, like I said, the man was a crook. Those *Galitzianers* . . ."

"*Grandpa!*"

"All right, don't holler on your poor old grandpa! Where was I! Oh yes, Rosalie has to fly back here from Philadelphia in two hours or I lose the bet. So what did that robber do? Instead of turning Rosalie loose according to our agreement, he first clipped one of her wings so that she couldn't fly ten inches. Then he dropped her off the back end of the rear car of the train. The last thing he saw of the poor little thing, she was squatted down between the tracks in the Philadelphia yard, dodging the switch engines."

Little Mike was aghast at this treachery. "You didn't pay the man all that money you bet, did you, grandpa?"

The old man shook his head. "I should say not! As a matter of fact I didn't have to—I won that bet."

"You *won!* How?"

"In exactly one hour and fifty-eight minutes by the clock, there came Rosalie into my yard . . .

"But, believe me, for the next three weeks her feet were terribly sore!"

* * *

Old Moishe, an octogenarian who had long since retired from the silk factoring business, was hardly a man of mystery. Yet, there were a few things about his past, especially those events dating back to his youth, about which he would not speak. Rumor had it that he might not have been as scrupulously honest as he was in his later life. For example, in the corner of his living room was a huge grandfather's clock he had once brought home without a word of explanation. That was more than half-a-century ago, but no one, not even the closest members of his family, ever learned how he had come by the valuable antique, and old Moishe had vowed to take the secret with him to the grave. They suspected that he had not purchased it, but they did not even know that for a certainty.

One evening, during the *Chanukah* holidays, his old friend, Rabbi Jacobson, dropped in for a chat. As they were sipping a glass of festive wine, the rabbi happened to think about that big clock.

"Moishe, it has been many years since you were young and perhaps a little wild," he began. "Now that you are older, wiser, and a citizen in good standing, why not satisfy my curiosity and tell me how you got that clock?"

"Very well," agreed Moishe, to the rabbi's great surprise. "It happened almost sixty years ago. I remember it well because it was the day before Passover and in my house there was nothing but poverty. There were no matzohs, no eggs, no meat—nothing! My bride was in tears and I was simply desperate. What to do?"

"Yes, yes! Go on!" urged the rabbi as Moishe paused to collect his thoughts.

"I went to the market place and wandered aimlessly about, praying for a miracle from heaven. Suddenly, a richly adorned carriage pulled up in front of me and a lady stepped out to enter one of the stores. She was dressed in beautiful satins and wore diamonds and jewels such as I had never seen before."

Again, Moishe lapsed into reverie and the rabbi, bursting with curiosity, begged him to continue.

"Well, as she passed me, the lady dropped her silk handkerchief, the four corners of which were tied together so as to make a tiny bundle. It fell right at my feet. 'Oh Lord,' I prayed, 'help me in this, my hour of need!' And the Almighty heard my prayers. I picked up that little bundle and opened it. There, in my very own hands, were ten gold coins, each worth a hundred dollars. I rushed home with an armload of food and from that very day my wife and I prospered."

"Is that all?" exclaimed the rabbi.

"That's all."

"But how about that enormous grandfather's clock?"

"Oh, the clock," added old Moishe innocently. "That was in the handkerchief also."

14

So Sue Me!

INTRODUCTION

Some 4,000 years ago, a Hebrew leader, not divine or perfect, but closer to God than other men, was commanded to promulgate the Law; not only the Ten Commandments, but the whole body of criminal and civil law as well. That man's name was Moses. It was he, the architect of the Hebrew people, who laid the foundation of a monotheistic religion based on the principles of love and justice. The great concern of this titan was to establish a social state in which perpetual poverty and degrading want would be unknown. Since that moment, when he descended from Mt. Sinai with his precious tablets, the influence of Moses has spread to all humanity.

Many Jews have been drawn toward the legal profession and who can doubt that Grandpa Moses is somewhat responsible. Yet, despite its noble roots, neither the profession nor the professors of the profession were held to be sacrosanct by their co-religionists. A people who can joke about their mothers, for instance, may almost be expected to aim barbs at mere lawyers—the Cardozas and the Frankfurters and the Brandeises and the Goldbergs and the Kissingers notwithstanding. Satire and irony tend to remind us that lawyers are also human and that ridicule serves the useful purpose of calling attention to correcting unjust or unnecessary legislation. Ludwig Bourne pointed this out in his jocular comment: "If nature had as many laws as the state, God Himself could not reign over it."

Hostility, whether conscious or subconscious, furnishes yet another reason for the plethora of jokes about lawyers and the law in general. There are times when our fate, our fortune, occasionally even our personal freedom, depend upon the sagacity and knowledge of lawyers, as well as the decisions of judges and juries. The hostility which some of us feel is actually directed at the figure of stern, unbending authority. Should our experience in court be unpleasant, our animosity is intensified. It remains in our psyche long after the ordeal itself is but a fade memory, and is directed at the law in general rather than at a specific case or personality. And, like the beneficial result that comes from lancing a festering boil, we feel a sense of relief when our resentment is released in the form of derisive laughter.

"Lawyers are just like physicians," observed Sholom Aleichem in *Finf un Zibtzig Toisnt:* "what one says, the other contradicts." The reason, however, may not be due solely to contrariness, if we can believe Judith T. Younger, Dean of the Syracuse University Law School, who said, "Most law students don't even know how to use commas, sentences or paragraphs; they haven't the foggiest notion of how to spell . . . Great men of the law speak brilliantly and beautifully, but most law students I've come in contact with—75 per cent of them—are illiterate. Nation-wide, I'd say that 50 to 75 per cent would be an accurate estimate." So the next time someone bitterly complains that he lost his case because of a stupid lawyer, just remember Dean Younger's value judgment, nod sympathetically and tell him you understand.

Fortunately, most lawyers have a keen sense of humor. They need it in their profession. *The California Law Review* once told of the lawyer who informed a siren, "My client wants you and himself to go your separate ways, and he's willing to pay you ten cents a mile." *The New York Law Review,* not especially noted for its comical articles, defined a jury as "the only thing that doesn't work right when it's fixed." In Chicago, the *Cook County Law Journal* related the story about the woman who told eleven exasperated male jurors, "If you men weren't so stubborn we could all go home." And the late Oscar Levant defined a lawyer as "a man who helps you get what's coming to him."

H.D.S.

Here is an unalloyed golden nugget of early Jewish Americana dealing with the high adventures of a "Jewish Indian" of bygone days— an anecdote that gives lusty voice to the expression popular in the 19th century: "The law is a ass." The subject of our present story is Edward Kantor, in later life a favorite of many Indians, who was accepted into their tribe and was known to them as "Bosh-bish-gay-bish-gon-sen," the Indian name for "firecracker," and a name he laughingly described as "more Jewish-sounding than my own."

Young Eddie was about 17 years old when he ran away from his home in Germany and came to America as a stowaway on a French vessel. After jumping ship in Charleston he took to peddling, then to clerking in a drug store. He was fired when he blew up the store during one of his "experiments." He then found a job as a stoker on a steamboat. Now it was the steamboat that blew up, but Kantor, who had to swim to shore to save his life, insisted that he was "only partly" responsible for the explosion. "The skipper wanted more speed and that's what he got," said Eddie.

He finally settled in Detroit where he opened a general store in 1849, trading mainly, at first, with the local Indian tribes. He soon won their friendship and they would often sit in a circle with their bearded, white-skinned comrade and smoke a peace pipe. Gradually he learned the languages of the Huron, the Chippewa and the Potawatami Indians, and they would listen, fascinated, as they heard of the adventures, told in their own tongues, of Edward Bosh-bish-gay-bish-gon-sen Kantor, the Jewish Indian.

Much of what befell Eddie can be verified. But there is much more that cannot. Among the legends attributed to him is the adventure which he is said to have experienced when he was 18 or 19 years old. The ancient classic has been heard in a dozen variants, with the proponent, as a rule, being Mexican, Irish or Indian. Most stem from the post-Civil War period. This one, however, a gem in the litany of Jewish-American folk humor, goes all the way back to 1817—about the time when another Jew, Abraham Mordecai, a veteran of the Revolutionary War, struck out from Pennsylvania and founded the city of Montgomery, Alabama.

It was a blustery day in March when the youthful horse-and-wagon peddler, Edward Kantor, pulled into Fort Deposit, Alabama, about four or five years after it was settled by Andrew Jackson. It was a crude, rough little town, inhabited by men and women who attended to their business with one hand while they kept the other on their rifles and powder horns.

Eddie's horse had gone lame, but the traveling young merchant was able to trade some of his goods with an Indian for another horse. Before the day was over, however, he was arrested by the sheriff for horse-stealing, a capital offense in those days. The Indian, it seems, did not have clear title to the animal he had sold to the young stranger. In fact, he had no title at all and promptly disappeared as soon as the transaction was completed.

Northern peddlers were none too popular in the Deep South, and this one, with his accent and strange ways, became the object of an intense and general aversion by the sheriff, the judge and the jury—but especially the judge.

At the trial, the jury heard the evidence and the speeches, then closeted themselves in the saloon for their deliberations, and within an hour returned with a verdict of guilty. But, short as the time of their deliberation was, the judge had not wasted it. During the recess, he had retired to his private chambers where he had consumed a quart of prime rye whiskey. When he returned to the bench to hear the jurors' findings and to pass sentence, he was weaving gracefully. He slumped down in his chair and when the foreman had announced the result just arrived at in the jury room, he focused (with some difficulty) a wavering eye upon the convicted peddler and in a thick tone gave the order:

"Edward Kantor, stand up!"

The prisoner rose in his place.

"Edward Kantor," said His Honor, "in but a few short weeks it will be spring. The snows of winter will flee away, the ice will vanish and the air will become soft and balmy. In short, Edward Kantor, the annual miracle of the year's reawakening will come to pass.

"The rivulet will run its purling course to the sea. The first timid flowers of the season will put forth their tender shoots. The glorious valleys of this enchanted region will blossom as the rose. From every treetop some wildwood songster will carol his mating song. Butterflies will sport in the sunshine and the busy bee will hum happily as it pursues its accustomed avocation. And all of nature, Edward Kantor, will be glad.

"But you—you miserable, thieving, horse-stealing, foreign son of a bitch—you won't be here to see it, because you are going to be hanged four weeks from this coming Friday."*

For the next four weeks, Eddie languished in the town jail, visited only by the judge's young daughter, Geraldine, who brought him his scanty rations. Through a tiny, barred window he witnessed the construction of the scaffold that awaited him. Now, all was ready. Today was the day. The circuit hangman had arrived, the sheriff had polished his shiny new boots, and the townspeople were dressed in their festive Sunday-go-to-meetin' clothes. The judge was prepared with a speech he had laboriously written for the gala occasion. Came the fateful hour in which the execution was to take place, and the sheriff entered the jailhouse to fetch the prisoner.

Lo and behold—the cell was empty! On the cot was a note addressed to His Honor:

> My dear Judge Murchison:
> Before the rising of the pale new moon in all its silv'ry glory, the Shenandoah Valley of Virginia will be fragrant with the scent of apple blossoms. The song of the meadow lark whistling in the grass will bring joy to the hearts of young lovers as they listen to nature's own music. Graceful swans will make silhouettes against the soft blue skies, and the setting sun will cast its amber glow upon that far-off area, bathing it in celestial beauty.
>
> And I shall be there to enjoy it, Your Honor, together with your daughter, Geraldine, whose permission was sweetly given to borrow your horse for my wagon.
>
> When Geraldine and I find pleasure in the fragrance of all the flowers, bask in the golden Virginia sun and bathe in the rippling stream as it runs its gentle course to the sea, we shall think of you, Your Honor, with affection and, most importantly, with happy forgetfulness.
>
> Edward Kantor
>
> N.B. You may call me Eddie.

* * *

---

* *There is nothing more sinful in the telling of a story than an anti-climax. The sheer beauty of the Judge's opening remarks and the sudden switch to his cold-as-ice conclusion is funny enough. Indeed, it has always served as the ending of this folk tale. But in this, the Jewish variant, there is a continuation of the narrative which is far more than an anti-climax, for without it, Edward Kantor's life would have ended in his early youth.*

Among the hardy souls who traversed the continent or sailed around the Horn to settle in California during the 1840s and early 1850s, was Samuel Ohrbach, an adventurous young attorney. In his later years, according to the California State Historical Society, Ohrbach devoted himself to the defense of the poor and downtrodden, and may well have been the first defender of civil rights for minority groups in the Golden State. This anecdote is especially rare because of its Oriental and Jewish cast.

On November 9, 1875, one of the first Tong wars broke out in San Francisco's Chinatown. A number of fatalities resulted in both factions. One morning, in the midst of the hostilities, a mild-appearing little Oriental came quietly into the office of the prominent criminal lawyer, Samuel Ohrbach. The caller opened negotiations without preamble:

"How much you charge, get Chinaman free for kill another Chinaman dead?"

"Two thousand dollars," answered the lawyer promptly.

"How much I pay down?"

"One thousand now—one thousand when I go to court for trial."

The visitor counted out a thousand dollars, placed it on the desk, and then started to leave.

"Just a moment, come back here," cried Ohrbach. "Where are you going?"

"I go kill him," said the Chinese client. "Be back bimeby."

*   *   *

Bloom, the button man, was charged with obtaining six boxes of buttonholes and two boxes of silk thread without notifying the owners thereof about the transaction. Having been indicted, he was arraigned before the court and the case against him was called. It then developed that he had no counsel.

"Why haven't you engaged an attorney to defend you?" inquired the judge on the bench.

"Who has money to waste on expensive lawyers?" demanded Bloom.

"Well, what do you propose to do, then, about the trial of your case?" asked His Honor. "The prosecutor tells me he is ready to go ahead and impanel a jury and present the evidence."

"Judge," answered the defendant, "as far as I am concerned, you can let the matter drop right here. I'll be better off, you'll be happy and the prosecutor won't have to work so hard."

But the court explained that this would hardly do. Glancing around the room, the judge noticed two fledgling lawyers just admitted to the practice, and the youngest and least experienced members of the bar.

"I shall appoint Mr. Newman and Mr. Levine to represent you," said the magistrate, indicating the striplings.

Bloom eyed the attorneys doubtfully.

"Your Honor," he said, "I'd like to make a little proposition, if it's all right with you."

"What's your proposition?"

"If you don't mind, I'll trade you both of these lawyers for one good witness."

* * *

The defendant was accused of sullying the honor of a pure young maiden, according to the lady's testimony, and he was having a difficult time explaining the circumstances.

"I'm innocent, Your Honor," he declared. "All I did was offer her a scotch and sofa, and she reclined!"

* * *

Judge Walter Meyers, of New York, usually a strict disciplinarian and stickler for the letter of the law, recently tititllated the readers of the staid *Law Review* with an account of the time he almost held a defendant in contempt of court. He decided against citing the man, claimed the judge, because he could not distinguish whether he had overheard a muttered swear-word or prayer-word.

It seems that the defendant spent the better part of half an hour attempting to convince Judge Meyers that he was innocent of the charge of beating his wife. On and on he droned, offering the most implausible explanations imaginable. When he had concluded his lame defense, the judge found him guilty as charged.

As the bailiff was leading the man away, however, the judge thought he heard him mutter an obscene, irreverent phrase.

"Just a moment, bailiff," called the outraged magistrate. "Bring the prisoner back here."

"What's the matter with you?" he barked. "Don't you know I can add to your sentence by finding you in contempt of court? How dare you curse me!"

"Yo' honah, I didn't cuss you," replied the defendant stoutly. "All I said was 'God am de judge!' "

* * *

The adage, "Truth is funnier than fiction," is borne out by the following actual cases, as reported by the National Shorthand Reporters Association, the organization to which most court reporters belong.

Q: Did you spend the night with Mr. Goldblatt at the Hotel Edison here in New York?

A: Such a question I'm refusing to answer.

Q: Well, did you ever stay all night with Mr. Goldblatt at the Chicago Hilton?

A: That question I'm also refusing to answer.

Q: Did you spend the night with Mr. Goldblatt at the Americana Hotel in Miami?

A: No.

* * *

Mrs. Kahan, a widow, had been served with a subpoena to appear as a witness against Mr. Abeloff, a gentleman-friend of whom she was quite fond. With the defendant, Abeloff, sitting in the front row, it became clear from the outset that she would be a hostile witness. The little drama that ensued is taken from the actual transcript:

Q: How long have you known the defendant?

A: Five years—six years—who knows?

Q: What is his name?

A: Abeloff.

Q: What is his first name?

A: This I don't remember.

Q: Madam, you've known your boyfriend for five or six years and you can't recall his first name?

A: No, I can't. Can't you see I'm excited? How can I remember when I'm excited? (Rising from the witness chair and pointing to Abeloff) Seymour, for God's sake, tell them your first name.

* * *

"Hello—hello. That you, Moe? This is Mr. Schmaltz. Sorry to hear about your auto accident, but when are you coming back to work?"

"I don't really know, Mr. Schmaltz. My doctor says I can walk, but my lawyer says I can't."

* * *

A young lawyer, recently graduated from CCNY and newly admitted to the bar, was determined to specialize in civil rights cases. An idealistic fellow, he looked forward to aiding the poor and the downtrodden, hoping that his shoulder-length hair and hippie-style clothing would not be a detriment in his battle against the "establishment."

Setting up shop in Spanish Harlem, he quickly found out all about what he considered "justice" when he lost his first case. Frustrated, he appealed the verdict to a higher court, but this time his presentation was far more detailed. He cited precedent after precedent, case after case, pointing out many instances where the defendant had been acquitted in what he believed were similar circumstances.

"Please, counsellor, desist!" interrupted the weary judge after listening to the droning voice for an hour. "You may rest assured that I understand the basics of equality under the law, and you can also take it for granted that this court is familiar with the elementary concepts of justice."

"Your Honor," sighed the crusading young lawyer, "that was the mistake I made in the lower court!"

* * *

Evelyn emerged from the courtroom waving the final decree of divorcement she had just been granted.

"Look," she exulted to her friend, Gloria, "I finally got it! Believe me, you'll never know the heartaches I went through with that man."

"What did you plead—mental cruelty?" asked Gloria.

"No, my lawyer suggested I should plead 'too much exercise,' and that's exactly what I did."

"Exercise?" echoed Gloria. "That's not grounds for divorce."

"You don't know my lawyer," retorted Evelyn. "He told the judge my husband got all his exercise by jumping to false conclusions, running me down in front of my friends, sidestepping his responsibilities, and pushing his luck too far!"

* * *

A customer bought some merchandise from Stanley on the installment plan, but refused to make the last payment. So Stanley went to see a lawyer.

"Before I take your case," said the counsellor, "you'll have to give me a $50 retainer."

"All right, here's the fifty," agreed Stanley, handing over the money.

The lawyer raked in the bills. "Thank you," he murmured. "This entitles you to two questions."

"What! Fifty dollars for just two questions! Isn't that awfully high?"

"Yes, I suppose it is," said the lawyer, nodding. "Now, what's your second question?"

* * *

Sol the sliced-salami salesman from Scranton was doing his unsuccessful best to evade the responsibilities of a concerned citizen.

"I can't possibly serve on the jury, Your Honor," he protested. "Just one look at that horrible prisoner already convinced me that he's guilty!"

"Silence!" roared the judge. "That's the district attorney!"

* * *

Finkel the *goniff* was accused of stealing a diamond-studded *mezuzah* from a rich man's doorpost. However, his attorney was a glib talker and the judge, after due consideration, decided that the evidence was insufficient to convict the defendant.

"You are acquitted," ruled His Honor.

"I *what?*" gasped Sol, unable to believe his own ears.

"You're acquitted," repeated the judge. "You may go home."

"Y-you mean," stammered Sol, "I can keep such an expensive *mezuzah?*"

* * *

Lawyer: Now let's get this straight. You say it was a very dark night, yet you maintain that you saw the auto accident 500 yards off. Sir, just how far do you think you can see on a dark night?

Witness: A million miles, maybe. How far is it to the moon?

* * *

The judge glared down on the far-from-contrite defendant.

"Melvyn R. Mishkin," he rasped, "you are charged with assault and battery, and with mutilating the plaintiff by biting off a piece of his nose. How do you plead?"

"I plead innocent, Your Honor," said Melvyn in a bold voice. "There were five of us in that pinochle game and we all got into the fight. It could have been any one of us who bit off his nose."

"No, it couldn't," retorted the judge. "The injured man saw you spit it out!"

* * *

The man had been hauled into court on a charge of reckless driving. But the story he told the judge was so sad, so poignant, so filled with the pathos of human heartbreak, that his honor had to brush the tears from his eyes before he could speak.

"I'm not blaming you," he finally said in a choked voice, "just fining you!"

* * *

Dep't. of Lost Causes: "Your honor, I have no defense except that she knew she had me on the spot so she took me to the cleaners."

* * *

Mr. Genzina and Mr. Gribben became involved in a controversy over who owed three thousand dollars to whom. So bitter was the dispute that they finally took the case to court. On the appointed day, they appeared before Judge Richard Watergate.

"Before proceeding with this case," announced His Honor, "I want to state right here and now that I received an envelope containing $500 from Mr. Genzina, the plaintiff, and another envelope containing $1,000 from Mr. Gribben, the defendant.

"The court wishes it known that it will return $500 to the defendant so that the case may be tried strictly on its own merit!"

* * *

Here's another Judge Watergate joke:

The quaking defendant had been charged with stealing two pickled herrings, an electric toothbrush, a button-stitcher, a tray of cheap costume jewelry, and a copy of last week's *Forvertz*. Being a well-dressed man, he could easily have paid for the merchandise, but he simply could not resist the compulsion to steal. It was obvious to Judge Watergate that the man was a kleptomaniac, and had a problem that required medical attention rather than a jail sentence.

"How many times have you been arrested for similar offenses?" asked the judge.

"Twelve," responded the frightened man.

"Well, spending time in jail doesn't seem to have helped you," commented His Honor, "What you need is rehabilitation, not prison. So I'll suspend sentence, but only on one condition: You must place yourself under the care of a psychiatrist. Do you agree to that?"

"Oh, yes, Your Honor!" gasped the overjoyed defendant. "I'll start this very day!"

"Very good. Now, will you kindly approach the bench? I have a few confidential words for you."

Choking down his sudden misgivings, the man slithered off the witness chair and apprehensively approached the bench.

"Listen," whispered Judge Watergate, leaning forward so that his mouth was only inches away from the defendant's ear, "if that psychiatry stuff doesn't work out, would you mind picking me up a toaster?"

* * *

Herewith and forthwith is the silliest courtroom drama in the annals of American jurisprudence:

Shulman the *shlepper* was summoned to court on the charge that he had ordered an expensive samovar from a mail-order import house and had thereafter responded negatively to the law of compensation. Rather than retain an attorney to represent him, he elected to plead his own case. Presiding was the eminent magistrate, Judge Farfelzup.

"First of all," began Shulman, "I never ordered that samovar. But even if I did, the plaintiff never sent it. And if he did send it, I never got it. And if I did get it, I paid for it. And if I didn't pay for it, then it arrived broken. Now, Your Honor, give me one logical reason why I should pay out good money for a broken samovar that the plaintiff never sent and I never got. That's normal by you?"

"No, I can't say it is," agreed the judge. "But the plaintiff states that you didn't even bother to reply to his several written requests for payment. You have to admit, Mr. Shulman, that isn't normal either."

"But, Your Honor, who cares what he says? Who are you gonna believe—me or that rotten liar?"

The judge turned to the court stenographer.

"Delete that word 'rotten,' " he ordered sternly. "That determination will be made later, in due course."

His Honor now faced counsel for the plaintiff.

"All right, we will now hear your ridiculous side of the story, and let us bear in mind the serious consequences of perjury, shall we?"

"But, sir, we haven't said anything yet!"

"Proceed, before I find you in contempt."

"Your Honor, we wish to introduce as evidence this signed receipt in which the defendant certified that he not only received the goods but that it arrived in perfect condition."

Judge Farfelzup again addressed Shulman.

"*Nu?*"

"My client—that's me, Your Honor—and I, we both deny that such a receipt was ever signed by me. But even if I did sign it, I never mailed it. And if I did mail it, the plaintiff never received it. And if he did receive it, the signature was a forgery. And if it was a forgery, then I shouldn't be held accountable."

"That's what I say!" declared the judge.

The opposing attorney, who happened to be one-legged, jumped to his foot.

"But, Your Honor, it couldn't have been a forgery," he protested. "We not only have a handwriting analyst who will testify that it is the defendant's own signature, but we also have a fingerprint expert who will attest to the fact that the defendant's prints are all over the receipt."

"You don't say!" exclaimed the judge. "How about that, Shulman?"

"Your Honor," Shulman began bravely, "even if—even—er—hmm— fingerprints, the man said? With handwriting experts yet? *Ai-yi-yi!*"

"Well, say something!" snapped the judge. "In this court you have to plead one way or the other."

"I'm standing pat on executive privilege and *nolo contendere.*"

Judge Farfelzup gave him a searching look.

"You know the meanings of those terms?"

"Sure! Executive privilege means I'm guilty but nobody can prove it. *Nolo contendere* means I'm innocent but how the hell do *I* prove it! So I'm asking you to show me mercy and I'm throwing myself on the ignorance of the court!"

* * *

"Can you tell me the difference between 'unlawful' and 'illegal'?" asked the teacher.

Little Nadine's hand shot up. The teacher smiled and nodded. "Yes, dear, you may tell the class."

" 'Unlawful' is when you do something the law doesn't allow," explained Nadine. "But 'illegal' is a sick bird."

15

Goniffs, Gamblers, Grabbers and Other No-Goodniks

INTRODUCTION

To be a practicing Jew is a career in itself—and a noble one. The trouble is that when some people finish practicing, they forget the nobility. Not that this makes them any different than gentiles—the lure of easy money tends to become an anesthetic that puts many a conscience to sleep, no matter what the race or religion. It also furnishes much of the grist for the American-Jewish humor mill.

A president can be pardoned for making tapes without the knowledge or consent of the tapee; but if *you* do it, you'll sit in the penitentiary for five years without benefit of connubial visitations: a respectable way of putting it, yes? The director of El Bandido Savings and Loan Association expropriates your deposits to buy his girlfriend mink-lined bras and panties with 24-carat gold filigree, and he gets off with a warning that henceforth he should mend his ways and be a good boy. The judge is not one of the depositors, of course —he's the bank president's golf partner. So they send him to Congress where he belongs. As to gamblers, has it ever occurred to you that the very kids who had too much *saichel* to believe in Santa Claus grow up and bet on horses? Go figure it out!

A current complaint is that prisons fail to do anything constructive toward the rehabilitation of inmates. Chief Justice Warren E. Burger, for one, believes that a man in prison without a trade should be taught one. Perhaps, he suggested, some incentive might be provided, such as a reduction of sentence for learning a useful occupation. In this, Chief Justice Burger seems to agree with the Talmud. Rabbi Judah Ben Ilai said: "The parent who does not teach his child a trade teaches him thievery."

Ancient Israel apparently had little need of prisons. For some offenses, stripes (beatings) were administered. For stealing, double restitution was required. There were cities of refuge to which perpetrators of involuntary murder might flee, but there is little mention, if any, of imprisonment. Perhaps the heightened Jewish sense of social justice made for less of the kind of poverty which breeds crime. Conditions such as exist in Latin America and other areas where a few own most of the land are not tolerated under the Mosaic law which proclaims that the land cannot be owned by anyone forever.

The Bible tells us that Joseph was cast into prison, but that was in Egypt. Where else? Actually, he had a good case. Had Joseph retained a wide-awake lawyer to appeal the verdict on that trumped-up charge of assault, he might have been freed; but who knows about those Egyptian lawyers and judges? However, things didn't turn out too badly for Joseph. He parlayed his ability to interpret dreams, going from prisoner to prime minister, and all the inmates—Joseph's erstwhile companions—did revel and rejoice to the tune of Mairzy Doats, for they were given an increase in their halvah allowance. But their joy was shortlived: what the prime minister giveth, the pharaoh taketh away. It was all very un-Jewish. The point is that, according to Jewish teachings, prison inmates need a dream—a dream of future usefulness. The absence of such a dream is symbolic of all the other problems associated with the penal system. And here, too, is a further source of the biting wit and humor that often voices a need more forcefully than the direct approach of indignation and outrage.

For the Jewish people, it was not merely law which was responsible for the general avoidance of crime; religion was perhaps the supreme deterrent. It seems to have been forgotten that our parents and grandparents did not blame poverty for all the ills and misfortunes that beset them. Yesterday's Jews lived in the ghettos with very little crime among them. When disputes arose, the parties involved brought their problems before the rabbi for a *Din Torah*.

Of course, not every litigant was satisfied with the rabbi's verdict. We recall the saintly Rabbi Salanter who once decided against a man who threatened to break every window in the synagogue if the rabbi did not change his verdict.

"And if you break the windows, do you think I will just stand there and do nothing?" said the rabbi.

What will you do?" demanded the belligerent defendant.

"I will immediately send for the glazier and have new windows installed," replied Rabbi Salanter.

The fellow shrugged resignedly and abided by the decision. "Who can fight with such a man?" he muttered.

Orthodox Judaism was never an especially convenient religion for the miscreant. In fact, it was difficult for a religious man to turn to crime. Imagine such a Jew who decides to become a robber. There is an ancient Jewish law which states that no one may enter a house without knocking. So the man, if he is serious about being a successful robber, and at the same time wishes to remain an observant Jew, is stumped at the outset. Even if he intended to enter through the window, he must first knock. That wasn't quite what Moses had in mind, but leave it to Jewish humorists (many of them rabbis) to create such zany analogies with the kernel of truth intact.

There is an old saying, "The Jews are like other people, only more so." That "more so" involves a heap o' *tsuris,* as they say down on the farm, when it comes to selecting judges. "A very old man, a eunuch or a childless person is not appointed to the Sanhedrin," averred Maimonides, "since they are apt to lack tenderness." Maimie—you should pardon the familiarity—must have been reading Mishna, which states, "The following are ineligible to serve as judges or witnesses: a gambler, a userer and a dealer in forbidden produce." By "forbidden produce," the sages probably meant such goodies as pickled pig's feet (or elbows, for that matter), and *escargots* which cannot be properly *kashered*. But it is the Talmud which lays down the toughest restrictions for aspirants to the bench: "Only those are appointed to the Sanhedrin who have stature, wisdom, good appearance, maturity, a knowledge of the tricks of sorcery, and familiarity with all the 70 languages of mankind." No wonder we have so few qualified judges.

Actually, and despite the unyielding injunction, "Thou shalt not steal," there are a number of Yiddish proverbs and expressions which take a compassionate view of the person who is compelled to steal because of dire stress. "He who would not steal to feed his starving child is an unworthy father," is one. The Bible itself tells us: "Men do not despise a thief if he steals to satisfy his soul when he is hungry." Also, we find, "Stolen waters are sweet."

Back in the third century, Rabbi Hiyya instructed: "Not the mouse, but the hole, is the thief." And another Jewish sage pointed out, "While forcing a lock, the burglar calls on divine aid." Nor can we forget Spinoza's challenge to hypocrisy, 300 years ago. In his monumental *Ethics*, the great philosopher declared: "Those who cry out the loudest against the misuse of honor and the vanity of the world, are those who most greedily covet it." A regular Jack Benny, that Spinoza.

As to gambling, the Talmud, surprisingly enough, seems to regard it with greater disfavor than stealing—probably because starvation may serve as an understandable reason for theft of food, but there is never an acceptable reason for heavy gambling. The Talmud speaks of two types of gambling: dice and pigeon racing. The Talmudic word for dice, *dubya*, seems to be of Greek origin, another example of the Hellenistic influence on the ancient Jews. Talmudic law held that a gambling debt was not legally collectable, and there was no Mafia in those days to force payment, either. What could the Greeks and Romans do about it? Cut your head off? Well, come to think about it, yes! But other than that, what?

The Mishna says, "A gambler is disqualified as a witness or judge," but doesn't say why. And Maimonides asserted, "A gambler always loses. He loses money, dignity and time. And if he wins, he weaves a spider's web around himself." In America, however, and with particular reference to New York's off-track betting, or the *meshuggeneh* antics around the crap tables in Las Vegas, Maimonides' spider would starve to death waiting for the big payoff.

One of the happy Jewish holidays has a gambling name: *Purim*, meaning "lots." Haman played bingo and cast lots on which day the Jews were to be annihilated. His game of bingo, however, didn't turn out too well for him, and he came down with a terminal case of *griener cholerya*.

Nevertheless, when it comes to moderate card-playing as a pastime, the Jewish position, on the whole, has been tolerant.

There is an old story of the poor widow who was about to be evicted from her home because she had no money to pay the rent. So her rabbi went looking for the president of the synagogue to see if something could be done for the unfortunate woman. He finally located the officer and some of his cronies seated around a table, deeply engrossed in a pinochle game. Flustered at the unexpected visit, they tried to hide the cards, but the rabbi urged them to continue. "Keep playing," he insisted. The men went on with their game and, at the end, the rabbi scooped up all the winnings to pay the rent for the poor widow.

Every vice contains a spark of virtue, and so forth. That's what sentimentalists like about Jewish stories. They turn out so nice.

The most famous Jewish work against gambling was written in the 17th century by a rabbi who was himself a compulsive gambler. Leon of Modena was a scholar in rabbinics, and also in the secular field. His erudition and renown were such that even Christians came to hear him speak—not that it ever did them any good. The thesis of his anti-gambling sermons was that wagering was as dangerous as playing on the edge of a roof—a comment made long before the Fiddler got up there and had a Broadway play named after him.

Leon of Modena never lost his fascination for the roof's edge. Perhaps he was waiting for Maimonides' spider to tip him off on a sure thing at Hialeah. Had the good rabbi been born 300 years later, he might have learned a little something from David Ben-Gurion. A hindu rajah wanted to take him to a horse race. Snapped Ben-Gurion: "I already know that one horse can run faster than another, and I am not interested in which one."

Once, long ago, to journey back in time for a moment, there lived a cobbler in the city of Chelm who committed a heinous crime and was sentenced to hang. But he was the only cobbler in town, so the Chelmites hanged one of the two tailors instead. "When the thief is needed," says the Talmud, "he is even taken off the gallows."

There are any number of contemporary folk tales which express the same general thought: The guilty person's social or economic position determines his degree of punishment—if, indeed, any. Old World traditional humor is not too different from its modern American counterpart. The crook, the gambler, the con man and others who depend upon cunning and stealth to turn a dishonest dollar have been with us ever since the Israelites took leave without asking permission of the Egyptians.

Some of the anecdotes in this chapter may appear to be new, but take heed, it is only the literary garments and change of time and locale which are different. The *goniffs*, gamblers and grabbers are the same.

H.D.S.

Not all descendants of Abraham earned their bread by the sweat of their brow. The connivers, *fenaiglers* and grabbers of Judaica Americana have a worthy counterpart in the old-time *schnorrer* of European Jewish folklore—that crafty beggar who lived by his wits. There is, however, a sharp line of distinction between the *schnorrer* and his American successor, the con man. The former was a clever panhandler; the latter was, and is, a *goniff*—a swindler.

Such a man, it turned out, was Sam Fenster.* He burst upon the lower East Side like a Roman candle—and like that candle he was just as quickly extinguished. The story, according to those few who are still alive to remember it, was finally pieced together by Gordon Kramer who rented his store to Fenster, and by a sign-painter named Max Bender, both of whom had ample reason to recall him with regret and reluctant admiration for his magnificent *chutzpah*.

From the information available, it seems that on July 3, 1919, Kramer looked up from his desk when a little old man entered his real estate office—actually a store located at 157 Grand Street. The stranger was at least seventy years old, but clean-shaven and dapper. Standing not more than five feet tall, he sported an elaborately-carved swagger stick and was wearing one of those African-style safari helmets one sees in travel posters. The odd-looking but instantly likable oldster was one of those men who radiates self-confidence and good cheer—the kind of man you would choose to share a pleasant evening with, over a few glasses of *schnapps*.

The visitor smiled genially, extended his hand and introduced himself: "Sam Fenster, from the Belgiumeh Congo. Here, give a look on my expensive calling card." he handed it to Kramer:

> FENSTER THE GREAT WHITE HUNTER
> —English Spoken Here—
> Also Yiddish, Congoleum & Belgium

"Lions and tigers I don't need this week," said Kramer, grinning broadly. "Come back better next Tuesday."

Fenster chuckled good-naturedly, retrieved his calling card which he carefully returned to his pocket, and then inquired about the sign in the window: Store for Rent—Reasonable.

"It's across the street," Kramer explained. The store had been vacant for several months and he was anxious to rent it.

"I want it only for a week, maybe two," Fenster said. "How much you're asking?"

Kramer rubbed his chin. He had hoped for a long-term tenant, but a week or two was better than nothing. "Well," he replied hesitantly,

---

* There are a number of versions of *Fenster and His Ferocious Flugel* in the Jewish communities of New York, Chicago and Los Angeles—and probably elsewhere in the United States. An Irish variant, *The Flyin' Flooheel*, places this humorous folktale in San Francisco, circa 1889. A later version, entitled *The Sky Floogle*, was reported in *Chillicothe and Ross County*, compiled in 1938 by the Federal Writers Project of Ohio, Works Progress Administration. The Jewish version, above, has been handed down from one generation to the next in the oral tradition of folklore and is published here for the first time.

"I'm usually asking fifty a month—it's a good location—but for such a short time . . ."

"I'll pay for a whole month," Fenster promptly declared. He opened his wallet and handed Kramer a crisp five dollar bill. "By me, business is business," he said briskly. "Here's my deposit. I'll put up a few signs and move in on Monday. The rest of the rent I'll pay on Grand Opening Night."

The quick-talking little man was on his way out of the door when Kramer called to him: "Hey, Mr. Fenster, what line are you in?"

"Wild animals," answered the Great White Hunter. "What else?"

"My good man," said Kramer, suppressing a wild urge to roar with laughter, "if you're thinking maybe you could organize a safari it should go to Africa, you're in the wrong neighborhood."

Fenster smiled indulgently. "A show I'm putting on like you never saw before," he explained. "For the first time anywhere in the civilized world I'm presenting, in person, the most ferocious, man-eating monster what ever lived—the sky flugel!"

"*Wh-whaaat!*" Kramer gasped. "What's a sky flugel?"

"You know what an alligator is looking like? Well, a sky flugel is twice as long, and higher even than an elephant. It got claws like a Siberian tiger and six rows of big teeth like from a shark. It also got wings from forty feet across, like a wampire bat, so what it's not catching on the ground it's flying up in the air it should get a little something to eat. The sky flugel got a rotten temper like a rhino and it's eating mostly eagles, gorillas and human beans."

"Now hold on a minute!" snapped Kramer. "In my stores I don't allow such kinds of goings-on. Suppose that sky flugel gets loose and starts killing people?"

"It can't happen, believe me," Fenster replied soothingly. "Didn't it just pass through Ellis Island? And didn't the Customs agent say the sky flugel was safe so long as it was chained inside its cage? You got nothing to worry about."

Sam Fenster departed. Next on his list was Max Bender, the sign-painter at 169 Grand Street. In Bender's shop, Fenster ordered 100 signs, each four feet long by two teet high. Headlines, in red paint, were to read: SEE THE FEROCIOUS, MAN-EATING SKY FLUGEL. DEADLY MONSTER NEVER BEFORE SEEN IN CAPTIVITY. TICKETS ONLY ONE DOLLAR! He also ordered twenty streamers, sixty feet long and three feet high, measured to stretch across the street, from building to building—these, too, with screaming headlines. He gave Bender a ten dollar deposit, promising to pay the entire balance on opening night.

The next several days were busy ones for Fenster. The signs were prominently displayed in a multitude of store windows on Houston, Rivington, Cherry, Grand, Orchard, Hester and Delancey Streets, with the blaring streamers strung overhead from one side of the street to the other. A reporter from the *Forvertz*, unable to collar Fenster for details about his remarkable animal, obtained his "inside story" from Kramer and Bender, and ran a feature article about the ferocious sky flugel.

On July 14th, Fenster ran out of tickets to sell. He had managed to scrounge sixty or seventy wooden boxes upon which the patrons were to sit. He would, he proclaimed, give a nightly performance for the next two weeks so that all ticket-holders could be accommodated. On opening night, the improvised "theatre" was packed with customers from wall to wall. The patrons were seated so that they were facing the back of the store, across which Fenster had hung a wide curtain, obviously to heighten the suspense and to separate the audience from the caged monster. They waited expectantly, and somewhat nervously, for their first glimpse of the huge and terrifying man-eater.

Suddenly, from behind the curtain, an ear-shattering, agonized scream caused the apprehensive customers to leap to their feet. There arose another scream—then another—piercing outbursts of mortal agony. There was a loud rattling of chains, a series of sharp cracks as though heavy steel bars were being torn asunder, and then, like a *golem* in a bad dream, Fenster himself staggered out from behind the curtain. A wave of unholy fright rolled over the audience. Fenster's hair was wildly disheveled, his clothes torn, his face and shirt-front smeared with blood.

"The sky flugel is loose!" he yelled hoarsely. "Run for your lives!"

The customers made a frenzied dash for the door, men yelling, women fainting, children crying out in terror. Fortunately, no one was killed or seriously injured in the mad stampede to safety.

The police soon arrived and, with drawn guns, searched the premises, but no sign of the sky flugel could they find. Nor could they find Sam Fenster. Nor could they find the money he had charged for admissions. All that remained behind the curtain and next to the open back door was a length of rusty chain and a bottle of ketchup.

So whatever happened to the Great White Hunter? Who knows? He simply disappeared as though he had been swallowed up by the earth itself. On July 20, 1919, the editor of the *Forvertz* began an investigation of the case that lasted until Labor Day of that year, but without success. The plain truth is that nobody ever found out what became of Fenster, or, for that matter, of the sky flugel.

* * *

Pity poor Pincus, the one-fingered pickpocket. Arthritis caught up with him and he can't work.

* * *

Complaint has been made from time to time about some of the so-called model homes which are put up so fast in the suburbs. The tenor of such complaints revolves around the theory that these houses are built to be sold, not lived in. It is our personal opinion, however, that real estate brokers and builders are just as honest as people in other trades and professions, such as used car salesmen, television repairmen, White House lawyers, meat-market managers and politicians.

With that disclaimer out of the way, we shall now relate a little story currently in vogue about the real-estate operator whose activities in the commuting areas have been highly successful. The only problem he encounters in the course of earning his livelihood is that he can't work the same side of the street twice.

Not long ago, he snared a prospective buyer—one of those fifty-dollars-down-and-pay-as-long-as-you-live prospects. The promoter took him out in his car to the site on Long Island, to look at the house which, he thought, would suit the needs of the customer, to say nothing of invigorating his own exchequer.

The building was in the process of construction. It had been started on Monday—on Friday it would be ready for occupancy. But this was Wednesday, and while the foundation was finished and the sides were tacked up and the roof had been pasted on, the painting and the interior trim and other finishing touches were yet to be added. The dealer led the proposed victim inside the structure. The plasterers were just concluding their part of the contract.

"Here you are!" said the operator with a great show of pride. "What do you think of *this* for a house?"

"To tell you the truth," said the homeseeker, "it looks kind of flimsy."

"*Flimsy!*" screeched the indignant realtor. "You call this fortress flimsy? Wait, I'll show you."

"Hey, Jim," he called to a workman on the other side of the partition.

"What?" responded Jim.

"Just step up close to the dividing wall between us. Get as close as you can."

"All right," said Jim, "here I am, almost touching it."

"Good! Now, Jim, you can hear me speaking through the wall, can't you?"

"Sure."

"But you can't see me through this wall, can you, Jim?"

"Nope."

With a smile of triumph, the promoter turned to the customer: "Now *that's* what I call a *wall!*"

* * *

Just as he was emerging from Hyman's Hoboken Haberdashery, Gedalia the *goniff* was caught red-handed with the loot he had just stolen.

"Before I read you your rights under the law," intoned the arresting officer, "I want you to know that I am charging you for possession of stolen property."

"Sorry," replied Gedalia, "I don't do business on credit!"

* * *

Shmuel, late for dinner, was confronted with the choice of facing an irate wife should he fail to arrive home on time, or taking a shortcut through Central Park. Choosing the lesser of two hazards, he took the short cut, even though the sun had set and it was growing dark.

He hadn't gone a hundred feet into the park when a man rushed up to him.

"Listen, Mac, ya seen a cop aroun' anyplace?" he asked breathlessly.

"No, I'm sorry," said Shmuel. "There's never a policeman around when you need one."

"Yer right," snarled the man. "Hand over yer watch an' wallet!"

* * *

The shifty-eyed stranger glanced around the lavishly appointed office and furtively approached the lawyer's desk.

"Are you Mr. Ginsboig, da guy what sprung Lefty Louie las' week? asked the gnome-like little man nervously.

"Yes, I'm Ginsberg," affirmed the attorney.

"Lefty's a frennamine. He sent me here. Y'kinaskim."

"I don't have to ask him: I believe you. What's your name and what can I do for you?"

"Jus' call me Hubcap Hymie. I need a mout'piece, but I ain't got no bread. In fack, I'm dead broke."

"Mr.—ah—Hubcab—er—Hymie—didn't Lefty tell you I'm one of the most expensive lawyers in the city?"

"Yeah."

"Then how do you expect to pay my fee?"

"Wouldja take a 1974 blue an' gray Cadillac Fleetwood Limousine fer payment?"

"I certainly would! Tell me, what are you charged with?"

"I'm charged wit' stealin' a 1974 blue an' gray Cadillac Fleetwood Limousine!"

* * *

Two cronies were discussing the ever-popular subject of law and order.

"There's a lot of crime going on these days," observed the Manhattanite, "but they don't have tough neighborhoods like they used to when I was a boy. In those days, on the Lower East Side, when someone asked 'What time is it?' you first thanked him for asking, *then* you told him the time."

"That's nothing," retorted the Brooklynite. "Back when I was a kid in Greenpernt, *nobody* asked for the time. They just took your watch!"

* * *

The telephone rang at the 23rd Police Precinct and Sergeant Clancey picked up the receiver.

"Yeah?"

"Police?" came a frantic voice at the other end of the wire. "I wanna report a burglar trapped in an old maid's bedroom!"

"Who are you, a neighbor?" asked Sergeant Clancey.

"No," cried the distraught voice, "this is the burglar!"

* * *

George Birnbaum, known to all as comedian George Burns, was always able to fracture the friendly folk around the Fulton Street Fish Market with this truncated description of his boyhood life.

"Our family was so poor," said George, "as children we used to help mother take in washing. We went around to other people's clotheslines!"

* * *

Davey and Sam were inveterate gamblers, and each weekend found them together at the local club where they played pinochle all night.

"Why the long face?" asked Davey as they sat down for their usual game.

"It's my wife," mourned Sam. "She gave me final warning that if I didn't give up cards she'd leave me."

"Hey, that's terrible," replied Davey. "I really sympathize with you."

"Yeah," muttered Sam disconsolately, "I'm sure gonna miss the old gal."

* * *

Felix, a professional crook, was taking his usual midnight constitutional down Broadway in search of business opportunities when he bumped into Simon, a fellow *goniff*.

"I hear you had some very good luck," observed Felix.

"Luck?" demanded Simon. "What kind of luck?"

"They tell me you were in Wanamaker's store when all the lights went out."

"That's right, I was. All of a sudden the whole place was in pitch black darkness. You couldn't see your hand in front of your face."

"Boy, what luck! Tell me, what did you get?"

"I got nothing—not a thing." moaned Simon. "When the lights went out I happened to be in the piano department!"

* * *

There is a delightful anecdote of ancient vintage concerning Diogenes who took up his lamp and went in search of an honest man. When he got to New York, somebody stole his lamp.

* * *

It was a balmy evening in June and Sam was enjoying an after-supper stroll when he was approached by a tattered, unkempt, whiskey-sodden figure.

"Sir," whined the stranger in piteous tones, "would you be so kind as to assist a poor, hungry, unemployed man? Believe me, sir, I have nothing in this whole wide world—except this gun!"

* * *

There's no use beating around the bush—Jay and Melvin were crooks and that's all there is to it. Everybody on the block knew it, too. But because of their ingenuity they had never been caught.

They had a *shtick*, these two. Jay posed as a deaf mute; Melvin as a cripple. They each carried a tin cup filled with pencils, and when suspicion pointed to them for some robbery or other, they would plead, in agonized tones, that they were only poor mendicants who just happened to be in the neighborhood at the time. How could a couple of impoverished beggars, one who could neither hear nor speak, and the other paralyzed so that he could hardly walk, be guilty of robbery?"

Their assumed afflictions were wisely apportioned; they could not have done better had they taken aptitude tests. Jay was far from bright —a first-class *shlemiel*, according to his partner in crime. His vow of silence protected them both whenever they were questioned by the authorities. Melvin, on the other hand, was a consumate actor and would have won acclaim in the theatre had he chosen so rash an activity as honest toil.

But the inevitable day came when a dedicated police officer outsmarted them. A clothing store on Delancey Street had been burglarized and the weight of evidence overwhelmingly established Jay and Melvin as the culprits. Two policemen arrived at their humble flat, paid them an anti-social call and transported them, at city expense, to the local precinct headquarters. There they were grilled for nearly two hours by the most astute detective in all New York—a career enforcement officer named Brutus Nero. It fit, too.

But at the end of the two hours they were still just as adamant about their innocence as they had been at the beginning of the interrogation. Nero, his patience worn to shreds and shards, felt his anger surging as he viewed the impudent lawbreakers.

"Listen, you guys," he roared at last, "you're a couple of phonies. I don't believe that you can hardly walk, or that you can't speak or hear. I'm gonna get the truth out of you if it takes me all week."

Jay paled and his lower lip quivered.

'Aha!' thought Nero. 'This is the weak one. I'd better concentrate on him.' Aloud, he commanded Jay to empty his pockets.

"Put all your stuff on the table," he ordered.

With growing apprehension, Jay complied, laying out a few coins, a house key and some stray bits of paper and such.

"What's this key for?" demanded Nero.

Melvin interrupted. "He can't hear a thing you say, officer. I told you ten times, he's deaf. He can't talk, either. Anyway, the key is for our apartment."

But Nero was far from convinced. Again he addressed Jay.

"I know you're pretending," he rasped. "Why don't you confess and save us both a lot of time and trouble?"

"Like I said," Melvin interfered again, "he can't hear you."

The detective had been studying the debris Jay had placed on the table. Suddenly his eyes gleamed. Seizing one of the papers in the pile, he waved it underneath Jay's nose.

"Here is a receipt from Bouncing Benny's Music Store—a receipt for two long-playing records. So you can't hear, eh? But you buy records!"

Jay shrugged, a look of resignation darkening his face.

"All right, so I'm guilty," he confessed in a perfectly normal voice. "I can hear, I can speak, and I like music." He turned to his partner. "I'm sorry, Melvin. I forgot about that receipt."

"Idiot!" screamed Melvin. "Why didn't you tell him you bought those records for *me?*"

* * *

Fire insurance is a more delicate problem than life insurance for the dishonest fenaigler, as it is somewhat easier for him to set his store or house afire than to cut his own throat to collect for it. That brilliant observation leads us to Mottel, the owner of a large dry goods store. Mottel conceived the idea of turning a fast dollar and not too incidentally to get rid of an overstock of last season's merchandise. He would accomplish this by having a big, well-advertised fire sale. Now before one has a fire sale, it is customary to have a fire. And before one has a fire, it is prudent to be covered by a fire insurance policy. So Mottel, a perfect paragon of prudence, called an insurance agent and they sat down to work out the details.

"Tell me something," said Mottel when he had signed the policy, "just suppose—mind you, we're just supposing—that my store burned down to the ground tomorrow night. What would I get under the terms of this policy?"

"About ten years," said the agent.

* * *

A month after he had taken out his fire insurance policy, Mottel's store burned to the ground, and with it his entire inventory of last season's merchandise. Surprisingly, none of the new merchandise had been damaged. By a strange and fortuitous coincidence, he had removed all new shipments to another location. Naturally, he notified his agent at once. The agent, in turn, was ordered by his office manager to bring an insurance adjuster with him and, together, they sifted through the charred ruins for a full eight hours. At the end of the day, they returned to their office where the manager, understandably nervous, awaited them.

"Did you find out what caused the fire?" he asked.

"Yes, friction," said the adjuster tersely.

"You mean something rubbed against something else?"

"Yeah," the adjuster affirmed. "The fire was caused by rubbing a $25,000 insurance policy against a $10,000 dry goods store."

* * *

"I didn't mind my husband cheating on me," Shirley wept. "As far as I'm concerned it's good riddance to bad rubbish. But what made me so angry is that he stole my brassieres and left me flat!"

* * *

Honest Daniel, the used car dealer with the heart of pure, unalloyed two-carat gold, was forced into bankruptcy—for the fifth time. Glumly, he watched his accountant add up a column of figures, arrive at a sum total and then attempt to deduct a greater amount from the lesser figure.

It's no use," said the accountant. "There's just no way you can pay more than four cents on a dollar."

"Now hold on there," retorted Honest Daniel, "I got a reputation to think about. "In all my other bankruptcies I always paid eight cents on the dollar and I'm gonna do it this time, too, if I hafta take it out of my own pocket!"

* * *

At a formal dinner party one evening, a Californian, on business in New York, found himself sitting next to the banker, Otto Kahn, with whom he was only slightly familiar. He attempted to establish a friendly footing by mentioning a few mutual acquaintances.

"One of my dearest friends happens to work for you, Mr. Kahn," he began for openers.

"Who?" asked Kahn with his usual testiness.

"Bob Albertson. I understand he is one of your most tried and trusted employees."

The banker's aloof reserve froze into even colder hostility.

"Sir," he replied icily, "Mr. Albertson was trusted, yes; and if we're fortunate enough to find him he'll be tried."

* * *

He was a runny-nosed little pickpocket, in court for the sixth time that year. The judge knew the usual charges against the offender by heart, but this time he raised his brow in surprise.

"What's this?" growled the magistrate. "Arrested for stealing a *fashion* magazine?"

"I guess I'm guilty," confessed the pickpocket meekly.

The judge glowered at the culprit.

"What in the world could possibly interest you in a fashion maga-zine?"

"Next season's styles," explained the *goniff*. "I wanted to see where the pockets would be."

* * *

Lubie the light-fingered luftmensch was caught in the very act of stealing a gold plated fly-swatter that had once belonged to Babe Ruth.

"It's my usual luck," he complained bitterly as the minions of the law led him away to his free room and board. "Here it is only Monday—a fine beginning for the week!"

* * *

Among the most expressive people on earth are the Israelis and our own home-grown Texans—especially when they are gambling. The unwary witness to one of their card-games is well advised to honker down, let the gale blow unimpeded and refrain from *kibitzing*. Having noted those three dictums, let us proceed.

Yaacov Eisen, of Tel Aviv, had heard so many favorable reports about his American cousin, Max Eisen, that he journeyed to San Angelo, Texas, for a visit.

They got along swimmingly, as the Pisces-born say. Max Eisen, who had changed his name to Montgomery Ironside, was the rootin' tootin' owner of the Double-Bar Mitzvah ranch, and he soon discovered that his Israeli cousin could not only equal his lusty penchant for windiness, but that he also shared his passion for America's favorite indoor sport— poker. So they sat down to play a few hands.

Unknown to each other, of course, Yaacov had drawn a full house, while Max—or Montgomery as we shall now call him—was holding an inside straight.

"I'll open with five," opined Yaacov.

"Raise you twenty."

"I'll see your twenty and raise you twenty pounds more."

"Twenty *what?*" exclaimed the startled Texan. "What the hell are you talking about?"

"Israeli pounds, what else?" said the cousin.

"Listen, Yaacov," exploded Montgomery, "if you wanna bet pounds instead of good ol' American dollars it's okay by me, but you better have the bankroll to back it up. I'm raisin' you a ton!"

* * *

"The one and only time I ever placed a wager on a horse turned out to be a disaster." complained Howard, a racetrack rookie. "It was the most affectionate race you ever saw. Imagine! The horse that I bet on hugged the rail, the jockey patted its behind, placed his arm around its neck and whispered tender phrases in its ear while it ran neck-and-neck with another horse, and I kissed my money goodbye?"

* * *

"Well, at least there's one consolation about your report card," sighed the youth's father as he scanned the long column of F's. "With grades like these you couldn't have been cheating!"

* * *

In 1849, during the Gold Rush days in San Francisco, more than 100 congregants attended *Yom Kippur* services, conducted by Joel Noah, brother of Major Noah (mentioned elsewhere in this book). There were no permanent structures available for the occasion, so the services were held in a tent-synagogue improvised by Hyam Joseph.

Now this fellow Hyam had a younger brother named Asher who was as unlike him as any two men could possibly be. Where Hyam was gentle, soft-spoken and pious, Asher was a rambunctious, card-playing, whiskey-drinking saddle-bum who was quick on the draw and took no nonsense from anyone. But, for all his swagger, bravado and rough ways, he was a learned young man. After he married and finally settled down to raise a family, he became a Hebrew teacher and lived out his long years as a model citizen of the Old West.

Asher Joseph's youthful exploits along the trail are now an integral part of Jewish-American folklore. Here is one of the humorous anecdotes told about this real-life adventurer. The tale has been doing yeoman service for these 120 years and has been adopted, adapted and embellished by the folklorists of other groups, but this earlier version belongs to Asher alone.

It was a Sunday afternoon in 1854, in the wide-open frontier town of Broken Bottle, Texas. In the rear room of the Thirsty Buzzard Saloon, a poker game was in progress. Around the table sat five silently intent men, four of whom were evidently cowboys, judging from their outfits. The fifth player was a professional gambler—a one-eyed card-shark who was working for the house. Before too many hands had been played, it became apparent that someone was manipulating the cards.

At last one of the cowpokes, young Asher Joseph, rose from his chair and stood up to his full height of five-feet-four. He directed a stream of tobacco juice into a nearby spittoon, reached into his pocket, pulled out a plug of tobacco, took a fresh chaw and leisurely put it back into his jeans. Next, he drew out a big hand gun and laid it on the table in front of him. then he cleared his throat and spoke his piece:

"Now, chentlemen, nobody is calling anybody a *goniff*—in fact, names I'm not even mentioning. By me I don't even have suspicions. All I got to say is this: If whoever is making monkey business with the deck don't stop it, the *momzer* is gonna get his *other* eye shot out!"

16

Politicians and Other Stalwart Champions of the Upperdog

INTRODUCTION

A hitherto Unmentionable Truth is that the average Jew is more interested in the *theory* of politics, than in its practical application. Never mind that a government program is working satisfactorily, or that a newly-proposed piece of legislation seems to possess merit; he waits for the next issue of *The New Republic* to make up his mind for him about the *theory*.

Another quirk worth mentioning is that he doesn't really *hear* a political speech, he *translates* it—just as rapidly as it is spoken. He can sit back and listen to the President making a speech on television about the state of the economy, but through his unique process of agile mental calisthenics, he understands the Chief Executive to say, "Let me make two things perfectly clear: First, the country is in excellent ˙shape; second, Congress is to blame for the mess we're in."

The Yiddish-speaking citizen won't even voice an opinion. He shrugs off all mention of Watergate-like scandals with, "Don't chop a tea pot" *(hakh nisht kein cheinik)*. He know the world is full of speakers prattling nonsense; of politicians who pollute the air with banana oil.

Gentiles, too, fall victim to specious verbiage. That is why the President, in the midst of the worst inflation to plague this nation in its history, was able to tell the American people in a major White Paper: "If you don't pitch in and do your part, and if we in the Executive branch don't pitch in and do our part, and if Congress doesn't pitch in and do its part, pretty soon none of us will have a part to pitch in."

Spiro Agnew learned, to his regret, that a knowledge of words alone do not a canny politician make. It's the manner in which he strings them together that counts. Agnew's vocabulary, probably the most extensive in modern political history, failed him one day when a visitor to Washington parked his car near the Vice-President's office. "If you are going to be here for the next few minutes, would you mind keeping an eye on my car?" asked the visitor of the man standing at the curb.

"Do you realize, sir, that I happen to be the Vice-President of the United States?" Agnew asked indignantly.

"No, I didn't realize it," confessed the motorist, "but that's all right, I'll trust you."

No one will ever be able to equal the wisdom recently enunciated by a senator who shall here remain mercifully anonymous: "Inflation comes at a very bad time just when prices are so high." That sort of astuteness is reminiscent of the congressman who refused to support an increase in gas and liquor taxes because he was afraid of losing the drunken-driver vote.

Former President Nixon will never offer any serious competition to Myron Cohen, but he is reported to have quipped, "If George McGovern had made just one more speech during the 1972 campaign, I'm convinced I'd have carried Canada." But if the talebearers can be believed, McGovern himself is no neophyte in the art of turning a funny phrase. "Talk about history repeating itself!" he said, "Forty years ago I can remember my father telling me, 'It's the Fords and Rockefellers who are running this country!'"

McGovern, as it later became evident, had the quality of integrity on his side—a commodity for which there were few buyers in 1972, but we can credit him for advancing the truth of an old American aphorism: He is living proof that not every American boy can aspire to be President. As to Ronald Reagan, he may have done irreparable damage to his presidential aspirations when, at a banquet honoring him as California governor, he blurted out, "Listen, Manny, I don't care what kind of a contract the William Morris office has. You're not getting 10% of the State Budget."

What has all this to do with Jewish humor? It has this to do with it: Every single one of the quotations in this Introduction which was attributed to a named politician was created by a Jewish writer. He observes and hears what others see and hear, but his rate of acceptance is very low. He's the scorner from Scarsdale, the cynic from Cincinnati, the doubter from Duluth, the berator from Brooklyn, the kibitzer from Kankakee, the jeerer from Jersey, the protester from Providence, the *yenta* from Yonkers, the hollerer from Hoboken, and the muttering *mishpocha* from Miami. They are everywhere, these Jewish wits, carrying within them the seeds of revolt against those whose political promises insult their intelligence. And it is they who have written this chapter. I have acted only as their recorder.

When a people has survived for so many centuries, under every conceivable kind of oppressive government, their reaction to specious campaign promises can justifiably be expected: "Look, we heard that *bobeh myseh* 4,000 years ago. So what else is new?"

And that is what this chapter is all about.

H.D.S.

Let us genuflect before the literati with some high-class original poetry. (Students seeking college credits are urged to make pertinent notes, always bearing in mind that neatness counts.)

Faigeleh-bageleh
Moisheleh Dayan
Casting a landlordish
Eye to the East,
Said in a manner quite
Characteristically,
"Jerusalem's ours, plus
The Gaza, at least."

Pocketa-shmocketa
Senator Javits, Oh
What do you think of the
Watergate scene?
"Nu, what can I say that's
Not un-Republican?
Elections are coming,
Ya know what I mean?"

Novena-mesheenah
Miz Bella S. Abzug
Campaigning for the high
Office of Pope,
Shouted fortissimo
(Not pianissimo),
"A Pontif by Yontif
On Pesach I hope."

Higgledy-shmiggledy
Reagan and Kennedy
Promised each other they'd
Play it by ear,
If elected to office
The winner would gladly
Dance a kazatske
With Golda Meir.

* * *

This anecdote is aimed specifically at those provincials who mistakenly believe that a Jew can always beat an Arab in an intellectual argument.

At the University of California at Berkeley, an Arab exchange student, Ahmed Halavah, was engaged in a debate with Martin Saper-stein, a political science major. Their topic was "Israel and the Arab States—Differences in Social Concepts."   Ahmed and Martin apparently were emotional types and before long they were hurling acrimonious charges at each other, together with unfavorable accusations about their parentage. Soon the debate took on all the fury of a free-swinging donnybrook.

"How can you stand there with your bare face hanging out and say that you Arabs give a damn about the great mass of poverty-stricken, undernourished and unemployed people in your countries?" demanded Martin, his voice dripping scorn. "Why, your own King Saud spent more money on his harem than he did for the social welfare of the people."

"Why shouldn't he?" Ahmed shot back in righteous indignation. "He spent most of his time there!"

* * *

When Senator Halfbright was defeated in the elections, he evidently felt he could at last give voice to his long-suppressed thoughts. After all, as a lame duck politician, what had he to lose? So, at the first opportunity, he filled the hallowed halls of Congress with his oratory, explaining why the United States should not interfere with the Soviet Union's treatment of Russian Jews who desired to emigrate to Israel. It was a very controversial speech and, to tell the truth, well delivered.

But it sounded better in the original German.

* * *

Arthur Goldberg, the former Supreme Court Justice and United States Ambassador to the U.N., was on a fact-finding mission to the Soviet Union. The first sight that caught his eye when he landed at the Moscow Airport was a huge banner proclaiming: *Everybody in Russia is Happy!*

Goldberg was understandably skeptical, but no matter who he asked, he always received the same answer, "Yes, I am happy."

After a week of such questioning, he visited the one and only synagogue in that area and asked the same question: "Are you happy?"

"Yes, very happy," answered the man, an ancient-looking patriarch who might have stepped right out of the Old Testament.

"Then tell me, why are you happy?" Goldberg demanded.

"It's like this," the aged one replied, looking furtively over his shoulder. "From the factory I come home tired after 12 hours of hard work for Mother Russia. I switch on the lights—*azay!* Thank God, no power failure! So I'm happy! Then I go to take a bath and I'm turning on the hot water. Aha—it works, and I'm happy! Then, in the middle of the night, there suddenly comes a knock on my door. It's the secret police. They say, 'Does Comrade Rabinovitch live here?' I say 'No, Comrade Rabinovitch moved away six months ago.' So they leave . . .

"And, Mister, am I happy I'm not Comrade Rabinovitch!"

* * *

Here's a suspender-snapper from none other than Israel's former Prime Minister, Golda Meir. The occasion was a state dinner in honor of West Germany's Willy Brandt who was visiting Israel. Mrs. Meir rose to speak:

"Let me tell you something that we Israelis have against Moses," she began. "He took us for 40 years through the desert in order to bring us to the one spot in all the Middle East that has no oil!"

* * *

Irv Krim, the volatile Washington correspondent, quit his job in disgust as part of the aftermath of the Watergate scandals.

"It's impossible for a political reporter to operate in Washington, D.C. anymore," he explained to his sympathetic readers. "All my unimpeachable sources have been impeached."

* * *

Fancy Philosophy from Phil the Furrier:
There is good cause for pessimism about our two-party system, considering their symbols. The Republican Party is represented by an overfed elephant with a snoutful of goodies, and the Democratic Party by a braying ass.

* * *

Some people never know when they're well off. Take Dubovsky, for example. He decided to return to Russia, the land of his birth, after living in America for thirty-five years. "I want to help make a success of the worker's Paradise," he gave as his excuse.

But Dubovsky was back in the United States three months later.

"In the Soviet Union it's just impossible to do anything right," he complained. "If you arrive for work five minutes early, you're a saboteur. If you're five minutes late, you are betraying socialism. And if you arrive on time—God forbid!—the commissar calls you into his office and hollers 'Where did you get the watch?' "

* * *

In July, 1974, President Richard Nixon was in the Soviet Union, hoping to achieve a non-aggression pact between that country and the United States. But he was having a hard time of it.

"Before we sign," declared Prime Minister Brezhnev, "you Americans will have to announce to the world that Adam and Eve were Communists."

Nixon, uncertain as to how he should cope with this dilemma, decided to consult an authority on Genesis—in this case, Henry J. Kissinger, who assured him that he had read several pages of the Bible in his younger days.

Kissinger retired to his study, poured over the Old Testament, and the next day he told Nixon to go ahead and sign the pact with the Soviet Union.

"The Russians are right," he said. "Adam and Eve were indeed Communists. After all, they didn't have a stitch on their backs, they had nothing to eat but apples—and they still thought they were in Paradise!"

* * *

The wheat scandal that erupted in 1972 brought anger to some and sadness to others. Typical was the reaction in the Frankel household.

"Grandpa, it says here that the speculators in Minnesota were responsible for the shady wheat deal," remarked the youth as he pored over the *New York Times.* "And here's an item that says Minneapolis got all the bad publicity but, actually, St. Paul cornered the wheat market."

"*Ach,* it disappoints me to hear it," murmured grandfather Frankel. "After hearing so much about his epistles I would never have believed it of him—but then, we live in such an irreligious age!"

* * *

"The main reason you Communists have never been able to make any progress in the United States," declared the patriot, "is that you don't believe in personal liberty."

"Sure we do," contested the Red. "We just feel that anything as precious as liberty should be carefully rationed!"

* * *

When former President Nixon visited the Soviet Union in July, 1974, he was successful in persuading Leonid Brezhnev to ease at least one of Russia's cruel restrictions against its Jewish citizens emigrating to Israel.

"In the new spirit of detente," proclaimed Brezhnev, "departing Jews will henceforth be allowed to take the following items with them, without payment of export fees:

Wooden rubles	Leaky milk containers
Used matches	Used theatre tickets
Shady sundials	Old calendars
Punctured drums	Weightless paperweights
Crushed lampshades	Silent alarm clocks
Wet newspapers	Dried-out flypaper
Cracked sunglasses	Meatless meatballs
Old light fuses	Bibles printed in Swahili
Shaky bridge tables	Used teabags
Patched underwear	Unwrapped Egyptian mummies

"As I have stated," declared Brezhnev, "export levies will not be made against the above personal possessions. However, all items taken out of the Soviet Union must be listed in the Official Exit Register. Therefore, a slight charge will be made for printing, not to exceed 100 rubles per item."

* * *

Alfredo Gonzales Shapiro stepped off the plane that had carried him from Havana to Miami. Together with the other refugees from Castro's Cuba, he lined up at the U.S. Immigration Office. When his name was finally called, the immigration officer looked at him suspiciously, noting his unmistakable Hebraic features.

"What's your nationality?" he growled.

"The same as everyone else's on the plane," answered the young man. "I happen to be a Jew but I was born in Cuba."

"That's funny," said the officer with a shake of his head, "you don't look Cubish!"

* * *

Old Sylvester had arrived in this country with his cousin Jake more than fifty years ago. Unlike Jake, however, who had settled in New York, Sylvester migrated to Georgia where he grew to manhood, prospered, acquired a southern accent and was a true-blue blown-in-the-bottle Dixie-crat to his very bones. Now both in their seventies, Sylvester was visiting his cousin in the Bronx. Before long, they were engaged in a heated political discussion.

"Ah tell ya, Jake, the only man fit fer the high office of president of this gran' an' glorious country is none othah than the guv'nah of the great state of Johja—Lestah Maddox hisself!"

"Very strange," replied Jake wearily. "A Jew talks with the dialect of a *schvartze*, has opinions like a Ku-Kluxer and expresses them from the wrong end of his anatomy. So tell me," he added none too gently, "what kind of qualifications does he have to be considered for the presidency?"

"Ah'll be glad to elucidate, cousin Jake. In all these heah Yewnited States, Lestah Maddox has no equal."

Old Jake nodded. "With this I must agree," he replied. "Superiors, yes. Equals, no!"

* * *

Back in 1935, when Mannie Fein was running for the New York State Legislature, he was labeled the greatest bore ever to hit the huskings in local politics. The man's campaign rhetoric consisted of one theme: "Crack the Big-Labor conspiracy." Mannie, in short, had a one-crack mind.

In October of that turbulent campaign year of '35, Mannie approached the colorful and recently elected Mayor Fiorello H. LaGuardia, seeking his support, even though he knew that the mayor had little liking for him.

"Mannie," growled LaGuardia, "why don't you go someplace where it would cost me a dollar to send you a postcard?"

"All right, be a comedian," said politician Fein, shrugging off the insult. "I'm throwing a big birthday party a week before the elections.

You know, of course, that my birthday isn't really until six months later, but I'd like you to show up."

"Why is it that you never seem to have a previous engagement before you visit me?" snapped the mayor. "Birthday party indeed! You could invite every friend you have and hold your big party in a telephone booth—and have elbowroom to spare."

"Tell me something," persisted Mannie in his usual dogged fashion, "just what is it that you have against me?"

Using the Yiddish tongue he had learned from his mother, LaGuardia replied evenly, "Just one thing, Mannie. Your supply of talk greatly exceeds the demand!"

* * *

Dr. Jonas Salk, architect Frank Lloyd Wright and Senator Abraham Ribicoff were deep in an argument as to which one of their professions was the oldest.

"Eve was taken from Adam's rib," said Dr. Salk, "and that surely was a surgical operation. The practice of medicine has to be the oldest profession."

"You're forgetting something," argued Wright. "Before the incident in the Garden of Eden you can't deny that an architect was required when order was created out of chaos."

"You're right," agreed Senator Ribicoff, "but who do you think created the chaos in the first place?"

* * *

Much to his grandfather's mounting annoyance, the college student was griping about the Watergate scandals, declaiming against the United States itself rather than placing the blame where it belonged—on the participants.

"Watergate-shmaughtergate!" rasped the old-timer. "You should consider yourself lucky to live in a country where you can vote people out of office if you don't like them. I remember, as a young man in Russia, I went to the polls to cast my vote. I was just about to open the envelope and drop my ballot into the ballot box, when a party supervisor stopped me.

" 'You're not allowed to open the envelope,' he yelled.

" 'You mean I can't even see who I'm voting for?' I asked.

" 'Of course not,' he told me. 'This is a secret ballot!' "

* * *

It was three o'clock in the morning when Barbara was awakened by her husband's wild thrashing and the exclamations of horror that burst sporadically from his lips.

"Nathan, Nathan, wake up!" she cried. "You're having a nightmare!"

Nathan slowly opened his eyes, and as the cobwebs of deep sleep cleared from his brain he breathed a thankful sign of relief.

"Oh," he moaned, "did I have a horrible dream!"

"What was so horrible?"

"It's kind of mixed up, but it all started with that damn Watergate business. In my dream, Nixon was still president and Spiro Agnew was still vice-president. All of a sudden Nixon resigns, so automatically Agnew becomes the new President. And what does President Agnew do? Don't even ask! He appoints Nixon as his Vice-President. Then Agnew gets impeached, so who is the new President? Yeah, Richard Nixon."

"A fine hoddya-do!" murmured Barbara.

"Wait, that's not all," Nathan continued, his face drawn. "There's a constitutional amendment that a President can't run three times in succession, but since he served as Agnew's Vice-President for awhile, the prohibition doesn't apply to him any more. Now he can start all over. So, in 1976, he runs against Ted Kennedy and gets re-elected. Then, in 1980, he runs against John-John Kennedy and he wins by a landslide. Finally, in 1984, when his term is up, the statute of limitations runs out on the Watergate business and the investigations are *kaput*."

"*Gevalt!* moaned Barbara.

"So he returns to his estate in San Clemente where he spends his days playing the missing tapes for his grandchildren."

"Look, Nathan, it was only a dream. Be glad it's over."

"That wasn't the end," he sighed. "After he retires, he decides to build a Nixon Museum on his property so he has the whole San Clemente place—the house and the land—condemned, so he needn't pay taxes on it. And his financial advisor, Bebe Rebozo, estimates the value at only ten cents on the dollar."

"*Nu*, that was good business," observed Barbara. "What do you care?"

"I care," groaned Nathan from the depths of his misery, "believe me, I care! I dreamed that I was holding the mortgage!"

* * *

If music hath charm to soothe the savage breast, then so hath the lulling magic of language. What you say is not as important as how you say it. Not that we originated that profound statement, but it serves to introduce the subject of our next story, an historical figure and a man of considerable proficiency in the practice of political palavar. We refer to the Rev. Dr. Arnold Fischel, minister of the Congregation Shearith Israel in New York City, a patriot of the Civil War era. His anti-slavery and anti-secessionist speeches and articles were widely quoted in the lecture halls and newspapers of the day.

In October, 1861, Rabbi Fischel applied to Secretary of War Cameron for a commission as chaplain in the "Cameron Dragoons," a volunteer regiment composed largely of Jewish soldiers. Cameron denied the application on the ground that the Acts of Congress relating to chaplains required them to be of a "Christian denomination." With the support of the Board of American Rabbis, Dr. Fischel fought the uphill battle to permit Jewish soldiers the right to spiritual representation by men of their own faith, and in December of that year he was granted an interview with President Lincoln. The Great Emancipator, in a letter to

Dr. Fischel, dated December 14, 1861, agreed that the law should be amended, and on March 12, 1862, thanks to the brave and persistent rabbi, the Act was amended to authorize the use of brigade chaplains.

Small wonder, then, that Dr. Fischel was so enthusiastic a supporter of Abraham Lincoln. Speaking at the unveiling of a monument to the martyred President, he uttered the phrase:

"Abraham Lincoln—that mystic symbiosis of stone and star: that man of peace with sword of gentle diadem." The comment was loudly applauded.

After the speech, a congressman approached Dr. Fischel.

"Rabbi, what in the name of heaven does that mean?"

"I don't know," replied Rabbi Fischel, "but it gets 'em every time."

17

Wine-Bibbers and Ad-Libbers

INTRODUCTION

The Jewish community in the United States seems to be plagued with an overabundance of savants who delight in intellectualizing humor on much the same level as a mortician explaining the technology of embalming. What's more, these wise men get paid for it! For them, a joke must have a psychological basis or they refuse to laugh. They apply psychology to humor in an attempt to endow it with neo-Freudian gibberish, always seeking to transform what is essentially an art form into a branch of medical science. The trouble with their reasoning, however, is that it stifles all jokes involving moral conduct which is in conflict with whatever standards happen to be in vogue. This, of course, includes their attitude towards the use of alcoholic beverages.

In 1892, Judah Leib (Leon) Gordon, the Hebrew poet, wrote: "Israel is ready to show the nations a phenomenon the like of which has never been seen: a peasantry not given to drink . . . laborers not given to brawls." But the estimable Mr. Gordon should have added the qualifier, "much" drink. It is difficult to conceive of a long succession of sages inveighing against the evils of drink to a people who never drank anyway. And how does one explain that jolly Jewish proverb: "Who blows foam from his glass is not thirsty!?" It is indeed true that most Jewish men imbibe only occasionally, and moderately: Jewish women hardly at all, although they are fond of the expression, "A little *schnapps* never hurt anyone."

Jewish drinkers seldom become aggressive; there are very few instances of a Jewish drunk declaiming that he can "lick any man in the house." Why, then, do Jews drink?

Dr. Freud would utter a loud and thoroughly disgusted "*ach!*" at this oversimplification: The average Jew drinks because it makes him happy. Brilliant, no? Happy, yes. Happiness, for him, is the agreeable sensation arising from contemplating the misery of the non-drinker, and reflecting on how miserable he would have been if he himself had not quaffed a few. As a rule, he prefers port or some other red wine—the fermented grape juice known to Temperance ladies as "liquor," and usually preceeded by "the curse of." After a few samples, the male imbiber is quick to remind the opposing sex that wine is God's next best gift to women.

But there is a good reason why Jews, on the whole, avoid whiskey: It is bad for the liver. Mothers impart that information at the time they warn their little boys about naughty girls. The liver (for the benefit of those not well informed on the subject) is the large red organ thoughtfully provided by God. It is attractive and utilitarian, and it enjoys a long, highly-regarded history. The sentiments and emotions which are now ascribed to the heart, for example, were anciently believed to infest the liver; hence its name: liver—the thing we live with.

The liver is the heaviest organ, and that's why it is called *kaved* (heavy) in the Bible. Next to the brain, the liver is the closest organ Man and goose have in common. The liver is the Almighty's most beneficial endowment to the goose: without it he would be unable to supply us with Strasbourg *pâté*, to say nothing of *genzineh gribbenes*.

There is yet another reason why some of the more gregarious Jews, emotionalists that they are, tilt the bonnie bottle: It gives them that lovely feeling of being "wanted"–usually by the pretty shikse in the poopik-revealing bikini who serves the refreshments. This romantic glow, which transforms Sol's Saloon into the Taj Mahal, may be described as the offspring of a liaison between a bank account and a bald head. Most Jews, however, drink at home because they refuse to pay the outrageous prices required to get all *shikkered* up in today's expensive emporiums. But even when they do get sozzled in a public facility, they are seldom inclined to belligerence. When pandemonium reigns, the Jewish drinker quickly and unobtrusively zigzags toward the nearest exit.

The man who "can hold more than a camel," be he Jew, gentile or gentilishly Jewish, is decried in equal measure by abstainers and teetotalers alike. There is an important distinction between the latter two. The "abstainer" is a weak person who yields to the temptation of denying himself a pleasure, and it can be definitely stated that the bride who marries him has a fine prospect of happiness behind her. The "teetotaler," on the other hand, is one who also abstains from strong drink, sometimes totally, sometimes tolerably totally. He's the guy you usually get stuck with as a brother-in-law.

"Man comes from dust and ends in dust," says the liturgy of the Jew, "but in between, what does it hurt to have a drink?"

You just can't beat that sort of creative thinking.

Le'chayim!

H.D.S.

We make the transition from politics to pixilation with the only Jewish story that comments humorously about Ulysses S. Grant—a notorious anti-Semite whose curbs against Jewish businessmen were summarily stopped by President Lincoln. Grant's proclivity for the bottle that cheers needs no embellishment here, and while this may not be one of those tales in which the denouement evokes uproarious laughter, its unfolding is one of high humor—and never mind the punch line. That it has survived for over 125 years speaks well of this bit of apocrypha.

Gold-crazy San Francisco, in the year 1851, was a rip-roaring gambling town with hotel rooms going at the rate of $100 a night. They came replete with hot-and-cold-running ladies of the evening. Whiskey was sold for $30 a quart, and there were plenty of customers.

A year earlier, Jesse Seligman, who with his brothers founded the internationally-known banking house which still bears their name, had just arrived in that boisterous city of the Golden Gate. With him was his youngest brother, 19-year-old Leopold. They opened a retail store and, since they received much of their payment in gold, they soon became brokers of that precious metal and, before long, were established in the banking business. But in that year of 1851 they were still retailers, only a few years removed from their peddling days.

One of the friends Jesse had made while managing their Watertown, New York store, was Ulysses S. Grant. By pure coincidence, Grant's Fourth Infantry was dispatched to the West Coast where he resumed his friendship with the Seligmans.

One evening, when Leopold was able to sneak away from his sober-sided older brother, he and the future president of the United States decided to partake of the various beverages offered by the tavern-keepers of San Francisco. For several hours they visited the establishments which specialized in potable concoctions until, with the dawn, the two bibulous gentlemen came to the simultaneous conclusion that it was time to lift their voices in song.

"Hey, Ulish—Ulishish—" ventured Leopold, "can you shing *Eli Eli?*"

"I don' shink sho," replied Mr. Grant.

"How 'bout *Di Klayneh Katchke?*"

"Don' know that one, either."

"F'heavenshake, Ulyshish, don' you know any shongsh at all?"

"Only two," replied Grant unsteadily. "One of 'em ish *Yankee Doodle* an' the other one ishn't!"

* * *

During Civil War times, there were many "dissenters" within the Jewish community. The most famous of those dissenters was Judah P. Benjamin, champion of the pro-slavery forces and ardent supporter of the Southern cause. He served as Secretary of State for the Confederacy and also as Secretary of War, refusing to relent even after the Confederates surrendered to the Union forces. Known as "the brains of the Confederacy," he fled to England where he remained for the rest of his life.

Judah P. Benjamin was a southerner through and through. He talked like one, thought like one and—yes—he drank like one. Among those heretofore unwritten myths and legends passed down through the years, many of which have the attribute of possessing at least a kernel of truth, we find this anecdote, told in the first person singular:

"Back before the War Between the States, around 1859 or so, a friend of mine came to visit our town in what is now Vernon Parish, Louisiana. His name was Judah P. Benjamin and he later became Secretary of War for our side. After the war he disappeared and I don't know what happened to him after that. But Mr. Benjamin—no one dared address him by his given name—was the only man I ever knew who, in appearance, mannerisms and tricks of voice, lived up to the popular conception of a typical southern gentleman of the pre-War old school.

"One day, returning from a duck hunt in the marshes, I dismounted from my mud-spattered horse in front of a white-pillared house set back among the magnolias and live oaks. My old friend, Mr. Benjamin, in his long frock coat, his wide slouch hat, his highly polished boots and his snowy-white shirt-front, stood on the porch to greet me. After salutations, I said:

" 'Sir, in case you are suffering from a drought in these parts, I have here in my saddlebag two quarts of guaranteed twenty-year-old whiskey.'

"A wistful light shone in Judah Benjamin's eyes and he mournfully shook his head.

"I gave a violent start.

" 'Can it be,' I asked, 'that you, of all men, have sworn off?'

" 'Such is the melancholy fact,' he stated.

" 'When?'

" 'Six months ago, but it seems an eternity since I imbibed my last drink of *schnapps*—otherwise known to the uninitiated as red-eye.'

" 'But why? What made you quit?'

" 'Well, son,' said Benjamin, 'it is an axiom among my people that an intelligent person refrains from ingesting that which is harmful to his body. And it is my studied opinion that the last barrel of likker I drank one weekend must have disagreed with me!' "*

* * *

The War of 1812 was mainly a war of the sea and its outstanding battles were on the water. One of the most valorous men fighting for the United States was the French-Jewish privateersman, Commodore John Ordroneaux, who gained renown for his bravery and skill during the naval encounter between the British frigate *Endymion* and the tiny armed vessel *Prince de Neufchâtel*, a brief but bloody battle which Commodore Ordroneaux won through superior strategy and sheer courage.

But Ordroneaux was also something of a martinet, and while he may not have been another Captain Bligh, he was about as stern a disciplinarian as ever commanded an American ship. A tough man, yes—a comedian, no. This whimsical bit of folklore is the only known humorous anecdote which involves him, and even then shows him bested by a junior officer.

---

*Adapted from *The New Orleans Delta*, Vol. XVII, No. 6, August, 1878. Introduction by the present author.

Shortly after his successful encounter with the British man o' war, Ordroneaux decided to allow a bit of shipboard revelry among the officers and crew for their gallantry under fire. But, immediately following the occasion, he entered a notation on the ship's log: "The first mate was drunk last night."

It so happened that the first mate, a new man on board and an able and conscientious individual, had never been drunk in his life until that night of celebration. He pleaded with the commodore for leniency, insisting that this was the first such offense he had ever committed and that it would never be repeated. He pointed to his record and reminded the commodore that he had been off duty anyway.

"This entry on the log will have a serious effect on my record, sir," he pleaded.

But the commodore was adamant. "You were drunk last night and I can't change the fact. The record will stand."

The first mate, deeply resentful, resumed his duties. That night, it fell to his lot to make the next entry on the log for the period of his watch. This he did, with what may be called a malicious scrupulousness of accuracy.

Next day, Ordroneaux found this innocently damning statement on the log:

"Commodore Ordroneaux was sober last night."

* * *

Here is a happy offering that was old—good and old—before Prohibition became the law of the land. It takes us back to an era when the newest dance vogue was the turkey trot; ragtime, the forerunner of modern jazz, was inching its way north from New Orleans and Memphis; the horse-car was the standard mode of urban transportation, and the neighborhood stable and blacksmith shop was a commonplace sight. It was a time when the huge wave of Jewish emigration from Eastern Europe had just begun to peak.

Ben, a baker, and Kalil, his friend, two gentlemen of ripened age, sat one evening by the wood stove in Ben's quarters when the shocking discovery was made that there wasn't a drop in the house to drink.

"Ronel! Ronel!" called Ben and, in prompt response, his young grandson appeared at the door.

"Listen, Ronel, I just found out that we ran out of—er—refreshments, and my friend Kalil and I are dying from thirst. So be a good boy and bring back for us a bottle of *schnapps*."

"But, grandpa," the youth protested, "the nearest place open at this late hour is ten blocks away. Besides, it's raining."

"Nobody's asking you should walk," said the oldster. "I already unhitched the horse from my bread-wagon. Just throw a saddle on him, get to the store as fast as you can and bring back the whiskey. If you'll hurry you should be back in fifteen minutes, and for that I'll give you a whole dollar. But don't lose any time—we can't wait a single minute longer than that. Remember—fifteen minutes!"

A dollar in those days was an unheard of gratuity for running an errand, and the grandson quickly agreed. "I'm on my way," he said, making a dash for the door.

"The streets are pretty slippery, Ben," observed old Kalil as the youth vanished. "I'm afraid the boy won't be able to get there and back in fifteen minutes. You didn't give him enough time."

"Don't worry, Kalil, " said Ben comfortingly. "That grandson of mine is the most punctual boy on the whole East Side." He glanced at his pocket watch. "He's just galloping out of the stable now."

He sat down, his timepiece still in his hand. Kalil, drooling slightly, produced his own watch and mentally proceeded to follow the grandson on his errand.

"He's now on Cherry Street," said Ben, after a few minutes' wait.

"Yes, and he's now going past the car barn," agreed Kalil.

"He's just crossed over to Orchard Street."

"Seven minutes exactly—and he's hitching his horse at Zopp's Schnapps on East Broadway.

"Now he's out of the store with the whiskey in only half a minute."

"Yes, seven-and-a-half minutes exactly. If he returns with the same speed, he'll be back here in fifteen minutes on the dot."

"Nine minutes, and he's back on Orchard."

"Now his horse is galloping along real good. The streets are slippery from the rain but he's making good time."

"Fourteen minutes!" shouted Ben. "He must be downstairs, putting the horse away in the stable. Kalil, in just one minute from now that boy will be standing in the doorway—take my word!"

Scarcely breathing, the pair sat in silence, listening with all four of their ears. In the hallway there were the sounds of running feet.

"Kalil," whooped Ben jubilantly, "didn't I tell you I had the most punctual grandson on the whole East Side? Fifteen minutes to the second —and here he is!"

The door was thrust open. The two thirsty gentlemen, fairly frothing with anticipation, leaped to their feet.

"Grandpa," said the young man, "for the past fifteen minutes I've been looking high and low for that horse's saddle but I just can't find it anywhere."

* * *

The mutual recognition pact with the Peoples Republic of China had been concluded and the Articles of Détente had been signed with the Soviet Union. Henry Kissinger, the architect of America's foreign policy, was jubilant. Here was truly an occasion that warranted celebration. In his New York hotel room, he put his feet up on the table, poured himself a manly hooker of bourbon and downed it with two gulps (and a twist of lemon). Ah, that was good! He poured himself another. Mmmm—that was even better! He poured himself a third—then a fourth.

Suddenly, he remembered that he was due at the United Nations to address the General Assembly. Frantically, he called the desk to get him a cab. Twenty minutes later, he rushed into the U.N. Building, raced to a crowded elevator and pushed himself into the last few inches of space.

He stood facing the passengers.

As the elevator expressed up to the U.N. floor, Henry cleared his throat and said:

"I shuppose you are all wondering why I called thish meeting . . ."

* * *

Sign in Fein's Fine Tavern on lower Broadway:

Never Drink While Driving
—You Might Hit a Bump and Spill Some—

* * *

Quoting from memory, here is another turn-of-the-century story told by the irrespressible Pitzy Katz during his vaudeville tours.

Jake the barber, passing by a tenement house in the predawn hours of the morning, saw a man leaning limply against the doorway.

"What's the matter?" he asked sympathetically. "Drunk?"

"Yeah, I'm 'fraid sho."

"Do you live in this house?"

"Yep."

"Want me to help you upstairs?"

"Yeah, shank you."

"What floor do you live on?"

"Shecon'."

With much difficulty, Jake half dragged, half carried the wilting figure up the dark stairway to the second floor.

"Is this your apartment?" he asked.

"Yep," affirmed the man, his eyes already closed in alcoholic slumber.

Jake opened the unlocked door and shoved the drunk inside. He then groped his way back downstairs. But as he was going through the vestibule, he made out the dim outline of another man, apparently in worse condition than the first, staggering in from out of the night.

"What's the trouble, mister?" he asked. "Are you drunk, too?"

"Yesh," came the feeble reply.

"Do you live in this house also?"

"Yesh."

"Don't tell me you live on the second floor, too."

"Yesh."

Again Jake half carried the stranger to the second floor. He pushed open the same door and shoved the man inside the darkened room.

As Jake was emerging from the building he discerned yet a third man, evidently worse off than either of the other two. This poor fellow was disheveled and bleeding from cuts and bruises on his head and face. He was about to approach him and offer his assistance when the object of his solicitude darted into the street and threw himself into the arms of a policeman.

"Offisher," he gasped, pointing a quivering finger at Jake, "perteck me from thish man. All night long he's done nothin' but drag me upstairsh an' throw me down th' elevator shaft!"

* * *

Horowitz of Dixie Fabrics, and Dormeir of Hudson Hi-Fashions, were unknown to each other until they happened to meet in a cocktail lounge one evening. Both had been imbibing freely of joy juice and they immediately experienced a bond of mutual congeniality. They fell into a somewhat hiccupy conversation.

"Seems to me like I've seen you somewhere before," said Horowitz as he vainly endeavored to light a sodden cigar stump with a dead match.

"I wouldn't be surprised," agreed Dormeir, always adept with a fancy phrase.

"Didn't I meet you at the Softwear Convention in Chicago, last year?"

"Not me. I never was in Chicago in my life."

"That's funny, neither was I."

"Well then," reflected Dormeir, pondering deeply, "the question now is, who the hell were those two guys who met in Chicago?"

* * *

Harry Baum, according to insiders who specialize in Los Angeles panhandlers, was usually called by his initials, which also stands for Hollywood Bum—an apt if inelegant nomenclature. H.B.'s place of business was on the sidewalk in front of the Brown Derby where he solicited alms from the passing gentry.

One Saturday evening, H.B.'s best customer, movie producer Darryl Zanuck, passed him by without extending the customary handful of coins. Indignantly, H.B. hailed the producer.

"Hey, Mr. Zanuck, you think I don't eat on Saturdays all of a sudden?"

Zanuck's mind had been elsewhere at the time and he hadn't even noticed the bum.

"I'm sorry," he said, "here's a dollar. Just don't give me that routine about starving. We both know what you really do with the money."

"All right," H.B. confessed. "I buy whiskey."

"Well, as long as you're so honest about it," said Zanuck, "come on inside with me and I'll buy you a drink."

They settled into a booth and producer Zanuck signaled the waiter.

"Two scotch and sodas," he ordered.

Said H.B. quickly: "Make mine the same."

* * *

Passing Beth Yisroel Synagogue in Staten Island, in the wee hours of the morning, a drunk noticed a sign that read: *Ring the Bell for the Shammes.* He did just that, and a sleepy-eyed old man came to the door.

"What do you want at this hour?" the *shammes* demanded crossly.

The drunk looked the old man over for a full 20 seconds and then retorted, "I want to know why you can't ring that silly bell yourself!"

* * *

Our next little tale dates back to long before the Prohibition era, when the Eighteenth Amendment finally gave Franklin D. Roosevelt a platform to run on. In those days there was a cozy, family-type saloon at 18 Chatham Square, in New York, called "The Schnapps Nook," but usually referred to by the local denizens as "The Shnookery." The specialty of the house was a mixed drink called "The Society Cocktail"— two of them and you wonder who's who.

Into "The Shnookery" one evening came two unsuspecting visitors to New York, eager to sample the "Society Cocktail," whose fame had spread even to their native hinterland. Obligingly, Harvey Roosevelt (born Henry Rosenfeld), poured a generous glassful for each of them. The concoction proved satisfactory in every respect.

When the two sojourners had finished their drinks, they immediately called for more of the same. The second service called for a third, but Harvey, the gentlemanly barkeep, raised a warning hand.

"No more, fellas," he said. "I'm sorry, but we never serve a customer more than two of these drinks. They're pretty strong."

"Just one more for the road," they pleaded.

"Can't be done. It's against the house rules. "I'd advise you gents to go along now and take a little stroll in the fresh air. You'll feel better if you do."

After further fruitless argument the visitors departed into the night, arm in arm. Presently, as they progressed along a dark and quiet side street on legs which had suddenly grown somewhat unsteady, one of the pair remarked:

"Say, listen—don't you hear footsteps behind us?"

The other hearkened.

"B'lieve I do," he said. "What of it?"

"It—it might be s-somebody f-following us."

"So what? Let him follow."

"But he m-might be one of those m-muggers."

"Well, just let him try something! Little does he know there's four of us!"

* * *

"Happy *Chanukah*, everybody!" shouted the stranger as he staggered into a small, neighborhood tavern.

The bartender laughed aloud. "For your information, mister," he said, still chuckling, "today happens to be the Fourth of July."

"*Ai*, am I gonna catch it from my wife," he moaned. "Seems like only yesterday she sent me out for the candles!"

* * *

Francis X. Lapidus, for many years cantor at the old Beth David *shul* on Greene Street, liked to hit the *schnapps* more or less—regretfully, more more, than more less. Not that Cantor Lapidus was a *shikker*. God forbid! But he did like to get "mellow" occasionally.

Some people, when they are in the mood, can be the biggest busy-bodies in the world, so it wasn't long before every *Yenta Tellabenda* in the congregation had complained to Rabbi Roth, and Roth's wrath was wroth indeed. Such kinds of un-cantorlike goings-on could not, and would not, be tolerated!

All cantors, as anyone who knows them intimately will attest, are undiscovered Carusos, with temperaments to match. So when Rabbi Roth confronted Cantor Lapidus, he knew what to expect.

"Enlighten me about something," the rabbi began gently enough. "Why do you drink so much?"

"Because my voice is not appreciated at the temple, and it makes me feel inferior," replied the disgruntled cantor. "When I drink I feel like a real somebody."

Rabbi Roth shook his head in sadness.

"If that were the case," he argued, "everybody who drank would be a somebody, and when everybody is a somebody then nobody is any-body."

Cantor Lapidus, to coin a few phrases, lit a cigar with a burning light in his eyes and froze the rabbi with an icy stare.

"If the congregation objects so much to my drinking," he demanded, "why did they give me for Chanukah an unbreakable cocktail shaker? And while I'm on the subject, who needs to shake unbreakable cocktails?"

"Please, be reasonable," urged the rabbi. "It just isn't seemly that a cantor should act like every weekend is an Irisher *yontiff*. I want you to promise me you won't drink any more." The good rabbi's voice grew urgent. "You don't know what all this wine and whiskey is doing to you."

"What wine and whiskey?" countered the miscreant, doing his best to needle the man who, to him, was meddling in his personal affairs. "I drink nothing but cucumber highballs—two drinks and I'm pickled. But you really have nothing to worry about," he added with a sadistic grin. "The only reason I'm drinking now is to avoid the New Year's rush."

The insolent reply hit home. Reluctantly, Rabbi Roth threw up his hands in a gesture of defeat.

"I'm sorry you forced me to say this," he sighed disconsolately, "but an alcoholic cantor is about as useful as a glassblower with the hiccups. I can see now that no matter what I say you intend to keep on drinking until your insides burn out and you've made an ash of yourself." The disappointed rabbi turned to leave. "Goodbye, ex-Cantor Lapidus," he murmured. "If you should suddenly disappear forever, it couldn't happen to a nicer guy."

Enraged at having been bested in the exchange, the cantor yanked open the door and ran into the hall, yelling his alcoholic defiance at the departing rabbi.

"You're not a rabbi, you're a capitalist!" he shouted. "You should change the *PRAY As You Enter* sign on the synagogue wall to *PAY!* You told your congregation that the temple was *prayer*-conditioned instead of *air*-conditioned just so you could save a little something on the electricity. You think it's hot in that temple? Wait'll you go to the *other* place!" Lapidus pulled a half-pint bottle of Schenley Number Five from his pocket and downed the fiery contents in one huge gulp. "Sure," he screamed, "you tell your people they're all going to heaven. Why not? You're selling them flight insurance on the side!"

Rabbi Roth pushed through the street door and found himself in the comparative quiet of the street—the traffic noises notwithstanding. He chuckled to himself.

It's a good thing, that no-goodnik didn't connect me with the one sign I really did put up," he said to himself—laughing at his cleverness— *"Come in and have your faith lifted."*

* * *

"Tell me, my good man," asked the kindly *rebbetzyn*, "why do you drink all that whiskey?"

"Madam," replied my good man, "what else should I do with it?"

* * *

Lend an ear to this exchange of dialogue, circa 1936, when Dr. William Goldman was professor of English at Brandeis University.

It was Graduation Day, and the father of one of the students had celebrated not wisely but all too well. He was in the parking lot adjacent to the university campus, peering owlishly at the cars, when Dr. Goldman appeared.

"Shay, mishter," called the weaving celebrant, "ish my car the one on the left or on the right?"

"Yours is the car on the right, sir," replied the professor. "The car on the left is a subjective phenomenon."

* * *

Jerry Miller, who used to travel for the Hecker's Flour people, found himself in Indianapolis one summer when he happened to run into his old friend, George, who was now living in that city. It was the first meeting between the two in many long years.

"Well, George," said the flour salesman after their initial greetings were over, "how are you getting along?"

The question seemed superfluous, for George was shabby, down-at-the-heels, out-at-the-elbows, and generally of a woebegone aspect. He permitted himself a hollow laugh.

"I never had such a run of rotten luck in my whole life as I've had these past few years," he began. "My wife's been an invalid since her car accident last August and it cost me all my savings for doctor bills. I had a nice business going, but my partner—that dirty crook—cheated me so badly I went bankrupt. In fact, I've been flat broke ever since. My oldest son is a loafer who won't work or go to school, and my younger one isn't much better."

"That sure is tough," observed Jerry sympathetically. "Back in New York, your brother Joe is doing very well. Haven't you heard from him?"

"Yeah, about a year ago. There sure is a big difference between me and my brother. Last I heard, he was just loaded with money. Listen, Jerry, I certainly would appreciate it, should you see him when you return to New York, if you'd tell him his poor brother George could use a little financial help. Right now fifty dollars in cash would look as big as a house."

"Believe me, I'll make it a point to speak to him," said Jerry. "After all, what are brothers—especially rich brothers—for? But, look, George, I've got a couple of bottles of good Mount Carmel wine upstairs in my hotel room. Come on up with me and we'll sample it. You'll feel better."

George accompanied his friend upstairs to sample the potables. He sighed deeply as he gazed into his well-filled glass.

"Makes me think of happier times," he said, downing the contents of the tumbler while his Adam's apple danced a visible jig in his throat. He then accepted another offering of the same.

"Jerry," he continued after a minute or two, "maybe I was exaggerating awhile ago. The trouble with me is that I've been brooding so much I get positively melancholy sometimes. Now, of course, my wife is still laid up from that auto accident, but it's beginning to look like she'll be better soon."

He held out his glass for replenishment. The third sample put a sparkle in his theretofore dulled eyes. He continued:

"Y'know, when I come to think of it, I'm not so sorry about the business going into bankruptcy. I never did care much for the line I was in, and being out of it has sort of given me a chance to look around. Next time, when I get a fresh start, I won't make so many mistakes, and I won't have a crooked partner, either."

George imbibed another glass of Mount Carmel's delight.

"About my sons—well, you know how modern boys are," he went on. "They're intelligent, and before long, I'm sure, they'll be acting like responsible young men. And—oh yes—by the way, if you see my brother Joe when you get back to New York, tell him you saw George out here and that George is getting along as well as could be expected."

An hour passed and they were starting on the second bottle. With an effort, the expatriate New Yorker raised himself to his feet. His eyes gleamed, his face glowed. he expanded his chest and reared back on his heels, his hands clasped behind him under his coattails; a perfect, living portrait of Baron de Rothschild.

"Jerry," he said somewhat thickly, "when you see my brother Joe, you just tell him that if he needs money or anything, and never mind how much, all he has to do is just call on me!"

* * *

We tell this one exactly as it was told in 1905, the only change being the substitution of a bus for a horse-car.

An inebriated old-timer, swaying unsteadily and his arms gesticulating wildly, flagged down a bus on the corner.

"Driver," he cried when the door was opened for him, "do you go to Forty-shecon' Shtreet?"

"Yes, I do," said the driver.

"An' Broadway?"

"That's right. Forty-second and Broadway."

"Well, g'bye," said the juiced-up old fellow, waving him on with a friendly gesture, "and have a good time!"

* * *

"There are three main reasons why a man is better off visiting his bartender than a psychiatrist," observed Bernie. "First, he's cheaper. Second, his medicine is guaranteed to put you in a good humor. And third, you can tell your troubles to a bartender standing up."

* * *

This piece of immortal prose has been ascribed to Lou Tendler's emporium in Philadelphia. True locale or not, it merits repeating.

A disheveled man, much the worse for wear and tear and things unsober, staggered out of the blind tiger owned by Tendler, the former great boxing champ-turned-tavern-owner. Laboriously, the drunk propped himself against the outside door and, for a few moments, owlishly surveyed the passers-by. Suddenly his knees gave way and he collapsed in a heap on the sidewalk and began to snore.

A short while later the local cop on the beat approached the scene, reflectively studied the fallen man and then poked his head inside the doorway.

"Hey, Lou," he called, "come out here a minute."

Lou Tendler emerged, blinking in the bright sunlight.

"Hello, Jim," he said pleasantly. "What's the trouble?"

The guardian of law and order jerked his thumb toward the slumberer on the sidewalk.

"Thought you oughtta know," he explained. "Your sign fell down."

* * *

Freddie and Rae were out on the town, celebrating their tenth wedding anniversary. Freddie, it soon became apparent, had imbibed more than was compatible with sobriety.

"Shweetie-pie," declared Freddie, planting a husbandly kiss upon her cheek, "my whole worl' revolvsh aroun' you."

"I wouldn't be surprised," said Rae coldly. "Didn't I tell you not to take that last drink?"

* * *

Two salesmen, one from New York and the other from Los Angeles, while attending a convention in Chicago, were indiscreet enough to succumb to over-indulgence in unholy potations. In other words, they got drunk. Several understanding fellow conventioneers carried them to a hotel room, stretched them out on adjacent beds and left them there to sleep it off. Let us call them Segal and Fliegel.

When they recovered consciousness a few hours later, it was broad daylight and they were still somewhat intoxicated. They stared at each other, their mutual suffering drawing them together in sympathetic brotherhood.

"Hello," said Segal.

"Hello," echoed Fliegel.

"Lemme introduce myself," ventured Segal. "My name is—hmm—I—I'm . . ." He furrowed his brow in thought. "Thash funny, I can't recall just who I am."

"Same here," confessed Fliegel. "Prob'ly it'll come to me in a minute, but right now I don't recall my name either. Tell you what, I'll look in my coat pocket: I got some cards there with my name on 'em."

Groggily, Fliegel rose to his feet and made his way to a heap of rumpled clothing on a chair. But here he made a mistake. Instead of fumbling among his own garments, he searched the pockets belonging to his new roommate until he found a card.

"Here it ish!" he announced. "Now ever'shing will be all ri'." With difficulty he read the words inscribed thereon.

"Louis Segal," he spelled out. "Don't soun' very familiar, still that mush be me."

Somewhere in the back of the real Segal's brain a chord of memory gave a very faint twang.

"Ver' glad ta meetcha, Mishter Shegal," he said dreamily. "An' I don't wanna offend ya, but it sheems ta me you got a bunch of in-laws that're a pain in the *tuchus!*"

* * *

A policeman appeared in court as a witness against Max Loeb, arrested for being drunk in public.

"How do you know the defendant was intoxicated?" inquired the magistrate.

"No doubt about it at all," said the officer. "When I saw him, he was dropping a penny in a parking meter. Then he looked up at the big clock on the City Hall building and moaned 'My God, I've gained eleven pounds!' "

* * *

The night clerk at the Hotel Algonquin was surprised to see a battered-looking man, wearing nothing but his undershorts, enter the lobby from the street. The stranger staggered to the desk and paused there, weaving groggily.

"What can I do for you?" inquired the clerk.

"I'd like to be 'scorted to the third floor—room 302," said the near naked man.

"Room 302?" repeated the clerk. He consulted the register. "I'm sorry, sir, but that room is occupied by Mr. Oscar J. Levine of Toledo. It's pretty late to be rousing a guest."

"I know what time it is, well as you do," retorted the inebriated one. "Jush show me to room 302 without any further con—conver—any further talk."

"Well, what's your name?"

"My name is Oscar J. Levine, an' fer your information I jush fell outta the window?"

* * *

It was a slow evening at the Tenth Avenue Bar and Grille. Baruch the bartender was toying with the idea of closing early when in walked a man with his dog. The stranger, his face flushed and his nose a Manischevitz-red, lurched to the bar and addressed Baruch in a confident if somewhat blurry voice.

"Look, Mac, I got a proposition fer ya. See this here dog? Well, his name's Pooch, an' he *talks!* Yeah, s'help me, he kin answer any question ya wanna ast him. Is it woith a straight shotta boibon on the house if Pooch answers a question?"

Baruch shrugged. After all, it was a very slow night—what could a little diversion hurt?

"All right, let's see what he can do."

The man gulped his bourbon down in one practiced swallow and then turned to his dog.

"Okay, Pooch, let's go. We gotta perduce fer this here good Joe, right? Here's the question: A guy is buildin' a boid house, see? He gets the floor laid an' he puts up the walls. But the foist time it rains, the boid inside gits all wet. Now, Pooch, tell this here man, what did the guy fergit to put on top of the house?"

"R-r-rufff!" went the dog.

"See? What'd I tell ya?" exclaimed the drunk exultantly. "Ol' Pooch knows his stuff, don't he? A real genius! Say, how's about another boibon, pal? My dog'll be glad ta answer one more question."

"Mister, believe me, you're not fooling anybody," Baruch told him. "I know there's a trick to it. But for the entertainment on a slow night, all right."

Another shot of bourbon was poured for the man and when he had tossed it down, he again addressed his dog.

"Now listen good, Pooch—pay close attention. A carpenter has a board with lotsa splinters on the edge. So he planes it down until he thinks it's smooth. Then he runs his finger over the board but it soitinly ain't smooth a'tall. Now, Pooch, if it ain't smooth, what is it?"

"R-r-rufff!" went the dog.

"Ya hear that?" shouted the stranger. "I told ya he's a genius! Tellya what, pal: One last boibon an' this here clever doggie will answer one final question."

"All right," agreed Baruch, "but this time let *me* ask the question."

"Sure! Anything ya say, pal. Whatsa difference who asts? This here dog is a intelleckshul. He got it up here—ya know what I mean? So gimme the boibon an' *you* ast the question."

Baruch brought the man his drink and then spoke directly to the dog.

"Tell me, Pooch, who is the greatest Jew who ever lived?"

The dog hesitated for a moment or two, perplexity clearly visible in its soft brown eyes, and then, in an uncertain voice, went—

"R-r-r—Tony Coitis?"

* * *

The gifted playwright, George S. Kaufman, once maintained that the following anecdote was his favorite drinking story. Having survived 100 years of circulation in one version or another, it seems well on the way toward achieving immortality.

As a young man, the distinguished critic, George Jean Nathan, enjoyed a bit of conviviality now and then. He attended a banquet given by some theatrical people one night and stayed late. It was three o'clock in the morning when he reached his home. In front of his house was a very small yard, hardly more than an ornamental grassplot; and in its exact center stood a maple sapling with a trunk about two inches in diameter.

Nathan made for the door, but he tacked off at an angle and bumped into the little tree. He made a fresh start, executed a wide detour, and came back—smack up against the maple. This time he put his back to its swaying trunk in order to be sure of getting the direction right, and off he went again, plowing up the grass. It was no use. He circled the lawn twice, but finished up holding on to the sapling.

Thereupon, Nathan sat himself down on the earth with great care, removed his hat, his shoes and his topcoat, and rolled up the coat for a pillow. As he sank to rest beneath the stars that shined down on Fourth Street and Ninth Avenue, he muttered in a voice of resignation:

"Lost, by heaven! Lost in the midsh of an impen'trable foresh!"

18

Cooking and Fressing

INTRODUCTION

The reader will notice a number of changes from the traditional humor of past generations as he reads this chapter. Some will be readily apparent; others more subtle. Unlike the "Yiddishe mama joke" which has, for the most part, retained its gentleness, the anecdotes in the following pages seem to have grown more sardonic. This does not necessarily mean that they are funnier or even more mature than yesteryear's jokes. They simply reflect the times in which we live. The flavor of *Yiddishkeit* is still there, albeit holding on with slippery fingertips.

The eating of *traif* (non-*kosher* food) by curious, careless or non-observing Jews, for example, has long been a staple of the people's humor. Following World War II, however, with memories of the Hitler obscenity still vividly alive, the emergence of the Arab threat to Israel's survival, and the Soviet Union's repression of its captive Jewish citizens, jokes concerning the religious injunctions about food all but disappeared —perhaps because the humorous stories seemed too inconsequential by contrast. Nevertheless, within more recent years there has been a mild reappearance of the quips and anecdotes, possibly due to the resurgence of interest in Judaism, especially among the younger men and women. But the dearth of such stories—at least of those comparable in excellence with the older jokes—is reflected in the collection presented in this chapter which contains only *one* funny story about the eating of forbidden food.

However, one facet of Jewish humor as it pertains to food and dining remains as popular as ever: the joke which revolves around that condescending, unflappable, arrogant, earthy and sullenly witty individual known, as "the Jewish waiter." He really did exist prior to the Great Depression of the early thirties, when, at last, hard times finally compelled him to adopt a more or less respectful manner toward his patrons. But the stories about him are still told and retold to this very day.

A few—*very* few—of these dour, sharp-tongued gentlemen continue their old and nefarious ways, mainly on New York's lower East Side, but regretfully, they too are becoming extinct. They shall be missed, those haughty remnants of an endangered species, for they not only exercised the right of veto over the customer's dinner selection, yielding with manifest reluctance to compromise, but they were usually right; the waiter was seemingly possessed of an unerring ability to match diner and dinner with the same analytical ingenuity as the old-time *shadchane* when it came to matching bride and groom.

The Jewish waiter, whatever else he may have been, was certainly no shrinking violet or cringing sycophant—and woe betide the patron who dared put on airs at *his* table! There is the delightful story about Sid Kramer, a waiter in Kaufman's East Side restaurant (a fabulous, turn-of-the-century eating place of which you will read more in the following pages). Back around 1920 or so, Edward, the Prince of Wales (who later became King of England only to abdicate his throne to marry Wally Simpson) entered the little East Side restaurant with his royal entourage. In those days, it was quite fashionable for upper strata socialites to go "slumming," so their appearance was not too great a surprise.

Kramer, who was not especially enthusiastic about slummers, straightened his apron, asked if anyone wanted water (he wasn't about to do unnecessary work for those who were not thirsty), and then listened carefully to their instructions. He was unable to write English, and simply memorized the orders. His power of recall must have been phenomenal, for he nodded after each of the party of 10 had stated their preference. He then sauntered off in the general direction of the kitchen, stopping meanwhile to pass the time of day with Kaufman, the proprietor, who saw nothing unusual, much less reprehensible, in such dalliance.

Returning to the visiting royalty with the first orders, which were perched precariously along the full length of his arm, Kramer leaned over Princess Elizabeth (to reign one day in the future as the queen), and murmured caressingly, "You're the cold salmon, Dollie?"

The astounded Prince of Wales looked up from his menu and was about to voice his displeasure, when Sid Kramer asked pleasantly, "Would you like, maybe, something superior for your interior, Eddie?" His face purple, the future monarch signalled for the proprietor, and Kaufman ambled over. He listened to the royal complaint, and then turned to his A-Number-One waiter.

"Listen, Sid, the man don't like you should call him Eddie," he explained reprovingly. "So call him Princie, or Harry."

Another interesting waiter episode involved the late Belle Baker, in those days a glittering star of show business. She went to Tomashevsky's, on Second Avenue, for an after-theater *nosh*. A young waiter took her order. He did not return for at least a half-hour, at which time Belle was fuming. "You mean to say you're the same waiter who took my order?" she asked incredulously. "Frankly, I expected a much older man."

Yes, there are countless jokes about the stereotypical Jewish waiter, but the joke is not on him—it is on society. The earliest of those impertinent waiters were the uneducated, unsophisticated immigrants whose insolence was really unintentional; they simply knew no better. There were also the educated newcomers who could find no work in their regular trades and professions, and were glad to obtain a paying job "waiting tables" in the new land. Unlike their illiterate colleagues, their impudence was intentional; they took out their personal frustrations on the customer. But, educated or not, those first waiters established a reputation for *chutzpah*—monumental gall—which has served as their image ever since. And the joke is on society because a succession of waiters, down through the years, perpetuated that image in one of the longest-running hoaxes in the people's folklore. As you read the jokes that unfold in this chapter, listen carefully and you may hear a mystic chuckle from somewhere in the room. It will be the ghost of that long since departed waiter having the last laugh!

Jewish humor, when it concerns the role of the sexes in the kitchen, is nearly always favorable to the male. Certainly, no female made the original observation that husbands usually miss their wive's cooking—every chance they get. Occasionally, of course, the missus emerges the winner: "You said you'd learn how to cook after we were married," growls hubby. And his bride of three months airily replies: "Oh, you know those campaign promises." It is one of those rare jokes about food in which the distaff side has the last word, but it is still an indirect put-down on the wife. And she doesn't exactly burst into gales of merriment, either, when the old man comes home from work and asks, "What's thawing?"

The mystery as to how our grandmothers and *their* grandmothers prepared all those bountiful, legendary meals without the aid of modern kitchen conveniences passeth all understanding. With that sort of family background in the culinary arts, one would think that today's husbands would be singing hallelujahs in praise of their wive's cooking. But if they are, it is not reflected in contemporary humor. Perhaps it is because the Jewish housewife—or houseperson, if you please—is more liberated than her grandma who subscribed to the theory of male superiority. If so, the subscription has been cancelled. Can you visualize ordering Bella Abzug to keep quiet already and fry the *latkes* or you'll give her *epis* she won't be able to sit down for a week? She'd holler for the fuzz. What's more, she'd tell you to go fry your own damn *latkes!*

Dietetics, the triumph of mind over platter, is yet another aspect of Jewish humor that was rarely evidenced in the older jokes. As might be expected, here, too, the quips and stories are slanted in favor of the male. Doctors tell us that more men than women are concerned about weight and dieting because of the higher incidence of heart attacks due to obesity among males. But you'd never know it by the jokes. It is no novelty to see a fat comedian unselfconsciously informing his amused audience that his wife has been on a diet for three weeks and all she has managed to take off is her hat. Actually, it is the woman who is the more careful weight-watcher. She knows that, while it may be true about a curved line being the loveliest distance between two points, when it gets too curvy it becomes a detour. She is now ready to diet—and let the hips fall where they may.

Liberated or not, grandma would have beaned grandpa with a chicken had he continually joked about her cooking in the manner of so many younger husbands. However, what with the ladies becoming rabbis and plumbers nowadays, they will soon be getting the quaint notion into their heads that they merit equal treatment in the joke department also. Comedians in bloomers! It is to weep! Wisecracking wives in the kitchen nobody needs. Traditionalists prefer the kind of joke in which the father turns to his son at the dinner table and remarks icily: "If your mother can take the time to defrost this meal, then you can take the time to eat it!"

But, let us end this Introduction, and have some real nourishment.

H.D.S.

Part One

DINING IN

The Pincus family fortunes had taken a turn for the better and nothing would do but that all the Pincii move to a nicer neighborhood. Grandpa Pincus, who had never lived outside a Jewish *gegent* in his life, had some difficulty adjusting to his new gentile acquaintances.

"How does a Jew make these *narishkeit mentschen*—foolish people —understand why a Jew boils water to make hot tea, blows on it in a saucer to make it cool, adds sugar to make it sweet and then adds a little lemon to make it sour?" old man Pincus grumped. "The way they're looking on me you'd think I just came over on the boat."

"It's not the way you prepare the tea," explained his granddaughter, trying hard to suppress a grin, "it's the way you pour the tea into your saucer and cool it by blowing."

Grandpa Pincus stared at her as if she had lost her powers of reasoning.

"So how else should I cool my tea?" he demanded. "Fan it with my *yarmulke?*"

* * *

Little Danny finished his dinner and his mother set a bowl of quivering Jello on the table before him. "Here, eat your dessert like a good boy," she said.

"I can't eat that, mama," he protested. "It ain't dead yet."

* * *

It has been said of the late Oscar Levant that he was the champion misanthrope of his time. If this story is any criterion, he deserved the dubious distinction.

Levant, according to impeachable witnesses, was on his way home one evening after a rehearsal.

"By the time I get home my dinner should be about ready," he declared. "If it isn't ready and waiting, I'm going to raise unmitigated hell. And if it is ready . . . I won't eat a damn bite!"

* * *

In these days of the impersonal giant supermarkets, we tend to forget that only yesterday the "Mom and Pop" grocery store flourished on almost every corner. These family-run groceries (as the stores were called) delivered purchases to the customer's home as a matter of routine. Orders were often telephoned to the grocer. The old-fashioned service which the customer received is nicely illustrated in this story.

Mrs. Zimmerman phoned her neighborhood grocery and and ordered a week's supply of food, including meat, vegetables and dairy products. The delivery boy soon brought the order to her house, but when she started to unpack she noticed that there were only ten eggs in the carton which was supposed to hold a dozen. She stalked to the telephone and angrily dialed the store.

"Hello, Mr. Gold, this is Mrs. Zimmerman. Listen, I got a complaint."

"*Nu*, unburden yourself," advised Mr. Gold soothingly. "You'll feel better."

"Well, I ordered a dozen eggs but you sent me only ten. That's a dozen by you?"

"Is that what you're making such a big *tsimmes* about?" asked Mr. Gold in genuine surprise. "To tell you the truth, you should be thanking me instead of complaining."

"What have I got I should thank you for?"

"The service. Believe me, Mrs. Zimmerman, two of the eggs in that dozen were so bad I threw them out for you!"

* * *

"Now you listen to me, Joey," said the boy's mother grimly. "I want you to eat up every bit of spinach on your plate!"

"No!" shouted Joey defiantly. "I ain't gonna eat no more vegetables until I find out where the Jolly Green Giant goes to the bathroom!"

* * *

A modern wife, according to Undernourished Untermyer, is one who can dish it out but can't cook it.

* * *

"Do you mean to say," asked Moe, his voice incredulous, "that after thirty years of marriage your wife still looks the same as the day you met her?"

"No," replied Ben sourly. "I said *cooks*, not looks!"

"Oh, sorry," muttered Ben. "I suppose you have to eat in restaurants to get a decent meal."

"To tell the truth, Moe, I haven't eaten out for at least twenty years."

"Then she must be very beautiful, to keep you home like that."

"Take my word for it, a beauty she ain't. With a face like hers she should nail a board over it."

"So why do you always eat at home?" asked Moe, puzzled.

It's no secret," Ben answered glumly. "I eat at home because sometimes her face takes my mind off her cooking, and sometimes her cooking takes my mind off her face!"

* * *

Cohen the Bensonhurst coin collector entered his brother's drugstore and asked for an Alka Seltzer.

"How come you got acid indigestion?" questioned the brother. "I thought your wife fixes three well-balanced square meals a day."

"She does," acknowledged Cohen wistfully, "but her square meals just don't balance in my round stomach."

* * *

"I'm not saying my family was poor," reminisced the late heavyweight boxing champion, Max Baer, "but when my mother sliced the corned beef it had only one side!"

* * *

Mrs. Umglik, a new arrival in America, was taking her first walk up Second Avenue, under escort of her older brother who had been living here for several years. In the window of a grocery store, she observed a great mound of cranberries.

"What are those?" she asked.

"Cranberries," explained her brother.

"They're good to eat?"

"Are they good to eat?" echoed the brother. "Listen, when those cranberries are stewed they make even better applesauce than prunes!"

* * *

Two-ton Tillie Sugarman answered a knock on the door, only to be greated by the neighborhood *schnorrer*.

"Mrs. Sugarman" he whined, "for three days I haven't had a bite to eat."

"Oh goodness!" she exclaimed. "If only I had your will power!"

* * *

A new arrival at a mental institution joined a fellow patient at the dining table.

"Oh, wow, you really are *meshuggeh*," he moaned, looking with unfeigned disgust at the other's laden plate. "Anybody who'd eat chocolate-covered meatballs *must* be nuts!"

"Oh, yeah?" snorted the the other derisively. "You ain't so normal yourself. I noticed you eating your soup with a knife."

"Well, that's certainly not because I'm crazy," retorted the new arrival. "It's just that my fork leaks!"

* * *

If you have ever tried to feed a six or seven-month old baby and keep its face clean at the same time, this line of dialogue should bring back fond, if messy, memories.

The young mother was busy elsewhere in the house and the father had undertaken the task of feeding little Becky in her highchair. The sloppy procedure went along about as expected, and after various and sundry starts, half-starts and accidents, he finally called out to his wife:

"Hey, honey, Becky finished the strained prunes but I think she wants more. Shall I give her a second coat?"

Part Two

WHINING OUT

In the mid-1920s there was a small combination delicatessen and eating place on the lower East Side called Rabinowitz's Russian Restaurant, on Rivington Street. There was certainly nothing spectacular about the little store-diner except for one thing—the signs that were lettered in soap on the window. Rabinowitz was a born humorist and no doubt missed his calling. Every few days, whenever he was seized by the whim, he would announce a "Special of the Day." Gentile visitors to the East Side who "went slumming" would gaze at the soap signs in wide-eyed wonder. But they provided merriment for the ghetto immigrants whose hard life in the *Goldeneh Medina* otherwise furnished little to laugh about.

The author, as a boy, jotted down some of the soap-signs; others were recalled from dim and distant memory. Here are a few "Rabinowitz Specials," most of them translated from the original Yiddish:

Golden Brown Sour Cream	Charcoal-Grilled Jello
Home-Made Calf's Liver	Iced Shish Kebab
Oatmeal Sandwiches	Hot Cold Cuts
Mashed Potato Chips	Braided Noodles
Gehakhta Leber a la Mode	Tossed Bread Pudding
Spaghetti in Syrup	Imported American Cheese
Caramel-Dipped Meatballs	Sauerkraut & Sardine Fruitcake
Lox Lollipops	Hard-Boiled Cantaloupe with
Onion-Flavored Ice Cream	Vegetable Fudge
Banana Borscht	Cauliflower Macaroons
Lokshn Soup Under Glass	Grated Salami

Hash-Brown Salad Dressing

Honorable mention must also be given to the drinks created by the irrepressible Rabinowitz:

Salted Orangeade
Condensed Schnapps
Tomato Juice Malted
Chopped Milkshake
Ice-Cold Hot Chocolate
Kosher Pickle Wine
Garlic Tea
Coffee with Chicken Gravy
Scrambled Eggnog

* * *

"Waiter," asked the naive customer, "how come the price for vegetable soup is the same as for hash?"

"Why not," replied the waiter. "They're really both the same, except that the soup is looser!"

* * *

"We sold over 200 hamburgers last night," boasted Walter, the wily waiter, "and I want you to know we did it all with a half-pound of meat!"

* * *

Once again we turn back the leaves of the calendar to chuckle at the highly imaginative but almost believable incidents that amused our parents and grandparents. These colorful stories were usually told as "true facts" and any number of people could always be found who could and would vouch for the truthfulness of the event. Needless to say, these "eyewitnesses" invariably named different locales and even different years in which the incidents supposedly happened. Our version of the following tale places the scene in "Kaufman's Essen," some time in the early 1930s.

Almost a half-century ago, a small restaurant on Grand Street, "Kaufman's Essen," achieved a sort of local fame on New York's lower East Side as a poor man's gourmet center. At prices for less than a dollar, Kaufman served such mouth-watering delicacies as stuffed *helzel*, roast goose with *genzineh gribben*, *hockflaish* wrapped in sweet-and-sour cabbage, *tsimmis*, *kreplach*, *kishkeh*, and, for dessert, there was always *kugel* or some other pudding or pastry.

But running a restaurant is like running any other kind of business—there is always one customer you wish had stayed in the old country. Kaufman had such a patron—an old man named Sokolov. If he wasn't complaining about the service, he was griping about the prices. If the soup was too cold, the coffee was too hot. Always something with this Sokolov—there was no satisfying the man. As far as Kaufman was concerned, his customer started out as a pain in the neck and worked his way down.

Tonight it was the bread. Sokolov was unhappy because he was served only two slices.

"Now just a minute!" Kaufman protested. "In here everybody gets treated equal. Two slices. You've been getting two slices ever since you started eating in this place, so why are you hollering now, all of a sudden?"

"Well, it ain't enough," Sokolov told him. "One slice I need with the soup, no? Another slice I need for the gravy, no? Another slice I need with the main course, no? Another slice I need with the coffee, no? Another slice . . ."

"All right, enough already!" Kaufman snapped. So he brought the man four slices of bread. After all, he was a steady customer, despite his complaining nature.

The next evening, Sokolov demanded still more slices. Kaufman sighed. "What can you do with a tightskate like this?" he muttered to himself. Teeth clenched, he put another four slices on the table.

On the following night, Sokolov looked at the ten slices of bread on his extra plate and then glanced up at Kaufman whose face was now grim.

"Kaufman, what's the matter—you're so poor you can't spare a few extra slices?"

In a rage, Kaufman sped back to the kitchen, grabbed a whole loaf of bread, cut it lengthwise in half, and rushed back into the dining area. He slammed the two halves down on the table, so infuriated he could not utter a single word.

Sokolov took one agonized look at the bread and cried:

"*Oy*, you're back to two slices!"

* * *

The diner ordered breaded veal cutlet, took a tentative first taste, frowned, took another bite, frowned some more and then called the waiter.

"I must say," he complained, "I've tasted better veal cutlet."

"Izzatso!" retorted the offended waiter. "Not in here!"

* * *

Josh, the talmudic student, was working his way through rabbinical college. On weekends, he served as a waiter at Sigmund's Seafood Stop-In. On this particular Sunday, the boss called Josh aside and informed him that the restaurant was stuck with over 50 pounds of flounder.

"I want you to recommend flounder to everyone who comes in," Sigmund instructed the youthful waiter. "Tell the customers the flounders were caught just an hour ago—fresh from the ocean, and the tastiest fish on the menu."

"But, Sigmund, the flounder is a week old," protested the future rabbi. "You know I can't tell a lie like that. It would be against all my spiritual beliefs."

"All right, so don't lie. Just push the flounder," demanded Sigmund.

A few minutes later, a customer sat down at one of Josh's tables.

"What do you suggest?" asked the patron.

"The flounder," said Josh promptly, "but it stinks."

*   *   *

It was a cold and rainy evening in December, and the diner entered Dov's Hester Street Deli-Restaurant in a foul mood. He made his way to his customary table and sat down, muttering angrily to himself.

"You're a little late tonight," observed Dov as he approached the ill-humored customer. "The rain hold you up?"

"Yes," growled the patron. "I had to drive around for twenty minutes looking for a parking place. Why don't you build a parking lot for this restaurant?"

"Mister," replied Dov with sweet reason, "if I had a parking lot, would I need a restaurant?"

*   *   *

From the *American Israelite*, we learn of a delightful little episode in the life of Gustav Poznanski (1805-1897), a widely known *chazan* of his day. It illustrates what can happen to an observant Jew who flouts the dietary laws of his people. In all fairness to the cantor, however, let it be said that it happened before he embarked upon his life's calling.

Visiting a Louisiana town, and being so far from home, Poznanski gave way to a wild and sudden impulse to taste forbidden food—just this once, he assured himself. He entered a restaurant which, being near the Gulf, specialized in seafood.

For Poznanski, the two opening courses were in the nature of novelties. Nevertheless, he partook freely of the crawfish gumbo and jambalaya Creole. But when the waiter brought him an individual oyster patty containing one large swollen Bayou Creek oyster enveloped in fluffy pastry, the *chazan's* eyes widened. Gingerly, he touched the contents with his fork. Then, with an expression of mingled surprise and distress upon his face he summoned the waiter who chanced to be passing his table.

"Whut's de trouble, boss?" inquired that functionary, ranging up alongside.

"Really, I'm not sure," stated Poznanski, his voice wavering from apprehension to outright disgust, "but it would appear that something has crawled into my bun and expired."

*   *   *

Not that it's the most important statement in the lexicon of American literature, but on Fairfax Avenue in Los Angeles there used to be a small restaurant named Della's Delicate Essen. Della herself is the authority for this whimsical exchange of dialogue.

A gentleman was sitting alone, staring malignantly at his order of fried fish. His lips were moving as though arguing with someone.

Della, who also served as waitress on the girl's day off, observed the diner's angry expression and, figuring that his demeanor was bad for business, she approached him in a deferential manner—a manner, incidentally, which she rarely indulged.

"Something is wrong, sir?" she inquired.

"Wrong?" spat the customer. "Of course not! Why should there be something wrong? I'm complaining?"

"I thought you were saying something, sir."

"I was. Me and this fish here, we were having a nice little discussion."

"*A meshuggeneh*," Della thought. Aloud she said: "That's very good, sir. Ha-ha-ha—talking with the fish!" She turned away, wondering what institution he had escaped from, but determined not to offend him.

"Hold on, lady," cried the customer. "On me you don't have to smile to yourself. What's the matter—you never before heard a fish talk? No? Well, you wouldn't understand his dialect so I'll translate for you the discussion we just had.

"First, I said to the fish, 'Hello, my fried friend, how's by you this nice evening?'

" 'I'm not feeling so good,' said the fish.

" 'You don't look too good, either; you should pardon me for saying so,' I said. 'Tell me, how are things down in the river?'

"And the fish said, 'How should I know? I've been here for two weeks!' "

* * *

A stranger in town went into the Greps Cafe in Burpee, California, and imperiously summoned the waiter with a beckoning finger.

"How's the food and service in here?" he demanded.

"Mister," replied the short-tempered waiter, "I just serve the food in this place; I'm not a character witness!"

* * *

Pencil and order book in hand, the waitress hovered over the early morning customer.

"I'll have scrambled eggs, toast and coffee," he said.

"Try the breakfast special for today," the young lady suggested. "It's better."

"No, just the eggs, toast and coffee, please."

"But the special has bigger portions and its fifteen cents cheaper."

"Madam, will you kindly bring me my order?"

"B-b-but . . ."

"See here, young woman!" growled the exasperated patron, "if I wanted a fight before breakfast I'd have eaten at home!"

* * *

Rose Berson, the *femme fatale* of East 114th Street, was on a vegetarian kick.

"Please bring me some raw bean sprouts, some raw carrot sticks, some raw cauliflower and some raw fresh cabbage leaves," she instructed.

"Lady," barked the waiter, "this is a restaurant not a meadow!"

* * *

"Waiter," protested the diner, "I hate to say it, but the tapioca tastes like glue."

"Sorry," muttered the waiter as he removed the plate, "this must be the rice pudding. The tapioca tastes from plaster."

* * *

A visitor from a small town had heard that Chicago waiters were a tough breed. He didn't believe it, however—that is, not until he entered the Bagel Basket on Jefferson Street in the Windy City.

"I'll have mashed potatoes, peas and lamb chops," ordered the out-of-towner. "And be damn sure you tell the chef to make the chops lean."

"Okay," said the waiter agreeably. "Any particular direction?"

* * *

"I see that tips are forbidden in this restaurant," said the pleased customer.

"Yes," said the genial waiter, "but so were apples in the Garden of Eden!"

* * *

"What in heaven's name did your cook put into this meatloaf?" cried the customer, after one small taste.

"Nothing to worry about," replied the waiter. "Perfectly good leftovers from yesterday's leftovers."

The diner tried another bite and then slammed down his fork in disgust.

"Who can eat this stuff? he demanded. "I don't mind eating leftovers and even leftovers from leftovers, but leftover leftovers from yesterday's leftover leftover leftovers is going too far!"

* * *

"Mister," complained the new patron, "these eggs smell bad."

"Well, don't blame me," retorted the waiter defensively. "I only laid the table!"

* * *

Gimpel the gourmet of Grand Street took one taste of his noodle soup and loudly called for the waiter.

"What kind of noodle soup is this?" he cried heatedly. "It tastes like dishwater!"

The waiter regarded him with an icy stare, and when he answered, his voice was just as frigid:

"How do you know?"

* * *

In his book, *Paul Muni: His Life and His Films*, Michael B. Druxman reminds us that Paul Muni believed that to be a good actor one had to prepare well, but the style and technique that each actor develops is the result of his own intuition and instinct. Muni was fond of comparing this approach, which he believed in strongly, to his wife's grandmother's method of making apple pie. She was an excellent baker, and when asked the secret of her delicious home-made pies, she would reply: "First I comb my hair. Then I wash my hands. Then I put on my apron. Then I make a pie."

19

Science and Scientists

INTRODUCTION

The number of Jewish scientists and inventors who have made lasting contributions to America's culture and prosperity are in the thousands. Charles P. Steinmetz, small in physical stature, but a giant in intellect, was the electrical wizard largely responsible for the early success of the General Electric Corporation. If it weren't for his contributions to science (to quote a new epigram), we would now be watching television by candlelight. And little need be said of the illustrious Albert Einstein whose wife didn't understand him. Whereas, the noted physicist could produce nuclear fission by putting atomic particles under tremendous pressure, Mrs. Einstein claimed that she could produce flawless diamonds by subjecting her husband to the same pressure.

The *luftmentsch* of Jewish folklore remains with us in the scientific community. Dr. Isaac Ellenbogen, of Harvard, whose research into the cause and removal of pollutants in our atmosphere has won him plaudits and cash from private foundations and government agencies, has stated that no one has ever really understood air. Had Dr. Ellenbogen taken the trouble to inquire more deeply, he would have learned what the average person—not versed in science—knows intuitively, that although cold air is a product of refrigerators, hot air comes out of Washington.

The field of anthropology does not seem to have much appeal for Jewish students. Few, to my knowledge, have attained eminence in that sphere, preferring, instead, the security of working in their father's store. The cause may have its roots in their theological training. As the old-fashioned Yiddishe papa protested to his college son: "Maybe *your* father descended from monkeys, but not mine!" The only scientific observation attributed to a Jewish anthropologist, and one which indubitably deserves mention here, was made by Dr. Gertrude Segal during her expedition to the Outback of Australia: "Look, you crummy aborigines, I'm just *studying* your customs. Keep your filthy hands to yourself!"

Anthropologists these days are mostly concerned with the worldwide problem of excessive human reproduction. There are two types of people responsible for the population explosion, according to the same

Professor Segal: the male and the female. The male, says the lady
scientist, is a member of the negligible sex, commonly known (to the
female) as chauvinist *chozzerei*. His genes contain two varieties: good
providers and bad providers, the latter usually dominant. It is noteworthy that most Jewish-American anthropologists are returning to the old
Malthusian theory, which pertains to Malthus and his doctrines. Malthus
believed in artificially limiting populations, but found that it could not be
done by talking. However, neither Malthus nor any Jewish investigator
into human behavior has ever matched Richard von Krafft-Ebing, who
left these immortal words to posterity: "Say, if you think *that's* racy,
listen to *this* one!"

It is only in the last 25 years or so that an appreciable number of
Jews have become geologists—who are more important than anthropologists if only because the costs of their college tuition's are higher.

We now come to botany, a repugnant branch of learning that has had
little appeal to the Jewish scientist—and he is undeniably right in ignoring it. Most aspects of this subject, especially those revolving around
pollination, cannot be discussed in this respectable book without running
afoul of the good people of Boston, but this much can now be revealed:
Botany is the science of vegetables—those that are good to eat even when
they taste rotten. It deals largely with the flowers and roots which are
usually badly designed, inartistic in color, and ill-smelling. Better to stick
to dairy and chopmeat—vegetarians to the contrary notwithstanding. A
little gout never killed anybody.

In retrospect, the "mad scientist" of legend, myth and movies may
yet prove to be mankind's (you should pardon the expression) savior. It
is he who seems to create the most practical consumer goods, such as the
new aspirin tablet that beats the *schnapps* through your bloodstream. A
mad scientist is one who does not conform to standards of thought,
speech, dress and action which are derived by the conformants from
study of themselves. He is at odds with the majority; in short, unusual.
It is noteworthy that persons are adjudged mad by officials who are
destitute of evidence that they themselves are sane.

In this brief Introduction, I have, by indirection, tried to establish
a frame of reference. The point is this: No area of science is immune to
burlesque; no scientist too lofty and important to escape the barbs of the
satirist.

Only one question remains to be answered: "Why is it that
American Jews, comprising a tiny percentage of the population of the
United States, and considered a race of mere dreamers, have been able
to attain pre-eminence in so many scientific areas?" The key word, I
think, is "dreamers." Rabbi Maurice Davis provides the answer:

"Every act of progress the world had ever known first
began with a dreamer. After him came the scientist or the
statesman, the expert on the technician. But first came
the dreamer."

And we laugh, because we are proud—and well pleased!

H.D.S.

"One beautiful thing about the photos of earth from outer space," declared physics professor Murray Klugman of M.I.T., "is that you can't see a single protest demonstration.

"The astronauts said the moon looks like a 'dirty beach,'" Klugman recalled, "Perhaps so, but to me it still looks cleaner than Coney Island after the Fourth of July.

"We have had many tangible benefits from space technology," concluded the professor, "although not all are adaptable to everyday needs. Take those new astronaut watches, for example. You can't tell time unless you're standing on your head."

* * *

Mrs. Frieda Rothafel, wife of nuclear scientist Dr. Emanuel Rothafel, currently on the NASA staff at Cape Kennedy, is justifiably proud of her famous husband. But a woman cannot live with a man for thirty years without realizing that these upper strata wizards may know very little else outside of their esoteric professions. Mrs. Rothafel explained it this way:

"My husband has one of the finest minds in the whole country. It starts working the minute he wakes up and doesn't stop until I ask him something!"

* * *

"Milton," the sixth grade science teacher called out, "can you tell me the difference between ohms and watts and volts?"

"No ma'am," replied Milton, "but I don't blame ya fer askin'."

* * *

Pincus the Pitkin Avenue presser is also a part-time scientist. He just figured out why summer days are longer than winter days. . . The heat expands them.

* * *

Professor Gregor Muzhik of the Soviet Union and Professor George Kaplan of the United States met during one of the ongoing SALT international conferences in 1974. They soon embroiled in an argument about genetics.

"I can tell you definitely," said Dr. Muzhik, "that in our classless society we have proved beyond the shadow of a doubt that it is environment, not heredity, that accounts for a person's appearance."

Dr. Kaplan frowned. "You Russian scientists have committed the sin of allowing your political ideology to run away with your common sense," he remarked drily. "Any college student can prove that heredity and environment each have their own characteristics and produce their own unique results."

"Prove it," demanded the Soviet professor.

"Very well," agreed Dr. Kaplan. "If a person looks like his father, his appearance will be the result of heredity. But if he looks like the milkman it will be the result of environment."

* * *

Dr. Klugmentsch, the scientist of advanced sonics, had made the remarkable discovery that turtles cannot hear the highest notes of a soprano, a flute or a violin.

"This explains," said Dr. Klugmentsch, "why turtles are seldom invited to concerts."

* * *

Shed a furtive tear for the poor professor who spent thirty years in intensive research, trying to find out why his colleagues were so absent-minded—then forgot the answer!

* * *

Dr. Albert Einstein, the most eminent physicist and mathematician the world has ever known, was on the podium explaining the rudiments of time-space calculations to an audience of graduating students and their guests. In the back row, sitting next to their son who had just received his diploma, were Mr. and Mrs. Meyers, ten years removed from their tiny *shtetl* in Russia. They watched with rapt if uncomprehending attention as Dr. Einstein illustrated his comments on a huge blackboard.

"The theory has been advanced," said the great scientist, "that the nearest habitable star is four light years from Earth."

"So what's four years?" whispered Mr. Meyers, *sotto voce.*

His embarrassed son silenced him with a fierce "shhh!"

Dr. Einstein continued: "There are 60 seconds in a minute and 60 minutes in an hour."

"This guy Einstein gets paid for such information?" demanded Mr. Meyers.

His wife gave him a wifely elbow to his ribs. "Sharrop already, you're disturbing the people."

"In a 24-hour day there are 86,400 seconds," Einstein went on, chalk-marking the blackboard with figures. "Multiply that by 365, the number of days in 12 months, and we arrive at a total of 31,536,000 seconds in a year."

"Big deal!" muttered Mr. Meyers.

"Now then, we enter the realm of astronomics," the scientist further explained. "Light travels at a speed of 186,000 miles per second. If we multiply that figure by 31,536,000—the number of seconds in a year—we find that the resultant number of seconds, 5,865,676,000, represents one light year. And as the nearest habitable star is four light years away, we know that it would take us 23,462,704,000 seconds to get there—provided we are traveling at a speed of 186,000 miles a second."

"Who has gas for such a trip?" asked Mrs. Meyers.

Mr. Meyers nodded. "The fare alone would set me back maybe a whole year's wages."

Dr. Einstein now concluded his address:

"In other words, ladies and gentlemen, relating those four light years to our own measurement of time, it would take us 744 years to reach another planet on which human beings could survive."

"I should live so long," commented Mr. Meyers.

"Maybe this Einstein doesn't like it in this country," surmised Mrs. Meyers, "so he's thinking *efsher* he'll emigrate."

Their son, who had been shushing them throughout the scientist's discourse, could no longer contain his irritation.

"What's the matter with you two? Have you got something against the great Einstein?"

His mother stared at him in surprise.

"Why should I have anything against him? He did me something? Personally, I think he writes very good on blackboards."

"Well, *I* have something against him!" snapped Mr. Meyers. "Here he's standing up on the stage and he's directing us like he's a traffic cop to a place that's a billion-shmillion miles away. But only an hour ago your great Einstein stopped me in the hall and asked me directions to the men's room!"

* * *

Dreyfus, the dubious doubter of Delancey Street never believed those U.F.O. stories until one day he pinched a waitress and saw flying saucers.

* * *

"Gee, grandpa, I sure wish I could be an astronaut," sighed little Mikey, his voice wistful.

"Then study astronomy."

"But, grandpa," argued Mikey, "I'm only seven."

"So what?" demanded the old-timer. "When I was your age, I was already self-taught. Like it was only yesterday I remember wondering where the sun went after dark, so I stayed up all night studying the sky."

"Did you find out?"

"I sure did!" affirmed grandpa with a broad grin. "It finally dawned on me."

* * *

Following the outbreak of the *Yom Kippur* War between Israel and the Arab States, the following editorial was prominently featured in the *Cairo Choleryeh:*

> It has been said that Israel's military successes have been due to its advanced technology and modern inventions. Chauvinistic Israelis have often asserted that they have achieved great progress because of their so-called inventive genius, while they deride the Arab States as still being in the 19th century.

Egypt wishes to give the lie to those typically Zionist lies. Arab ingenuity has forged far ahead of Israel's amateurish efforts since that State captured Palestine when we weren't looking.

As proof of Arab scientific superiority over the backward Israelis, the Cairo Choleryeh *is pleased to list the following Egyptian inventions which our primitive enemies have yet to equal, let alone surpass:*

* Salt and pepper shakers without holes, for foods that do not require salt and pepper.
* A piano with immovable keys, for those who would rather play the trombone.
* A stepladder without steps, for washing basement windows.
* A silent alarm clock for the unemployed.
* Fur-lined band-aids for cold cuts.
* A garden sprinkling can with no spout or bottom, for people who prefer artificial flowers.
* An electric sundial for telling time at night.

* * *

Doctor Fahni Halavah, distinguished president of the Egyptian Academy of Science, upon hearing of the electric sundial, was heard to comment learnedly, in Latin:
"Vos maynt electric?"

* * *

American Jewish folklore is replete with humorous incidents which illustrate the human side of heroic figures in our nation's history. The story of the devilish disappearance of Professor Einstein's check is an example. This true anecdote was reported by Dr. William Hess, Archivist, *RF Illustrated* (publication of the Rockefeller Institute), from letters dated 1923: *

Dr. Albert Einstein wrote from Berlin to Dr. Jacques Loeb of the Rockefeller Institute in New York, that he had an idea "which arouses the hope of solving the riddle of the quantum theory." To make the calculations to test this idea, he'd need a theoretical assistant; but he couldn't afford one. He thought $360 a year would suffice.

Dr. Loeb sent the request to Dr. Abraham Flexner of the General Education Board, adding his belief that "Einstein in his excessive modesty has reduced it to an almost impossible minimum." Dr. Loeb considered $500 more realistic. And so, Dr. Einstein was informed in a letter that the International Education Board had granted him $500 annually; the first check was enclosed in the letter.

Word next reached Dr. Flexner, from Dr. Heinrich Poll of Berlin, that Dr. Einstein had received the check but was not sure who had caused it to be sent; that he had mislaid or lost the check or someone had stolen it from him; and that "he is now in the greatest anxiety about what

---

*From *RF Illustrated*, publication of the Rockefeller Institute, Vol. 1, No. 4, Nov. 1973.

to do next."

Dr. Flexner wrote, while enclosing a replacement for the check:

"The last doubt is removed. Einstein is a great genius. Nobody but a great genius would be so careless in the handling of a check."

* * *

The above Einstein tale, occurring as it did in 1923, may be the first of the humorous anecdotes about the pre-eminent physicist to enjoy wide dissemination in Europe and the United States. But the following story is uniquely American, although it is not, of course, presented as fact. The imaginative incident gained currency shortly after the scientist, stripped of his citizenship and deprived of his possessions, fled Nazi Germany and arrived in the United States in 1934, where he accepted a post at the Institute for Advanced Study, Princeton. The story goes as follows:

Yoel the tailor was busily engaged at his pressing iron when who should walk into his humble shop but the great Albert Einstein, in person. Yoel, himself a refugee from Hitler's insane Third Reich and still unfamiliar with the English language, recognized the famous scientist immediately from pictures he had seen in the *Forverts*. When the visitor had concluded his business and was turning to leave, the tailor laid a hand on the physicist's arm.

"Before you go, Dr. Einstein, would you do me a big favor?" he asked, his voice brimming with respect and eager curiosity.

"If I can," Einstein agreed, smiling genially.

"Then tell me, what is this relativity business all about?"

"Well, to begin with," the great man responded, "relativity is a theory in physics which I happened to introduce. It discards the concept of time and space as absolute entities and views them as relative to moving systems or frames of reference. However, full comprehension of the mathematical formulation of my theory can be attained only through a study of certain branches of mathematics as, for example, tensor calculus."

Yoel nodded wisely and thanked the scientist for his explanation. When he was gone, the little tailor turned to his assistant.

"You know something?" he declared. "This Einstein thinks just like me!"

* * *

Zimmerman, the zoologist, recently informed a waiting world that he had successfully crossed a tiger with a parakeet. He doesn't know what to call the offspring, but when it talks you listen!

At least it's an improvement on his previous experiment when he crossed a mink with an octopus and got a coat with eight sleeves.

* * *

The second grade teacher had just finished explaining, in very elementary terms, how Sir Isaac Newton had formulated his theory about gravity. Now she was ready to test her little students with a few simple questions.

"Edith," she began, "what did Isaac Newton say when the apple fell on his head?"

"I know," replied Edith, smiling brightly: "The sky is falling; I must go and tell the king!"

* * *

Mr. Abraams was comfortably seated on the living room couch, reading the evening paper after a hard day's work. In the next room, his son was at the dining table studying for his college exams.

"Hey, dad, here's something interesting," the student called out, shattering the peaceful silence. "In my textbook it says that atomic scientists will soon have a way to heat a whole house on a single lump of coal."

"What's new about that?" snorted Mr. Abraams. "Our landlord has been doing it for years!"

* * *

Pincus the pessimist and Oscar the optimist were having a mild argument.

"I'm afraid that Arab technology is catching up with Israeli science," brooded Pincus.

"Impossible!" retorted Oscar.

"Not so impossible at all," replied Pincus. "Just the other day, Cairo Radio announced a new medical breakthrough—an appendix transplant!"

* * *

Mrs. Bloom was ecstatic when she read a letter from her daughter, a student at Vassar.

"What are you so happy about?" asked her husband. "Did our Joanie ask for only half of her usual monthly blackmail?"

"Listen to this," enthused Joanie's mother. "She says she got an *A* for her thesis, *The Influence of Science on the Principles of Modern Government*. Isn't that marvelous?"

"Yeah," grunted the father. "But when you write to her, tell her I said it would be a good idea if she began work on the influence of the vacuum cleaner on the modern rug."

20

Doctors, Nurses and Hospitals

INTRODUCTION

It is no secret that most Jews hold the medical profession in high esteem. If we are to believe the *bobeh mysehs* of folklore, Jewish mothers produce doctors; gentile mothers, patients. Yet, despite the favorable publicity engendered by the Yiddishe mama jokes, doctors have received a rather bad press in the people's oral and written literature. It is a situation I intend to encourage, for no other reason than the approval of my peer group—the happychondriacs of life.

The most illustrious Jewish doctor in history was Maimonides, whose "Physicians' Prayer" is not only a beautiful tribute to the practice of medicine, but provides a remarkable insight into the humane and spiritual qualities of that great and good man. But the veneration which has rightfully been accorded him for so many generations has not generally been proferred to other medical practitioners—allowing for the usual exceptions. A passage from the Mishna, for example, declares flatly: "The best of doctors are destined for Gehenna." Another ancient Jewish proverb warns: "Ask the patient, not the doctor" (especially if you want to know where it hurts). Even when a physician is moved by compassion for the poor and offers his ministrations without charge, he's "damned if he does and damned if he doesn't." The Talmud puts it this way: "A physician who heals for nothing is worth nothing"—a sentiment doubtless written by a scholar who practiced medicine on the side.

The humorous coupling of the *Malach-Hamoves* with the medical fraternity has long been employed in Jewish witticisms. In 1809, the *Chassidic* rabbi, Nahman Bratzlav, wrote: "It was difficult for the Angel of Death to kill everybody in the whole world, so he appointed doctors to assist him." But Rabbi Bratzlav was by no means the first to associate the two. Joseph Zabara, the 13th century Hebrew satirist of Barcelona, made the observation, "Both the doctor and the Angel of Death kill, but the doctor charges a fee." Nevertheless, we can all take heart and breathe a little easier. An American physician, Dr. Meyer Perlstein, in his book, *Amusing Quotations*, has given us these words of reassurance:

217

"If your time hasn't come, not even a doctor can kill you!"

Most of the characters of bygone days are still represented in American-Jewish humor through their modern counterparts. Occasionally, one can still find a religious Jew who, like his ancestors, is convinced that prayer alone will cure all sickness. He, too, is a legitimate target for humor. He believes that the laws of the universe can be annulled on behalf of a single petitioner. This devout person looks upon the Deity as a neurologist, proctologist, opthalmologist, chiropodist and celestial eye, ear, nose and throat specialist. Of the latter four parts of the body, the nose is given the least consideration, it being the farthest outpost of the face. As will be seen in this chapter, jokes about divine healing are limited, due, no doubt, to the large number of states in which the American Medical Association does not allow God to practice without a license.

Very few Jews are impressed by cultish health exercises. It is not easy to imagine Golda Meir, for example, sitting cross-legged in the approved Yoga position, and meditating with a guru who intones *hare krishna* with a Bronx accent, and whose costume matches her draperies. A similar disdain is felt for such occult beliefs as phrenology: the science of picking the pocket through the scalp.

Voodoo medicine is yet another area that has been shunned ever since a 19th century researcher, Dr. Emmanuel Isaacson, went to Africa to study the influence of insect venom on tribal health. He left this mortal coil involuntarily, but proved to medical science that the bite of the African tsetse fly is most efficacious as a remedy for insomnia. Isaacson's colleagues have since warned that it is easy enough to make jokes about witch doctors as long as you are far enough away so that when you look in the mirror you won't notice your head shrinking. There is no known antidote for this phenomenon, but there are plenty of jokes about it.

Nobody is neutral about dentists: you either dislike them or you hate them. The dentist is a latter-day prestidigitator who has mastered the art of putting forceps into your mouth while extracting currency from your wallet. He is adept at causing pain—a disagreeable feeling that may have a physical basis in something he is doing to your mouth; or it may be mental, caused by the good fortune of another patient whose appointment was cancelled. There are not many jokes about dentists. Getting them to say something funny is like pulling teeth.

Psychiatry, for the Jewish masses, is just coming into its own as a more or less respectable branch of medicine. For many years, psychiatry was thought to be a rather shady technique used by Jewish doctors to find out what the *goyim* were up to that they should be ashamed of. Nowadays, if you wish to talk therapy, you are required to lie down on an analyst's couch at the going rate of $25 an hour—and up. But old-timers can recall when talk on the East Side was free; and, because they were able to talk out their hostilities, it never even occurred to them to take such drastic steps as, for example, busing *Litvak* and *Galitzianer* children to each other's school.

Another source of humor is the psychiatrist's penchant for cloaking simple answers with the jargon of his profession. Tell him that you are depressed because of an unrequited love, and instead of telling you to find someone else, he will gravely inform you that "love is a temporary insanity curable by marriage or by removal of the patient from the influence under which he incurred the disorder. This disease," you'll be told, "is like cavities or diabetes, and is prevalent only among civilized races living under artificial conditions. Primitive people in backward nations, breathing pure air and eating simple foods, enjoy immunity from the ravages of love," he will conclude. He will then charge you fifty dollars, and all you will have learned is that love is sometimes fatal—and more frequently to the psychiatrist than the patient. And you will still feel lousy.

It should come as no surprise, in light of the foregoing, that Jewish humor is abundantly rich in those anecdotes which show the psychiatrist getting his comeuppance from the patient. One of them concerns the 86-year-old great-grandma, Mrs. Feldman, who sternly admonishes a young psychiatrist: "Look, mister, don't tell me I really got nothing to worry about. I was feeling rotten long before you were born!"

The average Jewish-American may pay lip service to the psychiatrist, but he secretly believes that most problems can be solved by an application of old-fashioned *Yiddishe saichel.* And, if he is unable to analyze his problem, he is more likely to consult his rabbi than a doctor. There is a well-known statement, attributed to the late film producer, Sam Goldwyn, which sums up this feeling of disbelief: "Anyone who goes to a psychiatrist ought to have his head examined." That, in essence, is the basis for many of the Jewish jokes associated with psychiatry.

Should you feel a slight attack of neurosis coming on as you read these pages, it is always helpful to realize that anybody who is *not* neurotic these days is probably underprivileged. In any case, this chapter is guaranteed to satisfy—or your mania will be cheerfully refunded.

H.D.S.

Part One
Oy, Doctor!

Mr. and Mrs. Roger Cohen proudly announce the birth of their son Bertram the doctor.

* * *

The new father-to-be paced the waiting room floor at the maternity hospital, wringing his hands and wailing, "Oh, my wife is so delicate! I just *know* she's too delicate for this!"

Finally, a nurse appeared. He rushed over to her, his face pale with worry.

"My delicate wife—she's all right?"

"Yes," she said, smiling reassuringly. "You're delicate wife is just fine."

"So tell me, quick," he cried, "is it a boy?"

She took a good look at the distraught husband's face.

"Well," she tactfully replied, "the middle one is!"

* * *

It is reported on absolutely unreliable authority that the following incident actually occurred to movie mogul Louis Selznick when he was a youth, newly arrived in this country.

It seems that Selznick suffered from a serious internal complaint, but his fear of surgeons and hospitals kept him from having the necessary work done to alleviate his condition. As might be expected, he became exceedingly low in spirits when a local practitioner told him it was now imperative that he undergo an operation. Tersely, the doctor ordered him to Mt. Sinai Hospital. There, after further diagnosis and X-rays, he was sent to the operating room.

Hours later, he recovered from the effects of the ether to find himself in a ward with other surgical cases in various stages of post-operative convalescence.

"Ohh," groaned Selznick, realizing he was still among the living, "am I glad that's over! I wouldn't go through that again for a million dollars—and thank God I don't have to!"

"Is that so?" inquired the patient in the bed on his right. "How do you know you won't have to go through it again—and soon?"

"Because my appendix is out," Selznick explained. "The whole thing's done. After all, how many times can you take out a man's appendix?"

"That's what I thought, too," stated Job's comforter. "But what happened? Fifteen minutes after I came to, they were rushing me back upstairs and opening me up again. One of those careless doctors left a sponge and a towel inside of me."

"Huh, you got off lucky," spoke up another patient from his cot nearby. "They had to hustle me back to the operating table and rip out all the stitches to get a pair of forceps and three scalpels they'd lost. Say, the way those doctors mislay things is . . ."

At that moment the surgeon who had officiated at Selznick's coming-out party opened the door to the ward and glanced at the sweating patient.

"I can't find that damned hat of mine anywhere . . ." he began, but got no further.

With a loud and anguished cry, Louis Selznick swooned.

* * *

"How's the missus?" asked the doctor in his usual jovial manner.

"She's better," replied the husband, "but if you want my opinion, the way she carries on when she's better I think she's better when she's worse!"

* * *

With the possible exception of Oscar Levant, Al Jolson was probably the most dedicated hypochondriac who ever gladdened a doctor's heart.

At a party one evening, one of the guests, a Hollywood medic, was telling Jolson about a new virus that had apparently been brought to this country by some Asian seaman.

"It's difficult to detect the virus," explained the doctor, "because the patient is outwardly unaffected. In fact, the man who gets the disease usually has a good, healthy complexion; his muscular and nervous systems are in perfect working condition; his digestion is good."

"Ohmygod!" cried Jolson, clutching his chest. "*My* symptoms exactly!"

* * *

The young student nurse was on duty in the maternity ward at Montefiore Hospital one day when she happened to see a new mother reading the book, *Doctor Zhivago.*

"Look," said the trainee, "about this doctor I don't know very much, but you can't beat Doctor Spock!"

* * *

Once again we enter that handy vehicle, the time capsule, and journey back through the sexy sixties, the nifty fifties, the fightin' forties, the dirty thirties, and on into the roaring twenties where we stop, hat askew and shirttails flying from that fast and breezy trip. We are at that "point in time," as our Washington friends used to say, when the transplanting of monkey glands and other such operations for the restoration of male vigor were in vogue.

Surgery for the restoration of youth had just been performed on a 70-year-old man who had hoped that, as a result, his chromosomes would henceforth be bouncing off the ceiling. As he came out from under the influence of the ether, he began to weep bitterly.

Mrs. Bernstein, the attending nurse, bent over him.

"Mister, it isn't necessary for you to feel worried," she said kindly. "The operation was a big success. Take my word, when you leave here you'll feel 20 years younger. Maybe more, who knows?"

But the poor old man only continued to wail, the tears coursing down his cheeks and losing themselves in his long white whiskers.

"Please, don't cry," pleaded Mrs. Bernstein. "The pain will soon go away."

"Who's crying from pain?" sobbed the patient. "I'm afraid I'll be late for school."

* * *

"How do you feel?" asked the doctor. "Sort of sluggish?"

"Sluggish?" echoed the patient wearily. "Listen, if I felt that good I wouldn't even be here!"

* * *

The patient was suffering from glaucoma of the left ear-lobe and the surgeon gently informed him that an operation was required.

"Doctor, I hope you don't mind," said the patient apologetically, "but I'm calling in another specialist before you operate."

"Certainly—I'll be glad to consult with him," the doctor readily agreed.

The next day, after the surgeon had consulted with the new specialist, he returned to the patient's bedside.

"It's only fair to tell you that I am in complete disagreement with the specialist about how to handle your operation," said the doctor. "Furthermore, I'm willing to bet that the autopsy will prove I was right."

* * *

"My father never went to medical school," averred Jenny the *balaboosteh*, "but he knew that the fastest cure for water on the knee is to hand the baby back to it's mother."

* * *

"I just wasted $1,100 on plastic surgery so my wife could have her face lifted," complained the unhappy husband to his friend. "I'll never go to that Dr. Bilik again!"

"But Dr. Bilik is supposed to be the best in the city," protested the friend. "You mean to say the surgery failed?"

"Well, not exactly," explained the husband. "He lifted her face all right, but when she saw the bill it fell down again!"

* * *

Doctor: I want you to understand, Mr. Chernoff, that this will be a delicate and dangerous operation. In fact, it is my duty to tell you that only one in five ever pull through. Now, before we begin, is there anything I can do for you?

Mr. Chernoff: Yeah, doc; hand me my shoes and pants!

* * *

Back during Prohibition days—that era when some of the people decided what was best for all of the people—Jack "Legs" Diamond, the black sheep of an orthodox Jewish family, was feuding with Dutch Schultz, Al Capone and sundry other gentlemen over the division of their respective territories.

One day, Jack ran into a crossfire from both the Schultz and Capone gangs and was taken to Bellevue hospital for the removal of miscellaneous bullets which had found lodgment in his innards. After the operation, he was wheeled into the intensive care unit where he slowly came out of the anesthesia. He looked about, puzzled.

"Nurse," he finally murmured in a weak voice, "why are the blinds drawn in this room?"

"Because there's a fire across the street," she replied coldly. "We didn't want you to think the operation failed."

* * *

The young intern had just completed an extensive physical examination of the taciturn old man.

"Tell me, sir," asked the medic." Do you suffer from arthritis?"

"Of course!" snarled the old-timer, glowering at the youthful doctor. "What the hell else can I do with it?"

* * *

Mr. Gross showed up at the Cedars of Lebanon clinic with a very rare skin disease. The intern, just two weeks out of medical school, gave him the usual once-over.

"Let me see your tongue," requested the young doctor.

Mr. Gross self-consciously complied. The medic took a good look, nodded wisely, and offered his studied advice:

"What you need is to get outdoors more—let the warm sun shine on that skin of yours. Do a little exercise in the open air."

"But, doctor," protested Mr. Gross, "I'm a mailman!"

"Hmmm," mumbled the doctor. "Let's see that tongue again!"

* * *

Sorrowful Sol: Doctor, I feel rotten. I'm afraid I'm not gonna last long.

Dr. Messer: Well, nobody lives forever.

Sorrowful Sol: I know, doc, but d'ya mind if I try?

* * *

There's a vignette that is told about the late Bugs Baer. It seems that he woke up one morning and discovered that he had no sight in his left eye. So he telephoned a friend to tell him the bad news. The friend offered his deep regrets and went on at great length to express his sympathy for the misfortune.

After several minutes of the tearful monologue, Bugs had had just about all he could stand.

"Look, do me a favor, willya?" he pleaded. "It's not all that terrible. I already saw all I wanted on that side!"

* * *

"Papa," asked the inquisitive daughter, "does a doctor ever doctor another doctor?"

The father laughed and gave the little girl an affectionate pat on the head.

"Why do you ask such a funny question?" he chuckled.

"Because Dr. Zucker gave me that nasty-tasting medicine even though I told him I hated it. So I was just wondering—does a doctor doctor a doctor the way a doctored doctor wants to be doctored, or does the doctor doing the doctoring doctor the other doctor the way he wants to?"

"Honey, take it from your papa," smiled the father. "By the time the doctor first gets his doctorate, he already knows too much about doctors to trust another doctor to doctor him!"

* * *

"My little brother, Baruch, went to the hospital yesterday," Rachel solemnly informed her second grade teacher. "They took his utensils out."

* * *

Stella had just returned home from the hospital where she had undergone surgery for hemorrhoids.

"Was the operation a success?" asked her sister.

"I suppose it was," replied Stella with a deep sigh. "But I'm afraid that for the rest of my life it'll be an eyesore!"

* * *

The physician finished examining his patient, an impoverished denizen of the lower East Side.

"I recommend that you take a long rest," he advised. "Go to the mountains for a few months."

"The mountains!" exclaimed the penniless man. "I can't even afford to go to Central Park. Why is it that you doctors always advise such expensive vacations? Don't you know what it means to be poor?"

"Now see here," said the doctor sternly, "I know exactly what it feels like. When I first started out to practice medicine I was so poor my stethoscope was on a party line."

* * *

"I want you to drink a cup of hot water every morning," prescribed the doctor.

"You gotta be kiddin', doc," said the patient crossly. "I've been doin' that for years, but my wife calls it coffee!"

* * *

Dr. Vaytig: No, Mr. Blum, your ulcers are not caused by business worries or family troubles. It's caused by eye-strain. That's what's causing your insomnia and loss of appetite, too.

Mr. Blum: Eyestrain? But, Doctor Vaytig, all I watch is the news on television.

Dr. Vaytig: Exactly! When you watch the six o'clock news you can't eat, and when you watch the eleven o'clock news you can't sleep. And when you worry about not eating and sleeping you get ulcers. See? *Eyestrain!*

* * *

Dr. Randolph Salinger of Beverly Hills was once summoned to the home of Chico Marx, one of the famous Marx brothers comedy team. The piano-playing entertainer with the Italian accent and funny hat was suffering severe stomach pains. According to Chico, the doctor gave him some pills and prescribed plenty of milk.

"I'll drop by again this evening to give you another once-over," said Dr. Salinger as he made ready to leave. "In the meantime, be sure to drink at least four glasses of milk. The more milk the better."

That evening the doctor returned as he had promised and examined the comedian once again.

"You're doing just fine," said the physician encouragingly. "Just be sure to stay away from milk."

"But, Dr. Salinger, only this morning you told me to drink plenty of milk," Chico protested.

"Oh, did I?" replied Salinger smoothly. "Well, that certainly shows the progress we've made in medicine since I last saw you!"

* * *

Nurse: That's a pretty bad cold you have, sir. What are you taking for it?

Patient: Make me an offer!

* * *

The boy had been playing baseball and, while sliding into home plate, broke his leg. His mother, who was watching the game, frantically rushed him to the hospital.

"Madam," said the staff doctor gravely, "I'm afraid your son has a compound fracture."

"Please, doctor," wailed the mother, "tell me in plain English. Who knows from arithmetic?"

* * *

Young Arthur Waxman, a first-year student at the Columbia School of Medicine, wanted to do something that was socially significant, so he got a summer job with Ralph Nader's task force.

Arthur's job was to investigate phony medical claims made by national advertisers. He was an instant success. At the end of his very first day with Nader's Raiders, he returned home brimming with enthusiasm and a true reformer's zeal.

"Boy, am I gonna fix those giant cigarette corporations!" he shouted happily. "Today I wrote a letter to every one of the big tobacco companies demanding that they prove their claim, 'Cigarette smoking is harmful to your health!'"

* * *

Mrs. Cohen met her neighbor, Mrs. Levy, at the laundromat. Mrs. Cohen had the sniffles.

"I'b id awful shape," moaned Mrs. C. "I thig I'b cobig dowd with the flu."

"I know just how you're feeling," sympathized Mrs. L. "But you got nothing to worry about. Just go see my doctor. He has a brand new drug it cures the flu in one day."

"This brad dew drug is so strog?"

"Strong? Listen, this drug is so strong," Mrs. L. said cheerfully, "you have to be in perfect health to take it!"

* * *

Coughing and wheezing, the skinny, stoop-shouldered old guy was on the examination table, getting a check-up for an insurance policy.

"I'm afraid the company will have to turn you down," said the doctor when he concluded his examination. "I don't think you are a good insurance risk."

"Why not?" demanded the man belligerently. "What's wrong with me?"

"Let's put it this way," said the unfeeling doctor: "If you were a building you'd be condemned!"

* * *

"If you ever expect to cure your insomnia," advised the doctor, "you'll have to quit taking your trouble to bed with you."

"But I can't" protested the unhappy patient. "My wife refuses to sleep alone."

* * *

The original Borden family, founders of the giant dairy concern that still bears the Borden name, included one young fellow who forsook the Guernseys to enter medical school. He became a well-known physician specializing in "female troubles."

Into Dr. Borden's office one day waddled Mrs. Ima Faird, the fattest woman he had ever seen outside of a circus. It seems the lady feared she might be pregnant and wanted a thorough examination. With a good bit of exertion and the added assistance rendered by the good doctor, Mrs. Faird managed to climb aboard the examination table.

"All right," commanded Dr. Borden from force of early habit, "open your mouth and say 'moo!'"

Part Two

The Meshuggeneh World of Psychiatry

Maxwell Shapiro, he of the nimble fingers who serves as *croupier* at the Gold Dust Casino's crap tables in Las Vegas, told this mournful story of his visit to a psychiatrist.

"Doc, I have a very serious problem," Max began. "I'm losing my memory—maybe I've already lost it completely. I can't seem to remember anything."

The psychiatrist smiled indulgently.

"I'm sure it isn't quite that drastic. You must remember *something*."

"No, nothing at all. I tell you, I can't remember a single thing."

"You mean, of course, such things as names and faces and dates? We all tend to forget them now and then."

"Doc, you don't understand. I mean *everything!*"

"Oh, that's pure nonsense!" snapped the doctor. "No one just forgets everything he has ever known. Even a person suffering from amnesia remembers *some*thing—such as whether he drinks coffee or tea or whether he smokes cigarettes or not."

"Listen, doc," Maxwell said despairingly, "I'm telling you for the last time; I can't remember anything at all. Everything I see, everything I hear, everything I read—it just makes a temporary impression and then goes out of my head forever. That's it, doc, I swear to you. I simply can't remember one—single—god—damn—thing!"

The psychiatrist frowned, leaned back in his chair and pondered this unique malady for several moments. Then he asked:

"How long has this been going on?"

"How long has *what* been going on?"

* * *

Psychiatrist: Tell me, Mrs. Stein, do you usually wake up grumpy in the morning?

Mrs. Stein: No, I'm usually letting him sleep late.

* * *

The intelligentsia along Pelham Parkway swear and avow that this story is true—but please, you shouldn't bet on it.

Two aged male patients at the *Goldeneh Medina* Sanitarium were sitting on a bench, sunning themselves on the front lawn of the institution. They were chatting amiably with Mrs. Berkowitz, their nurse, when a seagull flew over them and in passing dropped its calling card right on the bald head of one of the patients.

Mrs. Berkowitz, a most dedicated nurse indeed, rose to the occasion.

"Now Mendel, don't get emotionally upset. Don't move! You just sit right here on the bench and in two minutes I'm coming back with some toilet paper."

Mendel watched her as she scurried back to the main building and disappeared inside the door. He turned to the other patient and, in a voice tinged with sad disbelief, he gave voice to his suspicions.

"It hurts me I should say this, but for a nurse, Mrs. Berkowitz is setting us a poor example. By the time she gets back here with the toilet paper that bird will be fifty miles away!"

* * *

Senator Jacob Javits, may he live to a hundred-and-twenty, was inspecting the various hospital facilities in New York State. Toward the end of his tour, the Senator visited the *Sholem Aleichem Sanitarium* in Great Neck, Long Island. After inspecting the place and interviewing a few of the disturbed patients, he thanked the staff of administrators and started for the exit.

"Just a minute," snapped a guard as Javits was going through the gate, "you can't leave here."

The Senator smiled, realizing that he had been mistaken for one of the patients.

"Do you know who I happen to be?" he asked.

"No," said the guard, "but I happen to know where you are!"

* * *

Everyone thought that Harvey was just plain lazy, until a high-priced specialist finally diagnosed his case:
Voluntary inertia.

* * *

GEDALIA'S KAYNMOL GEVAYN TEEYATER
- Scene -
A palace room in ancient Egypt. The Pharaoh is reclining on a couch. Joseph, in his coat of many colors, is sitting on a chair beside him.

Joseph: It works like this, Phar. You just say the first thing that comes into your mind . . .!

* * *

The Modern Age of Exorcism began with the release of the motion picture, *The Exorcist.* Suddenly, all over the country, hundreds of otherwise rational people began screeching wildly that they were "possessed of the Devil." Thousands of others, somewhat more restrained, timidly suggested that they were being corrupted by satanic influences. The silly season had again arrived, overshadowing the flying saucer rage, the Loch Ness monster, the Abominable Snow Man and the latest discoveries of the lost continent of Atlantis. Exorcising the Devil from one's innards became quite fashionable.

In his study at Beth David Temple in Beverly Hills, Rabbi Oscar Green sighed deeply. His next appointment was with Mrs. Abel, wife of the famous movie producer and one of the most influential members of his congregation. Her 13-year-old daughter, it seems, had been invaded by the Devil and she was screaming for the rite of exorcism. 'A plague on those stupid films,' he thought harshly.

When Mrs. Abel and her young daughter were ushered into the office, their agitation was plainly visible.

"Rabbi," pleaded the tearful mother, "you got to do something quick for my little girl."

"What am I supposed to do?"

"Chase out from her the evil spirits."

"Madam," said Rabbi Green coldly, "I occasionally *drink* spirits, I do not chase them. Go to a psychiatrist."

"But I already took her to a psychiatrist," wailed the mother. "He said it was a case for a priest or a rabbi."

"So go to a priest."

Rabbi Green's icy response, his all-too-evident disdain for the whole silly business seemed to galvanize the Devil within the girl. She let out a blood-curdling scream, fell heavily to the floor, rolled about in a frenzy and frothed at the mouth. Mrs. Abel's frantic cries, added to those of her daughter, raised the decibels in the study to ear-splitting levels.

"All right already, enough!" shouted the rabbi above the mad bedlam. "I'll exorcise!"

Mrs. Abel was asked to wait in an adjoining room while the rabbi gave the Devil a good smack in his dirty face. Through the thick walls and the heavy door, the anguished mother could still hear her daughter's frightful screaming. And then, as suddenly as it had started, the yelling stopped. Ahh, sweet peace and quiet!

In a few moments, the rabbi and the girl entered the outer room and, to Mrs. Abel's joyous amazement, her daughter was serene, composed and even smiling a little.

"Take her home," said Rabbi Green. "She's cured."

After services on the following Sabbath, Mrs. Abel approached the miracle-working rabbi.

"I want you to know that my daughter is now a perfect little angel," she enthused. "No more evil spirits; no more Devil."

"And the screaming and the frothing and the rolling on the floor?"

"Gone. All gone. You did very good, Rabbi. Tell me, what did you say to cure her so quick?"

"I said to her: 'Now you listen to me, you silly girl. If I hear one more yelp out of you—just *one!*—I'll give you such a *potch in tuchus* you won't be able to sit down for a week!'"

* * *

At the Brighton Beach Home for Meshuggeneh Mentschen, a new patient was observed swaying from side to side like a pendulum.

"Are you *davening* sideways?" asked the institution's rabbi.

"No, I'm keeping time," replied the patient.

"Hmm. So what time is it?"

"Eight-thirty."

"You're wrong," said the rabbi, looking at his watch. "It's nine o'clock."

"Oh, my goodness!" exclaimed the patient, speeding up his motion. "I'll have to go a little faster!"

* * *

From the Presidium of Psoviet Psience and Psychiatry:

"All right, doctor, I'll lie down on the couch. Like this? Fine. Now, what questions do you want me to answer? My dreams? Well, as a matter of fact I do have this recurrent dream—at least two or three times a week. I keep dreaming I'm in this big city, see? And I'm surrounded by thousands and thousands of Poles, Czechs, East Germans, Rumanians, Hungarians and Lithuanians. And—get this doctor—they're all eating motzoh balls with chopsticks. Tell me, do you think there's a Freudian significance hidden away in that dream?"

"Well, that's hard to say, Comrade Kosygin . . ."

* * *

Feingold the blouse manufacturer had just experienced the worst season of his business life. So severe was the catastrophe that, as a consequence, he suffered a nervous breakdown. There remained nothing else for him to do but consult a psychiatrist.

"I'm feeling so low I'm even thinking of suicide," wept poor Mr. Feingold. "Doctor, can you tell me what to do?"

"Yes," said the headshrinker. "Pay in advance!"

* * *

"I've got a problem, doc," the new patient began.

"We all have problems," replied the doctor, smiling his assurance.

"My problem's this, doc: I get migraine headaches every time I think of my wife. I break out in a rash every time I think of my job. I get cold sweats every time I think of my bank account. Talk about problems! Boy, I got 'em!"

"Every problem has it's answer, of course, and I understand this one perfectly," said the psychiatrist, nodding. "You will need 100 sessions on the couch, at $25 per session."

The patient gulped. "Well, doc," he said after a painful pause, "that solves your problem. Now, how about mine?"

* * *

Rabbi Israel Walters tells of the time he served as an Army chaplain during World War II. Among his responsibilities was the spiritual ministering to the needs of the soldiers in Ward Eight—the "psycho ward" as it was called by the patients themselves.

"I was leaving the hospital one day when I noticed that my car, which was parked just outside the front gate, had a flat tire," recalled Rabbi Walters. "I jacked up the car and got the tire off, putting the nuts in the hubcap as most people usually do. However, while putting on the spare tire I accidentally tipped over the hubcap and the nuts rolled through the iron grille of a drain. I was standing there, no doubt looking as perplexed as I felt, and wondering how I was going to secure the wheel, when one of the boys to whom I had just spoken called to me through the chain link fence:

"Chaplain, sir, why don't you just take one nut off each of the other three wheels and use them on the fourth? They'll hold until you can get to a filling station."

"Say, that's a perfectly marvelous idea!" I exclaimed, full of admiration. "How did you ever think of it?"

"Why not? he answered with a cheerful smile. 'I may be crazy but

I'm not stupid!'"

* * *

Our penchant for digging in psychiatric pastures brings us to the grand master of mirth, Jack Benny.

"I went into analysis and was told to lie down on the couch and tell everything I knew," recalled Jack. "As a result, my analyst is now doing my act in Philadelphia."

* * *

The professor of psychology was instructing a class in Psych 1 at Columbia University. For some time he had been trying to explain the differences of the various terms used, but he could see that his students were still unable to sort out the unfamiliar words.

"Let me put it this way," the professor finally said. "These are the ABC's of the profession: 'A'—Neurotics build air castles. 'B'—Psychotics live in them. 'C'—Psychiatrists collect the rent!"

* * *

Sadie Goldsmith grew so weary of her mother's constant preachments that she "marry a rich doctor," the girl decided to get away from it all by joining the Peace Corps. After two years in the Congo she married a seven foot Watusi and returned to the Bronx with her ebony husband.

Mama Goldsmith took one look at the towering African in his loin cloth, feathers and pierced nose, and moaned; "*Oy*, Sadie, I said a *rich* doctor, not a *witch* doctor!"

21

Dollars and Scents

INTRODUCTION

Jokes are sometimes a gauge by which the attitudes and beliefs of a nation, group or individual may be measured. Probably nowhere else is this more manifest than in the many misnamed "Jewish" jokes which make an unsavory association between Jews and money. Many of them originated in the minds of 19th century bigots, and were crude caricatures whose primary function, it seemed, was to denigrate the ambitious German-Jewish immigrants and the Eastern European Jews who followed them in the 1880s and onward. The same scorn was seldom heaped upon the thrifty Scotsman. The canny New England trader who could "skin you out of a fly's eye" was likewise considered to be an altogether admirable character. Clearly, the abusive "Jewish money" joke was a veiled expression of anti-Semitism.

American-Jewish humor recognizes the simple fact that the good Lord created too many people for the available cash that's around, and that money and credit are curious articles: money is needed most when you haven't got it, and credit is something you have plenty of when you need it least. Contrary to the abusive nature of the old-time joke, Jewish humor advocated the wise use of money—never greed. "Look for cake and lose your break," declares a Yiddish proverb, cautioning against acquisitiveness. And the Talmud states: "Money legitimates a bastard"—which explains why there are so many oil-producing states sitting as legitimate members of the United Nations.

A cursory analysis of true American-Jewish humor provides a revelation: those anecdotes and witticisms revolving around the subject of money itself—that is, for its own sake—rank very low in the esteem of the Jewish people.

There are, of course, other subjects involving money which enjoy continuing popularity in the people's humor, but in those instances it is not the money itself that provides the *motif* or driving force behind the anecdote. Instead, money is considered for what it is: merely the accepted medium of exchange—the manner in which the energy expended in our labor is transposed into the things we use in our daily lives. Thus, in the following three chapters, "Commerce and Trade," "Yiddishe Blarney in the Workaday World," and "Keeping Up With the Kohnses," we find ordinary (and some extraordinary) people meeting the challenges of the business world, others coping with the ever-present problems of earning a living, and the fortunate ones enjoying the good life to which they hope to become accustomed.

In all these instances, the characters pursue their objectives with varying degrees of success and failure, courage and timidity, cleverness and foolishness. They are *people*, not just faceless names in a book, and many of the stories can be traced back to incidents that actually occurred. Some of the jokes, of course, depend for their humor on sheer absurdity. But they have this in common: money is only peripheral to the point of the story. Allow me, if you will, to illustrate with an anecdote in which the subject of money is understood but in which the word is never used— the main focus being on the legal complications of settling an estate:

"Your Honor," said attorney Klein as he rose from his chair, "what is the status, so far, of this case?"

"It's all over," explained the judge. "I have given a judgment for the residuary legatee under the will, put the costs upon the contestants, decided all questions relating to fees and other charges, and, in short, the estate in litigation has been settled, with all controversies, disputes, misunderstandings and differences of opinion thereunto appertaining."

"Good—very good!" exclaimed the attorney. "We're really making progress!"

"Progress?" echoed the judge. "Didn't you hear what I said, Mr. Klein? I just told you the case is closed; the matter is concluded."

"Yes, of course, Your Honor. In fact, it *had* to be concluded in order to give relevancy to the motion I'm about to make. Sir, I move that the judgment of the court be set aside and the case reopened."

"Upon what ground?" asked the judge in surprise.

"Upon the ground," replied the attorney, "that after paying all fees and expenses of litigation and all charges against the estate there will still be something left."

"Hmm, there must have been an error somewhere," said His Honor thoughtfully. "The court may have underestimated the value of the estate. The motion is taken under advisement."

Another example in which money is peripheral to a larger theme is found in this observation: "Many people complain that the mail service is slow, but let me ask you a civil question: When was the last time your gas, electric or phone bills were late?"

In the following little exchange of dialogue, we have a specific reference to dollars and cents, but here we are really concerned with the issue of inflation:

"That will be $3.50, sir," said the young lady in the box office as she handed the moviegoer his ticket.

The customer glanced up at the sign reading "Popular Prices" and demanded: "You call $3.50 a popular price?"

"Well," she replied sweetly, "we like it!"

It is clear, then, that the lively imagination with which so many Jews are endowed finds marvelous expression in jocular references to money matters—some of them oblique, others more direct. The characters in these jokes range from bank absconders to beggars. In that context, "abscond" means to "move in a mysterious way," commonly with other people's property. A "beggar" is one who asks for something with an earnestness that is proportioned to his belief that it will not be given. He is a descendant of the *schnorrer*, that grand anti-hero of Jewish folklore who was an *artiste* in the art of wheedling and fenaigling as compared with the crude American panhandler. Having passed through Ellis Island, the *schnorrer* surveyed his new territory and adapted his techniques to meet the challenge of New York's "tightskates and cheapwads," perceiving that his European tactics stamped him as a greenhorn—a designation that was something less than flattering.

For those not old enough to recall the meaning of the word, a "greenhorn" was an immigrant who arrived in this country two months after you did. The *schnorrer*, let it be said, quickly realized that the impoverished *griener* of the East Side, contrary to what he had heard in his home town, was no cornucopia and had little or nothing to give. Before long, after much soul searching and searing doubts, there came his moment of truth and he, too, joined the labor force. But he had one unexpected compensation: now that he had a job he could look down upon the next boatload of alms-seekers and coin his own hyphenated, scornful epithet—"Those *griener-schnorrers!*"

Jewish humor in America contains many allusions to overpricing and to the outrage of bamboozled customers. For some retailers, the price of an article is generally its value plus a reasonable sum for the wear and tear on their conscience in demanding it. Some of the jokes overlap into other categories. As an example, here is an illustration in which we not only have a confusion of price, but of accent as well:

Joseph, a comparatively new immigrant to the United States, purchased a suit of clothes which had been advertised at $58. But when he was presented with a bill for $89.50 he was horrified. There was an alterations charge, a city sales tax, a state tax, a federal tax, and a surplus tax—sort of a tax on taxes, or a tax-tax. Indignantly, he refused to pay anything above the advertised price. Flinging the original $58 down on the counter, he stalked out of the store with the new suit. The proprietor, seeing his 400% profit watered down to a measly 100%, called the police, and Joseph was hauled into court.

This was Joseph's first such experience in his adopted homeland and he shook with fear as he faced the bar of justice.

"Jotch," he said, after explaining his case in his broken English, "you should pliz haxcuse mine Hinglishe spitch, what mine heccent it shouldn't give me trouble I should losink this case."

"Sir," replied the judge, leaning forward, his manner brimming with kindness and understanding, "joosta because you talk-a like dat, you no gonna have-a no trouble long-a as I'm-a judge!"

Note, please, that while the theme of the above story concerns the subject of money, the surprise ending offers a resolution which has nothing whatsoever to do with money itself. It should also be noted that no racial or national bias is inherent in the tale, nor is it even implied that the defendant will receive anything other than a fair hearing. Jokes such as this bear little resemblance to some of the thinly-veiled canards which masquerade as "Jewish" humor, and whose characters exist only in the thoughts of their shadowy creators.

As I suggested earlier, money jokes are often linked with political sallies. At any moment, for example, we can expect an Israeli poet to compose an elegy to the United Nations: *They are Loyal to the Ones with Oyal.* But political situations change with the years, as does its humor. Those that endure are the witticisms and stories to which we can personally relate—those closest to home. Many express the wistful yearnings of a bygone generation of European Jews, now restructured to express similar longings in America. Others still retain their Old World simplicity, revived every half-century or so to delight a young generation for whom the stories are new. Such a joke is the one about the thrifty wife who cut off her cat's tail so that it would not take so long to leave or enter the house, thus saving heat. American-Jewish humor, however, when it involves money, is mostly native to this country. One of its many products is this witty observation: "Early settlers may have started this country, but it's those who settle on the first of the month that keep it going."

What is this business of money all about? Never mind the economists. Gertrude Stein figured it out for us when she wrote:

"Money is always there, but the pockets change. It is not in the same pockets after a change, and that is all there is to say about money."

H.D.S.

It happened at the start of the so-called energy crisis when the Arabs placed on embargo against the United States and halted their shipments of oil to this country. Chaim the yardgoods salesman was in dire need of cheaper transportation so he paid a visit to his cousin, Abe, proprietor of "Honest Abe's Used Car Caravanserie."

"Here's a nice, clean Chevvie," said Honest Abe, pointing to a heap of metal that might have been used by Paul Revere. "It gets 40 miles to the gallon and rides like a dream."

"Look, Abe, this is me—remember?" protested Chain. "Save the *bobeh mysehs* for somebody else. Just tell me, will this old clunker get at least 16 miles to the gallon?"

Abe shrugged. "Maybe, on the open road, going downhill and with the wind; but don't ask me to write it down."

"All right, how much are you asking?"

"It's yours for $700."

"*What!* Are you out of your mind? It's not worth $500. Tell you what: I'll give you $600 and we'll call it a deal."

Abe's face grew purple and his hands clenched into tight fists.

"I'm gonna give it to you straight, Chaim," he barked. "Just because you're my cousin doesn't mean you have to take advantage of me. I'm asking $700 for this car because I myself had to pay $300 for it. Are you gonna stand there and argue with me about a lousy four per cent profit?"

* * *

"Pop, any chance of you lending me ten bucks til payday?" asked the always-broke son.

"Why should I lend you money when you're wearing $200 suits?" demanded the father indignantly. "Look at me. All I have to my name is this old fifty-dollar rag—I'm even ashamed to call it a suit."

"Listen, pop, it's true my suit sells for $200, but I just put a few bucks down, that's all. I haven't made a payment in over a year."

For a moment or two the father was too surprised to answer.

"All right, I'll be glad to lend you the ten dollars," he finally said, "provided you get *me* a $200 suit on the same installment plan!"

* * *

During a fund-raising tour of the United States, after a State visit with President Richard Nixon in 1968, Golda Meir was asked, "How was it possible for Israel to defeat all those Arabs in 1967 in just seven short days?"

"It was our army," she replied. "It was the way we were organized. Our reserves saved the day."

"How so?"

"First," she explained, "we called up all the doctors and trained them well. Then we called up all the dentists and trained them well. Then we called up all the lawyers and trained them well. Then we called in our Minister of Defense, Moshe Dayan, and he gave the order: CHARGE!— and boy, *did they know how to charge!*"

* * *

Jack and Judy had saved their money for years and, despite Jack's limited income, they finally accumulated enough to buy a house in the suburbs.

"I hate to bring this up, Judy," said Jack hesitantly, "but in this high-class neighborhood it isn't nice for people to talk about their personal business. My salary, for instance. You'll have to stop talking about it to our new neighbors."

"Who's mentioning your salary?" yelled Judy. "I'm just as ashamed of it as you are!"

* * *

The husband had just taken out a new life insurance policy and was explaining the various clauses to his wife. Her eyes widened as she beheld the figures.

"Thirty-thousand dollars is a lot of money," she murmured.

"No, honey, the face amount is for $15,000," he explained patiently. "It pays $30,000 under the double-indemnity clause—but that's only in case something should happen to me through an accident."

The wife pondered this bit of financial manipulation which, to her, sounded as though it had been concocted by a Watergate lawyer.

"This double-indemnity business—it isn't fair," she complained when its full significance dawned on her. "Do you mean to say that just because you should die a natural death I only get half?"

* * *

There is a certain type of fellow who is automatically conditioned to raise unmitigated hell about the injustices he sees or hears about—or even imagines. He is a radical only when the conservatives are in power. When the radical or liberal element is at the helm he is just as apt to be a conservative—as long as he has something to rave about. His blood-thirsty curses are hyperbolic, not what he really feels; as for example, when he expresses that magnificent Yiddish malediction: "It should grow inside your stomach a trolley car!" Such a man was Peretz Weintraub who graced the lower East Side some forty or more years ago.

In 1929, after the Wall Street crash, banks everywhere were failing by the dozens. On Grand Street, Peretz strode up and down in front of the Bank of the United States (a misnomer that fooled thousands of hapless depositors), shaking his fist at the closed doors and literally snarling:

"In the electric chair they should put such people! A fire on their heads it should burn for ninety years and six months! By the neck they should hang, those crooks, until they're dead—dead—*dead*! The president from the bank, the vice-president, the board of directors—every-body—should be put on a guillotine and chopped off from them the heads —those bums, those *goniffs*, those gangsters!"

Officer Muldooney, the cop on the beat, walked up to him.

"Hello there, Mr. Weintraub. What're you so worked up about? Did you have your money in this bank?"

"No, I didn't," confessed the overwrought Peretz. "But if I *did*!— *ach*, would I give a *geshrei*!"

* * *

Two garment workers were bewailing the high cost of everything from lox to socks.

"This inflation business is sending me to the poorhouse," groaned one. "I don't know how, but we got to have more money."

"Making more money is no problem these days," sighed the other. "What's so hard is making a living!"

* * *

Joe and Edith decided to celebrate their fifth wedding anniversary by going to a movie—their first in as many years. When they got to the box office, the price of admission almost bowled them over.

"I wonder where the fifty-cent movie ticket went," murmured Edith.

"Ya wanna know?" rasped Joe, his face livid with outrage. "I'll tell ya where the fifty-cent ticket went! It went to three dollars!"

* * *

The late George Kaufman, playwright and critic, was visiting the country home of Moss Hart, another eminent writer.

Hart, inordinately proud of his estate, insisted on taking Kaufman on a personally conducted tour of the grounds. He pointed out where he had diverted a brook, created a waterfall and pond, transplanted several shade and fruit trees to provide a better view, and landscaped the terrain with various exotic plants—all at tremendous expense.

Kaufman was greatly impressed.

"Just think, Mosseleh," he enthused, "what God could have done with this place if He'd had your money!"

* * *

The late Sophie Tucker recalled the poverty into which she was born.

"We were so poor," claimed Sophie, "my parents couldn't afford children. The lady next door had me.

* * *

Meyer Lansky, the confidant of some questionable characters in Las Vegas, was being interrogated by the district attorney.

"Now that Howard Hughes has bought the Sahara, would you say that the mobster element is no longer involved in the hotel business here?"

Meyer looked the D.A. right in the eye—his good one.

"Hell, Mac, you got it all wrong," he explained in his own delicate way. "Howard Hughes did buy the Sahara all right, but not the hotel—the *desert*!"

* * *

There are tens of thousands of poor Jews in America. And they too have their stories. Here's a sample.

Mrs. Goldberg was in her Orchard Street flat, sipping a glass of tea and conversing with her next-door neighbor.

"This business of government assistance is all right, but it's taking away from us our dignity," she grumbled. "If it wasn't for the food stamps, the free day nursery for the children, free medical care, rent allowances, supplemental payments and the regular monthly check, I'd get off welfare tomorrow!"

* * *

"Talk about extravagant wives," complained Max. "Her idea of holding down the bills is to put a paperweight on them."

"You should teach her the virtues of thrift," counseled a friend. "Pursuade her to start saving."

"I tried that," explained Max wearily. "So she invented a new way to save money . . . She uses mine!"

*   *   *

It was a tender, poignant scene at the airport. The wife tearfully kissed her husband goodbye.

"Don't forget to write, darling," she said between sobs, "even if it's only a check!"

*   *   *

Here's a golden oldie that still retains its humorous charm. It goes way back to those days when a five-and-dime store meant just that, and not a place where a customer is offered a bedroom suite or a barrel of British chutney. The tale is about a mild-mannered, timid little man who had recently emigrated to this country. Without loss of time, he began to familiarize himself with American mores and institutions.

The newcomer to our shores was taking his first walk down Lexington Avenue when he was halted by a sign over a large red storefront. Laboriously, with his scant understanding of the English language, he made it out: *Five and Ten Cent Store.*

He considered the sign at some length. Next, he studied the contents of the wide show windows where domestic utensils, toys and a wide variety of other goods were displayed. Then he entered. Inside the wide double door, he encountered one of those impressive and dignified beings who seem to have been ordained by the Almighty to serve mankind as assistant store managers. To the little immigrant's vast relief, the store's major domo was Jewish.

"Is it true, sir," inquired the new arrival in Yiddish, "that nothing in this establishment costs more than five or ten cents?"

"That is correct," replied the store official.

"Good, good!" smiled the new American. "You'll be so kind, please, to direct me to the shoe department?"

*   *   *

One thing you have to admire about the present administration—its efficient Bureau of Statistics.

The Bureau just figured out that the best time to buy anything is about 30 years ago.

*   *   *

"Of course my wife and I are compatible," the husband told his analyst. "In fact we both like the same thing. It's just that I like to save it and she likes to spend it!"

*   *   *

The sweet-faced, white-haired old lady cashed her check at the supermarket and then profusely thanked the cashier.

"It's very nice you're helping me out," she said warmly. "You wouldn't believe it, but even the banks they're refusing to cash my checks!"

*   *   *

The frugal housewife was looking over the ads in the evening paper when she came to a full-page display.

"Ooh, Myron," she called to her husband who was watching a baseball game on television, "they're having a monster sale at Klein's!"

He looked up, irritated by the distraction.

"Listen, I ask you like a normal person," he growled: "Who needs a monster around the house?"

* * *

It was National Book Week, and for the past half-hour the English prof had been discoursing on the importance of literature in general. Now he addressed his first question to Miriam, the prettiest co-ed in the class.

"Young lady, if you could have only one book in your entire life, which book would you choose?"

"I think," replied Miriam after due and deliberate consideration, "I'd choose a checkbook!"

* * *

Mrs. Fein received a sternly worded notice from her bank that her checking account was overdrawn.

Embarrassed, Mrs. Fein sat right down, wrote a note of apology and sent them a check.

* * *

Willy Wexler, of West Weehawken Waterproofing, Window-Washing, Wood-Waxing & Wall-Wiping While-U-Wait, Inc., came home with furrows of care on his brow.

"Marianne," he said, "the way bills keep piling up is scandalous. I'm spending more than I can make. We've just got to cut down on expenses —both of us!"

"How?" asked Marianne.

"Well, we can start with a few personal sacrifices and then go on toward higher cost things. Now, what would you suggest to begin with?"

Marianne pondered a moment.

"I'll tell you how we'll begin," she said brightly. "Hereafter you can shine your own shoes. And I'll do my part too—I'll cut your hair!"

* * *

The college student was laboring over a letter to his folks.

"How do you spell 'financially?'" he asked his roommate.

His roommate spelled the word for him. Then, glancing over the learned one's shoulder, he added:

"And there are two r's in 'embarrassed.'"

* * *

"Papa, can I have a quarter?" begged the moppet for the fifth time.

"Stop making such a pest of yourself!" growled the father. "Why, when I was your age I asked for pennies."

"Okay, papa," said the little boy, his eyes lighting up, "can I have 25 pennies?"

* * *

Joey was only five years old but was very sharp indeed. The neighbors loved to play a game with him; one in which Joey was always glad to participate. They would offer him a nickel and a dime in their open palms and ask which one he would rather have. To the unending delight of the grown-ups, Joey always chose the larger coin.

One day, an older boy asked him the inevitable question:

"What's the matter with you, dummy? Don't you know that a dime is twice as good as a nickel?"

"Sure," answered Joey, "but business is business. Why should I spoil a paying proposition?"

* * *

A young college dropout had been searching for a job for a whole hour. He could find nothing suitable: the companies seemed to have no need for new vice-presidents, board chairmen, marketing consultants, efficiency experts or other positions paying $30,000 a year or more.

"I'm a victim of current inflationary tendencies," he sighed from the depths of his 18-year-old heart.

"Listen, if you think these are hard times," scolded the youth's father, "you should have been around during the Depression. I remember once I dropped a nickel in the telephone slot and the operator said 'God bless you, sir!'"

* * *

Abe and Dave, somewhat in their cups, were enjoying a convivial evening together at the local tavern. Their conversation drifted around to the subject of wealth, and who was the richest man in the world.

"It's gotta be Howard Hughes," said Abe. "His bank once returned one of his checks with a memo: 'Insufficient Funds. Us, Not You!'"

"That's nothing," retorted Dave. "I heard that old man Rothschild once sent a check to his bank and it bounced . . . Not the check, the bank!"

* * *

"Live it up while you can," advised the spendthrift. "Money is for the good life. Who needs money lying around in a bank?"

"But don't you believe in putting something aside for a rainy day?" asked his frugal companion.

"Of course not! Name me one person who ever really benefited by saving for a rainy day."

The friend considered the challenge for a moment or two and then answered tersely: "Noah!"

* * *

"I'm saving up for a new bike, dad," ventured the small boy hopefully. "Do you have any odd jobs around the house I can do?"

"I'm afraid not, son," replied the father.

"Well then," suggested the boy, "how about putting me on welfare?"

* * *

The two old codgers, brothers in their seventies, were as identical in appearance as twins could possibly be. But emotionally and intellectually they might as well have been strangers. One was a generous, outgoing type; the other was a taciturn miser.

It so happened that one day the generous brother called on his twin for a donation to the synagogue which they both attended.

"No," declared the surly miser. "I'm not giving my hard-earned money for any such purpose. I'll keep it where it belongs—in the bank."

"Listen, I know you are too old to change your ways," argued the generous one with a sigh. "But let me remind you of a Jewish proverb. It says in the Talmud—I don't remember exactly where—'Money is like fertilizer. It does no good unless it is spread around.'"

* * *

His full name was Marie Joseph Paul Yves Roch Gilbert du Motier, Marquis de Lafayette, but let us not hold that against him. The distinguished French general served with rare honor and courage in the American Revolution.

Among Lafayette's friends was Jacob Harte, a Baltimore merchant who loaned the General the sum of $7,256 with no more security than a handshake. Harte, who came to this country from Germany in 1775, was the father-in-law of Haym M. Salomon, son of the patriot Haym Salomon. But let us return to Jacob Harte.

"Jacob, my dear friend," said General Lafayette, "you need have no fears about the money I owe you. It will be repaid in full."

"I know that," replied Harte. "I have no fears whatsoever."

"You can be sure that every penny will be returned."

"Please, General, let us discuss it no further," said Harte with a wave of his hand. "I am not concerned about the repayment."

"My people have a very long history of honest dealing."

"All right already, you're an honest man," retorted Harte with some irritation.

"In fact," Lafayette persisted, "the records prove that my family goes back to Charlemagne, and I assure . . ."

"*Himmel*, enough is enough!" Harte interrupted. "My family lost its records in the Great Flood, but does that cast suspicion on me?"

* * *

Among the more interesting characters in American history was Mordecai Manuel Noah (1785-1851), writer, statesman and visionary; known to many as "Major Noah." Born in Philadelphia, he studied law but became a journalist and playwright. As a result of his worldwide travels and his diplomatic post in Tunis, North Africa, where he served as American consul (1813-1816), he became an advocate of Zionism. However, he realized that the creation of a Jewish state in Palestine was impractical at that time, so he conceived the idea of establishing a Jewish settlement at Grand Island, New York, near Buffalo. He named the proposed Jewish colony "Ararat," and on September 15, 1825, the foundation stone for the "City of Refuge for the Jews" was laid. But the plan was deemed fantastic and his appeal for followers and supporters was largely unanswered. The only remaining trace of this project is the foundation stone which is kept by the Buffalo Historical Society.

But Major Noah, it appears, was able to retain his sense of humor in the face of the almost universal hostility to his scheme for a Jewish State within the United States. In 1824, in an attempt to raise funds for the establishment of "Ararat," he traveled to Georgia where he made several vain efforts to meet with members of the influential Sheftall family who were not only wealthy but whose roots were established in the United States long before the Revolutionary War. The prestige of the Sheftall name would be almost as important as their money.

After a number of vain attempts to meet with the leading member of the famous family, and growing increasingly angry at the obvious snubs, Major Noah finally walked up the Sheftall mansion without an invitation and sounded the knocker on the door. When a servant responded, Noah wasted no time on preliminaries.

"Tell Mr. Sheftall I am here," he said, giving his name.

A few minutes later the servant reappeared. "I'm sorry," he apologized, "but Mr. Sheftall says he can't see you today. He has a sprained back."

"What kind of an excuse is that?" roared Noah in a voice that could be heard to the topmost rafters. "You go back and tell Sheftall that I just want to talk to him—I didn't come here to wrestle!"

22

Commerce and Trade

INTRODUCTION

American-Jewish business humor is characterized mainly by four rather unflattering elements: foolishness, cleverness, greed and resignation. I have excluded the designation of honesty because that attribute itself forms the general thrust of the jokes. One can be honest or dishonest at the same time that he is foolish, clever, greedy or resigned. Very few Jewish jokes laud dishonesty, but even in those rare instances where it does occur the emphasis lies elsewhere.

An old story tells of the man whose family was close to starvation and, in desperation, he stole an egg from a rich landowner who had 100 dozen eggs in his larder. But, goes the joke, the impoverished culprit did not feel he should have to bear the expense of cooking the egg on his own stove and was caught while frying it on the stove of the rich man.

In that illustration, of course, the thrust is upon the inequity of one man having nothing while another has more than he needs. This category of joke often goes to extremes, however, as in the following folk tale, obviously mythical, wherein the moral is *caveat emptor*—let the buyer beware.

In the year of 1879, shortly after he was appointed a justice of the State Supreme Court, Judge Robert Weiss purchased a lake-front summer home. One day, he and his wife, Faye, were sitting on the bank, in front of their residence when a stranger approached.

"I wish to cross over to the other side," explained the visitor. "Would you be kind enough to rent your boat to me? I will return with it before the day is over."

"Yes, of course," replied the judge.

The stranger paid the rental in advance and also left a substantial deposit to be returned when the boat was brought back. He then got into the boat, pushed off, and rowed away. A hundred yards off shore, the boat suddenly sank and the man drowned.

"Oh, Robert," cried Faye, "that was a terrible thing to do to that poor stranger—and after taking all that money, too! Why didn't you tell him that the boat had a hole in it?"

"Because," said Judge Weiss patiently, "the matter of the boat's condition was not brought before me."

The above bit of piracy, according to time-honored custom, is excusable on the ground that piracy is simply another name for business without its frills and customer relations departments—just as God made it.

But not all anti-heroes do so well as Judge Weiss. Consider the tragic story of Weinberg, the miller. Back in 1883, Weinberg made millions by extracting all the nutrients from his wheat flour and selling the bleached, white residue throughout the nation. Having saturated the market with his unwholesome product, he then packaged and sold the extracted wheat germ at a fancy profit to those whose health had failed by consuming the white flour.

Misfortune then struck—misfortune being the fortune that never misses. Weinberg tripped over his gold shoelaces one day and fell into a barrel of his own flour. He was then carted away by an unsuspecting wagoner and transported to Beckerman's Bakery where he was converted into 4,238 bagels at 29¢ per dozen, the going rate in those days. Thus, while the celestial choir sang, "Try a Little Tenderness," the nutritional value of Weinberg's flour was restored by a Power greater than his own, at no extra charge to the consumer.

The obvious moral is that unappetizing things happen to naughty people. But that is not the sole reason we are recording the two aforementioned stories. As you doubtless know, there is no letter W in the Hebrew alphabet. It follows, then, that neither Judge Weiss, Weinberg the miller, nor anyone else whose name is spelled with a W could possibly be Jewish. It is my studied opinion that all such persons (with the exception of Chaim Weizmann who, I am convinced, was really a Hindu) are actually "passing," having abandoned their natal religions in order to get a foot in the door of the dry goods business. Moreover, it is my further belief that jokes involving Jewish malefactors with a W in their names are Arab inventions whose sole purpose is to discredit the Jews, all of whom are trustworthy, loyal, helpful, friendly, courteous, kind, obedient, cheerful, thrifty, brave, clean and reverent—including those in jail.

The cries of anguish emanating from American manufacturers, usually accompanied by the shedding of copious tears acquired from the nearest crocodile farm, have for many decades served as a legitimate target for Jewish humor. This is especially true of such centers of commerce and trade as New York, Chicago and Los Angeles, where they have been most successful in the fine art of separating the fleece from the sheep in sheep's clothing. The producer's problem arises from the low tariff or scale of taxes placed on foreign-made goods. His complaint is that these import duties should be much higher in order to protect him from his greedy consumers.

It should be noted that the hostility which is evident in Jewish jokes involving commerce and trade is commonly directed toward "big business"—the larger corporations, cartels, national chain stores, and the like. But these very same jokes preserve a spirit akin to paternal affection and amused understanding for the small merchant who, in his never-ending struggle to remain afloat in the changing financial tides, displays an aptitude for competitive ingenuity and resourcefulness so dear to the Jewish heart. The effort need not even bring success: a man can be tripped by his own cleverness in this type of humor, just as long as the effort, *on the surface*, appears to be intelligent. An example is found in the shoe-biz caper that occurred in the Windy City not long ago:

Sid Michaelson, proprietor of the shoe store at the intersection of LaSalle and Washington in Chicago's loop, prided himself on his self-taught scholarship; that condition in which a person knows a little about a lot of subjects. It was his belief, for instance, that the word "mind" derived from the Latin *mens*. So, seized with an inspirational idea one morning, he proudly displayed a sign over the door of his shop with the motto, *Mens conscia recti*.

Across the street, Irv Gold, Sid's equally learned competitor, not to be outdone, emblazoned his window with his own sign: Men's, Women's and Children's conscia recti."

Another illustration of the lighthearted touch is apparent in a story that was popular during the depths of the Great Depression. A young man who suffered a nervous breakdown was sent by his parents to see a psychiatrist. After a lengthy and involved examination and series of tests, the doctor recommended that the youth be put someplace where he would not be disturbed . . . so they put him in business.

Now, having said all I know and don't know about the subject of commerce and trade, I refer you to the following anecdotes about those stalwarts who valiantly keep their shops and factories open during war and peace—peace being that period of fenaigling between two periods of fighting.

H.D.S.

The owner of a big textile plant hired one of those so-called efficiency experts to cut down on waste, speed up production and nail down loose ends.

Filled with self-importance and determined to exercise his authority, the expert made a tour of the factory on his very first day of employment. He had made his way through only one department, doing whatever it is that such people do for a living, when he came upon a spectacle that shocked his efficient being to its very core.

On a bench before him was a languid-looking young woman in a rumpled smock, busily engaged in sitting. That's all—just sitting. Only the jaws of this girl showed any signs of activity: she was masticating Juicy Fruit with a vigor that would have brought delight to Mr. Wrigley. Presently she stopped chewing, drew in her breath and blew an orange-sized bubble. Then she resumed her former posture of *rigor mortis*.

With mounting indignation the expert watched her. Then, approaching her, he fixed a stern, accusing eye upon the delinquent.

"See here, young lady," he snapped. "What do you think you're doing?"

"Who, me?" inquired the girl in a brilliant bit of repartee. "I ain't doin' nothin'."

"If you don't mind telling me, what do you expect to do when you get through doing nothing?"

"Nothin'."

"Well, what have you been doing?"

"Nothin'."

"And how long have you been sitting here doing nothing?"

The girl opened a cavernous mouth and yawned.

"I been sittin' here 'bout an hour—maybe an hour-an'-a-half."

"Is that so! How much do you earn a week?"

"Sixty-fi' dollars."

"Well," said the expert, "we'll stop that right now. When is your week up?"

"T'morrer."

"You needn't wait until tomorrow. You can go right now."

The efficiency man reached into his pocket, hauled out his own personal bankroll, peeled off six tens and a five and pressed the total into the sitting gum-chewer's outstretched hand.

"Here!" he rasped. "Take your money and get out of here. I don't ever want to see you inside this plant again."

"Yes sir," promised the young lady meekly. She rose from the bench, smiled a weak farewell and slouched out.

"I guess that's inaugurating a little rough-and-ready reform right at the outset," said the expert to himself. He beckoned to the foreman of the department and the latter came forward.

"Who is that girl I just chased out of here?" he asked.

"Her first name's Becky—that's all we ever called her. I don't know her last name," replied the foreman. "She works for Knickerbocker Fabrics downtown. She was waiting here for a receipt!"

* * *

There's a nice Biblical ring to the following announcement of the 1890s, reminiscent of Abraham's sacrifice:

Entire Stock of Clothing of Isaac a. Co's
—at a sacrifice—
by
Abraham

* * *

"These long-haired hippies will ruin me," moaned Sam the barber. "Just today one kid came into the shop and told me to take just a little off around the hips."

* * *

The American Jewish Committee decided to cut its budget, so the well-known efficiency expert, Dr. Felix Kaplan, was appointed to carry out the task.

Determined to reduce costs wherever possible, he snooped around the AJC offices, pencil and pad in hand, to see what he could learn.

On the first floor he found a clerk with his feet propped up on the desk, sipping a cup of coffee and reading a copy of *Commentary* magazine.

"Just what do you do here for a living?" asked the visibly irritated Dr. Kaplan.

"Just what it looks like—nothing!" came the answer.

Kaplan wrote it down on his pad and went to the second floor. There he found another clerk, also with his feet propped up on the desk. And he, too, was drinking coffee and reading *Commentary*.

"What are *you* doing to earn your keep?" demanded Kaplan.

"Nothing," replied the clerk.

"Ah-*hah!*" cried Dr. Kaplan triumphantly. "So that's what's wrong with AJC's labor force—duplication!"

* * *

Newsboy: Swindle! Big swindle! Read all about it! Thirty-nine victims!

Tightwad: Here's your money, boy. Gimme a paper . . . Hey, wait a minute—I don't see anything about a swindle!

Newsboy: Swindle! Big swindle! Forty victims!

* * *

Secretary of State Henry Kissinger had just returned from Peking where he had successfully concluded arrangements for a rapprochement between the Peoples Republic of China and the United States. In America, the business community hummed with anticipation as visions of immense trade with China appeared on the horizon.

At his curbside pushcart on Hester Street, Yankel perused the news account of Kissinger's trip, one eye on the *Forvertz* he was reading and the other on his display of merchandise.

A woman with slanted eyes, high cheekbones and yellow-tinted skin —clearly Oriental—stopped in front of his cart and speculatively fingered some of his goods.

"How much for this?" she asked.

"Missus, believe me, that goods is 60 cents a yard," he answered eagerly. "But for you I'll make it 40 cents—I want the China trade!"

* * *

Two cloak-and-suiters were complaining about the demands of the labor unions.

"It's gotten to the point where my own secretary is now on a four-day week," moaned one.

"So's mine," agreed the other sadly, "but it takes her six days to do the work."

"Well, at least they always hurry back to the office after their last coffee break," said the first boss. "They don't want to be late for quitting time."

* * *

Al Uhlman, sales manager for Aunt Bertha's Undies, Unlimited, was called into the big boss' office.

"Al, you're the smartest man we ever had in this company," the chief began. "You've demonstrated your ability by working your way up from rookie salesman to manager of the whole sales department in just two years. You've outsold all the other men combined. You know all there is to know about our whole line of undergarments and your suggestions for next year's line are really brilliant."

Al smiled, wondering how big his raise was going to be.

"Thank you, sir," he murmured with false humility.

"And so," concluded the boss, "you're fired!"

"*Fired!*" the sales manager gasped. "In heaven's name, what for?"

"I'll tell you what for!" exclaimed the boss, his voice rising. "It's guys like you who always start their own companies and give me all that *tsuris* with the buyers!"

* * *

Stanley, traveling for Fabulous Frocks of Flatbush, expected to be on the road for several weeks, so he had his mail forwarded to his Nashville customer, Leo Levy, of Lee's Ladieswear.

But no sooner did Stanley arrive at the store when Leo handed him a special delivery letter. He read the terse message and a pallor spread across his face.

"What's the matter?" asked Leo. "You look worried."

"It's my wife," explained Stanley. "She just had triplets. Holy mackerel—we never expected anything like this! And take a look at the size of this hospital bill!"

"Congratulations," said Leo, grinning. "Now you know how it feels to be billed for more merchandise than you ordered."

* * *

The season had been one of the worst in the garment manufacturer's memory. He was on the verge of bankruptcy.

"Miss Tellabenda," he called to his secretary, "get my broker on the phone."

"Which one?" she asked sprightly. "Stock or pawn?"

* * *

Old man Shlepper and his equally aged friend, Kolboynik, had known each other ever since they arrived together in the United States, some fifty years ago. Shlepper was in the used car business, Kolboynik in retail clothing, and they always made it a point to patronize each other—and always with a certain amount of haggling. After having kept up appearances, they would then enjoy a glass of *schnapps*.

A week or so before Passover, Shlepper came to see his old pal to buy a new suit. After some picking and choosing, a proper garment was selected.

"Well, here we go," sighed Shlepper from long experience. "How much?"

"For you—eighty dollars," replied Kolboynik. "A real steal."

"*Eighty dollars!* Of all the *chutzpah!* What do I look like—a *griener tuchus* from Ellis Island?"

"All right, don't carry on like a *meshuggeneh!* . . . Seventy dollars, and I'm losing money."

"Forty I'll give you; not a penny more."

"*Forty dollars!*" screeched Kolboynik. "You should be in a mental institution! That suit is *insured* for more than that!"

* * *

An ambitious young man once asked philosopher-statesman-financier Bernard Baruch if there was a formula that would absolutely guarantee success in business.

"Yes," replied Baruch. "Think up something that costs ten cents or less to make, sells for a dollar or more, and is habit-forming."

* * *

Berel the butcher from Williamsburg had been in this country for less than a year and was experiencing some difficulty with the English language. His friend, old Guri the grocer, had arrived in the United States 15 years earlier and often helped Berel with his linguistic problems.

One afternoon, when they met for lunch, Berel brought up a subject that had perplexed him for days.

"Guri," he asked, "what means 'recession' and 'depression'? There's a difference?"

"Of course," said Guri patiently. "To tell the truth, they both mean *gehakhta tsuris*, but people interpret it differently. For instance, if you lost your job, that would be a recession. But if I lost mine, *that*, my friend, would be a depression!"

* * *

"Grandpa, listen to what it says here in the morning paper," cried Herbert. "The price of postage is going up again!"

Grandpa shook his head. "I just don't understand those people in Washington," he said dolefully. "If I was running the Post Office Department, instead of increasing the cost of postage I'd just decrease the size of the stamps."

* * *

Paul Muni took great delight in narrating this minor adventure story. It happened in his earlier years when he was playing an engagement in Chicago. One day he went for a stroll along South Clark Street and came to a district of second-hand clothing shops. A sight that greeted him there sent him back with great haste to find three of his friends and take them with him to help him enjoy his discovery.

They halted in front of a store window filled with garments bearing seductively worded legends purporting to represent that these offerings had been cast back upon the makers' hands through no fault of their own but rather because of the captiousness of the original purchaser.

The words "Misfit," "Not Claimed," "Tailor's Sample" and so on, recurred time and again. But in the central display, originality in the gentle art of advertising phraseology had scored a triumph. Behind the glass dangled a pair of trousers of a most startling cut and an even more startling pattern. The colors fairly leaped through the window to smite the passerby in the eye. To the garment was affixed a card bearing the statement:

THESE PANTS WERE UNCALLED FOR

* * *

Now that his oldest boy was of age, the father changed the sign over the store from "Kaplan's" to "Kaplan & Son."

"Well, well," commented the neighboring storekeeper, "you and your son are now carrying on the business together?"

"Fifty-fifty," Kaplan grunted. "I run the business and my son does the carrying-on."

* * *

Mr. Birnbaum, sales manager for Modern Men's Clothes of New York, was returning to America after a business trip to Israel. On the way back, he decided to stop off in Rome and take in the sights. Two weeks later, he finally arrived home.

"How was the trip?" asked the big boss.

Fantastic!" enthused Birnbaum. "In Israel I sold a thousand more suits than any of us expected. Then I stopped off in Rome and saw all the historical sights. I got in with a sight-seeing group and we had an audience with the Pope."

"The Pope himself? You don't say!" marveled the boss. "What does he look like?"

"Oh," ventured Birnbaum, "I'd say about a 38-short."

* * *

"Hello, Ralph. How's by you?"

"Don't talk to me!"

"Hey, what's the matter?"

"Did you or didn't you sell me the shop as a going business?"

"I did."

"Well, it's gone!"

* * *

Mr. Zabarsky was sole owner of My Cups Runneth Over Manufacturing Company, the giant producer of high fashion brassieres. So it was no wonder that the foreman of the shipping department was somewhat nervous when he was handed a note from Zabarsky—Mr. Z himself.

With trembling hands he opened the envelope. Then he gulped as he read the message:

I'm sending my son to your department so he can learn the business from the ground up. But don't show him any favoritism. I want you to treat him like any other son of mine.

* * *

When Morris, the insurance broker, heard there were no agents within 200 miles of Broken Bottle, Wyoming, he was overjoyed. "At last!" he exulted. "No competition and a wide-open field!" Within a week he left New York and opened his new insurance office over the Broken Bottle Saloon.

On his first day of business, a cowboy applied for a policy.

"Have you had any recent accidents?" asked Morris as he busily filled in the insurance form.

"Nope."

"Well, have you had any accidents at all in your life?"

"Nary a one, unless you count the time a steer once busted most of my ribs and a sidewinder set his durn fangs in me."

"For heaven's sake!" Morris exclaimed. "Wouldn't you call those accidents?"

"No, I shore wouldn't," drawled the cowpoke. "Them varmints done it apurpose!"

* * *

The clothier was boasting about the sagacity of his new sales assistant.

"That fellow Eisenman I just hired is the smartest guy who ever worked in this store. You don't believe me? Listen: only yesterday there comes in here a poor woman whose husband just died. She wanted a cheap suit, but nice-looking, to bury the corpse in.

"So what did Eisenman do? I'll tell you what Eisenman did: he not only sold her the most expensive suit we had in stock but he got her to buy an extra pair of pants!"

23

Yiddishe Blarney in the Workaday World

INTRODUCTION

The dignity of honest toil has long been rooted in Jewish history. Indeed, the work ethic has been associated with Judaism ever since the Pharaoh commanded the Israelites to make bricks from straw. The edict did not meet with their enthusiastic approval. "You gotta be kiddin'!" they protested to the Strawboss of the Nile. The controversy led to the first organized labor dispute of record. They walked off the job and kept on walking for forty years.

Having reached their own homeland (and never mind what the Arabs claim), the Decalogue served as a handy labor-management device with which to shaft the bosses of the day. The ancients formed two unions, each consisting of six locals, or tribes. In Israel, there was the COI (Chosen Ones, Industrialwise), later changed to the CIO to accommodate the Unchosen Ones. There was also the AF of L (Ashkenazic Federation of Litvaks), whose hiring hall was in Judea. Additionally, there was a 13th local, or tribe, comprised of Galitzianers, but they signed a sweetheart contract with the indigenous management, and were not heard from again until they surfaced in New York to establish the costume jewelry business. The lost local's motto was: *Ver Fahrblunjhet!*

Then came King Solomon with big ideas for the construction of hanging gardens and a splendid palace with a thousand master bedrooms, each with a golden sink so his pampered wives could do the dishes in bed. Now, Sol wasn't a bad sort of fellow if you didn't get to know him, but the unauthorized demands for fringe benefits and other aggravations he suffered from the hired help soon gave him a royal pain in the assets. So he decided to have it out with the architect—once and for all.

"Now see here, Archie," Sol began, "I don't want you to think I forgot my campaign promises or that I'm anti-union, but the place you selected for my garden is so hot, it even killed my artificial flowers. Then, there's the problem with the plumbing. I know I ordered running water in every room, but who needs it should run down from the ceiling? Another thing, I didn't complain when the goldfish pond caught fire and burned to the ground, but whoever heard of going downstairs to get to the attic? This is efficiency by you?"

It pains us to report that Sol's trouble didn't end there. When he moved into the palace and carried his thousandth bride over the threshold, the poor man got a hernia.

In America, the organized labor tradition not only continued, but reached new heights. It also reached new lows, depending on which side of the bargaining table you happened to occupy. It even invaded the hallowed temples of worship. The following vignette is an illustration:

Cantor Rosenblatt, accompanied by two burly workmen in overalls, entered the synagogue a few minutes before services were to begin. He introduced the strangers to the rabbi: "This is Pat Murphy, and this man is Mike O'Sullivan."

Puzzled, the rabbi drew Rosenblatt aside. "Why did you bring them here, of all places?" he asked.

"Who had a choice?" the cantor replied dolefully. "Last week I bought a new hearing aid, and the union ordered I should hire two electricians!"

But, to give the labor organizers their due, they themselves realize that their demands can sometimes jeopardize management's financial stability. Consider the case of Mannie Manischevitz, mogul of the baking empire. After a month of negotiations in which neither side would yield, Mannie finally caved in to the union's demands.

"Okay, you win," he told the bargaining agent. "The employees get the ten-dollar-an-hour minimum wage with an escalator clause, 60 days a year paid sick-leave, with three-months paid maternity leave for men as well as women, retirement at full salary at age 38, a 20-hour work week, and 20-minute coffee break every hour—all clauses guaranteed by the management."

"I'm sorry, but our membership will need one more guarantee," said the union agent brusquely. "With all those corporate expenses, we'll require a guarantee that you won't go broke!"

Jewish workaday humor does not exclude the onerous household chore. Unlike the man of wealth, the ordinary citizen can always find work that needs doing at home. The rich man, for example, may boast of a fine, dry wine cellar, but the average workingman's basement is so damp he can't even set a mousetrap down there for fear of catching a herring. Then there's the electric appliance that always needs fixing. Usually it's the toaster that works on A.C. or D.C., but not on bread. It goes without saying that disaster enters the picture when terrified little Rosie rushes into the house yelling, "Mommy, Mommy! Daddy just fell off the roof!" And Mommy answers pleasantly, "I know, Rosie dear. I just saw him pass the window."

Jewish humor also allows the hapless victim to complain about the complaint department. It permits him to confess, "I like my job; it's just the work I hate." What he cannot smite he bites—with a sharp-toothed quip.

Even his annual two-week vacation is not immune. The hotel's condescending desk clerk who asks, "Do you have a reservation?" is slapped down with the retort, "What do I look like, an Indian?"

The bellboy, with his ever-present palm extended, is another target. "Carry your bag, sir?" The hotel guest glares and squelches him with, "No, let her walk!"

Back home again, the weary, unrested vacationer indulges in some rueful recollections. "The hotel was so big," he muses, "that by the time I got from the lobby to my room, I owed for another day. I even had to dial long distance to call the desk. And the arrogant waiters in the hotel's dining room! I had a tip-top waiter. If I didn't tip, he blew his top. I remember asking him how to get to the washroom, and he snarled, "Mister, this is no place to do your laundry!" Even the water he served was positively cloudy, and I told him so. But he just brushed aside my complaint. "The water's okay, go ahead and drink it," he assured me. "It's just the glass that's dirty!"

Another guy we can't fight, but whom we can smite with a derisive joke is the frozen-faced boss with a heart to match. It's the familiar old story: he is free to joke and ridicule at your expense, but you dare not reply in kind. Jewish humor, particularly the audacious *American*-Jewish humor, provides the outlet for marvelous escapist fantasies. The boss calls you into his office in the morning when business is so quiet you can hear the overhead piling up. You are dying to say, "Don't worry, boss, business is always slow at this hour, but it's sure to drop off in the afternoon." Instead, you maintain a discreet silence. With his usual rasp, the boss launches into the subject at hand—*you:*

"This is just a suggestion and you don't have to follow it, unless, of course, you don't want to keep your job."

Then comes your moment of triumph. You've had all you can take from this pompous ass, you should pardon the expression, and so you give it to him straight from the clavicle:

"Sir—and I use the title advisedly—my aptitude test shows that I'm best suited for prolonged vacations. I quit!"

For the first time since you've known him, he actually smiles.

"Are you really quitting?" he croons, "or are you just trying to brighten my day?"

The incorrigible old reprobate! He simply *must* have the last word! You feel like telling him your only regret about quitting is that now you'll be drinking coffee on your own time, but you have an uneasy feeling he'll top that one, too. He's had more practice with the put-down than you. So, on your way out, you slam the door and yell, "Goodbye, Fido! Don't forget to give your mother a bone!"

No, it isn't like that in the real workaday world, but that's the way it is in Jewish humor—bless it!

H.D.S.

The owner of a closed union shop was on an inspection tour of his fabricating plant when a large scaffold accidently toppled over and landed on him, pinioning him beneath the wooden structure.

"Help!" he yelled to an electrician who was working nearby. "Get this thing off me!"

"Sorry, but you'll have to ask a carpenter," apologized the electrician. "My union doesn't allow me."

* * *

Your grandparents laughed at this one, and we pass it along so that your own grandchildren will enjoy hearing it from you.

In 1916, President Wilson appointed Louis Dembitz Brandeis to serve as a Justice of the United States Supreme Court. In due time, Judge Brandeis found a suitable residence in the Georgetown area of the District of Columbia. It was a lovely, post bellum house and the eminent Justice-scholar-Zionist was very pleased with it. But he had no sooner taken possession of his new home when he learned, to his chagrin, that the most important element of the plumbing system was not in proper functioning order; or, to put it indelicately, the toilet drain was stopped up.

But let the departed spirit of Judge Brandeis tell the story as he himself related it so long ago:

"The plumber who was recommended to me was an individual named Plotnik who combined the practice of a rather unromantic calling with a poetic temperament. Even in the midst of his professional labors he was much given to studding his conversation with quotations from the poets. Rarely did an occasion arise when he was at a loss for a classic reference.

"The plumber arrived at my home equipped with the tools of his trade. He removed the coupling of the drain where it connected with the bowl and then, for several long moments, he paused to contemplate the situation. The job was of such a magnitude as to temporarily abash even so experienced a hand as Plotnik. Slowly, almost reluctantly, he rolled up his sleeves, at the same time dubiously eyeing the prospect that confronted him. And, as he contemplated the fearsome project, the most horrible, disgusting, nauseating, sickening stench billowed forth from the drain pipe.

"Kneeling beside the bowl, Plotnik the plumber looked up at me, standing above him, and he shook his head. Then, in all that foul miasma, he said:

"'Well, Judge Brandeis, I suppose I might as well get started. Faint heart ne'er won fair lady!'"

* * *

Melvin and a co-worker were at lunch in *Lottie's Latke and Leber Luau*, on Fairfax Avenue in Los Angeles. As usual, Melvin was complaining about his boss.

"That man is so dumb he can't spell DDT," he grumbled. "He thinks a blood vessel is some kind of Red Cross ship."

"You oughtta be glad he's so dumb," said his co-worker, shrugging. "If he was any smarter he'd fire you!"

* * *

Pauline had been hired as the new secretary only two weeks earlier, but already she was having notions about her handsome boss. What worried her, though, was that he was engaged. Oh well, a girl can dream, can't she?

One morning, Mr. Right called her into his office to take some dictation. His fiancée was visiting her mother in another city and he had promised to write regularly. Dutifully, he dictated a warm and affectionate letter.

Pauline expertly took it all down in her flawless shorthand, went back to her desk to type the letter and then brought it to her boss for his signature.

"What's this?" he snapped as he was about to sign it. "You left out 'I love you.'"

"Oh," she whispered in her best sultry voice, "I thought you had stopped dictating."

* * *

It was the salesman's first day out pounding the pavements. He returned to the office that evening and was greeted by the sales manager:

"Get any orders?"

"Two," moaned the unhappy huckster: "'Get out!' and 'Stay out!'"

* * *

Bang the cymbals, twang the lyre! Hackensack is checking in with one.

Hal Bruck, sales manager for the New Jersey Jobbing Company, distributors of tobacco products, candy and other vital necessities, assembled all the salesmen on his staff for a meeting.

"Gentlemen," Hal began, "I've called you together to announce a big sales contest—the most important one our company has ever conducted. It will run for eight weeks and each of you has an equal chance to hit the jackpot."

The salesmen, naturally, were excited at this rare opportunity. From the rear of the room an eager voice rang out:

"What does the winner get?"

"The winner," declared Hal, "gets to keep his job!"

* * *

Eighteen-year-old Walter—that stalwart member of the Great Unwashed—sauntered into the State Employment Office and informed the placement clerk that he would consider a position in keeping with his sense of values and philosophy.

The employment couselor stared at the long-haired youth, noted the holes and patches in his faded, unfragrant jeans, and regarded his four-inch unkempt whiskers.

"I'm not sure we have anything in your line," she finally said. "Tell me, what have you done?"

"Who, me?" exclaimed the puzzled young man. "About what?"

* * *

Sammy the labor leader, age fifty-one, had been a widower for five years and now he wanted to marry again. So he went to one of those Jewish introduction firms with fancy computers that are advertised to match personalities "and make your dream come true with a scientifically selected mate."

Sammy took one look at the computers and demanded: "Is this a union shop?"

"Certainly," said the manager. "*Shadchans* Local 102."

"All right, then, let's see some pictures."

The manager brought out a large album and Sammy glanced through the pages until he came upon the photograph of a curvaceous young lady of about twenty-four.

"Here's the one for me," he announced. "Wrap 'er up."

"Sorry, but you'll have to take Mrs. Umglik instead," declared the manager, pointing to the photo of a wrinkled, toothless old crone, clearly a widowed great-grandmother of Napoleonic vintage.

"*A klug tsu Columbus!*" howled the outraged labor leader. "What the hell for?"

"Because this is a union shop," explained the manager, "and this one has seniority!"

* * *

"It really doesn't pay to hire relatives," moaned Bernie the furrier. "Only last week I hired my niece as a bookkeeper and the first thing she did was to bring me a column of figures with a wrong answer. So I told her to go back and add it up again five times. After about an hour she came into my office and gave me the results—five different answers!"

* * *

Finkel, employed by Amalgamated Clothing Company, timidly knocked on the boss's office door.

"Come in, it ain't locked!" hollered Mr. Amalgamated.

Finkel shuffled over to the boss's desk and, in his usual diffident manner, asked for a raise in pay.

"After all," he added, summoning up what little boldness he possessed, "I'm entitled. I have twenty years experience."

"Finkel, you ain't had twenty years experience," barked the brains of Amalgamated. "You've had one year's experience twenty times!"·

* * *

The shop foreman, irritation showing plainly in his face, strode over to Sheldon, a hippie.

"Listen," he grated, "do me and everyone else in the shop a big favor and quit whistling while you work."

"Hey, man," retorted Sheldon defensively, "who's working?"

* * *

In September, 1974, William Roth, president of Queensborough Woollens, Inc., put up a sign on the bulletin board which the International Ladies Garment Workers Union found offensive. The union jumped all over him and made him take it down, but the announcement was salvaged for posterity:

ATTENTION, ALL EMPLOYEES!

It would be appreciated by the management if, somewhere between starting and quitting time—without infringing on lunch time, coffee breaks, rest periods, ticket-selling and vacation planning—each employee finds some time that can be devoted to what we, in our old-fashioned way, like to call the Work Break.

It is our earnest opinion that this will be an aid to steady employment and regular pay checks, and it is our hope that each employee will give it a fair trial.

* * *

Bella the bookkeeper was due at the office at eight-thirty sharp, but this morning she sauntered in at nine. There was an indefinable something in her manner that seemed to indicate that her tardiness was deliberate.

"Good afternoon, your highness," greeted the boss, his voice oozing sarcasm. "This is the earliest you've ever been late."

"My dear Mr. Bergdorf," replied Bella coolly, "I'm giving it to you straight from the elbow. When a person does not like another person she does not have to work for such a person. To be employed here is no longer my glass of tea."

"You mean you're quitting because there's somebody here you don't like?" he asked, genuinely surprised.

"Precisely, Mr. Bergdorf."

"Who?"

"You, Mr. Bergdorf!"

* * *

Lazy Herschel slouched into the State Employment Office and asked for a job.

"How long have you been out of work?" asked the placement clerk.

"I dunno," answered Herschel. "I lost my birth certificate."

* * *

The young man had just graduated from the New York College of Optometry and was lucky enough to find an immediate position at "Cheap Charlie's—the Eyeglass King of Mosholu Parkway."

"The rules around here are very simple," instructed Charlie. "When a customer comes in for a pair of glasses, you must first get the examination part over with as soon as possible. Then show him a few samples, always starting off with the most expensive frames we have."

"Okay," agreed the neophyte, "but I don't see any price tags. How much do I charge?"

"We don't have a set price," explained Charlie. "When the customer asks you the cost, just tell him 'forty dollars.' If he accepts without saying anything, you add, 'That's for the frames—the lenses are ten dollars more.' And if he still doesn't complain, you say, 'each!'"

* * *

Izzy, the top salesman for a large publishing house, returned to the New York office after a book-selling journey to the West Coast where he had called on the distributors and retailers in the trade. Pleased with the results of his trip, he triumphantly laid a batch of orders on the desk of his boss and then presented him with his expense account.

The boss scanned the expense sheet for a few long moments and then glanced up at the salesman who was hovering over him.

"Look, Izzy," he said, "I'll okay this expense account on one condition—that you give me the fiction rights!"

* * *

The recent college grad found a job and, after working for a whole week without a raise in pay, went to the boss to find out why he had been so sorely neglected.

"Now just a herring-pickin' minute!" protested the boss. "You can't just waltz into my office like this and ask for a raise. You have to be like everyone else around here and work yourself up."

"Work myself up!" echoed the young fellow indignantly. "Whaddya think I been doing for the past hour? Look, I'm trembling all over!"

* * *

Monty Segal, of the Segal Mail Order Company in Chicago, tells of the time he caught one of his typists asleep at her desk—for the third time. Apparently the young lady enjoyed partying until the wee small hours and caught up on her beauty sleep during the daylight hours of nine to five. Monty shook her gently.

"I'm sorry, Miss Goldilox," he said apologetically. "I wouldn't wake you up like this if it weren't something important . . . You're fired!"

* * *

The distinguished Guggenheim family, prominent in metal smelting and refining, as well as in philanthropy, was founded by Meyer Guggenheim who came to the United States from Switzerland in 1847, when he was 19 years old. He started out as a peddler, eventually entered the embroidery importing business and then bought a mine in Colorado. From that point on his industrial empire grew.

But we are concerned here with Meyer Guggenheim's first venture into business in America, when he trudged through the mining towns of Pennsylvania with a pack on his back, selling stove polish, ribbons, thread and a few other items, such as spices and lace.

It was a cool autumn day in the year 1848 when young Guggenheim, his peddler's knapsack secured to his aching back, turned into the short road leading to a farmhouse. At once he noticed that the roof of the house was ablaze. He gesticulated wildly to an elderly woman who was standing in the doorway.

"Lady, lady!" he yelled. "Your houze iss alreatty on vire!"

"What?"

"Your houze is burning."

"Wha'ja say? I'm a leedle deef."

"I said your houze iss ge-full mit vire."

"Oh, is that all?"

"Vell," said Guggenheim, taken aback, "dot's all I can t'ink of right now."

24

Keeping Up With the Kohnses

INTRODUCTION

The average American of the Jewish faith has prospered since those days when he lived in an East Side flat overlooking the rent. A few have even attained wealth, and therein lies a paradox: the rich man is often someone you like better the more you see him less. He worships bigness. Even his bank is so huge it has a special window for robbers. That enormous house he owns is another example: if you happen to be in the living room and you gotta go, you'll just make it. And have you ever seen those 18-inch *mazuzahs* on his front portal? He keeps his checkbooks in them.

It is a fact to be regretted, but too many of our wealthy *landsleit* have forgotten when they were so poor they could afford to buy only one shoe at a time, or had to walk to the opera to save carfare. And they have the *chutzpah* to laugh and invent little jokes about the poor, yet! It makes you wonder how some people can look so clean and laugh so dirty. The rich man will grin and tell you that in these hard times you should be happy about your poverty because it's so inexpensive. "Poverty," he will announce like *Moishe Rebbenu* with the tablets, "is the one thing money can't buy."

So you ask him for a little financial help: "Can you lend me a fiver for a week, old boy?" And he makes with another flippant retort: "What does a week-old boy need with a fiver?" Witticisms like that you don't need, so you tell him he should only live to be so old as his jokes. What that Wall Streeter neglects to tell you is that he was fooling around with the birds and the bees instead of the bulls and the bears. He put half of his money in revolving doors and half in Ex Lax, and was cleaned out before he could turn around. It's different with small investors like us. We buy a little stock in a company that pays quarterly dividends, and every three months they send us a quarter. *Nu*, go fight the Stock Exchange!

A few of the *nouveaux* Rolls Roycers now have unlisted wives. But Jewish humor has long espoused equal rights for women—it clobbers the female as well as the male—especially the affluent lady who pays her

Diner's Club card with her American Express card. She's the woman who goes to the corner store and buys two corners. The less well-heeled observer, particularly if his credit is so bad the stores won't even accept his cash, views her as a pampered pet who would fall down and *plotz* from sheer fright if her fortune cookie contradicted her horoscope. Yet, he's fascinated with her because she never opens her mouth—she's had so many face lifts she talks through her eyes. As for her pompous, rich hubby, the poor man sees him as an arrogant braggart, a selfish *chozzer*, a snob and a first-class exploiter—and those are his *good* points!

The difference between the Jewish woman of means and her poor working sister is even apparent in (how shall I phrase it?) their climactic heights of intimacy. Velma van Papilary moans, "Oh, Myron, we just can't go on like this, as if we were strangers. All you want is my body." Sophie the sewing machine girl groans: "*Oy*, Jake, stop this very instant —I forgot the Pill! Jake, *stop*! You're deaf all of a sudden? Jake, I'm ordering you, st . . . *Oyyy*, Jaaake!"

The opposing attitudes between the haves and wish-they-hads include such esoteric preferences as, of all things, birds! For example, the wealthy American Jew likes the Tarrytown titwillow; the poor one settles for little Rubin redbreast. The rich man is smitten with the fortnightly nightingale; the working man is happy with the Israeli six-day warbler. The man of means adores the Bar Harbor bluebird; the poor man is contented with the Bronx blueberg, to say nothing of the Golan Heights goldberg. And the rich man loves the California condor; while the poor man, in his patriotic zeal, is happy with America's national symbol, the bald-headed siegel.

These jokes, of course, do not pretend to mirror the lifestyle of the privileged classes, but rather how we think they live—or ought to live. And underlying all this satirical humor is its theme of equality. We can almost hear a biblical Israelite protesting: "So enlighten me, mister *balaboosteh*! Who gave you permission you should eat *challeh* while I get stuck with all the manna? And where does it say I must *walk* to Jericho in this desert for 40 years while you ride around on a camel, *noch?* You, too, were born in the bulrushes you should be maybe more chosen than the rest of us?"

The monetary disparity between the rich and the poor has long been a staple of European-Jewish humor. In the United States, its gets downright hilarious. When Mr. ShapEYEro, for instance, loses on the stock market, it means his 7-Up dropped 2-down—but if *you* drop anything in the market it's because your shopping bag broke. What makes it such a coincidence is that ITT and your shopping bag split on the same day. Rich people, of course, don't shop at supermarkets or buy from Pincus the pushcart peddler. Instead, they patronize those fancy shoppes where they sell gifts you wouldn't have as a gift, including barometers made in Japan so you should always know when it's raining in Yokahama. Those Park Avenue shoppes even have a specialty grocery department where Mrs. LevEYEne buys steak, caviar and truffles—for Fifi, her French poodle!

Should you make the mistake of entering one of those exclusive shoppes in search of a wash-and-wear mink coat for your wife, don't even bother asking. Better to go see Pincus who'll sell you an Indian washing machine—a rock. You don't think your wife would be too impressed with such a gift, so you settle for a ring with a stone that's so tiny you need a magnifying glass to see it. Your wife complains, "Why did you buy me such a small diamond?" And that quick Jewish mind of yours is ready with a plausible answer: "Because, honey, I didn't want the glare to hurt your eyes."

If you are like most of us, you have enough money to last you a lifetime—unless you buy something. That "something" is usually an automobile. Actually, for those who are intent on keeping up with the Kohnses, it isn't a cheaper car that's wanted, but an expensive car that costs less. But rich folks have their problems, too. Every time Mr. Kohn's auto is in the middle of a car wash, his dashboard phone starts ringing. With you, it's different. Your wife wants a mink stole and you want a car. So you compromise—you get the mink stole and keep it in the garage. I know just how you feel, friend. When she demands a foreign convertible, you'd secretly like to buy her a rickshaw.

A very brief parable, please. Two goldfish in a bowl were having an argument about religion. Finally, one said in disgust: "But if there's no God, who changes the water every day?" My point is this: In Jewish humor, the differences between the Jews, like those goldfish, are outweighed by their similarities. Rich or poor, their responses are much the same. Wealthy or not, a Jewish boy becomes a man on his 13th birthday when he stops asking his father for money and requests a loan. *Yiddishe* mamas are also the same. In Texas, mama tells her kids, "Be careful when you go to school today, children. We had another well come in last night and it's slippery out." And in New York, mama is finding out that English is a funny language. A fat chance and a slim chance mean the same thing. When you're tight, your tongue's loose. Her educated daughter tells her, "Mama, your main trouble is with your vowels." And mama replies anxiously, "Maybe I should see a doctor."

But, whether you bought your wife that lovely fur coat or whether you killed it yourself, this chapter is for you!

H.D.S.

The fancy-shmancy Fagins of Mamaroneck have a perfect marriage, according to that authoritative and distinguished journal, the *Yonkers Daily Yenta*. He's got what it takes and she takes what he's got.

* * *

Two brothers-in-law, Sol and Myer, were intensely jealous of each other's business successes and, as a result, the competition between them always raged at fever pitch. Even their wives, sisters though they were, joined in the rivalry.

One evening, when Sol returned home from the office, his wife greeted him with some disconcerting news.

"That sister of mine told me today that Myer just bought the latest model Cadillac," she cried, almost tearfully.

"Oh, he did, did he?" growled Sol, heretofore the proud owner of a Chevy. "Well, the first thing tomorrow morning we'll buy a Lincoln Continental. That'll show him who's who and what's what!"

Myer's wife soon learned from her sister that their social status was again quo, with Sol now a little quoer, alas. Upon hearing of this act of one-upmanship, Myer waxed wroth indeed, and proceeded to grow wrother by the hour. The very next day, he had a telephone installed in his Cadillac.

"Now," exulted Myer, "let that cheap chiseler beat this!"

Myer's wife, of course, could scarcely wait to tell her sister about the engineering coup.

As might be expected, Sol immediately had a phone installed in *his* car. This time, however, he decided to do a little gloating. So he made a call to his brother-in-law.

"Hello, Myer," he crowed, "this is Sol. I'm calling your Cadillac from my Lincoln Continental. Just thought I'd let you know I have a phone in my car, too."

"Glad to hear from you, Sol," answered Myer briskly, "but, say, would you mind holding the wire for a minute? I'm on another line!"

* * *

From our Entrancing Trivia Department: The Internal Revenue Bureau knows just what to give the man who has everything—an audit!

* * *

Mrs. Guggenheim and Mrs. Loeb, members of the Park Avenue Dividend and Capital Gains Chapter, Hadassah, attended a symphony concert sponsored by their chapter to raise money for the poor on West End Avenue. Both were music lovers and listened to nothing but classical offerings, in contradistinction to the cheap, vulgar kind lesser mortals usually enjoy. They adjusted their jewels, tuned up their hearing aids and settled back in their seats to enjoy the concert.

To their surprise, the orchestra swung into a soothing rendition of *Stardust*, albeit dressed up in a Wagnerian arrangement. Neither Mrs. Guggenheim nor Mrs. Loeb recognized it. There seemed to be something vaguely familiar about the main theme but they were unable to recall it, try as they did.

"I wish we had thought to get programs as we came in," said Mrs. Guggenheim in a well-bred whisper.

"So do I," agreed Mrs. Loeb. "But it wouldn't have done me much good anyway, even if I had remembered to get a program. I left my reading glasses at home."

"Oh, I did want to know the name of that refrain," sighed Lady Guggenheim. "Look, there's a printed sign beside the stage—probably an announcement."

"Yes, I see it, dear, but without my glasses I can't quite make it out. Your eyes are better than mine—can you read the title of that haunting refrain?"

Mrs. Guggenheim squinted through her lorgnette.

"Ah, yes, it gives the name of the refrain," she murmured. "I never heard it before. I imagine it's from one of the lesser known operas. It's called *Refrain from Spitting!*"

* * *

Now that her papa had made it big in the kosher-leather shoe business, teenaged Lisa decided to break into "society." The best way to demonstrate her new breeding, she felt, was to inject a few well-chosen French words into her everyday conversation. So she bought a French-English dictionary.

A few evenings later, as she and her family were watching television, President Ford was shown speaking a few words to the Ambassador of France, and conversing in the Ambassador's own tongue. When Ford finished his brief comments, the girl's father turned to her.

"*Nu*, Lisa, you're the expert around here since last week. Tell me, does the President speak good French?"

"Papa, believe me, I'm really too-too shocked," murmured Lisa in her newly-acquired ladylike manner. "He made not one, not two, not three, but *faux pas!*"

* * *

Sol Lapidus never did change his miserly ways after he became rich. When he was poor he knew where his wife hid her nickels and dimes. Now that he's wealthy he knows where the maid's quarters are.

* * *

Becky, a five-year-old little girl, lived with her parents on the East Side of New York. Her rich cousin, Frieda (now Frederika), who was six, lived in a mansion near Halfshell-on-the-Hudson. One day, the wealthy part of the family invited their poor relations to spend the day at their estate. Becky and Frederika met for the first time.

"Tan oo say 'Dere was a 'ittle dirl an' she had a 'ittle turl inner forrid?'" asked Becky.

"Perhaps not in the prescribed phraseology," replied Frederika. "If memory serves me correctly, it runs about as follows: 'At a recent period in the annals of organized society, there existed a diminutive feminine specimen of the human family whose conspicuous decoration was a capillary spiral appendage of minute dimensions descending perpendicularly from the forefront of her head. When she was amiably disposed, she produced the impression of being excessively agreeable, but when she abandoned herself to the natural inclinations of an unregenerate spirit, her deportment became unacceptable.'"

"Oh, wow!" exclaimed Becky, wide-eyed with admiration and curiosity. "How tum oo know Jewish so good?"

* * *

Newly-created socialite Mrs. Yetta Yifnif adjusted her monacle and smiled at Carl Sandburg, her guest of honor at the literary tea.

"I'll tell you a secret," she commented to the famous author. "Mine favorite writers are George Boinard Schwartz and Stephen Vincent B'nai B'rith."

* * *

Another Mrs. Yifnif story:

Now that she was rich, Yetta Yifnif bought a French poodle, dyed it pink like the other fancy poodles in the new neighborhood, and joined the Larchmont Kennel Club. She then entered her poodle in the forthcoming show for purebreds.

As the handlers prepared the pampered canines for the showing, the Ladies Poodle Society members got together in the clubhouse for cocktails. Proudly they discussed their entries: Henri, Andre, Babette, Lamour and Suzette.

"Mine poodle's name is Fido," said Mrs. Yifnif.

"Fido!" they exclaimed. "What kind of French name is that?"

"By me it's very French," replied Mrs. Yifnif huffily. "On the registration papers I'm spelling it P-h-i-d-e-a-u-x."

* * *

"Beulah, did you clean out the refrigerator like I told you?" Mrs. Schmaltzbottom asked the new maid.

"Yes'm," said Beulah. "An' I gotta admit, the filet mignon an' the champagne wuz delicious!"

* * *

They were an old established family of bankers and great merchants, the descendants of the German-Jewish peddlers of the 1840s who, by diligence, brains, luck and pluck, created vast financial empires. The particular branch of this much-intermarried clan was named Kuhn-Loeb, a nicely-hyphenated euphemistic cognomen even without the familiar "Inc."

These Park Avenue Kuhn-Loebs had a seven-year-old son who had been carefully reared, as would be expected. His manners were impeccable, his language ditto. He was the pride of his mother's heart, the envy of all mothers in the neighborhood of Park Avenue, Fifth Avenue, Central Park West and adjacent areas where never is heard a Yiddishe word. He was, in short, a model and a pattern for other youngsters of his age.

But Clarence—wouldn't you just know?—was in some respects like everybody else. He was, after all, human, or close to it. So it was inevitable that he would slip just once. Having thus slipped, he sought, with lagging steps and drooping head, the presence of his mother. Carefully, he averted his face so that she could not see the greenish complexion with which it was now decorated. But as he came near she caught the odor of tobacco on his breath.

"Oh, Clarence!" she cried. "Naughty-naughty! You've been smoking! You'll be sick!"

Politely but wanly, Clarence made reply:

"Sick, mother dear? Hell, I'm dying!"

* * *

In the year 1915, Ben Margulies was well along on the road to becoming a hardware magnate, although he could not know, of course, that World War I would earn him additional millions within a few years. But to the day of his death in 1939, at the age of 80, and despite his great wealth, he remained a simple, good-natured and well-liked man. The story that is told about him and his wife sounds almost too good to be true, yet there is a ring of verisimilitude about it. Judge for yourself.

Unlike her husband, Mrs. Margulies had a ball bearing jaw. One day in June, 1916, she and Ben arrived at a so-called dude ranch in Montana for their summer vacation. For most of the good folks in that state it may have seemed a reasonably short summer, but to the residents in the immediate vicinity who were within earshot of Mrs. Margulies' rapid-fire tongue, it was a century.

The woman proved to be one of the most durable pests the gentle cowhands and hotel-keepers had ever seen or heard. She worried and harried the cowboys. She sat on the veranda and talked everybody into a coma. She spread gossip, meddled in the management of the place, criticized the cooking until the chef quit, and three times a day made life miserable for the dining room help. She was, in short, the Queen Mother of all the *yentas* extant in the United States of America. When she departed for home at the end of August, the local gentry attired themselves in their best store-boughten clothes and threw an old-fashioned fiddlin' hootenanny.

The following summer, however, Ben reappeared alone.

"Where's your wife, Mr. Margulies?" inquired the proprietor.

"She's dead," explained the widower.

"Ya don't say!" responded the host. "Who shot her?"

* * *

"Chrysanthemum, look at this!" chided Mrs. Klaynekeit. "I can write your name on the piano with my finger, it's so dusty."

"Yes'm," replied the cheeky maid, "an' you done spelt it wrong."

* * *

There was great excitement in the Prinzmetal family. A real English lord was coming to pay them a visit! Mr. and Mrs. Prinzmetal had met His Lordship while returning from their latest European trip, and the important man had graciously accepted their invitation to spend his first weekend in the United States as a guest under their roof.

Now he had arrived and, after an effusive welcome, he was sitting at the Prinzmetal's table. Mrs. Prinzmetal, flustered and flattered, urged

My Lord to eat heartily. Her husband, beginning or ending every sentence with the noble-sounding "M'lord," was swollen with a sense of the honor which had descended upon his household. The dinner hour was being invested with a reverential, not to say worshipful, air.

As a special privilege—something he might talk about in his later years—little Charlie, age five, had been permitted to attend the function, on condition that he refrain from speaking unless first spoken to. Mindful of his pledge, the youngster remained quiet, his large round eyes fixed in a stare upon the face and form of the British lord.

But an innate sense of Jewish hospitality moved him to break his vow of silence when he noticed His Lordship's eyes roaming hither and yon across the table as though in search of something.

"Mama," said Charlie. "Oh, mama!"

"What is it, Charles dear?"

"God wants a pickle!"

* * *

It was one of the most fashionable weddings of the year, if not the decade. Everyone, but *everyone*, my dear, was there: the Loebs, the Guggenheims, the Rothschilds, the Kahns, the Strausses, the Cardozas, the Lehmans and the Morganthaus. The exclusive Park Avenue temple glittered with jewelled matrons and their suave and handsome escorts.

Rabbi Schwab finished his ceremonial functions, stepped back and smiled. A hush fell over the synagogue as the groom slipped the wedding ring on the bride's finger. At that moment, the reverent silence was shattered by the excited voice of a little girl in the rear of the temple:

"Mommy, is this where he sprinkles the pollen on her?"

* * *

Now that Jake and Irma were rich, they decided to add a little culture to their hitherto shallow lives. At their first opportunity, they went to the Metropolitan Museum of Art and took a guided tour of the exhibits.

"Say, this is a fine bust of Michelangelo," said Jake admiringly.

"That's not Michelangelo," explained the guide. "That's Leonardo da Vinci."

Irma, acutely embarrassed by her husband's ignorance, tugged at his sleeve.

"Jake," she hissed, "why do you have to open your big mouth when you don't know a single thing about the New Testament?"

* * *

The affluent have just as many problems with their offspring as do the rest of us. They differ only in degree. Take the case of the pretty sophomore at Radcliffe, Gloria de Sable, formerly Gertrude Fox. For weeks on end she had badgered her father for a fast and flashy new car, but the old man, aware of his daughter's wild nature, had stubbornly refused. At last, however, her persistence wore him down and he gave in—with a brand new Mercedes Benz. But he also warned her that the car would be taken away if she received so much as one traffic ticket. He meant it—and she knew it.

Gloria promptly took the Mercedes to one of those outfits that specialize in "customizing" stock cars. The chassis was widened, the body lowered and the engine souped up so that it would do 130 with ease. Now Gloria was ready to drive.

She was tooling down the highway at a mere 110 when, in her rear-view mirror, she spied a motorcycle cop in hot pursuit. With her father's warning still fresh in her mind, she pushed down on the gas pedal and the car leaped forward like Secretariat at the Kentucky Derby. But the police officer somehow managed to tail her. She grew increasingly worried. One way or another, she thought, she must evade that policeman. A citation for speeding and perhaps reckless driving was a certainty should she be caught.

But Gloria was a resourceful as well as a pretty girl. Seeing a filling station about a half-mile ahead, she slowed down just enough to turn into the driveway without overturning the car, and then, with the cop not far behind, she jerked open the door and raced into the ladies room. When she came out a few minutes later, there was the motorcycle officer, one foot on the bumper of her car, his citation book in hand.

Without a word she got back into her new Mercedes Benz, looked at him with a knowing smile on her face, and cooed:

"Bet you thought I wouldn't make it!"

* * *

Mrs. Vanderkatz reminded her housekeeper that her husband had invited a number of his business associates and their wives to spend the weekend with them.

"You done tol' me," said the housekeeper. "Wunst wuz enough."

"You're all prepared?"

"No ma'am," snapped the housekeeper. "I'm all *packed*!"

* * *

Big executives have their problems, too. Julius Rosenwald, head of Sears, Roebuck and Company, put in such long hours and hard work that he finally suffered a physical collapse. He was rushed to a fancy private hospital where he was given a sedative. He awoke the next morning to find a crisply starched young nurse in his room.

"Good morning," she greeted him cheerfully. "You're due for surgery in an hour."

"Surgery? What for?"

"Ulcers."

"Oh," he responded nervously, "I hope I'll have a strong anesthetic. What about this twilight sleep I've heard so much about?"

The nurse smiled. "That's for labor."

"I see," replied the big executive thoughtfully. "So what do you have for management?"

* * *

Let it be said that members of the Jewish aristocracy are just as attentive to *Chanukah* as the gentile elite are of Christmas. Witness:

Back in the 1900s B.T (Before Taxes), old Lazarus Strauss called his son, Nathan, into his study and asked: "What would you like for *Chanukah?*"

"A chemical outfit," said Nathan promptly.

So Lazarus shopped around for the best chemical outfit on the market and finally bought one—

DuPont!

* * *

All her life, Flo Malkes had lived on the shadowy edge of poverty, but such was her nature that she saw not the dilapidated tenements, the pushcarts and the shabbily dressed people among whom she lived on Henry Street. In her mind's eye she saw only the midtown mansions, stunning gowns and all the other habiliments of the very rich. Perhaps it was better that way: It saved her much suffering.

But, miracle of miracles—she was notified one day that she had been bequeathed a substantial fortune by a distant relative whom she only vaguely remembered from her childhood.

Flo Malkes became Fifi Midas. She moved uptown, into a plush condominium on Fifth Avenue, acquired a Rolls Royce and a chauffeur, and generally lived it up in high style.

Naturally, she dined only in the best establishments and, as befits a lady of her refinements, the day came when she entered *Pierre's*, the most exclusive French restaurant in all of New York. The menu was printed in French, of course, but Mrs. Malkes, or Midas, had no intention of admitting that she lacked acquaintance with that language. She took the bill of fare from the hovering *maitre d'* and studied it with an air of great intentness. Then she aimed a pudgy finger at an item near the top of the card.

"To start off with," she said, "please bring me that."

"But, *madame*," the headwaiter protested, "ze orchestra ees playing zat!"

* * *

There is an old, thrice-told tale about the society woman who looks down her nose, raises her lorgnette and says to her housekeeper, "We usually spend our summers in Europe." And the housekeeper replies matter-of-factly, "So what? I was born there." The affectations assumed by the few have long provided mirth for the many. Stella Adler, the truly great actress, was especially adept in the art of lancing inflated egos and laughing at false pretensions. Here is a story that illustrates the point.

One autumn day during World War II, shortly after the Nazis had launched their all-out buzz-bomb attack on London, Stella was preparing to go to the theatre for a rehearsal when she noticed that one of the jewels in her favorite ring had fallen out. She promptly went to Cartier's to have the stone reset.

The deferential clerk, impressed by her grand manner, her precise articulation, her obvious *savoir-vivre*, said:

"Please accept my sympathy, *madame*, for the difficulties you British people are experiencing in England these days."

Always the consummate actress, Stella drew herself up in that awe-inspiring, regal manner of hers.

"My deah man," she replied haughtily, "Ay'm not Br-r-itish, Ay'm just affected!"

* * *

LA PLUME D'MINE TANTEH TEEYATER
Scene
—A lavish hotel room in Paris—

Nouveau riche, Mama Hirshberg and her daughter, Rose, are in earnest conversation.

Rose (complainingly): Mama, we've been here in Paris a whole week and I haven't been to the Louvre yet.

Mama (anxiously): Rosaleh, maybe you better take a little physic.

* * *

Mrs. Shayneh Balabatish was guiding the new maid, Amanda, around her Park Avenue mansion, explaining the maid's duties and acquainting her with the various furnishings and the individual care they required. She pointed out the Chippendales, the French Provincial and Italian Renaissance pieces, the Louis IV bedroom suite and the Victorian dining room ensemble.

As they entered the library, they were confronted by the Balabatish grandchildren, all five of whom were cavorting, laughing and shouting with glee as they pounded nails into the valuable furniture. The maid gasped in horror.

"Oh, it's perfectly all right," smiled Mrs. Balabatish.

"But," protested Amanda, "how can you afford to let them?"

"Nothing to worry about," said Mrs. Balabatish reassuringly. "Nails we can always get wholesale."

* * *

Shlomo Shnookelman, starting out in America as a humble fish peddler, at long last managed to tip the scales in his favor and wound up with a rash of cash. He moved from his former tenancy in lower Manhattan, purchased a town house in the East Sixties and joined one of those posh synagogues whose rabbis are more interested in tax and syntax than they are in traditional observances.

The rabbi of this particular temple, a King James version of an orthodox synagogue, appointed Shnookelman to serve as an usher for the approaching Passover services. Eager to please and anxious for social acceptance among these fancy coreligionists, he grimly resolved that he would maintain a sharp vigilance for anyone who might desecrate the proceedings with unseemly conduct.

The doors had no sooner opened when the elderly Mrs. Jacob Schiff, matriarch of all the Jewish banker families in America, entered the temple. She settled into her customary place in the front row and withdrew from her enormous purse an old-fashioned ear trumpet so she would be better able to hear the sermon.

Shnookelman took one look at the hearing device and he strode over to the dignified, imperious Mrs. Schiff.

"Lady," he barked, "one toot from that horn and out you go!"

* * *

Newly-rich Mrs. Glick was showing one of her poor relations around her new home on Riverside Drive. Proudly, she led her wide-eyed relative to the spacious kitchen and the cavernous living room.

"And this is the dining room," announced Mrs. Glick. "Here we can feed twenty people, God forbid, at one time."

"What about the bedroom?" asked the relative. "It's big, too?"

"The bedroom sleeps twelve.

"And the bathroom?"

"Ah, in the bathroom I can seat eight!"

* * *

Now that I.J. Fox had made his second (or maybe it was his third) million dollars, he decided that the time had arrived when he could afford to emulate his fellow millionaires and do a little relaxing. But sitting around a fashionable country club or playing golf with a bunch of old duffers was not to his liking. I.J. Fox was an adventurous soul. He craved excitement. Then came an inspired thought: He would go on an African safari to hunt big game.

The next morning found him at the offices of Congo Safe, Sane & Sanitary Safaris, Inc., an organization that promoted such expeditions. After listening to the sales pitch and studying the colorful brochures, the prospective Great White Hunter nervously cleared his throat.

"Tell me something," he began. "It's true that a berserk elephant or a rhino will sometimes charge a safari truck?"

"Well, yes, it's true to a certain extent," replied the office manager haughtily, "but I assure you, sir, we frown on the practice!"

* * *

Oscar and Beatrice of Orchard Street were overwhelmed to learn that a distant relative had died and left them a million dollars. Nothing would do but that they leave the lower East Side immediately and rent an apartment on Central Park West. Now they were busily engaged in planning the artistic decor in keeping with their new station in life.

"I think," suggested Oscar, "that on the dining room wall we should have something in oil."

"You mean," asked Beatrice hesitantly, "a sardine?"

* * *

At a United Jewish Appeal rally, speaker after speaker exhorted the vast audience to contribute to its utmost ability. Finally the moment came when the speeches were finished and the donors were expected to make their pledges. Suddenly, from the rear of the auditorium, a booming voice rang out:

"My name is Howard Mishkin, of Mishkin Furs, Inc., 128 East 37th Street, New York City, New York, and I pledge $1,000 anonymously!"

* * *

Jack Benny, speaking of a heritage-happy, ancestor-worshipping, self-important snob:

"He wasn't brought by the stork. He was brought by a man from the Audubon Society personally!"

* * *

Abe Kantor had struggled all his life to make a success of the little manufacturing concern of which he and his wife were the sole owners as well as workers. They made wallpaper paste from a secret formula their janitor had sold to them for a dollar many years before. Then, one day, by the sheerest of accidents, they found out that their wallpaper paste was not only edible but very low in cholesterol. Overnight, they became wealthy.

Abe and his wife bought a co-op apartment on Fifth Avenue and furnished it sumptuously. Then they hired a butler—right out of Buckingham Palace.

On their first day of residence in the fashionable new quarters, they celebrated with a dinner by candlelight. The butler served them beautifully, as though they were born to royalty. When they finished dining, the impeccable butler bowed over them and asked, "Will the marster and moddum have their arfter-dinnah brandy in the library?"

Abe looked up at the butler in genuine surprise, then stared helplessly at his wife.

"How do you like that?" he asked. "Here's a guy who buttled for the king of England and he don't even know the library closes at six!"

25

Sports

INTRODUCTION

Jewish intellectuals, adhering to long tradition, continue to view excessive interest in athletics as an unhealthy phenomenon, but you know how those intellectuals are: let anyone get a little pleasure out of life and they can give you more reasons to abstain than can the Lubavitcher rebbe. Nevertheless, some of their observations are very well taken.

"Exaggerated respect for athletics," said Albert Einstein in 1934, "is hostile to the ripening of the character and the desire for real culture. It stamps our age as barbarous, materialist and superficial."

Dr. Sigmund Freud was equally vehement in his denunciation: "The preference which the Jews have given to spiritual endeavor for 2,000 years has had its effect; it has helped against brutality and the inclination to violence which are usually found where athletic development becomes the ideal of the people."

Needless to say (but I'll say it anyway), neither Al nor Siggie ever yelled themselves hoarse at a baseball game and consumed indigestible hot dogs and warm beer that tasted like it had been bottled in a barn. But, as grandpa used to say, what's right is right: Einstein and Freud were opposed to the *idealization* of athletics, rather than to the sports themselves, especially when they tended to overshadow education or supercede the spiritual and cultural values of a supposedly civilized people.

When we speak of Jewish prize fighters, we must go back in time a bit—quite a bit—about 2,000 years. Had I been alive at that time, and my typewriter already invented, I would have written a biography titled, *Resh Lakish: The Gladiator Who Became a Famous Rabbi*. Who could resist such a title? It would have become an immediate best-seller. Resh Lakish, who became one of the foremost Talmudic sages, fought in the Roman gladiatorial arenas. He must have been a mighty fighter, for there is no record of his having ever suffered a defeat. Of course, when a man was defeated in the arena he was dead, and Lakish lived to a respectable old age. He believed in beating his sword into a plowshare and then attacking with the plowshare.

How does a fighting champion become a spiritual leader? It all started when he went for a swim at a Mediterranean beach. There, he was seen by a great rabbi and his youngest and prettiest daughter who marvelled at the gladiator's handsome features and beautifully muscled body—at least the daughter marvelled. Her father was just interested. At her gentle, indirect, ladylike hint ("Papa, I want that guy!"), the old man arranged a match—but only on the condition that Resh Lakish catch up on his Torah lessons. Resh studied, married the girl, and became one of the shining lights of the Talmud. He is quoted in the Talmud as saying that in every crime there is a bit of insanity, an observation frequently used by psychiatrists these days, particularly when paid to say so in court.

Having thus covered the last 2,000 years of Jewish sports figures, let's turn our attention to more recent times.

In America, the once lively Yiddish press had no sports section, nor did it need one. Few of its readers were interested in who made a home run. The immigrants from Kovno or Bialystok were sufficiently happy that they were not required to run home from work, but could take the trolley car. Billiards and pool hustling failed to answer their cultural needs (like pinochle, for instance), and a game between Minnesota Fats and Wisconsin Skinny was, for them, a *goyishe* curiosity. ("So you hit a cue ball with a stick it should hit another ball it should roll into a corner pocket! *Nu*, this makes you a *shammes* in the Swiss Navy?")

Football and basketball were even less interesting to the turn-of-the century immigrants. There were no wails of anguish on the East Side when CCNY lost to Bryn Mawr in the *Lokshen* Bowl.

As for prize fights, anyone who fought with his fists was a bum, a loafer, a no-goodnik. Those early immigrants would not pay a nickel to see two men beating each other up in Madison Square Garden. They thought they should be arrested.

But that attitude was not entirely shared by the second generation of American Jews. Prior to World War II, boxing was one of the most popular sports among the Jewish masses, though we must admit that the intellectuals still preferred violin lessons. The greatest interest in prize fighting was evident during its heyday when Irish, Italian and Jewish boxers vied for the purses that could provide escape from the slums in which many of them lived. And it was during that period when nearly all of the classic boxing jokes arose.

Returning to the nostalgia theme, the boxing ring produced a number of outstanding fighters in the various weight divisions. Among them were Max Baer, Al Singer, Benny Leonard, Maxie Rosenbloom, Barney Ross, Lou Tendler and King Levinsky. Many humorous anecdotes about them have survived, some of which are presented in this collection.

I have coupled the words "intellectual" and "sports" more than once in this Introduction, and may the *Mosheeach* show compassion for my indiscretion when and if he gets here to tally up the Divine score. However, although it pains me to admit it, the intellectuals are quite right, for a change, in their denunciation of excessive college sports as being detrimental to education.

Several stories in this chapter deal with the supposed ignorance of women when the subject involves sports. One such joke tells of the annoyed husband who snaps at his wife: "Why do you always cry and sniff at a movie over people you never met?" And the wife retorts: "For the same reason you scream and holler when a man you never met hits a home run." However, let us be fair to the ladies. In all honesty we must agree that today's generation of young women knows all about the national pastime. They understand baseball, too.

Also represented in this chapter are a few humorous anecdotes aimed at the more technically-minded baseball fan. To illustrate: A rookie had just walked six batters in a row, then hit two, then balked, then threw wildly in three pick-off attempts. The manager strode out on the field to take him out of the game. "What!" cried the indignant kid— "When I've got a no-hitter going!"

And now, let's hear it for good ol' Yeshivah . . .

Gimme a G; gimme an E; gimme a V; gimme an A; gimme an L; gimme a T. *Oyyy Gevaaalllt!*

H.D.S.

In New York City, a teacher asked a boy: "Who defeated the Philistines?"

"If they don't play the Mets," snapped the kid, "I don't keep track of 'em!"

* * *

Some people are just not born to be athletes. Spectators, yes. Participants, no. Take Sonny Saperstein, for instance. Sonny, you may recall, was the first judo student ever to win the yellow belt. He really should have known better.

Sonny's wife gave him a stern ultimatum that if he didn't quit this *meshuggeneh* judo business there would be no more visits from the tooth fairy. So he took up boxing instead. For a while it seemed as if he had at last chosen a sport in which he could excel. In fact, he was finally matched with Muhammed Ali in Madison Square Garden. There were two hits in the whole fight. Muhammed hit Sonny and Sonny hit the floor.

By this time, it was clear even to Sonny that he would have to involve himself in a less violent sport. So he took up tiddley winks. Believe it or not, he worked his way right up to a world championship match.

But, alas, we bring melancholy tidings:

Sonny tiddled when he should have winked!

* * *

Now that Berman was retired and finally had the time, he yielded to his lifelong ambition—golfing. He went to the best golf pro in the city and they made an appointment to meet on the links for his very first game.

On the following Friday, the instructor showed Berman how to tee up the ball and then said, "Hit the ball as near to that flag as you can."

Berman took a mighty swing and the ball soared to within four inches of the flag.

"Not bad," complimented the instructor. "In fact, that's pretty good."

"So what do I do next?" asked Berman.

"Now you have to knock the ball into the hole."

"What?" roared Berman, outraged. "Why the hell didn't you tell me that in the first place?"

* * *

Several decades ago, when the world of pugilism ranked such champions as Al Singer, Benny Leonard, Barney Ross and "Slapsie" Maxie Rosenbloom, among many others, there was a little boxing club on East Broadway owned by one Murray Adelson, a tough, shrewd little man. Murray's gym was not merely undercapitalized, it was shaky to the point of collapse, and one night the attendance was woefully slim.

This situation prompted some deep thought. Having done his heavy thinking, Murray entered the ring before the first scheduled bout and, his accented voice ringing with sincerity, he made an announcement:

"Gennelmun, I received today a letter from the Markweezy from Queensberg, and he's telling me, straight out with no baloney, I got to pay him $25 for using his rules here tonight.

"The hat will now be passed!"

* * *

Nathan had been going over his old scrapbook, rereading the college newspaper accounts of his former exploits on the gridiron. He had even saved his old football. Full of nostalgic self-admiration, he turned to his mother.

"Just think, mom, I've been out of college for five years now, and I still have my pigskin."

"*Oy*, Natie!" she gasped. "Maybe you should quick see a doimatologist!"

* * *

The late L. Wolfe Gilbert, affectionately known as "Wolfie," was scarcely over five feet tall but was as active physically as he was mentally. He was a sharp but lovable character. Long before he attained fame as the composer of such popular songs as *Waiting for the Robert E. Lee, Ramona, Down Yonder, The Peanut Vendor* and *Jeannine, I Dream of Lilac Time,* among a score of other hits of the day, Wolfie had a vaudeville act with Pitzy Katz, the comedian. They were billed as Gilbert and Katen—a song, dance and patter team. Wolfie was later to become board chairman of ASCAP, but he always delighted in reminiscing about his early days on the theatrical circuit. This little gem occurred in 1912 or thereabouts.

Wolfie and his vaudeville partner, Pitzy, found themselves in London one summer. The balmy days made the pair homesick for baseball. They combed the Savoy Hotel and the theatre where they were appearing and found just enough Americans who loved the sport to form two scratch teams. Then they borrowed the use of a cricket field for an afternoon and marked out a rough sort of diamond. After taking care of these preliminaries, plans were concluded for the All-American Baseball Championship of the British Empire, the game to be held on the following Sunday, Wolfie serving as captain of one team and Pitzy the other.

When they arrived at the scene of conflict, a difficulty arose. There were exactly 18 Americans present and all of them expected to play. Where would they get an umpire? Choice fell upon a Britisher among the spectators. He was selected because he had served as a referee at cricket games. He had no knowledge of the rules of baseball but he thought he could learn. His name was Walberg.

So Walberg was given a drilling. He grasped the fine distinctions between a strike and a ball and a foul; the matter of what happened when a fielder caught a fly was easily explained to him, but at the end of a half-hour he was still unsure of the more subtle aspects of the game. Still, the rival teams were anxious to start and the commanders decided to get on with it.

After some extra coaching, umpire Walberg stationed himself behind the catcher and the battle began. The lead-off man on Wolfie's team whanged the first offering of the rival pitcher squarely on the nose and sent the ball high in the air. The centerfielder caught it.

"You are through, sir; quite through," called the umpire, leaping forward.

There was loud applause from both sides. Pleased at having so quickly mastered the intricate phraseology of the Americans' pastime, Walberg strutted back to position.

The next man slammed a wicked grounder toward Pitzy's shortstop. The latter scooped it up and threw it to first base. But the play at the bag was close.

The catcher swung on the umpire.

"How was that?" he barked.

With unfeigned admiration in his voice, Walberg gave his decision: "Ma-a-h-velous, sir! Absolutely ma-a-h-velous!"

* * *

Moses and Jesus were playing a round of golf at the Celestial Country Club. First, Jesus teed up and made a hole in one. Then Moses also drove a hole in one.

"Well, Moe, we're even so far," said Jesus.

"Now look here, Jake," Moses protested "we made our point. Now whaddya say we cut out the miracles and play a little golf?"

* * *

In his heavenly abode, the patriarch Abraham lit the *shabbes* candles and then, over a glass of tea and lemon, he settled back to read the *Forvertz*.

Suddenly, from down below on Earth, he heard a raucous tumult.

"Now who could be desecrating the Sabbath like that?" he wondered.

With his new laser telescope, he looked down and there he saw a crowd of at least 80,000 people in the Houston Astrodome watching a baseball game. A quick count showed him that over 30,000 Jews were among the spectators. Outraged, he picked up the phone and dialed G-O-D. After a few rings, the Boss picked up the receiver.

"Hello," said father Abraham, "that you, Joe?"

"Now look here, Abe—the name's Jehovah! Show a little respect!"

"All right, Jehovah then, I have a complaint."

"*Nu*, what is it this time? Those people from the New Testament picking on you again?"

"Nothing like that. But you really must do something about all that *goyishe* conduct back on Earth. Did you know that at this very minute 30,000 Jews are watching a baseball game at the Astrodome?"

"You got something against baseball?"

"No, of course not. But that's not the point. This is Friday evening and it seems to me our people ought to be a little more observant of the holy day."

"What's the big attraction they're all watching the game?"

"Hank Aaron is coming to bat and he's about to break Babe Ruth's record."

"You're absolutely right, Abe. That's no excuse they should act like a bunch of wild Republicans. Call me back after the game and I'll do something about it. . . and by the way, what channel is it on?"

* * *

"Just remember," consoled the trainer as his bruised and battered fighter staggered back to his corner of the ring, "if the other guy was any good he wouldn't be fighting you!"

* * *

Benny Leonard was thrashing the daylights out of Lefty Louie, his opponent in the ring. The bell sounded, signaling the end of the third round and the opponent returned unsteadily to his corner.

"Did I land any good shots?" Lefty asked his manager.

"Not yet," said the manager, "but keep on swinging. Leonard might catch a cold from the draft!"

* * *

This story was imported into the everyday world in 1923 from its native birthplace in the Harmonie Club, New York's select German-Jewish counterpart of the gentile Union League Club. The membership required that all new applicants be of "genteel environment" and socially acceptable—meaning, they were required to have a cosmic bank account.

One day in June of the aforementioned 1923, a new member was welcomed into the Harmonie Club—a Mr. Hellman who made a living selling sixty million jars of mayonnaise a month. He was socially acceptable because he came from the "genteel environment" of the Corn Exchange Bank and never associated with *Galitzianers*.

Actually, Hellman wasn't a bad fellow, until you got to know him. He enjoyed his vintage *schnapps*, fast horses and, above all, golf. It was his predilection for the game of clubs and little round balls that drew him into animated conversation with another new member, a fellow named Rosenwald who owned a modest dry goods store called Sears, Roebuck and Company. Both of these gentlemen learned, to their mutual delight, that their love of golf allowed them to simmer in the city while their wives summered in the country.

"What do you generally go around in?" asked Hellman.

"Oh," replied Rosenwald, "about 105 or 106, when I'm on my game."

"Me, too," said Hellman. "If I break 110 on any course, I'm doing pretty well. I guess we're about matched. What do you say we play together for five dollars a hole?"

"Sure!" said Rosenwald.

The next day, on the Harmonie Club's golf course, they played 18 holes.

The following evening, Hellman showed up at the Club, but Rosenwald was absent.

"I don't blame him for staying away," grated the mayonnaise man. "If I were as big a damn liar as Rosenwald I'd be ashamed to show my face around here, too. You know what that dry goods salesman did? He made an *82*—and I had to play my *tuchus* off to beat him!"

* * *

"Pop," asked the sports-minded youngster, "what's the main difference between an amateur and a professional?"

"As far as I can see," replied the father, "the *only* difference is that the pro gets paid by check!"

* * *

Hubby took the missus to see her first game of baseball. It was the last half of the ninth inning, with the bases loaded, two out and three balls called. The pitcher threw a red-hot sizzler and the batter for the visiting team lifted a fly ball to left center. The center fielder for the home team, leaping high into the air, made an "impossible" catch, fell backwards and then rolled over on the ground—but he held on to that ball!

Thirty thousand fans lost their minds and went wild in the stands, roaring their approval. Hubby yelled and jumped about in a frenzy of delight. And through it all, his wife looked at him with mouth agape.

"Why were you hollering and jumping like that?" she asked when he had quieted down somewhat.

"Are you blind?" he demanded. "Didn't you see him catch that ball?"

"So?" replied the missus, shrugging. "That's not what he's getting paid for?"

"You'll have to scratch my horse," he sighed.

"All right," replied Mrs. Straus with an uncertain smile, "but where?"

* * *

American Jews have a long and comparatively honorable history in the breeding and racing of horses. After all, it was August Belmont (Schoënberg), the immensely wealthy banker of the last century, who founded the Belmont Stakes. So, without further flummery we fearlessly foist the following flippancy upon the unfortunate reader.

Mrs. Frederic W. Straus, of *the* Straus family, was aware, of course, that her famous socialite-financier husband was active in the "sport of kings," as they say in the expensive books, but this was the first time she had been asked to help out in a charity horse race. Understandably, then, she was a little puzzled when an owner came to report that his entry had a stiff knee.

* * *

Two middle-aged men were walking off the tennis court after only a few minutes of play. The older, somewhat corpulent fellow was puffing heavily.

"I guess I'm in pretty poor shape," he confessed ruefully.

"How long have you been playing, Herbie?" asked the younger man.

"About two weeks."

"Then let me give you a little practical advice. Try the Christian Science way—mind over matter."

"I already have," admitted the fat one. "When my opponent serves the ball to me, my Christian Science mind says, 'Now, Herbie, you just race right up to that net, slam a blistering drive to the far corner of the court and then jump back into position.' That's exactly what my Christian Science mind tells me . . .

"But my Jewish body says, 'Herbie, to make a *shlemiel* out of yourself you don't need!'"

* * *

Harry, the high school football player, injured his back in a tackle and went to the school clinic for an examination.

"Have you ever been troubled with sciatica, meningitis or muscular atrophy?" asked the nurse.

"Yeah," confessed Harry, "whenever I try to spell 'em."

* * *

There are still a few oldsters wandering about this mortal coil who will recall with fond nostalgia the vaudeville team of Potash and Perlmutter. The two comedy stars regaled their audiences with Jewish-accented jokes, as was the style at the turn of the century, but they were equally adept with "straight" stories which they often told off-stage. One of their favorite exchanges concerned an athletic event in which a young American lad had just broken the world pole-vaulting record. As the applause died away, Potash remarked:

"He did real good, that boy, and I'm proud he's an American. But in the old country I saw a young man who jumped a foot higher than this new champion . . . I said a foot? *Two* feet, maybe!"

"What kind of foolish talk is that?" demanded Perlmutter. "Don't you understand this boy set a new world's record? Don't you understand that nobody in the whole world ever jumped so high before? Don't you understand that it may be years and years before anyone jumps so high again? Two feet higher, you say? How can you make such a stupid remark?"

"I don't care," said Potash stubbornly. "Back in Minsk I saw the boy jump so high with my own eyes. In fact, I knew him personally. He was a neighbor."

"What?" blared Perlmutter incredulously. "You knew him, you say? Who was he?"

"It was your own kid brother, Morris," stated Potash gently.

"Oh-h-h, you mean my kid brother, Morris!" exclaimed Perlmutter in an altered voice. "Well, it stands to reason . . ."

* * *

The battle-scarred prize fighter strode into the manager's office.

"When ya gonna sign me up fer a fight?" he demanded, weaving about and shadowboxing with an opponent who did not happen to be present at the moment. "I'm really ready! Looka 'at footwoik! Watch 'at lef' jab! Obsoive 'at ol' reflex. I'm inna bes' shape of m'life. So when're ya gonna get me a match?"

"Well, if you're as ready as you say," the manager replied somewhat dubiously, "I'll get you a match. Anybody in particular you'd like to fight?"

"Yeah, one guy in pertickla. I wanna fight King Kohen."

"Now look here," said the manager sternly. "If I told you once I told you a hundred times—*you're* King Kohen!"

* * *

Reuben, billed as "The Roaring Rassler from Rochester," arrived home in a dark mood. His wife, Ida, met him at the door.

"I saw the match on TV," she said, her voice full of sympathy. "I'm sorry you lost."

"I just can't understand why they gave the decision to the other guy," answered Reuben disconsolately. "How could I lose the bout when I won the two rehearsals?"

* * *

"A one-hundred per cent American boy," avowed Sandy Koufax, "is one who studies arithmetic just so he can keep the baseball scores. He's also the kid who knows the complete lineup of all the games, but only the first line of the *Star Spangled Banner*."

* * *

Due and proper credit must be given to Al Brancato, former Toronto infielder, for the most fascinating alibi in all the history of baseball.

One night Al went out on the town and had a great time, living it up until three in the morning. As he weaved up the steps in front of his house, he slipped and gave his backbone a whack. The next day, he came to practice limping, and slightly stooped over.

"What happened to you?" demanded the worried manager.

Al was not about to confess his previous night's misconduct and run the risk of a heavy fine.

"Wrenched my back," he said evasively.

"Yeah, I can see that. But how?"

"You won't believe this," declared Al, a devout Catholic, "but on my way home from practice yesterday I just 'happened to step inside a synagogue and before I knew it my spine went out of joint while I was *davening!*"

*   *   *

"It's easy to spot a golf nut," averred one mournful golf widow. "He'll jump traffic lights to save seconds and wait patiently for two hours for the first tee."

*   *   *

There is no record of this event in any of the official sports annuals. But the story has been so persistent it would be a shame to ignore it. It goes like this:

Hank Greenberg, when he was a top Yankee star, was having a running feud with Iz Goodman, the umpire. Hank was an articulate guy and a fast-thinker, but poor Iz could never win an argument—except on the field, of course, where his word was final. Oh, how Iz longed to put Hank "in his place"—just once—to show the world that he could defeat his nemesis with his intellect and not just with the authority of his office.

The Great Umpire in the Sky must have heard his prayers. The day came when Iz was presented with his shining hour; when, before 50,000 wildly cheering fans, he not only vanquished the pride of the Yankees but absolutely demolished him. It happened thisawise:

Greenberg drove a high, deep fly to center. He raced to first base, the ump running right alongside him, making absolutely certain that he touched the bag; then on to second, third and home, with Iz accompanying him all the way, calling "touch that base!" Hank, understandably, was burned up—to a crisp. "Oh, well," he thought, "what the hell, it's a homer."

But as Hank slid into home base, umpire Goodman yelled—

"You're out! Fly ball to center!"

*   *   *

At the ball park, the husband's wife began to pester him with a running barrage of questions about the game until his disposition went from sour to bad to horrible. Yet, he somehow managed to restrain his temper and politely answer all her innocent questions.

"Now tell me this," she said, pointing to the catcher: "Why is that man wearing a mask?"

But this time the dam broke and hubby's soigné reserve evaporated in a red mist.

"That, my dear wife," he said in a voice that hovered at thirty below zero, "is to prevent him from biting the batter!"

* * *

Bobby: Riddle me this, grandpa: What has 18 legs and catches flies?
Grandpa: Nine birds?
Bobby: No.
Grandpa: All right, so what has 18 legs and it's catching flies?
Bobby: The New York Mets.
Grandpa: Impossible! The Mets is popping, not catching!

* * *

Mr. Finkel, the haberdasher, was known on his block as something of a baseball expert. One Saturday afternoon, a couple of stern-faced, hulking young men came into his store and demanded that he umpire their Sunday game. Their regular unpire, it seems, had been stabbed, shot, beaten and poisoned after having rendered a decision which did not meet with the popular approval of the home team. Mr. Finkel, who stood an even five feet in his socks, took one analytical look at their glowering faces and decided that discretion was definitely the better part of valor. He agreed to be at the local ballpark early the next day, Sunday.

The game was between the Black Panthers and the Hell's Angels. The man at bat weighed about 240 pounds, was at least six-foot-three and had the arms and shoulders of a gorilla. The catcher was built like Grant's Tomb, only stronger. The pitcher could have passed for the Abominable Snowman. Tiny Mr. Finkel looked like a grasshopper beside them.

The first ball came over the plate. "Strike one!" called the nervous umpire, as the batter glared at him menacingly.

The next offering whizzed over, just outside the plate.

"Ball one!" called Mr. Finkel. This time the pitcher, Joe Behemoth, gave him an icy stare.

Now the third pitched ball whipped over a corner of the plate. The catcher tore the mask from his snarling face and waited for the umpire's decision.

"Two!" called Mr. Finkel.

"Two *what!*" yelled the batter, the pitcher and the catcher in ugly unison.

Shrinking back into his padding, Mr. Finkel stammered—

"Too close to call!"

* * *

There's a fanatical doggedness about a fight fan that will not be swayed. Nothing can divert his attention once he starts to expound on his favorite sport. A case in point was the man with the asbestos stomach lining. The late heavyweight boxing champion, Max Baer, claimed that it really happened. Here is the story in Max's own words:

"After I won the crown, my face became familiar to the general public. Wherever I went, people who knew me only by my picture would stop me, introduce themselves and want to talk with me. At first, so much fame was agreeable—I was flattered. But after a while, when the novelty had worn thin, I began to cherish my privacy. I found out what many other men had learned before me: being in the public eye had its drawbacks.

"One summer night, being alone for a change, I slipped into a quiet tavern for a cool glass of beer. Besides the bartender there was only one other person in the place—a middle-aged Jewish man in his shirtsleeves. The bartender recognized me and, when he spoke my name, the little stranger gave a happy yell and threw himself at me and grabbed my hand and pumped it up and down and wouldn't let go of it and began talking excitedly, sometimes in pure Yiddish which, thankfully, I had a working knowledge of, but mostly in his heavily accented English.

"I understand how these boxing fans are and I didn't want to hurt his feelings. But he almost talked my ear off. He asked a thousand questions. How did I beat Carnera? What was my opinion of Max Schmeling, the darling of the Nazis? Did I think I could take Joe Louis? Was it true that Jack Sharkey wanted to make a comeback? And so on and so forth. Language poured out of that guy in a steady stream. I broke in just long enough to invite him to join me in a drink, hoping that would silence him for a few minutes, but, without missing a beat, he downed his beer with two swallows and kept right on talking.

"I was getting desperate. I tried to dodge him by edging away but he followed me down the bar, hanging on to my elbow and firing more questions at me like bullets out of a rapid-fire machine gun.

"All of a sudden, I spied a bottle of Tabasco sauce on a table behind me. I reached out with my free arm and grabbed the bottle, unscrewed the cap and winked at the bartender. He caught my meaning—after all, it's an old custom in New York bars—and he quickly drew two more beers and placed them in front of us. Then, on another signal from me, he distracted the man's attention for a few moments and I emptied the whole bottle of that red-hot hellfire into the guy's beer.

"It wasn't a nice thing to do, I admit, but like I said, I was desperate. I figured the tabasco would heat up that non-stop mouth of his, and while the bartender was extinguishing the fire I'd make my escape.

"The man swung around—the bartender and I watching him intently —and he lifted his schooner.

"'Vell, Max, mine boy,' he said, 'le' chayim!'

"With one gulp he swallowed that fiery brew and, as we waited for him to give a howl of agony and for the flames to burst out of his mouth, nose and ears, he set the emptied mug down, wiped his lips with the back of his hand, and said:

"'Tell me, Maxeleh, you t'ink maybe did Gene Tooney beat Dempseh mit a long count?'"

* * *

Feibush was flabby-fat and sixty. His doctor suggested that he take up golf for his health. So he joined the Gotham Golf Club, and though he had never played a game before in his life, his scores were amazingly low. On his first day, he played the course at par. On his second day, he shot a seven below par, and on the third day he made it at ten below par.

"Look here," said a fellow golfer who had been keeping a sharp eye on this astounding golfer from the beginning, "you know perfectly well that you didn't make this course with those low scores. I've been watching you. What's the idea of cheating like that?"

"Mister," replied Feibush calmly, "my doctor said I should play golf for my health, and low scores make me feel much better."

* * *

Sandy Koufax, the unparalleled pitching star of the New York Yankees, was in Japan with his team where they were playing a couple of exhibition games.

On behalf of one of the host villages near Tokyo, a little girl brought a bouquet of lovely flowers and presented the gift to Sandy. Struggling with her limited English, the child said:

"These flowers will die, Sandy Koufax *san*, but you will smell forever!"

* * *

For years, Sidney had been a rabid baseball fan. When he wasn't at a ballgame, he was watching one on TV. He read nothing but the sports pages of his newspaper and, even then, only the baseball articles. He subscribed to all the baseball magazines and had lately taken to claiming that he, himself, was one of the greatest pitchers and hitters who ever lived—a startling statement considering the fact that he had not played a single game since his first year in high school. Things got so bad that, at last, his family sent him to the almond and pecan orchard for treatment.

The resident psychiatrist, who hadn't deviated from Freud's teachings for the past thirty years, began with the customary question: "Tell me about your dreams."

"I dream every single night," declared the new patient.

"What about?"

"About baseball, of course!"

"But surely you dream about girls."

"What!" demanded the outraged Sidney, "and miss my turn at bat?"

* * *

Harry Shreiber, sports columnist for the Los Angeles *Herald*, was covering the Olympic games for his paper. Everywhere he looked he could see athletes representing almost every country on earth. All were busily engaged in setting up their equipment, practicing, huddling with their teammates or talking with their coaches. They included swimmers, divers, gymnasts, runners, basketball and volleyball players, boxers, wrestlers and many other athletes.

Usually, Shreiber could tell at a glance which sport the contestants represented, but there was one fellow who did not seem to fit in any category. Try as he might, he couldn't match the man with his particular field of athletics.

Suddenly, the fellow picked up a long pole. The newspaperman's eyes lit up. 'Aha,' he thought, 'now I know!' But to make sure, he decided to ask. So he walked over to the stranger.

"Pardon me," he began, after introducing himself, "but are you a pole vaulter?"

The guy looked at him in complete amazement.

"*Nyet*," he replied, shaking his head, "I vas being Russki. But how did you know my name vas Valter?"

* * *

A knock sounded on the door of apartment 3-C and an elderly gentlemen opened the door.

"Good morning, sir," said the caller. "Is your son at home?"

"No, he's not here," said the oldster.

"I'm a friend of his. May I ask where he is?"

"He's by the lake in Central Park."

"Oh, he went ice skating?"

"Well, it all depends," reflected the old man. "If the ice is thick like my boy expects, he's gone skating. If it's thin like *I* expect, he's gone swimming!"

* * *

Frankie Farfel the Florida fistfighter and Peter Popkin the Pough-keepsie pugilist had been signed for a bout by an unscrupulous match-maker who knew perfectly well that Frankie wouldn't stand a chance with the more experienced Popkin.

As expected, Popkin's powerful left hand found Frankie Farfel's chin an easy target and, for the next three rounds, the Florida fighter took an awful pounding. When the bell sounded, ending the fourth round, Frankie staggered back to his corner where his trainer carefully scrutin-ized his battered features.

"Listen, Frankie," the trainer sighed, "ya better let Popkin hit ya with his right fer a while. Yer face is gettin' lopsided."

* * *

Arnold was taking an unusually long time to finish his homework. "What's the matter?" asked his father. "Stuck for the answers?"

"Yeah," said Arnold. "I'm supposed to pick the nine greatest Ameri-cans, but I can't decide who to put on first base."

* * *

Back in the 1940's, at DeWitt Clinton High School, a popular basket-ball coach of the school team was called "Doc" Walters. He wasn't a real doctor, according to the players: they just called him that because he was a real operator.

* * *

During his presidential years, Dwight D. Eisenhower spent much of his leisure time at the Burning Tree golf links on the outskirts of the nation's capital. An Arnold Palmer he was not, but sometimes he made the course at par, and once in a while below par. His favorite caddy was Danny Marcus, formerly of New York but at the time living in nearby Arlington, Virginia, with his parents.

Despite President Eisenhower's liking for his caddy, however, he was growing increasingly irritated with the young man's habit of denigrating his best shots.

"My pop could do better than that," he would comment, no matter how far or how accurately the ball had been hit. The day finally came when Ike reached the end of his patience.

"This father of yours; how old is he?" demanded the President.

"Seventy-six," replied Danny promptly.

"And how long has he been playing golf?"

"Well, to tell you the truth, sir, he only played three times in his life. Still, if you'll pardon me for saying so, Mr. President, he could beat you easily."

"He's seventy-six years old?" exclaimed Ike, understandably incredulous. "And he's only played three games in his life? You have some nerve comparing him to me! I'll bet you fifty dollars he can't beat me."

So it was arranged. The next day the elder Mr. Marcus, a short man with shoulders about three feet wide, appeared on the links where his son introduced him to the Chief Executive. Ike reaffirmed that he would play the old man 18 holes for a $50 bet. Ground rules were established and it was agreed that the visitor should drive first.

Old Mr. Marcus stepped up to the tee, squared his huge shoulders, and then, using an extremely unorthodox stance, he gave the ball such a mighty slam that it was flattened on one side. The ball rose to the upper reaches of the atmosphere—God knows how high—and sailed four hundred and fifty yards right to the rim of the green.

Eisenhower's eyes grew as big as saucers.

"Good heavens," he cried, "this man can't be beaten!" He threw up his hands in defeat. "I'm calling it quits. I give up! Here's your fifty dollars. There's no use going any further!"

Grinning, Danny accepted the money and started to walk towards the car where his father was waiting for a ride back home, when Ike commented:

"I must admit, Danny, that your father hit that ball farther and straighter than anyone else in all the history of the sport. But tell me something, how does he putt?"

"Same as he drives," said the proud son. "Wham! Zoom! Four hundred and fifty yards!"

* * *

At a show business "roast" in which Jack Benny was the guest of honor, or "roastee," one of the speakers was Olympic swimming champ Mark Spitz.

"The nearest Jack Benny ever came to participating in sports," commented the famous athlete, "was when he got a job shagging flies in a zipper factory."

* * *

Among the all-time great boxing champions was Barney Ross, who captured the triple crown in the lightweight, junior welterweight and welterweight divisions. He also won the Distinguished Service Cross for outstanding bravery during World War II, as a fighting Marine. But that is another story that belongs properly to the rich heritage of American-Jewish folklore. We are concerned here with an incident that occurred when Barney was on his way toward achieving the welterweight title.

A new, young sparring partner, William Brophy, otherwise known as Wild Bill, was anxious to impress Barney with his skill and aggressiveness—a good but rather obvious way to "psyche" an opponent. So the Irish product of New York's lower West Side—a character straight out of a Damon Runyon story—proceeded to lay it on thick.

"I'm one helluva tough guy," said Bill, swaggering back and forth across the room and flexing his muscles. "In fack, I'm da toughes' guy who ever came outta Hell's Kitchen."

Barney smiled patiently, quite aware of the young fellow's purpose.

"Just how tough are you, kid?" he asked.

"Oh, ya callin' me 'kid', huh? Well, aroun' my neighborhood, when anybody called me 'kid' I knocked 'im out in one roun'. Dat's why dey call me Wild Bill."

"I have news for you, kid," said Barney, unperturbed, but tiring of the brash youngster's big mouth. "After I get through with you, Wild Bill will be known forever as Sweet William!"

* * *

Twelve-year-old Jennifer, whose latest "cause" was ecology, had been listening to the news on her pocket transistor radio.

"I think people should be stopped from shooting the rapids," she cried indignantly. "They have just as much right to live as we have!"

* * *

Seymour and Stanley decided that if the *goyim* could climb mountains, so could they. Whereupon, they traveled to Switzerland to climb the Alps.

By the afternoon of the first day, they were way up near the clouds when Seymour lost his footing, fell fifteen hundred feet and landed spread-eagled on a snow-covered ledge.

Stanley peered down over the precipice and yelled at the top of his lungs:

"Seymour! Seymour! You're all right?"

"Y-e-e-e-s, I'm o-k-a-a-a-y!" came Seymour's voice in a long, far-away echo. "But my hands are fro-o-ozen!"

"Listen, Seymour, don't worry about your hands. I'm letting you down a rope. Just grab it with your teeth and I'll pull you up."

Stanley lowered the rope and Seymour managed to get a good grip on it with his strong teeth. Little by little, as Stanley pulled, his friend was hauled up the steep side of the mountain. It took nearly two hours but finally Seymour was only three feet from the top.

"Keep your teeth in that rope, Seymour. In a minute you'll be safe. How do you feel?"

"I'm *f-i-i-i-n-e!*"

* * *

You never see it on television, of course, but those Rose Bowl games on New Year's day call for a lot of drinking by the fans, either to keep warm or just for the sake of conviviality.

Last year, the Pasadena bottlers came up with a newly-invented highball. It's called a "Football Special"—three drinks and you kick off!

* * *

It is a well-known fact that a man looks larger with his clothes off than he does when fully dressed. The point was driven home one day when Max Baer, a huge, powerfully-muscled hulk of a man, stretched out on a couch in the cooling room of a Turkish bath. A stranger, coming in from the steam room and blinking as the sweat ran down his face, spied the giant of a man and halted. He wiped his eyes clear and approached the reclining figure.

"I beg your pardon for addressing a perfect stranger," he said in a deferential voice, "but would you mind telling me who you are?"

"Not at all," said the other affably. "My name is Max Baer. I'm a jockey."

26

Interfaith Ecumania

INTRODUCTION

Throughout history, a nation's moral health and cultural maturity could usually be determined by its treatment of the Jews. But the word "treatment" has little significance in America where, as a policy of state, the Jewish citizen is not "treated" as a separate entity but "accepted" as an integral part of society. Freed from the mailed fist of arbitrary power in Europe, enjoying the same rights accorded any other American, he is at liberty to express himself as prophet, sage or fool, dependent only upon his individual talents and proclivities.

The uninhibited exchange of interreligious banter with members of the various Christian faiths represents a departure for the Jew. In the Old World, it was unusual in some countries and unthinkable in others. Derision was acceptable when applied to Jewish religious beliefs, but blasphemous when the same joke was deflected back to the teller. What was sauce for the goose was vitriol for the gander.

To the credit of the American Jew, his interfaith jokes bear no resemblance to the barbs which passed for humor on the continent—particularly in Eastern Europe. The difference is that the American joke in this category is a concord of good will, good nature, good humor and good taste—told with playful intent; sometimes to make a point, but more often because the anecdote or quip is simply funny. These inoffensive jokes, some of which are represented in this chapter, revolve around the similarities as well as differences between synagogue and church practices, theological and philosophical viewpoints, rabbis and priests, and the tongue-in-cheek "misunderstandings" that arise from these similarities and differences. If there is any undercurrent of hostility in the jokes, they are well hidden beneath layers of absurdities and ludicrous characters.

According to the late Ralph Weingart, the waggish, turn-of-the century rabbi of Baltimore, "it sometimes appears that the only true Christians are found among the Jews." But what is a Jew? That thorny question has been plaguing Jewry for eons; but, as a sort of extra bonus to the reader, I shall answer it and settle the argument once and for all. And, like a lion in a den of Daniels, I shall not only emerge unscathed, but earn the undying gratitude of a noble people.

First, to be a Christian is a fate; to be a Jew is a destiny. I am not quite sure what that means, but we have to start somewhere, and it does sound intelligent.

Isaac Bashevis Singer wrote that Jews are "a people who can't sleep themselves, and let nobody else sleep." Singer sang a sad song with that observation, but we note a suggestion of frivolity in it which may be a little out of place in this serious quest for eternal truth.

Let us consider a few other sources of enlightenment. Isaac Peretz, the famed Yiddish novelist, stated, "We are more than a people . . . . We are of pure blood." But no less an authority than Rabbi Stephen S. Wise declared, "We are a race by religion, *not* of blood!" And that about sums that up.

Now that you know what a Jew is, let us discuss our Christian brethren. It seems to me that every Jewish humor book should also have something nice to say about gentile humor, if for nothing else than to show there are no hard feelings. After all, look how good they've been to the Jewish people all these years.

Gentiles claim there are only seven basic jokes. Here they are, in the order of their unimportance:

1. On West 53rd Street and 10th Avenue, there's a sportsminded fellow who spent all evening trying to get the English Channel on his TV set.
2. A pretty girl is like a melody—after you marry her you have to face the music.
3. There once was an ambitious band leader who hired more musicians than he could shake a stick at.
4. The Madison Avenue bus was so crowded last week that even the driver had to move to the rear.
5. A banker called his stockbroker for some quick cash, only to learn that the broker was broker than he.
6. A cannibal finally left the Congo for the big city to visit a psychiatrist because he was fed up with people.
7. Pat McNulty was ordered to get an immediate flu shot, but his bartender didn't know how to mix one.

Those are the funniest of the elemental gentile jokes—and now you know why there is such a crying need for *Jewish* humor!

The cement that bonds Christian and Jewish humor is "understanding"—a cerebral secretion that enables one having it to know a house from a horse by the roof on the house. Its nature and laws have been intensively expounded by Locke, who rode a house, and by Kant, who lived in a horse.

Another ingredient of interfaith amity is common sense. One simply does not call up the pope and tell him he can resign because he's in good hands with Allstate. Nor is it necessary to remind priest or rabbi that purgatory is hell.

Having exhausted all the similarities in the Judeo-Christian relationship, we now turn our objective attention to its differences. The modern

American Jew, it has been pointed out by the philosopher, Boris Blue-belly, believes in the religion of Jesus; he just cannot bring himself to accept the religion *about* Jesus. One area of disagreement which is frequently mentioned—at least in this book—is the idea of a soul, a spiritual entity concerning which there hath been brave disputation. Bluebelly held that the soul has its seat in the liver and he has often been quoted as saying, "He who destroyeth his liver through strong drink loses his soul and shall suffer eternal damnation," a viewpoint which gave rise to the phrase, "That damned drunk!" The Jewish view, especially among the Reform and Reconstructionists, is that the soul resides in the upper duodenum where ulcers attack the less pious. The thoughtful reader would be well advised to accept a little of both theories and thus assure himself a front-row seat in heaven.

We are not yet done with this business of a soul. A difference of opinion exists between gentile and Jew concerning the transmigration of the soul—or reincarnation. Jews believe that the Messiah will someday put in a personal appearance and revive all the dead, restoring to them their original bodies whether they like it or not. Christians, on the other hand, believe that people live an incalculable number of times on this earth, in as many new bodies, because one life is not long enough to attain moral and spiritual perfection. The True Believer is so keen-sighted as to have observed that everyone desirous of perfection eventually attains it through the maturity of the traveling soul. Less competent observers are disposed to exclude Arabs, who seem neither wiser nor better than they were last year.

A majority of the interfaith jokes in this section can be traced back to the latter part of the 19th century and the first two decades of the 20th. A few are obviously new, such as the quip about the banning of Xerox machines by the Catholic Church because they interfere with natural reproduction. One quip, dated at about 1890, describes a saint as a dead sinner, revised and edited. Another of that era announces that New York's priests were planning to organize a union because they wanted Sundays off.

The closeness of Catholic and Jewish humor in the United States probably had its start in the 1870s, at a time when Jewish immigrants began to inherit the East Side tenements from the Irish who preceeded them to this country. Both lived together amicably for as long as the dwindling Irish cave dwellers inhabited the East Side, and until their improved financial circumstances permitted them to leave for better neighborhoods—with the empty caves being quickly occupied by tens of thousands of new Jewish residents. These immigrants, let it be noted, were not the first cave men and women in Jewish history. A famous community of troglodytes dwelt with David in the Cave of Adullam. The colony consisted of "every one that was in distress, and every one that was in debt, and every one that was discontented"—in brief, all the socialists of Judah.

The caustic humor that emanated from the lower East Side of New York may best be explained by David Ben Gurion's witty statement: "The outlook of the ghetto divided the universe into two: this world for the gentiles, the hereafter for the Jews." The Scriptures, for another example, were described as the sacred books of the Old Testament, as distinguished from the false writings on which all other faiths are based. The Sabbath was known as a weekly festival having its origin in the fact that God made the world in six days and was arrested on the seventh. Observance of this day, according to humorists of the 1890s, is enforced by the commandment: "Remember the seventh day to make thy neighbor keep it wholly." In that connection, a point of controversy still exists between Jew and Christian as to whether the week begins or ends with the Sabbath. To the Creator, it seemed fit and expedient that the Sabbath should be the last day of the week, but the Early Fathers of the Church held other views.

Nevertheless, despite all this psuedo-intellectual badinage, the most enduring of the interfaith jokes will still be found among those that depend for their humor on naivete, inoffensive impertinence and the stereotypes (gleefully promoted by the Jewish people themselves) that have long been associated with this genre. They should be. Despite their simple-mindedness, these jokes are often the funniest. We are reminded of the time Mrs. Lefkowitz was granted an audience with the Pope. "Mr. Holiness," she said boldly, "how come a man so successful like you never got married?"

H.D.S.

Ask anyone you happen to meet along Tremont Avenue in the Bronx if he ever heard the one about the local Jewish kid who once enacted the role of the infant Jesus in a school play, and he'll slap his thigh, roar with laughter at the very mention of the tale, and then say, "No, tell me about it." That reaction notwithstanding, let us now spread the cheerful story beyond the confines of the East Bronx and far from the madding I.R.T.

On the momentous day of November 10, 1943, Wally Wexler, a kindergarten pupil at P.S. 67, was about to be touched by the hand of destiny. Mrs. Murphy, the assistant principal, was directing that year's Christmas pageant and, since few babies are normally registered in grade schools, the lady was feverishly casting about for a handsome little boy to portray the infant Jesus. The moment she laid eyes on Wally Wexler's angelic face she knew in her heart that he would be perfect for the part. Because he was Jewish, she experienced a few hours of anxiety until she secured his parents' permission, and then she joyfully went ahead with the rehearsals.

As for Wally, he was about as ecstatic as a six-year-old budding actor could possibly be. His role called for him to lie on a nice, soft cushion inside a laundry basket and remain "as quiet as a mouse" while the older boys and girls performed. Everyone was in costume, and Wally himself was wrapped in a sheet which served as swaddling clothes.

Came the great night. The curtain went up and there, stage center, was Wally, but hidden, of course, in his "manger." A trumpet sounded and Herod gave a soprano cry of rage. Other actors in their costumes representing sheep, goats and cows, milled about, baaing, bleating and mooing. Mary and Joseph, looking a little young for their age, gave forth with the glad news of the first Yuletide, and at the door of the impromptu stable the Three Wise Men prepared to enter onstage.

Wally's performance, thus far, had been exemplary—in fact, just marvelous—as he lay in the "manger" without sound or motion. He could not see over the rim of the basket and he wondered how the other actors were faring. The sounds of the "farm animals" and the dialogue and murmurings of the players increased his curiosity. But it was the reaction of the audience that intrigued him most. He could hear their whispers, the rustle of their clothing, the creaking of their chairs and an occasional cough. Then came a round of applause beyond isolated Wally's understanding.

Whatever Biblical teachings, traditions and history had been imparted to him in his six years of life, they were sadly deficient in the details surrounding the birth of the Galilean. Nor had his limited knowledge of Mosaic law prepared him for receiving such gifts as precious stones and frankincense, to say nothing of myrrh. Vaguely, he comprehended that somebody was about to offer him a bunch of presents, and that he was somehow important in the general scheme of things, but a laundry basket tends to shut off the view.

Wally could stand it no longer. The unseen activity proved too much for an inquisitive little boy. He raised one experimental eye over the side of the manger. A rolling chuckle spread through the audience at the unexpected debut. This appreciation of his acting ability encouraged him to sit up in full view of the spectators. Now Mrs. Murphy groaned in anguish, the other participants in the Nativity play joined the audience as interested observers, and the pageant ground to an inglorious halt.

Wally smiled happily. All eyes were fastened on him! He was the *star*!

Surrounded by King Herod, Mary and Joseph, the Three Wise Men and all the players representing the farm animals, Wally aimed both index fingers at the audience like two spraying machine guns and went—
"*Ack-ack-ack-ack-ack-ack-ack-ack-ack-!*"

* * *

Six-year-old Rachel persuaded her friend Constance, a little Methodist girl, to attend synagogue with her. All went well. On the following Sunday, Rachel's parents agreed that their daughter could go to the Methodist Sunday School with Constance as a return courtesy.

The Sunday School teacher spoke at length of the Good Samaritan, adding a few gory details of her own that made Rachel's stomach a little queasy. When the teacher finished, she decided to put the moral of the parable to practical use.

"Now, children," she began, "if you saw a man lying in the street after being hit by a speeding car, and he was bleeding all over from ugly wounds, what would you do?"

Volunteered Rachel: "I'd frow up!"

* * *

A wealthy black executive hired a butler who was Jewish. On the first New Year's Eve after his employment, as the family sat down to dinner, the butler was summoned by the man of the house:

"Sam, would you please bring a bottle of '59 Beaujolais?"

The butler, fingers snapping, danced out of the room, singing:

"Bring out de cream cheese,
Slice dat bagel,
Spread on de schmaltz, please,
Taste dat knaidel—
Ya dig, man?"

The Negro employer smiled indulgently.

"You have to give those Jews credit," he commented to his family at the table. "They sure got rhythm!"

* * *

It was St. Patrick's Day in New York and the annual parade along Fifth Avenue was about to begin. Tens of thousands of spectators lined the sidewalks on each side of the thoroughfare, among them Father O'Malley and his friend Alex Zimmerman.

"I just noticed something that puzzles me, Alex," said Father O'Malley, almost shouting to make himself heard above the laughter and gaiety that surrounded them. "You're wearing a shamrock."

"Take a good look around you," grinned Alex.

The priest let his eyes rove up and down the street. "It seems to me," he said, rather surprised, "that there are many Jewish faces in the crowd—and, yes, they're all wearing shamrocks, too."

"Well, the answer is quite simple. This is a unique occasion for my people."

"Unique?"

"Sure," said Alex, chuckling. "How often can a million Jews gather together just to watch the help marching by?"

* * *

Patricia, a Catholic girl, and David, a Jewish boy, were very much in love. However, because of her religious convictions, she refused to marry him unless he converted to Catholicism. After much soul-searching, he finally gave in to her tearful pleading and agreed to undertake the Church's required course of study. And now that he had made up his mind, he threw himself into his labors with a vengeance, poring over his books night and day, speaking with Church officials and asking profound questions of his instructors.

One evening, three months after her sweetheart had begun his studies, Patricia came home sobbing.

"What's the matter, dear?" asked her mother. "Why are you crying?"

"It's David," she wept. "He's decided to become a priest!"

* * *

Let us go back to the second decade of this century.

Father Ducey, a famous New York clergyman, was the resident priest at St. Leo's, one of the most widely-known Catholic churches in the downtown area.

One weekend, in the spring of 1919, Father Ducey became ill, as did many others during the flu epidemic that claimed so many victims that year. His assistants had also fallen before the rampaging virus, so, out of desperation, he sent an emissary to the equally famous Rabbi Stephen S. Wise, pleading that he conduct the Sunday confessional hearings in his stead. The good rabbi, possessor of a sharp and cultivated wit, saw the humor as well as the urgency of the situation, and he consented to sit in his friend's place.

Early the next Sunday morning, a woman entered and coughed nervously. From the other side of the partition she heard a voice—a voice that was kindly and inviting:

"Well, my daughter, what have you to tell me?"

"F-f-father Ducey," sputtered the lady, "I-I-I'm embarrassed to say this—I've always b-b-been a good Catholic . . ."

"I absolve you of that," interrupted Rabbi Wise. "Go on with your confession."

But the horror-stricken penitent had fled.

* * *

Avner, who had recently arrived in the United States from Israel, was taking a stroll down Lexington Avenue one afternoon to familiarize himself with his new surroundings. During the course of his walk, he happened to meet his gentile neighbor who was in earnest conversation with his pastor. The neighbor introduced them.

"Where are you from?" asked the minister, noting Avner's Hebrew-accented English.

"From Haifa," said the newcomer to our shores.

"Oh, yes," exclaimed the cleric, beaming, "we have a mission there."

"A mission in Haifa?" echoed the surprised Avner. "What for?"

"Why, to spread the Word—'Jesus Saves.'"

"Reverend, pardon me for saying so," said Avner haltingly, "but your mission has no chance. In Israel, the words are 'Jesus Saves—Moses Invests!'"

* * *

Patrick and Marvin were walking home from school one afternoon when they encountered Father O'Toole who was hobbling along in a painful, bent-over posture.

"Good morning, Patrick," said the priest, every word an effort. "How's my little parishioner today?"

"I'm fine, Father, thanks. But why are you walking all crippled up like that? What happened?"

"Frankly," said the cleric, somewhat embarrassed, "I fell off the commode and injured my back."

The boys expressed their I'm sorries and then walked on. After a minute or two of silent reflection, Patrick blurted out:

"What's a commode?"

"How should I know?" retorted Marvin. "Am I a Cath'lic?"

* * *

The Prime Minister of Uganda called in his most famous architect. "I want you to build me a palace," he demanded. "I want it to be ornate, breathtaking, imposing—the most magnificent palace anywhere in Africa."

"Very well," said the architect, "but first I'll have to go to New York. I'll need time to study the latest building methods, learn about new structural designs and engineering techniques."

So the architect went to New York and studied for a whole year. When he returned to Uganda, the Prime Minister asked, "When can you start building my grand palace?"

"With God's help I can begin sometime between *Yom Kippur* and *Succoth*," replied the architect.

"Why are you using all those strange words?" asked the Prime Minister suspiciously. "Have you forgotten that you are a Ugandan?"

"No, of course not," replied the architect. "But after six months in Manhattan, two months in Brooklyn and four months in the Bronx, one tends to use the local idiom."

* * *

Inside a little country church near Landover Hills, Maryland, the rector was in the midst of a Sunday morning sermon. Mrs. Anderson sat in a front pew with her daughter, Catherine, and the little girl's friend, Mildred Cohen, age nine.

Mildred had never been to church before and the activities held her interest for a while, but soon she began to fidget. To make matters worse, the three candy bars she had eaten without her parents' knowledge had upset her stomach. Presently, she glanced up with a distressed look on her face.

"Mrs. Anderson," she whispered.

"Shh!" hissed the lady.

"But, Mrs. Anderson, I feel sick," persisted Mildred.

"Sit still and think of something else," suggested Mrs. Anderson, regretting that she had allowed herself to be talked into bringing the child.

"But, Mrs. Anderson, I'm gonna be awful sick in just a minute!"

"Oh, all right!" snapped the irritated woman. "Just slip out very quietly and go behind that big tree in the churchyard. When you feel better you can come back."

Her eyes now glassy, her skin tinted yellow and her jaws tightly locked, Mildred trotted down the aisle. In what seemed to be an amazingly short time, everything considered, the little girl returned to her seat.

"Feel better?" inquired the lady rather testily.

"Uh-huh, I feel okay now."

"You weren't gone very long. You must have found the big tree very quickly."

"No, ma'am. I didn't hafta go way out in the yard. Right outside the church door, in the lobby, I saw a box and it had a little sign on it. And the sign said—

"For the Sick!"

* * *

When a Jew converts to Christianity all he gets is a new religious title. But when a Christian converts to Judaism—ahh!—he at once becomes retroactively eligible for 2,000 years of persecution!

* * *

It has been said that Judaism is not only a religion; it is a state of mind. For some, it approaches religious chauvinism, which isn't necessarily bad. Witness:

Pincus and his family of little Pincii were returning home from *shul* one day when his youngest son stopped to talk with another boy. In the course of their brief discussion, the youngster asked the other boy his religion. After some hesitation, he replied that he was a Catholic.

"Son," asked papa Pincus a little while later, "did I hear you ask that boy his religion?"

"Yes, I did."

"Let me give you a word of advice, young man," counseled the father. "Never ask a person his religion. If he's Jewish he'll tell you soon enough. If he's not, there's no point in embarrassing him!"

* * *

Four separate shipwrecks occurred and four survivors were cast up on a lonely island far off the regular shipping routes. Two of the men were Americans, the other two were Englishmen. After several months, a passing steamer hove to and took the four aboard. The Americans, Sidney and Stanley, were escorted to the skipper's cabin, there to relate their experiences.

"Captain," said Stanley, "it would really grieve you to see the way those two Englishmen ignored each other. In the whole time we were on that island neither of them said a single word to the other. You ask why? Simply because they weren't properly introduced."

"And how did you two fellows make out?" asked the skipper.

"We didn't need introductions," said Sidney. "On the very same day I found Stanley on the beach, we organized a reform and conservative temple a debating society, a golf club, a Bonds for Israel chapter and an Impeach Nixon protest!"

* * *

Orthodox rabbis do not, as a general rule, attend Catholic church services—at least not in Milwaukee where this story has been making the rounds since the last Iroquois uprising.

A gentile friend cajoled Rabbi Berkowitz into attending St. Joseph's in the city that made Schlitz famous. The old rabbi, long since retired, finally agreed when it was explained that a visiting dignitary would speak about the Jewish influence on the formation of the Church.

In the front row, Rabbi Berkowitz's eyes widened as the visiting lecturer announced his topic: *My name is Joseph, father of Jesus.*

At the conclusion of the talk, when they had been introduced, the rabbi said drily:

"My friend, you have had a most unusual experience!"

* * *

Two youngsters were arguing the relative merits of their respective faiths.

"Bet you don't even know the difference between a Methodist, a Baptist and a Jew," taunted the Protestant boy.

"Oh, yeah? I do so!" retorted the Jewish boy. "A Baptist gets dunked in water over his head, but a Methodist only gets sprinkled."

"What happens to the Jew?"

"A Jew—well—hmm—a Jew, I think, gets dry-cleaned!"

* * *

The members of St. Thomas Aquinas Church in the Bronx were so fond of their priest that they presented him with a brand new Cadillac.

Across the street, at Temple Yisroel, the congregants watched as the priest came out, inspected the car appreciatively and blessed it by making the sign of the cross.

Not to be outdone, the Jewish worshipers immediately bought their rabbi a new Cadillac also. Then he came out, inspected the car, and snipped off the tip of the radiator hose.

* * *

Groucho Marx, who once said of a woman, "She speaks 120 words a minute with gusts up to 160," is well known for his jaggedly serrated tongue. Not long ago, he was approached by a certain highly-respected priest.

"I want to thank you for all the joy you've brought into the world," said the good father.

Snapped Groucho: "I want to thank you for all the joy you've taken out of it!"

* * *

A spiritualist séance was in progress. The medium, Mrs. Hannah Goldberg, specialized in summoning the spirits of great historical figures from the Other Shore. Tonight was especially rewarding for the assembled True Believers. The Czarina rapped on a table and made a chair waltz on two legs. Albert Einstein strummed a guitar and sang excerpts from *Fiddler on the Roof*. King Solomon recited his famous passages with a pronounced Flatbush accent.

At this juncture, Louis Goldberg, the medium's husband, made a special announcement. If anyone present wished to communicate with the shade of some illustrious one who had not already taken part in the evening's program, the medium—for a slight fee—would endeavor to materialize the individual desired.

A visiting True Believer, Mrs. Sullivan, spoke up. She would give anything, she stated, if she could just have a direct blessing from her Lord and Saviour.

"Oh," she cried, "if only I could have His personal benediction!"

"A benediction!" called out someone else in the audience.

"A benediction! A benediction! A benediction!" chanted the others in unison.

Madame Goldberg agreed to try. As her husband hastily retreated, she went off into a trance, uttering muffled, moaning sounds. Presently, the black draperies at the entrance to the room were agitated and then, in the pale bluish light that shone dimly upon the curtains and left the rest of the room in darkness, there appeared a ghostly figure swathed in white.

In the midst of the ensuing silence that was as still and quiet as death itself, the apparition took one step forward, raised two fingers of its right hand in the gesture of apostolic blessing and, in impressively deep tones, uttered the word they had all been waiting to hear:

"Benedictine!"

* * *

It isn't often that an honest-to-goodness true anecdote is offered which is genuinely funny, but this one was reported in the staid *Catholic Beacon*. The ending fairly bursts with unconscious humor:

Arthur Feldman, formerly of the Jewish faith, has completed his training period and has taken the required Communion. He will shortly graduate from the Church of the Transfiguration.

* * *

The Rev. Billy Graham was putting on his biggest revival meeting in the history of Los Angeles and Shirley Rapoport decided to attend. So persuasive, so powerful a speaker was the popular evangelist that before his sermon was over, Shirley was "saved."

"Oh, Dr. Graham," she gushed, completely overwhelmed in her new-found faith for the evening, "before you came, I didn't know what sin was!"

* * *

Mr. Kramer was not too happy with the news that his daughter was keeping company with a gentile fellow. "A million fine Jewish boys in America," he would scold, "and you have to pick a *shaigetz*!"

One evening the daughter brought her boyfriend home to dinner.
The young fellow, not a bad sort of chap, thought it might be prudent
to ingratiate himself with old man Kramer. What better way than to
claim a small bit of Jewish ancestry? In any case, it was rather stylish
to be Jewish these days.

"You'll be surprised to know, sir," the boyfriend began, "that I am
part Jewish."

"You're right," snapped the father. "With a name like Patrick Clancey, I *am* surprised. So enlighten me."

"It happens that I have one-sixteenth Jewish blood in my veins."

"In that case I'd be very careful if I were you," said Kramer, his
voice grim. "One nosebleed and you're out of the tribe!"

* * *

An episode in interfaith relations occurred recently at the Church of
the Immaculate Heart in Los Angeles.

It seems that Ethel Rosen's labor pains began several days earlier
than either she or her doctor had anticipated. Her husband, Phil, quickly
bundled her into their car and he began a wild ride to the maternity
hospital. But he had not driven more than four or five blocks when Ethel
emitted a fearful scream:

"Ohhh, Phil! Ow-wow-wow-wow! It's happening! The baby is coming! Yowww-wow-wow!"

Phil brought the car to a screeching halt and frantically looked about
for help. He noticed that he had parked right in front of the Catholic
church, so he dashed inside and, in a complete panic, told the priest what
was going on at his very doorstep.

"Don't worry about a thing," the priest said reassuringly. "I've
delivered several babies. No problem at all."

He went outside, entered the back of the car and, in a most professional manner, he brought the baby into the world, smacked its little
behind to start it breathing, and then he went to the hospital with them
to make sure everything progressed smoothly. He was indeed a good
Samaritan—a true man of the cloth.

In the hospital, the doctor warmly complimented the priest for his
timely and humane actions. He put Ethel to bed, made the baby comfortable, and then turned to Phil.

"That was a mighty nice act of kindness on the part of the priest,
Mr. Rosen. Why not show your appreciation by naming the baby after
him?"

And that is exactly what he did. He named the baby "Father"!

* * *

Did you ever wonder why the Jewish people have for so long been
termed "stiff-necked"—even by their own prophets? Perhaps a clue is
provided in the following exchange.

A rabbi and a priest were discussing the differences between the Old
Testament and the New. It was the priest's contention that the New
Testament gave more proof of Divine cooperation because of all its

purported miracles.

"Remember," argued the priest, "our Lord walked on water, he raised the dead, he fed hundreds of people with a few loaves of bread and some little fishes, he changed water into wine, and he ascended bodily into Heaven."

"So what does that prove?" insisted the rabbi. "The Old Testament includes such miracles as parting the Red Sea, making the sun stand still, Moses ascending bodily to Mt. Sinai to talk personally with God and to receive the Decalogue from the very hands of the Almighty."

The priest nodded. "I believe in those miracles, too," he acknowledged. "But be honest about it—do you really think your miracles have as much substance as ours?"

The rabbi glared at him.

"What's the matter with you?" he snapped crossly. "Can't you distinguish between fact and fiction?"

* * *

To be orthodox in everything in which a policeman figures, the said policeman should be of Irish extraction. Any departure from this is a violation of all folklore tradition. Nevertheless, convention notwithstanding, the hero of this story is a policeman who was not an Irishman. He was a Scot. But, before introducing him, it is necessary to present the other principal character involved in this little tragedy, circa 1890.

That other character was Jewish, but he was not a police officer. He was, in fact, an elderly civilian who had stopped during a stroll to watch a job of street repairing.

Three stories up above his head, a housewife placed a large platter of cheese *blintzes* to cool on the front window ledge of her tenement. The ledge had a slant to it. The platter slid off and, descending, struck the elderly gentleman squarely on the head, bruising his scalp and covering him with the contents of the dish.

He gave a loud cry of pain and astonishment and sank to the sidewalk. He was not badly hurt but he had suffered a rather severe shock. As sympathetic onlookers pulled him up to a sitting position, the Scot policeman ranged up alongside and took in the sight.

"Well," he said, "I kenned you Jews were fond of *blintzes*, but, laddie, you're the first one I ever knew to decorate himself with 'em."

* * *

Theodore Roosevelt's dislike of bigotry can be traced back to his early days in politics when he served as Police Commissioner of New York City from 1895 to 1897.

"While I was in that post," he reminisced, "an anti-Semitic preacher from Berlin, Rector Ahlwardt, came to New York to preach a crusade against the Jews.

"Many Jews were quite excited and asked me to prevent him from speaking and not to give him police protection. But this, I told them, was impossible, and even if it were possible it would have been undesirable because it would make a martyr of him. The proper thing to do was to make him appear ridiculous.

"Accordingly, I sent a detail of police under a Jewish sergeant, and the Jew-baiter made his harangue under the active protection of some 40 police officers, every one of them Jewish.

* * *

Houses of God often take on peculiar and humorous nicknames in America.

The Catholic church in California where the families of many of the wealthy stars (like Loretta Young and family, Danny Thomas and family) would go each Sunday to worship, was nicknamed "The Church of the Cadillacs." The orthodox synagogue in Brooklyn on Eastern Parkway and Albany Avenue, where wealthy families like the Rokeachs and Bronfmans once worshiped, was called Murphy's Shul because the land on which it was built was once owned by Murphy.

27

Religion

INTRODUCTION

Tristan Bernard, the French-Jewish writer, was asked what he thought of life after death. He replied: "With regard to the climate, I would prefer Heaven, but with regard to company I would give preference to Hell." Bernard, to be sure, was no thundering voice of Judaism, but his comment is a valid illustration of the Jewish view of humor which not only laughs at its own shibboleths but also at those of others. That laughter, however, contains within itself an innate understanding of Jewish strengths as well as frailties: the characteristic which distinguishes it from the kind of anti-Semitic derision which for too long masqueraded as "Jewish" humor.

There is nothing new about coupling levity with religion: the Talmud and the Bible themselves contain a fair share of biting wit and humor. Eliezer, the first-century Talmudist, sardonically observed that the time to pray and the time to act do not necessarily coincide. "When the children of Israel came to the Red Sea and Moses prayed too long," wrote Eliezer, "the Holy One said to him: 'My children are in trouble: the sea before them, and the enemy behind them, and you stand here indulging in long prayers!'" For further authority, we turn to the Bible—the Book of Psalms—where we find that even the Almighty has a sense of humor: "He that sits in Heaven laughs." We can only conclude that if humor is good enough up there it ought to be good enough down here.

The noted wit, Robert Orben, quipped, "My wife was the answer to my prayers—which could explain what is happening to religion these days." But it wasn't always thus. For instance, there was the day of the miracle—an act or event out of the order of nature, such as beating a normal hand of four kings and an ace with four aces and a king. And there was the omen—a sure sign that something will happen if nothing happens. These Divine gratuities began in the era of the pre-Adamites, a group of experimental and apparently unsatisfactory races that antedated Creation and lived under conditions not easily conceived. Duuvid Jacobson, the Darwinian geologist who was recently arrested for stealing a shovel from the custodial room at CCNY, believes that these pre-Creation beings inhabited the "Void" and were something between fishes and birds. Little is known of them beyond the fact that they supplied Cain with a wife and theologians with a controversy. Professor Jacobson is currently writing a book entitled *Sacred Songs My Warden Taught Me.*

The intellectual quality of Jewish religious humor is usually at its sharpest and funniest when it revolves around the opposing theological views of Judaism and Mohammedanism. The witticisms are funny because the humor often derives from a straightforward comparison of the two, rather than a "punch line." Consider the differences between Mohammedan and Jew in their respective ideas of Heaven. The Moslem envisions his Mohammedan Paradise as the abode of the *houri*, a comely female whose sole function is to make things cheery for him when he takes up post-Earthly residence there. His belief in her existence marks a noble discontent with his mortal spouse to whom he denies a soul. That lady, it is said, holds the *houris* in deficient esteem.

Conversely, the Jew sees Heaven as a place where the wicked refrain from annoying him with their silly opinions, while the good listen with close attention to his own intelligent views. All this cerebral conflict arises not only from a study of the Bible, but the Koran as well— a book which the Mohammedans believe to have been written by Divine inspiration, but which Jews and Christians know to be contradictory to the Holy Scriptures. This does not, of course, absolve the Christians who prefer King James' version to God's. Professor Jacobson has proposed that an orthodox *cheder* be opened in Cairo and in Vatican City for remedial teaching.

Infidels are found in all races and in all climes (if the reader will pardon an original observation). In Rome and Madrid, an infidel is one who does not believe in the Church; in Tel Aviv and New York, he is one who does. As Jewish humor defines it, impiety among Christians is the belief that a certain party was conceived in the same pleasant manner as was Moses. Among Jews, piety is reverence for the Supreme Being based upon His resemblance to man, excluding U.N. delegates. But, however hard they try, Jews are simply incapable of understanding the Pygmies of Equatorial Africa who happen to be monotheists, each having no other god than himself, and whom he worships under many sacred names. His religious symbol is neither a Magen David, a cross nor a crescent, but an elevator shoe. The Pygmies are so called to distinguish them from the bulkier Caucasians—who are Hogmies.

American-Jewish humor thrives on controversy. To mention just one aspect, the Jewish people, like their Christian brethren, are divided in their views about predestination and free will. The predestinarian believes that Adam's fall was decreed from the beginning, but the freewillers hold that he need not have sinned unless he had a mind to. Men and women have been sinning in a like manner ever since that little affair in the Garden of Eden, and the Creator, who was responsible for the built-in habit in the first place, has yet to offer a satisfactory reason for his opposition.

Man alone, it appears, must assume all responsibility for his actions. But some ultra-modern Jews regard responsibility as a detachable burden easily shifted to the shoulders of fate, fortune, luck or a neighbor. Believers in astrology unload it upon a handy star. Some of the young Jewish males become Jesus Freaks and remain so until their next change of underwear, at which time they are usually too old to resume their studies of Torah. Also, as some of the anecdotes in this chapter indicate, there is the individual who seeks revelation, edification and solace in the mysticism of the clairvoyant—a person, usually a woman, who has the power of seeing that which is invisible to the patron; namely, that he is a *shnook*.

The comments made in this Introduction only suggest the wide scope of Jewish humor as it pertains to religion. It ranges from the incisive to the bland. An example of one of the more innocuous expressions of Jewish wit is represented in a sign on the front lawn of a Reform synagogue in Beverly Hills. It reads:

EVERYONE WELCOME
Entertainment–Refreshments
Hear Veronica from Santa Monica
Play Her Harmonica this Chanukah!

As for the sharper Jewish humor, we offer this prediction, made by the late columnist-author Lawrence Lipton in the Los Angeles *Free Press:*

Pope Paul VI will settle the Church's birth control problem by proclaiming immaculate conception as the holiest and most effective contraceptive, having resulted in only one case of pregnancy in 2,000 years.

The Black Jews of America have a credo which, though stated a little differently, is essentially the same as that of their white coreligionists. I offer it as a parting benediction:

"You should so live that when the roll is called up yonder you won't have to cram for the final exams."

H.D.S.

Let us begin the stories and jokes in this chapter with the reiteration that the age of a good and lively yarn need not be the criterion for its telling. The very fact that an anecdote has endured the wear and tear of many years is ample proof of its excellence; had it lacked merit, it would have died a natural death long ago. So, for a new generation of readers, here is a tale that had its vogue a few years after the Spanish-American War—some time between 1903 and 1908.

In Baltimore, at the turn of the century, an itinerant *maggid*, or preacher (looking for all the world like a prophet of old with his majestic white beard and flowing, snow-white robe), was invited to speak at the Sanhedrin Temple (located on what is now the site of Sears, Roebuck). The synagogue's regular rabbi was somewhat apprehensive about the old man's ultra-orthodox views, but he had come highly recommended. The rabbi's fears, as it turned out, were justified. The *maggid* harangued the congregation with a scorching sermon that would have done credit to a Bible-thumping, fundamentalist Baptist preacher. As the venerable patriarch brought his sermon to a close he shouted:

"And I say unto you, the Day of Judgment is at hand, and unless you have lived in strict accordance with the Law as handed down to us by Moses himself, there will be weeping and wailing and gnashing of teeth!"

An old lady in the front row, frightened half out of her wits, cried out:

"But, *rebbe*, I have no teeth."

"My good woman," thundered the righteous *maggid*, "teeth will be provided!"

* * *

Shadrach, Meshak and Abednego, having survived the fiery furnace, offered up their prayers to the Almighty. When they had finished, Shadrach made his complaint:

"Lord, not that I'm criticizing, you understand, but that last idea of yours wasn't so hot!"

* * *

Mrs. Jacoby went to the post office to mail her son a Bible. He had just enrolled in a Yeshiva the week before, and she wanted him to have it as soon as possible.

"Anything in this package that's breakable?" asked the postal clerk.

"Only the Ten Commandments," said Mrs. Jacoby.

* * *

Those avant-garde temples designed by modern-minded architects can inspire religious fervor, arouse our pagan instincts or incite our indignation, depending on individual reaction.

For example, when Philadelphia contractor Max Engel visited Beverly Hills for the first time, his son, who had moved to California several years before, drove him along the "Miracle Mile" on Wilshire Boulevard. There he beheld a breathtaking sight—an ultra-modern synagogue whose lines were apparently borrowed from the Taj Mahal, the Roman Amphitheatre, the Vatican, King Solomon's Temple and a Lord Baltimore filling station.

"That's my synagogue," boasted the son. "Temple Beth Nishtgedeiget—Reform. How do you like it?"

"To tell you the truth," replied conservative Mr. Engel, "I wouldn't know whether to pray in it, at it, or for it!"

* * *

"And now, Shirley," said the Hebrew School teacher after the Bible lesson was finished, "please tell the class—what were Dan and Beersheba?"

Twelve-year-old Shirley, who had been watching some pigeons on the window ledge when she should have been paying attention, hesitated and then answered uncertainly:

"I—I think they were a husband and wife—something like Sodom and Gomorrah!"

* * *

A member of the International Ladies Garment Workers Union paid a social call at the home of his shop steward. As he rang the bell, he noticed with surprise that the *mezuzah* on the doorpost had been replaced with the likeness of an apple.

"What happened to the *mezuzah*?" he asked when he had been admitted inside the house. "Since when have apples become our symbol?"

"You're forgetting something," replied the ILGWU steward calmly. "If it weren't for the apple, where would the garment industry be today?"

* * *

A teacher was checking her students' knowledge of proverbs.
"Cleanliness is next to what?" she asked the class.
Replied a small boy, with feeling:
"Impossible!"

* * *

Laurie Goldstein, teacher at the Prospect Avenue Hebrew School in the Bronx, reminds us that it doesn't hurt to be prepared with a quick comeback when confronted by the inevitable fresh little kid in every class. One such youngster attempted to stump her with a trick question.

"Who was the straightest man in the Bible?" asked the boy.
"I don't know," replied Miss Golstein innocently. "Who?"
"Joseph," responded the fresh kid, grinning broadly. "Pharaoh made a ruler out of him."

"I'm glad to see that you've studied your Bible," she said evenly. "Perhaps you can tell the class who was the *smallest* man in the Bible?"

He gave her a blank look. "I don't know," he admitted.
Smiling, she told him:
"Bildad, the Shu-ite!"

* * *

Twelve-year-old Gary came from a very strict orthodox home and, of course, attended an orthodox synagogue with his parents. One day, a reform family moved into the apartment next door and they soon became friends. The neighbor's child, a girl of Gary's age, persuaded him to accompany her to the reform temple.

"*Nu*, what did you think of the *goyishe shul*?" asked the boy's parents when he returned home.

"Well," he said, shrugging, "the music had a pretty good beat, but the commercial was too long!"

* * *

Tomorrow was *Chanukah*, and little Clifford, kneeling beside his bed, his hands clasped in fervent prayer, was making his pitch:

". . . and I want a new ten-speed bike, a basketball, a football and a new English teacher. These demands are non-negotiable!"

*   *   *

The teacher at the Hebrew Day School had just finished telling the story of Moses to the children in her class.

"Now, tell me," she concluded, "what would you do if you found a little baby in the bulrushes, just like the Pharaoh's daughter did?"

Little Susie's hand shot up. "I know what I'd do," she cried. "I'd change him!"

*   *   *

Davey put away his toys for the evening and, as usual, began his bedtime prayers in a low monotone.

"Honey," said his mother, "I can't hear you."

Retorted Davey: "I wasn't talking to you!"

*   *   *

Most Jews have some sort of knowledge about the three main branches of Judaism—Orthodox, Conservative and Reform. At least they know which ones to ignore at fund-raising times.

*   *   *

For almost a year, Grandpa Sulzberg had been a constant embarrassment to his family. He would mount a soap box on street corners in his neighborhood and proclaim himself the Messiah. Then he would proceed to harangue the amused crowds that gathered, hurling fierce warnings and injunctions, reminding them of the dire consequences of their evil ways. In his long white robe which he had fashioned from a bedsheet, and his flowing, silvery beard, he did indeed look like a Biblical patriarch.

Old Sulzberg's delusion gradually worsened, and finally his sons and daughters and grown grandchildren held a conference and reluctantly agreed to send him to an institution. There, they hoped, with proper treatment, he might regain his sanity and then return home.

At the Cedars of Lebanon Home for the Mentally Disturbed, the "Messiah" got along famously with his fellow patients. Until, that is, he made the mistake of exhorting them to abandon their Godless ways.

"I am Moses reincarnated," he thundered like a prophet of old. "I am the Messiah!"

"Oh, yeah?" yelled one of the patients. "Who said so?"

"I'll tell you who said so," yelled Mr. Sulzberg-turned-Messiah. "God said so."

And from the outer circle of patients an indignant voice rang out: "I did nòt!"

*   *   *

Sign in the window of Kaplow's Book Store, on La Cienega Boulevard, in Los Angeles:

REMEMBER THE REAL MEANING OF
CHRISTMAS THIS YEAR.
Attend the Church or Synagogue
of Your Choice!

* * *

The little girl insisted that she be allowed to say her prayers without any help, and her parents proudly agreed.

Wide-eyed, they heard her intone:

Our father who art in Heaven,
Howard be thy name;
Give us this day our jelly bread;
Lead us not into Penn Station,
And deliver us from people—amen!

* * *

In his column, syndicated by the Jewish Telegraphic Agency, David Schwartz commented on the student unrest which was then sweeping the country.

"The students really grew worrisome when one group charged the college dean's office yelling, 'Take no prisoners!'

"Some Jewish students at a Minneapolis high school are calling for Jewish Power," added the witty journalist. "They are demanding two sets of dishes at school functions. Also, curly hair is beautiful, they say, and everyone should wear *yarmulkes.* Another plank in their platform calls for *hamantashen* on *Purim,* dairy foods for *Shevuoth* and *gefilte* fish on Saturday."

* * *

Lot, the unfortunate one of Biblical history, was stumbling blindly through the torrid sands when a Voice spoke:

"Just to keep the record straight, this has nothing to do with your being Jewish!"

* * *

Moses stood on the shore of the Red Sea—stopped cold. Behind him, in the distance, clouds of billowing dust arose from the Pharaoh's chariots as his legions closed in on the fleeing Israelites. Suddenly, with a mighty roar, the waters parted into two mountainous columns—opening up for them an avenue of escape. Moses looked ahead at the gloomy, forbidding roadway, and then up at the towering cliffs of water on either side. He lifted his anxious face toward the heavens:

"Tell me something," he sighed. "How come I always have to go first?"

* * *

Mr. and Mrs. Chotnik had hoped that their son, Stanley, would follow in the path of their own orthodox ways and pursue his higher education at Yeshiva University. Instead, despite their voluble concern, he entered Notre Dame. But when he returned home for summer vacation they were vastly relieved to see that their fears had been groundless. Stanley had not forsaken his ancestral faith, he had not been converted, he had not, it was clear, been affected in the slightest by his non-Jewish environment. In fact, on the very next Friday, he readily agreed to accompany them to synagogue.

That evening, at the close of *shabbes* services, the rabbi, an old friend of the Chotnik family greeted the young Notre Dame student with a wide smile.

"It's good to see you here in temple again, Stanley," said the rabbi, shaking the youth's hand. "Frankly, your parents and I were afraid you might be Catholicized there at South Bend."

Stanley's eyebrows lifted in surprise. "Impossible!" he declared. "No one will ever convert me, Father."

28

Rabbis

INTRODUCTION

Since pre-Colonial times, the American rabbinate has distinguished itself as a source of inspiration and leadership for the nation's Jews. It has also produced a vanguard of leaders who contributed greatly to the ethical and physical well-being of the United States itself—promoting the human rights of all citizens, Jew and gentile alike, in their struggle for a better society. America's rabbis participated in the War of Independence, the Abolitionist crusade, the struggle to organize and maintain a viable labor movement, the establishment of the public school system, non-sectarian hospitals for the poor, and many other affairs of state and community.

But it is not the purpose of this book to recount the honorable achievements of the rabbinate. We are concerned here only with Jewish humor as it applies to rabbis. The jokes by and about them are not confined to their role as teachers and scholars. The anecdotes concern their attitudes and personalities. They tell of every kind of rabbi: the serious-minded and the jocular, the simple and the profound, the tolerant and the intolerant, the placid and the combative.

True rabbinical humor, some of which is incorporated in this Introduction, is almost invariably on a higher intellectual plane than are the "rabbi jokes" told by the laity. The former are best enjoyed by those with at least a working knowledge of the Bible, a history of the Jewish people, and some familiarity with world events. The latter is not nearly as cerebral, but is usually more "human" and relies for its laughter on the outrageously comic, rather than on clever wit. Both have equal stature in American-Jewish humor, and can be equally funny.

According to the Talmud, "A rabbinic decree must not assume the character of a jest." A few of the ultra-orthodox rabbis have interpreted this to mean that they themselves must be excluded from all humorous references. "To that opinion," snorted one reform rabbi, "I must reluctantly bow-wow!" Since rabbis do not or are not supposed to argue among themselves, they *discuss* matters, their discussions being a method of calling attention to the errors made by those who disagree with them. The orthodox rabbi is a strong believer in strict allegiance to traditional beliefs and ritual—more so than are the conservative and reform, but the *tzaddik*—the *Chassidic* leader—takes a dim view of strict orthodoxy. Nephtali Zevi Horowitz, an articulate *tzaddik* with a broad sense of humor, made this cynical (but funny) observation about what he believed to be unfounded loyalty to any of the other Judaic sects:

> This thing "allegiance," I suppose,
> Is a ring fitted in the Jewish nose,
> Whereby that organ is kept righteously pointed,
> To smell the sweetness of the Lord's anointed.

Unlike most other rabbis, Horowitz made no grand claims of a Heavenly call when he decided to enter the rabbinate. He said:

"At first I did not want to be a rabbi, for a rabbi has to flatter his flock, and so I thought of being a tailor. Then I saw that a tailor has to flatter his customers, and so does a shoemaker, and a bath-attendant; and I asked myself, 'Where, then, is a rabbi worse off?' And so," he concluded, "I became a rabbi."

Intra-Judaic squabbles have produced numerous gems of wit. The *Chassid*, Reb Yitzhok Levi, once took it upon himself to defend the Jewish people against God: "Lord, if ever Thou shouldst issue a hard decree against the Jews, we *tzaddikim* will not fulfill Thy commands!" The statement apparently did not coincide with the views held by the Yiddish writer, Shmuel Jaffe, who retorted, "One more rabbi like Yitzhok Levi and God will cancel our contract!"

In all fairness to Levi, let it be said that he was a kind and good man, deeply involved in community affairs. Indeed, his philosophy of communal involvement was supported by none other than Dr. Kaufmann Kohler when he delivered his inaugural address in 1903, upon becoming president of Hebrew Union College. "All the knowledge the future rabbi acquires," he told the assembled rabbinical students, "must be subordinate to the higher tasks of practical communal service which he is expected to assume."

That comment elicited a blast from the Hebrew scholar, Abraham Kahana, who made a brief icy reference to Rabbi Kohler, but saved his heavier ammunition for Reb Levi:

"For community affairs we have politicians, not political rabbis. Dr. Kohler should go back to *cheder* and study all over again for his *Bar Mitzvah*, and never mind presiding over a college. As for that *person*, Yitzhok Levi, when he was about to be born, Satan complained that if Levi's soul were to descend on earth it would reform the world, and his own power would come to an end. Then the Holy One comforted Satan and said: 'But he will be a rabbi and he will be too occupied with communal affairs!'"

Solomon Schechter, the rabbinical scholar and author, once discussed the intra-Judaic controversy with Rabbi Louis Finkelstein, the noted leader of American conservative Judaism and his successor (once removed) as head of the Jewish Theological Seminary. "Whatever the faults of the rabbis, consistency is not one of them," grinned Schechter, refusing to take the matter seriously. "As I see it, the only problem these days is that unless you can play baseball, you'll never get to be a rabbi in America."

Another writer, Israel Lipkin, dismissed the whole argument of creed and deed with a few brief words: "The *Chassidim* think they have a rabbi; their opponents think they need no rabbi. Both are mistaken." To which Herschel Mishkin, an othodox rabbi, added: "I pay no attention to the silly chatter of the *Chassidim*. Of course, I pay no attention to the prattle of the reform and conservative, either. I only hope and pray they will all return some day to the Jewish faith!"

American-Jewish humor takes a tolerant view of the disputes among the Judaic sects, kept alive, in the main, by the rabbis themselves. The only real difference among them is that a reform rabbi speaks *about* God, a conservative rabbi *to* God, and an orthodox rabbi answers them according to the holy dictates of his conscience.

They all believe in the Decalogue: a series of commandments, ten in number, which are just enough to permit an intelligent person to make a selection for his own degree of observance, and not so many as to embarrass him by those he overlooks. A good Jew, therefore, in the modern tradition, is one who believes that the Decalogue is Divinely inspired, and is admirably suited to the spiritual needs of his neighbors. He follows the Mosaic Laws insofar as they are not in conflict with the little pleasantries of life.

The Ten Commandments are highly respected in the North Temperate Zone. We are assured that if we obey the Divine injunctions, our prayers will be answered. Most people, the rabbis tell us, pray for good health, happy marriages and riches. The trouble arises from our interpretation of all these celestial favors. For example, riches is considered as a gift from Heaven signifying "the reward of toil, virtue and piety," said Rabbi Stephen S. Wise. It is "the savings of many in the hands of one," said Golda Meir.

All rabbis, regardless of the branch of Judaism they may represent, are in accord in their reactions to the Neanderthal who mouths anti-Semitic jokes. Prejudice, to the rabbi, is a vagrant opinion with no visible means of support. The bigot who repeats the hoary canards under the guise of humor is looked upon as a prevaricator—a liar in the caterpillar stage who, at molting time, blossoms forth as an adult cretin upon whom a scathing retort would be wasted. Another point of agreement among modern-minded rabbis is their doubt as to the physical existence of a place called Hades, the nether world where the dead live. Among the ancient Greeks, Hades was not synonymous with our Hell. Many of the most respected citizens of antiquity resided there in a very comfortable manner. Indeed, the Elysian Fields themselves were a part of Hades, though they have since been removed to 42nd Street and Eighth Avenue.

The greatest area of agreement among orthodox rabbis is found in their unyielding conviction that all observances must be in strict accordance with the ancient religious laws, particularly those concerning ritualism, that Garden of God where He walks in rectilinear freedom, keeping off the grass. But if there is any one rallying point around which all rabbis can gather in unanimous certitude, it is in their hostility to the agnostic posing as an iconoclast—the self-appointed breaker of idols. It makes no difference that the Jewish people have not fraternized with idols since the Golden Calf episode: when a Jew sets his mind to it, he can argue about anything. So, as a substitute for idols, he inveighs against ritual and even the basic beliefs in God and Torah to advance his notions. The rabbis most strenuously protest that the Jewish iconoclast pulleth down but pileth not up. For, should he have his way, the poor worshipers would soon have other idols or beliefs in place of those he wacketh upon the noggin. The iconoclast saith: "Ye shall have none at all, for ye heed them not." And the rabbi respondeth: "If the rebuilder fooleth around hereabouts, behold, we shall depress his head and sit thereon till he squawketh."

The foregoing clearly demonstrates—or should have by now—that American-Jewish humor as it pertains to the rabbinate is pretty hairy stuff, profound and intellectually stimulating. It bears no resemblance to the frivolous jokes one usually hears about the old-fashioned *rebbe* preparing a class of fresh kids for their *bar mitzvahs*.

By-the-bye, as they like to say in the more elegant circles, have you heard the one about the old-fashioned *rebbe* who was preparing a class of fresh kids for their *bar mitzvahs?* Read on, but just smile, smirk or grin a little—it isn't nice to laugh at old people.

H.D.S.

Rebbe Saul Isaacson, who for 45 years conducted the store front *cheder* at 157 Grand Street on the lower East Side, was a very old man when he finally went to his reward in 1927. How old he was, God only knows—and He won't tell. In that last year of his teaching, Rebbe Isaacson had 18 pupils. The smarter boys—those with retentive memories—could sail through the hour-long sessions with little more than a cuff on the ear and a few glowering looks—just to let them know who was who and what was what. The fumblers got their smacks along with pertinent and unflattering commentaries on their mental processes. The slow learners received the royal treatment, with whacks to whatever portion of their anatomies was most convenient, or whose backsides were in perihelion, so to speak, with his ruler. It was with these latter that Rebbe Isaacson, bristling through his salt-and-pepper whiskers, would demonstrate his most unrabbinical talent for sarcasm, disparagement, contumely, affront and derision.

In his defense, however, let it be said that the fathers of the youngsters had themselves, in many cases, been prepared for their own Bar Mitvahs by the irascible old man and they were aware that his scowling demeanor hid a deep anxiety that his *boychiks* might not be ready for their communion. He was, in short, a born teacher—an East Side Hebrew Mr. Chips straight out of Jewish-American folklore. His boys were carbon copies of the fathers and, in some families, the grandfathers he had dragged, kicking and squirming, to the thresholds of their Bar Mitzvahs. For him, the tricks they loved to play on their aged teacher were all part of the burden a Talmudic scholar in his position was destined to endure. His departed wife once remarked that he would arrive home in a ferocious mood because of some prank played on him by one of his pupils. "But after supper, and over a glass of tea and lemon," the *rebbetzyn* smiled, "he would recount the episode and chuckle. 'A wild one, that stinker, but not as bad as his father was at his age, nor even his grandfather: Now *there* was an incorrigible one! So today he's a rabbi in a big, fancy temple with a rich congregation. And how does he repay me? He sends his son's offspring to torture me in my old age!'"

One such "offspring" was twelve-year-old Ira Shmulowitz (later a judge of the Circuit Court in New York). On this particular afternoon in 1927 of which we speak, Rebbe Isaacson's disposition had deteriorated from vile to unspeakable. Unfortunately for young Ira, it was his turn for reading and answering questions. The rebbe glared at his victim, his ever-present ruler gripped firmly in his bony hand. Ira was one of the slow learners, and to compound the teacher's aggravation, the boy also fancied himself as something of a kibbitzer. On that day, however, Isaacson's foul mood intimidated the class in general and, at least for now, even Ira. He listened carefully as the rabbi spoke:

"Mister Intellectual, you remember yesterday I spoke of Moses?"

"Yeah, sort of," mumbled Ira, slouching alongside the teacher's table.

Splat! went the ruler across Ira's behind.

"Sort of?" fumed the rabbi. "You will be *sort of* Bar Mitzvah when you reach thirteen? You will be *sort of* Jewish?" He made a valiant effort to compose himself. "Now, without 'sort-ofs', and if it isn't putting you out too much, what can you tell me about Moses?"

"He led the Israelites outta Egypt an' acrosst the Suez Can . . ."
Splat!

"Oww!" Ira howled. "You said so yerself! Ask the other kids!"

"I have to ask those idiots what I said? They're your character witnesses all of a sudden?" *Splat!* "Now, do me a big, personal favor and answer the question."

"I fergot what it was."

"I asked about Moses. Maybe you heard of him somewhere in your world-wide travels."

A gleam came into young Ira's eyes. So the *rebbe* wanted to make jokes, eh? Okay, he asked for it.

"I know about Moses," he said, nodding. "I saw him in the movies. He got them tablets, see, an' he came down offa Mount Sinai, an' there was this girl, see, an' . . ."

Splat!

"Dumkopf!" Isaacson exploded in wrath. "May the waters of Jordan back up into your *lokshen* soup! What has Hollywood to do with the noblest rabbi of all time?"

Ira dared not show the slightest of smiles. He had really provoked the old man this time, and the other students, vastly entertained, burst into joyful laughter, a reaction which did little to improve the old man's disposition. They were silenced only upon his snarling command that they cease their hilarity forthwith or suffer a physical confrontation of their own.

But Ira was enjoying his co-starring role and he was in no hurry to relinquish the spotlight. He waited for the rabbi to resume his questioning.

"We will try another subject," Rebbe Isaacson said darkly. "I assume you can at least *daven*."

"No," replied Ira, unable to suppress a grin, "but I can somersault."

Splat! Whap! Splat!

"Comedians in *cheder* we need, hah, *yingatsh?*" In a red fury, Rebbe Isaacson rose from his chair to deliver a *coup de' état* with his upraised ruler. Ira, in an effort to dodge the descending blow, lurched to one side and inadvertently bumped the table with his body. The table slammed into old Isaacson and knocked him off his feet.

"Well, don't just stand there!" the rabbi barked as he struggled to get up. "Give me a hand!"

And the students, for the first time in his memory, complied with waves of enthusiastic applause, giving him the biggest hand he had ever received in his life.

* * *

You heard maybe about the unemployed cantor who is now making a fortune? He learned the Wedding March backwards, and now he sings it at divorces!

* * *

During the Civil War, one of the most loyal supporters of emancipation for the slaves and an important fund-raiser for the Union cause was Morris Raphall, the rabbi of B'nai Jeshurun. Numbered among his friends were many high government officials, including President Abraham Lincoln himself.

One day, just after *Purim*, Rabbi Raphall went to Washington to see if he could get a commission in the army for his son. Lincoln listened to the good rabbi's request and then commented drily:

"I understand your reason for coming here to Washington, but tell me, aren't you supposed to be back home, praying for the success of our soldiers?"

"Our prayers are going on just the same," the rabbi assured him. "My assistant is doing that."

"Very well," said Lincoln, the trace of a smile on his lips, "here is the signed commission for your son. Now you can go home and do your own praying."

* * *

A rabbinical student returned to his room at the seminary, his sullen face clearly indicating distress.

"What's with you?" asked his roommate.

"I just asked permission to smoke while praying but I got turned down—and in no uncertain terms, too," moaned the unhappy future rabbi.

"You should have used a little psychology and done what I did," suggested the other prospective spiritual leader. "I just reversed the question and asked if it would be okay if I prayed while smoking!"

* * *

This author once referred to his dear friend, the late rabbi Montagu Katz of Los Angeles as "Holy Katz," at which he did wroth exceedingly wax, or whatever. But he was, nevertheless, possessed of a delightful sense of humor, as witness this tale—one of his favorites.

Rabbi Katz had an old friend, another rabbi named Solow. It seems that Rabbi Solow was afflicted with a galloping tongue—a man who, from time to time during the course of his sermons, would begin a new phrase with the line, "Just one more word, my dear friends," and then never keep his promise.

On this particular Sabbath, Rabbi Solow droned on and on and on, interminably. The congregation grew impatient and fretful. A hum of conversation could be heard, at first an almost indiscernible whisper until, growing in volume, it threatened to drown him out entirely.

Now Rabbi Solow, if it has not yet been established, was a unique character. As an accoutrement of his calling, and with good reason, he kept a gavel on the lectern beside the *Torah* so that he could rap for silence when necessary—and he would indeed find it necessary at least once during each of his long-winded sermons. The irreverent buzzing in the audience was now so audible that he felt it his duty to God and his own honor to bang for order. As he brought his gavel down with emphasis, the handle snapped. The hardwood head hurtled through the air and struck with a resounding thud squarely on the forehead of a congregant in the front row. The victim sank back in his seat, glassy-eyed.

A horrified hush followed the accident. Rabbi Solow took advantage of the quiet to go with his sermon.

At this, the injured gentleman revived slightly. With his eyes still closed, he murmured in a voice that could be heard by all:

"Hit me again. I can still hear him!"

* * *

Rabbi Edgar F. Magnin, spiritual leader of the prestigious Wilshire Boulevard Temple in Los Angeles, tells of the time he resigned as General Manager of the Universe.

"I had been unable to sleep for several nights. I would lie awake, worrying about the Arab intentions toward Israel, about the poor and downtrodden in this country, about the state of the world in general.

"One night, as I turned and tossed in my bed, an eerie light grew within the darkness of the room, and from within that light there came a majestic Voice. And that Voice said:

"Edgar, you can go to sleep. Tonight *I'll* wait up!"

* * *

"Rabbi," said the worried father, "I wish you'd speak to my son. Here he is, *Bar Mitzvah* age, and all he ever thinks about is baseball."

The rabbi sighed to himself. 'With so many delinquent children getting into trouble,' he thought, 'this is indeed a minor problem.'

"I'm sorry to disappoint you," he said, suppressing a desire to show his annoyance, "but I cannot scold your boy for something we Jews have been practicing for thousands of years. In fact, there are several references to baseball in the Bible."

"Are you serious?" demanded the father incredulously. "What are they?"

"Well, for example, you will recall that Eve stole first and Adam stole second; Gideon rattled the pitchers; Goliath was put out by David; and the prodigal son made a home run!"

* * *

The *shammes* of the Utica Avenue Synagogue and the *shammes* of Temple Beth Israel, both in Brooklyn, were bewailing the unkind fates that had brought them into association with their respective rabbis.

"Our rabbi is an educated man," grumbled the first, "but he just doesn't think before he speaks. Only last Friday he organized a Young Mothers Group—and did he embarrass me! He gets up in the pulpit and announces, 'All ladies of this congregation who wish to become Young Mothers should see the *shammes* this evening and he'll give you the best dates for the recreation room.'"

The other *shammes* nodded sympathetically.

"And that's what everybody calls executive ability," he sighed. "Believe me, my friend, when they say a rabbi is a good administrator it means he's taking credit for all the hard work done by the *shammes*. Sometimes it shakes my religious faith."

"Well, I wouldn't go so far as to say that," replied the first *shammes*. "I've seen nine rabbis come and go at the Utica Avenue Synagogue, and I still believe in God!"

* * *

To make a brief story briefer, when a Canadian railroad journal published an advertisement seeking 200 sleepers for a new cross-country line, Rabbi Albert R. Coleman of Detroit offered them his entire congregation.

* * *

The rabbi was expounding on the various interpretations of Biblical lore when sounds of a heated debate in the rear of the class brought his lecture to a halt.

"All right," he snapped, "what's so important back there that you're interrupting the class?"

"We were just arguing about reform and orthodox Judaism," explained one of the students.

"What's to argue?"

"He says there is no difference of real importance," said the student, pointing to the young man sitting next to him. "But I say there is."

"Then I'll settle the argument for you," said the rabbi, impatient to get on with his discourse. "The difference is actually very small. Orthodox Jews believe that the Pharaoh's daughter found Moses in the bulrushes. But reform Jews believe the Pharaoh's daughter only *said* she found Moses in the bulrushes!"

* * *

Bill Bennett the barber, was a good Christian and widely known for his religious fervor. His deep respect for the clergy was the talk of the neighborhood.

One day a Protestant minister came into his barbershop and got a haircut. When Bennett was finished, the minister reached for his wallet but the barber shook his head and smiled.

"Put your wallet away, Reverend," he said. "I never charge a man of the cloth."

The minister thanked him and left, but he soon returned and presented the pious barber with a Bible.

A few hours later, a priest entered Bennett's shop and he, too, got a haircut. Once again the barber refused to accept any payment.

"Forget it, Father," he said. "I never accept money from a priest."

The priest left and shortly thereafter returned with a crucifix which he presented to the barber as a token of his appreciation.

Toward evening a rabbi entered the shop. He also got a haircut. When the rabbi reached into his pocket, the barber waved the money aside.

"That's all right, Rabbi," he said. "You don't owe me a thing. I never accept payment from men who do the Lord's work."

So the rabbi left, and soon returned—with another rabbi!

* * *

Three rabbis, representing the three main sects of Judaism, were having a mild argument about religious matters.

"It seems to me," said the reform rabbi, "that the best way to approach Jewish theology is from the standpoint of an umpire at a ballgame. For example, as a reform rabbi, I call 'em as I see 'em."

"Well," said the conservative rabbi, "I call 'em as they are."

"As far as I am concerned," countered the orthodox rabbi, "you can call it a ball or you can call it a strike—but it's neither until *I* call it!"

* * *

The old rabbi listened patiently while the youthful agnostic expounded his views.

"According to Nietzsche," observed the non-believer, "God is dead."

"According to God," said the rabbi calmly, "Nietzsche is dead!"

* * *

Cincinnati's Rabbi Roger Kahn, to his congregation: "I have always publicly stated that the poor are welcome in this synagogue at all times, and I see by last month's receipts that they have indeed come!"

* * *

Forget what your rabbi told you! What does he know about romance? Here's the way it *really* happened.

"Adam, baby," said Eve as she presented him with a bouquet of forget-me-nots she had picked in the Garden of Eden, "do you absolutely and truly love me?"

"Sure," said Adam. "Who else?"

* * *

Rabbi Langbleibt of Far Rockaway had a well-deserved reputation for being long-winded. On this Sabbath, he was in especially good form. His topic for the day was "Prophets of the Bible."

"Now then," he added after speaking for a half hour, "we have disposed of the major prophets. Next we come to the minor prophets. To what place, my dear friends, shall we assign them?"

From a seat in the rear of the temple, a bored-looking stranger arose. He waved an explanatory hand at the seat he had just vacated and said:

"One of them can have my place!"

* * *

The 1920s produced a large number of humorous stories in which the "fresh little kid" is pitted against the short-tempered Hebrew teacher. Here is another from that period.

Mortie, the sporty shortie, did not exactly endear himself to the *rebbe* at the Delancey Street *cheder* when he asserted, "David just couldn'ta been a psalmist!"

"*Nu,* supply me please with information to the contrary," demanded the *rebbe.*

"Because a psalmist tells fortunes by reading palms," replied Mortie, grinning.

"Ah-*hah*! A regular Eddie Cantor in our midst, *noch*!" growled the *rebbe.* "All right, *ingel,* as long as you are such a *galernter,* such a *dinchazzan,* I have a question for you."

"I din't unnastan' all them Joosh words," Mortie mumbled.

"I'll be happy to articulate my query in lucid English."

"I din't unnastan' that, either."

"*Klayneh nahr,* my question shall be asked in plain English, but first I want to know something," the *rebbe* went on, his voice ominously low. "Did it ever occur to you that you might study for your *Bar Mitzvah* on Broadway where Charlie Chaplins are more appreciated? No? Then perhaps you might enjoy receiving your instructions on the vaudeville stage where you could make jokes and be confirmed at the same time. This too did not occur to you?"

Mortie made the mistake of laughing and the good *rebbe's* eyes blazed. "You see, young man, I can also make with the jokes. But there is a time and a place for everything—and *cheder* is definitely not the place for anything except study."

"But I *was* studyin' ", argued the irrepressible Mortie. "I was studyin' how long it would take before I could go home."

The *rebbe* groaned and rolled his eyes toward heaven as though beseeching aid from above.

"I'm giving you one more chance—only one question to answer—and then you may go home," he said wearily. "And" he added, consulting his watch, "you'd better hurry—the zoo closes in an hour."

"Okay, what's the question?"

"In the year 165 B.C.E.,the Maccabees celebrated a great victory. We still commemorate that occasion by lighting candles for eight days, children play *dreidel* games, and we have lately taken to exchanging cards and gifts during this festive week. Now, to what holiday do I refer?"

"Christmas?" responded Mortie tentatively.

"Gottenyu!" the teacher exploded, his beloved *Chanukah* thus desecrated. He managed to compose himself and, with a resigned wave of his hand he dismissed his student.

"To my deep regret, Mortie, I shall see you again tomorrow," he sighed. "But, for me, the intervening 24 hours without your presence will seem like a month in the Catskills!"

* * *

Rabbi Simon Mendes, who settled near the headwaters of the Susquehanna in 1840 or thereabouts, was a good man—pious but full of humor and adept at quick repartee.

One Sunday morning, he was presented with a fine string of pickerel, caught by one Heinrich Herrman, a member of his tiny congregation.

"Rabbi, I want you to have the fish," said the man somewhat nervously, "but it's only fair to tell you that they were caught on *shabbes.*"

"Heinrich," replied Rabbi Mendes as he reached for the string, "the Lord and I both know that the pickerel were not to blame."

* * *

Although Rabbi Isaac Mayer Wise (1818-1900) is remembered as one of the outstanding pioneers of reform Judaism in America, it seems to have been forgotten that he possessed a keen wit and could, when the mood was upon him, be quite amusing. And when he chose to turn a joke upon himself, he could be savagely satirical. This tale, dripping with irony, presents the articulate rabbi at his humorous and intellectual best.

It was a lovely day in May, 1899, and Rabbi Wise, age 81, was slowly and feebly walking down a street in Cincinnati. As he faltered along, he met the young and vigorous Rabbi Yosef Alman, professor of languages at the Hebrew Union College, the institution which Wise himself founded in 1875.

The young rabbi shook his older colleague's trembling hand and respectfully murmured, "Good morning, sir. And how is Isaac Mayer Wise today?"

"Isaac Mayer Wise is well, quite well, thank you," said the aged rabbi. "But the house in which he lives at present is becoming quite dilapidated. It is tottering upon its foundations. Time and the seasons have nearly destroyed it. Its roof is pretty well worn out. Its walls are much shattered and it trembles with every wind. The old tenement is becoming almost uninhabitable, and I think Isaac Mayer Wise will have to move out of it soon. But he himself is quite well, thank you."

(Wrote Rabbi Alman in his *Memoirs of a Challenger:* "I had an almost irresistible impulse to enfold him in a bear-hug, and I would have, had I not been certain that the old boy would have belabored me with his cane for such an affront to his dignity.")

* * *

Questions rabbis have had to face:
*   "Do rabbis have to work for a living?"
*   "Do Jews make the best rabbis?"
*   "Do rabbis have any other hobbies besides talking to God?"
*   "Is it against the Jewish religion for rabbis to smile when they make speeches?"
*   "Does God eat kosher food?"
*   "Is Moses or Sandy Koufax the most famous Jew who ever lived?"
*   "Can Friday evening services be changed to Thursday night so we won't miss the good TV shows?"
*   "How many of the Ten Commandments can you break, and still go to heaven?"

29
Death, Where Is Thy Sting-A-Ling-A-Ling?

INTRODUCTION

Among the vigorously original contributions to American art in general is the art of Jewish wit and humor. No other land could have served as the catalyst. Only here in the United States did the Jewish people feel incomparably superior to whatever mother country in the diaspora they had left behind. And without feeling incomparably superior to everybody, especially your mother, what can you accomplish in creative art? That robust humor, distinguished by its recklessness, its willingness to take things laughingly right up to death's door and the throne of God, trusting for redemption not in some delicacy of expression or mystic reverence for ultimate truth or the angels, but in an underlying faith in social laughter: that has been the Jewish contribution to the unique art of American humor!

Why a separate chapter about a subject so unpleasant as death? Because death, however unwelcome, is the ultimate adventure into the unknown that must befall all living creatures. And whatever happens to mankind in an important way must inevitably have its humorous aspects. Philip S. Bernstein, in the *Long Island Builder*, aptly observed: "We have no right to ask, when sorrow comes, 'Why did this happen to me?' unless we ask the same question for every joy that comes our way."

Death, of course, is a proper occasion for grief, but without grief there could be no humor, for, as noted in an earlier chapter, we cannot truly know joy if we have never experienced sorrow as a comparison. Behavioral scientists tell us that the closer humor is to pain the more likely we are to laugh. It is the astute *telling* of a story or a quip that makes it an art. Once again, we are reminded that laughter may be a response to any pleasant stimulus as well as to any unpleasant one that can be playfully told, and playfully accepted by the listener.

American-Jewish folk humor abounds in jokes revolving around the broad subject of death. The anecdotes differ from the European tales in that they are seldom harsh. They are told for the pure joy of evoking laughter, rather than to teach a lesson, as was the case in much of the humorous *folkskeit* of yesteryear's Europe.

326

For example, the following folk tale of Mrs. Stein's welcome to Paradise, while it retains the traditional elements of the exemplum—the allegorical sermon used by medieval rabbis to illustrate or support a moral point—it is still typically American. It not only embodies the gentler characteristics of the American-Jewish "death joke," but in its own simple, unassuming way, offers a heartwarming answer to the new wave of "anti-momism" writings affected by some contemporary Jewish authors who lacquer their self-disdain with Freudian gilt.

Old Mrs. Stein, after a very long and fruitful life, passed away and quickly found herself at the Gate of Beauty.

"What have you done in your lifetime on earth that merits your admittance here?" asked the stern-visaged patriarch, Abraham.

"*Rebbe*," quavered the frightened Mrs. Stein, "I was only good at one thing."

"And what was that?"

"Cooking," she replied dolefully. "Only cooking."

Father Abraham's face softened in a kindly smile—the most ineffably sweet smile she had ever seen.

"Please come right in," he said warmly. "You are entitled to every blessing Paradise has to offer."

"Why do you honor me so, dear *Rebbe*?" asked the puzzled lady.

"Because, *mamenyu*," he crooned, "you have saved more men from perdition than a dozen rabbis!"

Nearly all Jewish jokes relating to women and Heaven are gentler than those involving men in the same situation. This preferential treatment is even apparent when the female, unlike sweet Mrs. Stein, is a thoroughly reprehensible person. Here is an appropriate illustration:

Mrs. Faird presented herself at the Gate of Heaven and knocked with trembling hand.

"Madam," said Father Abraham, peering suspiciously through a peephole, "from whence did you come?"

"From Flatbush I came," replied Mrs. Faird with embarrassment, as great beads of perspiration spangled her spiritual brow.

"Never mind, my daughter," replied the patriarch compassionately. "Eternity is a long time; you can live that down."

"Mister, I got something to confess," she went on, obviously worried.

"In our religion we don't have confessions."

"But this is different. If you'll give a look in your records, you'll see that maybe I don't belong here. I—I—well—I poisoned my husband and I chopped up my brother-in-law. Not only that, I . . . ."

Father Abraham suddenly grew stern. "Your aggressive behavior does indeed present a problem, madam. Were you a member of the Women's Liberation movement?"

"No."

The gates of pearl and alabaster swung open upon their golden hinges, making the most ravishing music, and the patriarch bowed low.

"Enter into thine eternal rest."

But Mrs. Faird hesitated.

"The poisoning, the chopping, the . . . the . . ." she stammered.

"Of no consequence, I assure you. We are not going to be hard on a lady who did not belong to Women's Lib. Take a harp."

"But I applied for membership. They wouldn't let me in."

"Take two harps."

Another distinctive feature of Jewish humor is that it does not dwell on the *causes* of death, or the *manner* of dying (although the humorous recitation of symptoms are popular in jokes when they do not evoke unpleasant reactions in the listener). In this respect, the Jewish joke has changed but little from its older European origins. When causes of death are mentioned at all, there is usually a valid reason for their inclusion, but they are given without clinical detail and are in good taste. However, when we speak of "good taste" we are referring to an intangible value judgment which can mean different things to many people. When Simon Blumenthal, a motion picture producer who was also a successful "gentleman farmer" passed away some years ago, the late Jack Benny mournfully observed that he had died of chestnut blight. And in Miami Beach, Rabbi Walter Hahn, delivering a funeral sermon, solemnly intoned, "Chopped liver on shtrudel was highly esteemed by the remains." These, of course, are examples of wit rather than the humor of a constructed joke.

By way of contrast, here is a typical Russian joke which, according to the editors of *Krokodil*, the Soviet Union's famous mass circulation humor magazine, is one of the most repeated in that country:

A Russian went to a wake for his friend's mother-in-law, extended his condolences and asked: "What did she die from?"

"Poisoning," the bereaved man replied.

"Poisoning?" the friend said in perplexity. "Then why is the body so bruised and battered?"

"Because," answered the son-in-law, "she didn't want to take the poison."

There are a number of reasons why that story could never be regarded as a Jewish joke. First, because of its ill-concealed violent nature. Secondly, because it would be too easy for the Russian Jew to envision the tale as referring, instead, to a Jewish citizen attempting to leave for Israel. Thirdly, it simply does not have the Jewish "feel"—the flavor of *Yiddishkeit* which is completely absent in the jokes told by the Russian people, be they peasants or party officials.

Can a death joke retain the "human touch" and still be funny? American-Jewish humor assures us that it can and does. It can pierce the gloom of an open grave and describe it as a place in which the dead are laid to await the coming of the medical student. It will inform us that the modern American hearse is especially designed for the guy who always yearned for the fanciest car on the road.

Embalming, that desecration of the holiest of Jewish beliefs, is seen as a method of interfering with the ecological balance by cheating vegetation of its natural sustenance. The metallic casket enhances this unnatural process, according to Jewish humor, and many a dead man who should be ornamenting his neighbor's lawn as a tree or enriching his table as a bunch of radishes is doomed to a long period of post-mortem uselessness. The earth will eventually claim him, but in the meantime the rutabaga and the rose are languishing for a nibble at his *gluteus maximus*. As the weary rabbi sighed after hearing of all this disgraceful conduct: "It's the cross we must bear!"

H.D.S.

To prove that romance can even blossom at the gravesite, who can forget Mrs. Goldfarb?

She stood weeping at her husband's grave when a courtly stranger approached her.

"Madam, I regret the unfortunate circumstances under which I say this," he began in a respectful manner, "but I must tell you that I have fallen in love with you at first sight."

"Loafer! Bum!" cried Mrs. Goldfarb indignantly, aghast at this monumental impertinence. "Get out of my sight this instant or I'll call a policeman! Is this a time to talk about love?"

"I assure you, madam, that I did not intend to reveal my feelings at this sad time," the gentle stranger explained, "but I was simply overwhelmed by your exquisite beauty."

"Listen," said Mrs. Goldfarb, "you should see me when I haven't been crying!"

* * *

Moishe, the janitor, was in the cellar of his tenement, shoveling coal into the furnace, when his twelve-year-old daughter, Rosie, burst in.

"Papa, papa, come quick!" she cried. "Mama can't breathe, and she's blue in the face! I think she's dying!"

Moishe dropped his shovel and bounded up the five flights of stairs to the top-floor apartment where he and his family lived. But when he opened the door, there was his wife sitting up and smiling.

"I'm better," she announced. "Nothing to worry about."

A couple of days later, little Rosie again rushed down into the basement, screaming, "Papa, papa, come quick! Mama can't breathe, and she's blue in the face! I think she's dying!"

Once more Moishe raced up the five flights of stairs and hurled himself into his apartment. And, as before, his wife was sitting up, smiling bravely. Again she said, "I'm feeling better now. Nothing to worry about."

A third and then a fourth time, Rosie brought her father the dire news, but when he got to the apartment, his legs numb from climbing the stairs, his wife would be sitting up and "feeling better."

A week passed without further incident, and then it happened again. Rosie rushed into the furnace room to announce for the fifth time that her mother was "blue in the face and dying!" Again Moishe ran all the way up to the fifth floor and rushed into the apartment. But this time he found his wife on the floor, her eyes closed, her face blue. Kneeling beside her, he lifted one of her eyelids with his thumb. Then he pressed his ear to her chest, but could hear no heartbeat. He felt her pulse but could detect no sign of life.

'Well!" exclaimed Moishe, rising to his feet. "This is more like it!"

* * *

Karl Kravitz, of the Cravat Company of Canarsie, attributed the success of his necktie business to his lifelong policy of postdating all his checks.

Upon his death, his headstone was engraved with this immortal legend:

HERE LIES
KARL KRAVITZ
DIED DEC. 18, 1972—AS OF JAN. 3, 1973

* * *

If you have ever harbored any suspicious thoughts about the relationship between doctors and deaths, this news item should answer your unspoken question:

DEATHS DECREASE AS DOCTORS STRIKE

> TEL AVIV (WINS)—The number of funerals have dropped by nearly half since a doctors' strike began in Israel, according to statistics released by the Jerusalem Burial Society. No explanation was given for the coincidence. But the archives of the Tel Aviv Burial Society showed a similar drop in the number of funerals when doctors went on strike 20 years ago.*

* * *

Mrs. Saperstein had just sent the children off to school when the phone rang.

"Is your husband's name Philip Saperstein?" asked a sepulchral voice at the other end of the line.

"What else?" replied the lady.

"This is the coroner's office. I'm sorry to tell you this, but we have a traffic death here. We found your telephone number in his pocket. Would you please come down here to the morgue and identify the body?"

Mrs. Saperstein arrived within a half-hour and an attendant escorted her to a figure covered with a white sheet. The attendant then lifted a corner of the sheet and uncovered the victim's face.

"Was this man your husband?" he asked.

Mrs. Saperstein's eyes widened.

"*Ai-yi-yi!* How did you—yes, that's my husband—ever get your sheets so white?"

* * *

---

*B'nai B'rith Messenger, Los Angeles, June 29, 1973.

The séance was at its height. Various spirits had responded to invitations from the medium to commune with the audience. The one and only Moses himself rapped on a table until his ghostly knuckles must have been sore. George Washington obliged with a tambourine solo. David Ben Gurion responded with the first two bars of "Eli. Eli," apologizing for his huskiness which, he said, was due to a bad cold. Cleopatra floated overhead, dimly revealed in regal robes of white cheesecloth to which the price tags were still attached, Altogether, it was a successful séance. Houdini would have been tickled half to death.

The mistress of ceremonies, Mrs. Medium's daughter, announced the second phase of the program. If anyone present wished to establish liaison with the shade of some departed dear one, Madame would do her best to accommodate, for a modest little something extra.

From among the awed spectators, Mr. Chernoff spoke up:

"I would like a few words with my wife, Anna, who died last year."

Madame went off again, into the Great Silence of which Man knows not. There was a breathless pause. Then the black calico draperies at the door were agitated by a mysterious wind, and from behind the curtains a muffled voice issued forth:

"Dearly beloved, this is Anna, speaking to you from the Beyond."

"Hello, Anna," greeted Mr. Chernoff. "How's by you these days?"

"I am well and happy, heart of my heart. And how are you faring?"

"I had a rotten season, but who's complaining?"

"It delights me that you are happy, dear one."

"Listen, Anna," said Chernoff after a few seconds of thought, "I got something to ask you."

"Proceed, my dear husband. I shall be happy to answer your question."

"Tell me, where the hell did you learn such good English?"

* * *

New York is a big city.

Speaking of New York . . .

Montgomery Eisenkop, the Pulaski Street pretzel bender, passed away at the respectable old age of 91 and went to the Hereafter.

"Well, whaddya know!" he exclaimed, gazing all around and taking in the scurrying crowds, the tall buildings and the general hustle and bustle. "I'd have bet a million dollars Heaven wasn't like this. Feels like I'm right back in good old New York."

"Mister," sighed a fellow ex-New Yorker, "who said this was Heaven?"

* * *

To avoid all charges of discrimination against certain people, the following is an Arab joke. *Azoi:*

An Israeli who, regrettably, had not led a good and decent life, passed away and went below. But his despair soon turned to incredulous wonder as he looked upon the lush vegetation, rambling brooks and pretty little lakes that surrounded him everywhere.

"You look surprised," said an Arab resident of the place.

"Why shouldn't I be surprised," answered the Israeli. "I expected Hell to be hot and dry and arid. But all I see here are rivulets, ponds, fruit trees, vegetables, flowers and green grass. You call this Hell?"

"As a matter of fact, it used to be as hot and barren as you expected," explained the Arab. "But then those Israelis started coming down here and they irrigated the hell out of the place!"

* * *

The *shammes* and the cantor, although attached to the same synagogue for more than 20 years, had never liked each other. Came the day when the cantor went to his reward.

"He died on Tuesday," said the *shammes* maliciously, "because he found out his life insurance expired on Wednesday!"

* * *

On her deathbed, Beatrice was giving final instructions to her husband.

"Eli, you've been so good to me all these years. I know that you never had a thought about another woman. Now that I'm going, I want you to marry again as soon as possible, and I want you to give your new wife all my expensive clothes."

Eli shook his head.

"That I can't do, Beatrice darling," he said unhappily. "You're a size 16 and she's only a ten!"

* * *

Yasher, the dry goods jobber, had just returned from the cemetery where he had served as pallbearer for a retail merchant who had died owing him $3,000.

"It's the story of my life," he complained to his missus. "When he first started in business I carried him for ten months, which is a month longer than his own mother carried him. And today," he concluded bitterly, "I had to carry him all the way to the grave!"

* * *

Mr. Peyger of Poughkeepsie was not expected to last out the night. But, miraculously, as the first rays of dawn filtered through the lace curtains and began to lighten the room, old man Peyger stirred and opened his glassy eyes. The nurse immediately summoned the doctor.

"Well, this certainly is a pleasant surprise," commented the medic as he listened to the old-timer's heartbeat and thumped him on the chest and back. "I have some very good news for you."

A wild hope blossomed in Mr. Peyger's tired heart. He had not dared to dream that, at the age of 96, he would live through this latest coronary.

"Y-y-you mean I—I . . .?"

"Exactly," boomed the doctor. "My prediction was all wrong. You're not sinking quite as fast as I thought you would!"

* * *

For a whole week after her husband Benny died, Mrs. Levy wept day and night. On the following Monday, the insurance agent called at her home and presented the grieving widow with a check for $50,000. She brushed a tear from her eye.

"Believe me," she said with a little catch in her voice, "I miss my Benny so much I'd give half of this just to have him back!"

* * *

The beloved Lubavitcher rabbi of Beth Stuyvesant Congregation in Brooklyn was breathing his last.

"My blessings go to you, my dear wife; and to you, my sweet daughter; and to all my friends and the members of my congregation," he said haltingly. "And please tell cantor Groshen that I especially wish him well—his voice notwithstanding!"

* * *

When much-married Sadie, the shady lady, finally went to her ultimate rendezvous with that Great Marriage Broker in the Sky, she departed with the knowledge that she had planned her life well.

She was halted at the pearly gate by a rather disapproving Father Abraham.

"I notice," he said as he consulted his *chasseneh* book, "that you first married a banker, then an actor, next a rabbi and lastly an undertaker. What kind of a system is that for a respectable Jewish woman?"

"A very good system, dearie," replied the new arrival: "One for the money, two for the show, three to make ready and four to go!"

* * *

In the late 1920s and early 1930s, the late Borrah Minevitch was the world's acknowledged harmonica virtuoso. For a brief period, the present author as a boy was one of the "Harmonica Rascals" under his direction. A quip about Borrah's entrance into Paradise is recalled with much affection.

It seems that Gabriel, in charge of the celestial music department, was not at all pleased with Minevitch.

"Everybody else up here is satisfied with a harp," complained Gabriel, "but *he* has to have a harmonica!"

* * *

The lecturer on the occult was warning to his subject of supernatural manifestations.

"Ah, my friends," he exclaimed, a look of dedicated zeal animating his face, "if you could but be made to believe! If only the world would cease its scoffing and come to realize that visitations from the Mystic Shore happen all the time."

The lecturer searched the faces in his audience to find those sympathetic souls who agreed with his philosophy.

"I have told you about my own experiences," he continued, "but surely one of you has also had direct communication with a departed spirit. If there is any such person here in this audience who has been in touch with a ghost, I would appreciate it if he or she would stand up."

From her seat in the front row, Mrs. Faigel Frume got to her feet.

"Me," she said loudly. "Such a 'sperience I had you wouldn't believe."

"This is very gratifying," said the delighted speaker when the applause died down. "Behold, a volunteer witness; one who is a total stranger to me, arises to give her testimony. My dear lady, do I understand you to say that you have been in touch with a ghost?"

"In touch with him?" echoed Mrs. Frume. "Better even than that. When I was a little girl in Russia one of them butted me till I was black and blue."

"A ghost *butted* you?"

"A *ghost*, you said? *Vay iz mir!* I thought you said a *goat!*"

* * *

It was during World War II, and some of the members of Plumbers Local 102 were down at Union Hall, chatting about the events of the day. The conversation eventually got around to President Truman's ouster of General MacArthur and the General's famous phrase, "Old soldiers never die, they just fade away."

"He's not alone," grinned one of the plumbers. "Old lawyers never die, either. They just lose their appeal."

"And old pilots never die," laughed another plumber, "they just fly away."

"How about old violin players?" chortled a younger member of the plumbers' union. "They just fiddle away."

"Now hold on a minute!" protested one of the old men. "Instead of picking on other trades, how about us plumbers? Do we just die—period?"

"No," replied the younger man gleefully. "Old plumbers never die, they just flush away!"

* * *

(The following anecdote, a classic in mounting irritability, has been part of Irish, Russian, Polish and American Negro humorous folklore for at least half a century.* This Jewish variant dates all the way back to 1887 when it was privately and anonymously published in a folio titled *I'm So Leffink!* Peculiarly enough, considering the pamphlet's title and the times, there is not a hint of dialect in the story—the only one in that booklet which is free of accented English.)

Hilda and Herman were spending a quiet evening at home. That is to say, Herman was quietly engrossed in a book, but Hilda was in a

---

*The Negro version: *Encyclopedia of Black Folklore and Humor*, by Henry D. Spalding, Jonathan David Publishers, Inc., © 1972. (Preface, pp. xvi-xvii.) The Jewish variant, above, has been edited and partially modified so that archaic or passé words and phrases may be more easily understood.

talkative mood.

"Honey," she began, "if I should die before you do, will you promise me something important?"

"Yeah," grunted Herman without lifting his eyes from the page he was reading.

"Promise me you'll always keep my grave green."

"Aw, don't be so morbid," he replied. "What's the use of talking about dying? You look pretty healthy to me."

He buried his nose in the book, completely absorbed, once more, hoping he would not again be distracted.

"Well, yes, I feel healthy, dear," Hilda interrupted again after a minute of blessed silence, "but I want to be sure my final resting place won't be neglected. You might want to remarry or something, and forget all about me."

"Look, Hilda, I'll remember you forever. Stop shopping around for an undertaker and let me read!"

This time he was rewarded with three whole minutes of peace and quiet, when his wife again took up the thread of conversation exactly where it had broken off.

"I'd hate to be forgotten by my own husband. I suppose it's because I'm so sensitive—because I have so much emotion. Darling, you're positive that you'll keep my grave green?"

"Yeah, I'm positive," he growled, his eyes glued to the page.

"Well, that's a great consolation. Only, I'd like for you to say it with more feeling . . . Precious, are you absolutely, positively sure you'll keep my . . ."

"Hilda," shouted the pestered man, casting his book aside, "I'll keep that damn grave of yours green if I have to paint it myself!"

* * *

Lightning flashed across the leaden sky, momentarily illuminating the pitch-black night. Thunder crashed. The rain fell in torrents.

Inside the little apartment, old Zelig awaited the end. At his bedside, his wife wept silently.

All at once the ancient one opened his glassy eyes and spoke in a hoarse whisper:

"I'm dying, my dear Bat'ya. Send for a priest."

"I should send for a *what*?" exclaimed the shocked wife.

"A priest."

"Zelig," she cried, "you mean a rabbi!"

The old man managed to lift a feeble hand in protest, and with a final touch of his old fire he snapped:

"A rabbi should go out on a night like this?"

* * *

Baruch Goldwasser, known to all of his nine followers as Barry Goldwater, knocked on the Heavenly Portal and was admitted by the sergeant-at-arms, Joshua.

"We're putting you up temporarily at the Paradise Hotel," said Joshua, "but first you'll have to sign the register."

Barry signed.

"Now for a little information," continued the celestial guardian of the gate. "How old were you when you left the vale of tears?"

"Ninety-one."

"Hmm, you must have seen a lot of changes in your time."

"I sure did," moaned Barry, "and I want it clearly understood that I was against every one of them!"

* * *

The venerable old rabbi, known throughout the land for his wisdom, lay in a coma, very near death. On either side of his bed, hovered his most worshipful disciples.

"*Rebbenyu*," pleaded the spokesman for the grieving congregants, "please do not leave us without a final word of wisdom. Speak to us for the last time, dear rabbi."

For a few moments there was no response, and the weeping visitors feared he had passed on to his well-earned reward. But suddenly the rabbi's lips moved, ever so slightly. They bent over him to hear his final words:

"The Jewish people are the twin stars of the night," he whispered in a faint voice.

The disciples looked at each other in perplexity. What did he mean? What great secret of life was hidden in that mystic statement? For the better part of an hour they exchanged opinions, analyzing the sentence from every conceivable standpoint, but they could not decipher the deeper meaning.

"We must ask him before it is too late," said the leader. Once again, he leaned over the still figure of the revered sage.

"Rabbi, rabbi," he called out urgently, "we implore you to explain: Why are Jewish people the twin stars of the night?"

With his last spark of energy, the rabbi lifted his palms and croaked:

"All right, so they're not the twin stars of the night!"

* * *

This one goes back to the year 1939 when the UJA was founded as a single fund-raising body in behalf of the American Jewish Joint Distribution Committee, the United Palestine Appeal and the National Refugee Service.

An old reprobate, one who had spent his life as an excessive drinker, gambler and general defiler of decency, finally and unlamentedly died. At the services, neither the rabbi nor any member of the old scoundrel's family could think of anything good to say about him.

In the midst of the embarrassing silence, a member of the rabbi's congregation stepped forward and announced:

"If nobody has anything to say for the deceased, I'd like to say a few words about the United Jewish Appeal!"

* * *

Jewish humor abounds in tales of cheapwads and tightskates, but the all-time champion of close-fisted penny-pinchers is presented in this little vignette.

Skolnik, the Scarsdale skinflint, awoke one morning to find that during the night his wife had died. After one glance at the stark form lying there beside him, he leaped out of bed and ran into the hall.

"Daisy," he called down to the maid in the kitchen, "come to the foot of the stairs, quick!"

"Yes," she cried. "What is it?"

"Only one egg for breakfast this morning!"

* * *

Plotkin the painter was working on a third-floor scaffold when he fell off and was severely injured.

At the hospital, the doctor told Plotkin's grieving wife, Miriam, that her husband had only a 50-50 chance of surviving, and that he had suffered some brain damage. One of the peculiar oddities of his confused mind was a compulsion to scribble everything he heard or even thought about.

"He'll probably insist on writing you a note or two," cautioned the doctor. "Just remember, it's only a symptom of his brain injury. Don't pay any attention to it. With God's help and the science of medicine he'll get over it some day."

When Miriam was finally allowed to visit her husband, his eyes lit up. He smiled when she kissed him and he even tried to say hello, although still unable to talk. Suddenly, without warning, his eyes grew wild, he began to gesticulate violently, making frantic motions with his hands, indicating that he wanted to write a note. She tried to ignore him, as the doctor had suggested, but after enduring two full minutes of his agonized actions, her wifely heart melted and she handed him a sheet of paper and a pencil.

He scrawled something on the paper and then his head fell back on the pillow. To her immense shock, he was dead.

Later, at home, and alone with her sad thoughts, Miriam remembered the note her husband had so frantically written in his last moments of life. Still weeping, she retrieved it from her purse and read:

"You're sitting on my oxygen tube!"

* * *

In the mid-1700s, demonology formed a significant part of the myths and legends of the day, just as remnants of those superstitions are being revived in modern times with such anomalies as exorcism and necromancy. The following legend, handed down from generation to generation in the oral tradition of Jewish-American folklore has the saving grace of being humorous.

One evening, when Hayman Levy, one of the most important merchants in all the colonies, was working late at his warehouse, and alone with his ledgers and manifests, his youngest and favorite son rushed into his office.

"Father, I beg you, let me have your carriage and your fastest team of horses," he cried breathlessly. "I must leave at once!"

"Why all the haste?" asked the elder Levy.

"Because," answered the youth, "only an hour ago, as I was working in the garden at home, I saw Death standing there. And when he caught sight of me, he stretched out his arms. There is no doubt at all that he was threatening to take me with him. I beg you, father, help me to escape!"

"Yes, of course I'll help," said Hayman Levy, thoroughly shaken. "You will leave for Boston at once and stay with your uncle, Nathaniel. He will be glad to shelter you. Now go, my son, and take the carriage and the fastest horses in our stables. With speed, you should be in Boston on Tuesday."

The father then hurried home and burst into the garden where he found Death still there.

"Are you the *Malach-hamoves*?" he demanded.

"I am," replied the Angel of Death calmly.

"How dare you make threatening gestures at my son!" he fumed.

"Why, sir, I assure you" gasped Death, clearly astonished, "I made no move to threaten your son. I only threw up my hands in surprise to find him here in New York when I have a rendezvous with him in Boston on Tuesday!"

* * *

When we speak of Gertrude Stein, we refer to a more or less contemporary figure whose name has often been associated with the folklore of literature, but never with *folkskeit*. Born in Allegheny (now part of Pittsburgh) in 1874, the author and patron of the arts was a celebrated personality of her time. After attending Radcliffe, where she was a student of William James, she began premedical work at Johns Hopkins, but in 1902 she relinquished her studies and went abroad, spending the rest of her life in Europe, chiefly in Paris. There, through her own writing and patronage, she influenced such young writers as Hemingway, Sherwood Anderson, F. Scott Fitzgerald and a host of others. She also encouraged many new painters and purchased the work of such unrecognized newcomers as Picasso and Matisse. Her talents brought her into contact with people on every level of life, from struggling young artists to members of the French nobility. She passed away in 1946 at the age of seventy-two, and therein lies another bit of folklore.

Miss Stein was breathing her last in an upstairs bedroom of her Paris home when an acquaintance, a distinguished noblewoman who was not aware of the writer's mortal illness, came to call. Alice B. Toklas, Miss Stein's companion-secretary, conveyed the message to the sickroom and, in a few minutes, returned with a note. The answer sent down from the chamber of the departing sufferer demonstrated that, while she could be as earthy as a stevedore, she could also reach the heights of exquisite politeness.

The eminently unique note read:

Gertrude Stein sends her compliments to Madame de Calais, but begs to be excused, as she is engaged in dying.

30

Travails on Travel

INTRODUCTION

It goes without saying that any group of people who would wander for 40 years in a hot desert, with nothing but matzoh from Heaven for sustenance and a burning bush to read by, must indeed possess an urge to travel in their genes. Moses, the wagon-master, was rewarded with a marvelous rave notice in the Bible for his leadership, especially after he headed the bad guys off at the pass. It was there, you will recall, that he parted the waters with an upflung palm, like the traffic cop who used to part the waves of traffic in the old days at the intersection of Lafayette and Canal Streets. Moses also changed his staff into a serpent, according to Exodus—whoever *he* was. It was a good trick—but the Israelites had experienced enough *tsuris* with serpents in the Garden of Eden without having another such creature in their midst. "Better you should concentrate on more practical miracles," they suggested, "like turning your staff into a nice box of halavah."

Those four decades in the desert must have been a terrible ordeal, but 40 years cannot be compared with the 2,500 years during which the Jewish people wandered over the face of the earth after the downfall of the Kingdom of Israel and the destruction of the Kingdom of Judah. The ancient Hebrews were a prime target for exploitation by the Assyrians and Babylonians who conquered them. A hard-working, imaginative people, the Jews would find a few square miles of land no one else wanted —barren, arid, forbidding. They would dig wells for water, irrigate the desert wastelands until they bloomed and became fruitful. They would build cities and engage in commerce. Once accomplished, however, each of those formerly unproductive and forbidding lands became like a rich and juicy orange, waiting to be plucked by more powerful neighbors.

That is precisely what they did—and what their descendants today are still trying to do. But, now, the orange is riper and juicier, and this time the Jewish people have decided to eat it themselves, and to save the seeds for replanting. The Word has been issued straight from the horse's mouth in Israel to the other end of the horse in Araby.

The Wandering Jew has finally found his home, but his record for travel remains unbroken. His journeys have taken him around the globe, from the most primitive areas whose inhabitants think television is a city in Israel, to the metropolis of New York—home of taxi drivers who peek. In that city, another exodus is taking place because of the mounting crime rate. Killings—those acts which create a vacancy without naming a successor—are a prime concern of the new refugees. According to them, there are four kinds of homicide: felonious, excusable, justifiable and praiseworthy, but it makes no great difference to the victim whether he fell by one kind or another—the classification is for the advantage of lawyers. They have to live too, even if we don't know why.

Flying is the newest mode of travel for the modern Wanderer; that is, flying in an airplane: soaring around on gossamer wings occurs only after the plane falls down. There are still a number of obstacles to be overcome before flying can be called perfect. For one thing, in most cities you need a plane to get to the airport. For another, it is too easy for an honest citizen to get arrested at the airport. Take the case of *Zaftik* Zelda who landed in the pokey for doing take-offs on the runway. However, reform rabbis love those big 707 Jets where they can hide in the first class section, away from the prying eyes of their congregants, and smoke Corona-Corona cigars-cigars.

Barry Goldwater is a Major-General in the Air Corps Reserve. He is our authority for quoting the dangers involved in flying. One day, according to Barry, he was bringing his plane into Los Angeles and, while he was still at an altitude of 30,000 feet, his radio crackled ominously:

"This is the Tower at L.A. Airport—your landing gears have not descended. Repeat—your landing gears are not down. If you can hear me, waggle your wings."

And Barry radioed back:

"Out of gas. If you can hear me, waggle your tower."

It is not always the physical act of travel itself that causes problems, but the complications that arise after the destination has been reached. The story of Gwendolyn's vice arrest that followed her trip to Europe is a case in point. It is a story that is rapidly assuming the status of a folk tale, and has been quoted as an actual occurrence by almost every segment of society in America. Did it ever really take place? Travelers have described it as happending to members of their tour in Shanghai, in Rio de Janeiro, in Rome. It has been told as gospel truth in every suburban bar and country club across the nation. Surely it was once told for the first time—about the real Gwendolyn. Here is the American-Jewish version:

When her husband became an overnight millionaire by discovering a method for making two gallons of wine out of one gallon of wine (by the simple process of adding lots of water), Goldie Nathan blossomed forth as Gwendolyn Abernathy and prepared herself for the good life. Having absorbed all the culture she could locate in the United States, she decided to visit France and acquire a little extra polish. It was there that tragedy struck. Somehow, Gwendolyn became separated from her tour group in Marseilles and wandered unwittingly into the red-light district. She was trying to find her way back to her hotel when the gendarmes raided the place.

Gwendolyn Abernathy, age 42, from 63rd Street and Fifth Avenue in the City of New York, president of her Hadassah Chapter, important contributor to the Zionist movement, and an eminent and respectable society leader, was thrown into a paddy wagon with a dozen ladies-of-the-evening. To her further horror, she was booked at the local police station for practicing prostitution without a license. It was several hours later that her husband appeared to gain her release.

He fumed and roared, threatening to call the U.S. Consul, the U.S. Ambassador, the U.S. Cavalry. An apologetic official explained that a terrible mix-up had occurred, but for a slight fee of $3,00 and Gwendolyn's signature, she would be freed immediately. The husband shrugged. Three dollars was such a trifling amount, and the police seemed to be truly sorry about the arrest. He paid the sum and, as they left, the official, lavish in his apologies, pressed a document into Gwendolyn's trembling hand.

It wasn't until the couple returned to New York that their daughter, a student of French, told them what the document really was: a license for Gwendolyn!

American-Jewish humor contains very few jokes relating to interstate bus travel. Whoever heard of a long-distance bus going through a Jewish neighborhood! Prior to World War II, it was not the airplane, but the auto on land and the ship at sea which accounted for nearly all of the anecdotes. Some of these stories have survived as classics and a few of the newer ones also show signs of durability. It is regrettable, however, that with the passing years they seem to grow less identifiable with the traditional Jewish joke. Still, it is pleasant to note that the people's humor ebbs and flows with the economic, political and social tides. One can only be heartened by the recent warning sign on the back of a Schwartz Bakery truck in Chicago: *This Truck Has Been in Ten Accidents and Ain't Lost Any! Nu?*

Whatever the hazards of driving a car, traveling by train isn't made any easier by the railroads. The late Jack Benny reported one of the reasons for the waning popularity of the rails when he reminded us of a Kansas law still in effect: "When two trains approach each other on the same track both shall come to a full stop and neither shall proceed until the other has passed." Laws like that make us wonder where the automobile industry finds all those empty roads for filming its TV commercials.

The identification of the travel joke with the hotel joke is another facet of American-Jewish humor. The connection is obvious, of course, but unlike the humor of other peoples, they are seldom classified separately. It is assumed that the subject of the anecdote is away from home, but the act of travel itself is only incidental to the story. Here is an illustration:

Sam, the Syracuse suspender salesman, in Florida as a hotel guest, was completely fed up with the whole system of tipping, tipping, tipping! Every time he turned around, it seemed to him, somebody's hand was out for a tip. After a week of taking care of doormen, waiters, bellboys, maids, desk clerks, hat check girls and such, he decided to call a halt to the whole sorry business. "I didn't have to travel a thousand miles just to give my hardearned money away," he muttered to himself.

Then came a knock on the door.

"Who is it?" Sam called out.

"The bellboy, sir. Telegram for you."

"Well, just slip it under the door," said tip-tortured Sam, a crafty gleam in his eye.

"I can't, sir."

"Why not?" growled Sam.

"Because, sir," explained the determined bellboy without a moment's hesitation, "it's on a tray!"

H.D.S.

The year was 1934. The *Queen Mary* was two days out of New York and, although the sea was not as heavy as it had been for the past 24 hours, the huge ship still rolled in the heaving swells.

On board were Benjamin Nathan Cardoza, in his second year as an Associate Justice of the Supreme Court, and the brilliant Harvard Law School preofessor, Felix Frankfurter, already nationally known but still six years away from his own appointment as a Supreme Court judge.

Frankfurter, although 12 years younger than Cardoza, was having the worst of the foul weather. His face had taken on a pea-green cast and his stomach churned violently as he staggered weakly toward the rail for the time-honored ritual that is no respecter of rank or privilege.

"Is there anything I can do for you, Felix," asked Cardoza, his voice full of sympathy.

"Yes, there is, Ben," gasped Frankfurter. "Overrule the motion!"

* * *

"The trouble with flying on those big jet planes," grumbled Grandpa Graubyen in his usual testy voice, "is that we see less and less of more and more, faster and faster, at prices that are higher and higher!"

* * *

The following story tells of a minor crisis that once beset Mike Todd when he was married to Elizabeth Taylor.

Shortly after their marriage, they found themselves in New York where Mike had an important *Cinerama* deal in the works. With the financial part of the contract signed and sealed, it was imperative that he fly back to Hollywood immediately to secure the production end of the arrangement. Without warning, however, the weather turned against him and it began to snow. He called the airport and was told that unless it cleared up, all air traffic would be halted until it stopped snowing. However, the planes would still be taking off for about an hour, so if he hurried he might catch the last flight to California.

Scrambling around the room, Mike grabbed up all his clothing and jammed it willy-nilly into his suitcases. Elizabeth was taking a shower so he opened the dresser drawers and closets and snatched all of her clothing and stuffed them into her suitcases as he had done with his own things. The speed with which he packed, helter-skelter though it was, gave him the extra time to call a bellboy who arrived at the hotel suite within a minute. The boy grabbed the luggage and rushed it to the airport. Then Mike called the desk again and ordered a taxi to be waiting downstairs for him and his wife.

A few seconds later, Elizabeth stepped out of the bathroom, wrapped in a towel.

"Mike," she said, puzzled, "where are my dress and shoes?"

* * *

For this one, we are indebted to the late Eddie Cantor.

Father Abramowitz, mother Abramowitz and master Myron Abramowitz, age seven, were taking a sea voyage—a first-time experience for them. The weather was bad and the sea was rough, as they usually are at vacation time. Unlike his parents who had suffered almost immediate gastronomic disturbances, little Myron seemed immune to seasickness. He frolicked about the ship with merry cries, got underfoot and in people's way, and generally deported himself as any healthy, active seven-year-old may be expected to do on a holiday.

On the second day of their indisposition, Mr. and Mrs. Abramowitz dragged themselves up on deck. If they must die—as seemed to them probable—they would die in the open air under the skies rather than in a stuffy and crowded stateroom. Commiserating stewards guided the Abramowitzes to two steamer chairs placed side by side in a sheltered place, eased them down gently, covered them with lap robes and shawls, and left them to suffer together.

Presently, Mrs. Abramowitz, tossing an aching head from east to west, with occasional changes of direction to north and south, beheld a spectacle which, under ordinary circumstances, would have caused her to leap to her feet and dart to the rescue. For, 20 feet away, her only son was in peril. Unobserved, restless Myron had climbed the guard rail and then straddled it, one leg dangling freely over the bounding billows, crowing his joy as the motion of the ship now lifted him up, now plummeted him to the depths.

His mother tried to rise but failed. She strove to cry out to her endangered son but her voice issued forth as only a thin, horrified wheeze. In this emergency, she clutched with a trembling hand at her husband's listless form.

"Quick, for God's sake," she hissed fiercely, "speak to Myron!"

Mr. Abramowitz's lackluster gaze followed where her finger pointed.

"Hello, Myron," he said in hollow tones.

* * *

A traveling salesman, on a train from New York to Chicago, entered the club car and was agreeably surprised to note that the other occupants, also salesmen, were as unmistakably Jewish as he was. They introduced themselves all around:

"My name's Connors," said one.

"I'm Callahan," said the second.

"I'm Calhoun," said the third.

"I'm Conrad," said the fourth.

"Glad to know you," said the newcomer to the group, nodding comfortably. "My name's also Cohen!"

* * *

A pretty young American girl, visiting Israel, entered the lobby of the *Areyngekrokhn in Frimorgen* Hotel and confidently approached the desk. She picked up a pen, looked around for the guest book, and beamed at the desk clerk.

"Do I register with you?"

"You sure do, lady," he sighed, taking in her luscious figure, "but I'm sorry to say there's no vacancies."

* * *

Tannenbaum the tailor had saved up his money for years so that he could fulfill a longtime dream—to take a Caribbean cruise. But he hadn't reckoned with seasickness. On the second day out from port, the captain noticed him, green-faced, hanging on to the ship's rail.

"Sorry, sir," said the captain politely, "but you can't be sick here."

"No?" said Tannenbaum. "Watch!"

* * *

The art of gesticulating with the hands to emphasize or clarify the spoken word—and it *is* an art—is not confined to the Jewish people. The practice is less common to Jews, as a matter of fact, than to other nationalities; for example, Arabs, Armenians, Turks, Greeks, Portuguese, Latin Americans, American Indians and Italians.—*Especially* Italians!

Professor Milton Eichorn of New York University always claimed that the following actually happened to a friend of his. This modern Greek tragedy had its beginning when Dr. Eichorn's supposed friend, Sigmund Marks, was traveling through Italy. He dined one night at a café in Naples where the behavior of two Italian gentlemen at an adjacent table intrigued him deeply. What they said made no difference to him inasmuch as he spoke no Italian, but the pantomime between them gripped his attention. His interest was quite understandable. His own parents utilized the well-known gestures to strengthen their spoken words, their conversation aided and abetted by elevated eyebrows, shoulders, elbows and palms. Italians, too, he noted, seemed to regard language as a calisthenic exercise.

After watching the nearby pair for some time, the vacationing Sigmund Marks beckoned to the headwaiter. The waiter was Swiss and knew half a dozen tongues, including English.

"You've been standing just behind those two men at the next table," began Marks. "Probably you overheard everything they've been talking about."

"Oh, yes," said the waiter. "One of them said . . ."

"Hold on," interrupted the American, "I don't want you to tell me, yet. I want to see if my deductions are correct. You see, my own people use the same sort of hand and arm movements. Now here's the way I figured out their conversation:

"One of them—the one with the beard and the educated eyebrows— is an inventor. Yes, I'm sure of that. And lately he perfected a new type of airplane—a vast improvement of some kind over the older models. He has just described its design to his friend at some length. From his gestures I could make out that the propeller revolved much more rapidly than the old-style propellers and that it also used a jet engine. The test flight must have taken place very recently. Everything went smoothly until the plane had climbed to a very great height. Then something broke.

"Down, down, down came the ill-fated airplane. It struck the earth with a tremendous crash. It was literally dashed to pieces. The pilot, apparently a friend of the inventor, was instantly killed. His body was horribly mangled. Yes, it was a terrible spectacle, a horrible tragedy. The poor man is still filled with distress and remorse; probably his nervous system will never be the same again. And never again will he have anything to do with aircraft—he is through with them forever. Meanwhile, I can tell that his dinner companion, listening to the gruesome story, has been almost overcome by emotion. He, too, is grief-stricken.

"Now then, waiter, tell me—was I right?"

"Not exactly," replied the waiter. "What happened between them was this: The bearded gentleman was complaining that only this morning his wife ordered him to pull in his stomach, and he already had. So she told him his get-up-and-go had gone and went. He then informed her that, for exercise, he'd try chasing girls, even if he had to do it downhill.

"And the other fellow replied, 'When you get all the weight-lifting you need just by getting out of a chair, and your thoughts turn from passion to pension, and you begin to feel friendly toward insurance agents, then it's later than you think and sooner than you expected!'"

* * *

Comedians like to tell stories about traveling salesmen and their infidelities. But Hershel Baumgarten, who used to travel for Feldman's Fancy Furnishings in East New York, wasn't like that at all. He really loved his wife. When he was on the road he spent his nights praying, not carousing. And when he died he left his wife 654 Gideon Bibles.

* * *

Isidor had worked hard all his life and, now that he was retired, he decided to do a little traveling. His first stop was Mexico City, and like many other tourists he looked forward to seeing his first bullfight. But, when he arrived at the ticket window, he was dismayed at the high admission price. He simply couldn't afford it.

Disconsolately he wandered to a side entrance, hoping at least to catch a glimpse of a real live bull. Suddenly his interest was aroused by three men who strode confidently to the entrance and gave a secret password:

"Picador," declared the first man, and he was promptly admitted into the stadium.

"Toreador," asserted the second man, and he too immediately walked inside.

"Matador," announced the third man, and he also went inside.

Our hero got the idea.

"Isidor!" he proclaimed, strolling nonchalantly toward the ringside seats.

* * *

Octogenarian Louis Langtseit was driving peacefully along at his usual speed of 20 miles an hour when suddenly a siren sounded behind his 1938 Studebaker. Dutifully, he pulled over to the curb. A stern-faced officer approached.

"Mister," he began, his manner ominous, "this is a one-way street."

"So sue me: I'm only going one way," responded Mr. Langtseit, clearly puzzled.

The policeman's face reddened. "Look," he growled, trying valiantly to retain his temper, "there are signs on both sides of the street. Didn't you see the arrows?"

"Arrows!" exclaimed the old man. "On what are you talking, on what? I didn't even see any Indians!"

* * *

Then there's the American businessman who went to Tel Aviv where he quickly learned that a cop is a cop.

The American was new in Israel so he approached a traffic officer near the airport.

"Sir," he began politely enough, "can you direct me to the nearest bank?"

The cop glared at him. "Mister," he snarled, "do I look like a bank director?"

* * *

Irv Fox, who made a mint in the julep business, had never been more than 20 miles outside of his native New York. Now that he could afford to relax and do a bit of traveling, he decided to make up for lost time and, as a result, found himself enjoying an entirely new life in America's unfamiliar (to him) frontier.

That first summer away from his old haunts found him fishing in the upper peninsula of Michigan. His guide was a typical woodsman. One night, in the cozy glow of the campfire, the guide regaled Irv with accounts of the severity of the winters in those parts—how deep the snowdrifts were and how biting the winds from Lake Superior could be and how thick the ice was and how low the thermometer fell and how long the cold weather lasted.

"Well," exclaimed the New Yorker when the native finally halted for breath, "we have some pretty bad cold snaps along the seaboard but nothing to equal what you describe. How do you manage to stand such terrible conditions?"

"Me? I don't even try to stand it. Before it freezes up solid I pack up and get out of here and go down south for the winter."

"To Florida," I suppose," ventured Irv.

"Nope," said the native, "Grand Rapids!"

* * *

"Mr. Policeman, could you kindly give me a direction?" asked Mrs. Yomtov as she rolled down the window of her car. "I'm looking for the first turn to the left."

* * *

Fifty years earlier, when Mrs. Rabinowitz landed on Ellis Island as a young girl, she was bustled off to a little town in Louisiana where her cousins had a general store. Now, silver-haired and bent with the years, the dear old lady was visiting New York. And it was the first time she had ever ridden in a taxi.

As the cab swung away from the airport and began to weave its way through the traffic, Mrs. Rabinowitz noted with growing alarm that the driver kept removing one hand from the steering wheel and putting it outside the window. When he had negotiated the turning of the third corner, each time repeating this movement, the passenger could contain herself no longer.

She bent forward and tapped him on the shoulder with a determined forefinger.

"Mister, do an old lady a favor," she said. "You take care of the driving and look where you're going. I'll tell you when it's starting in to rain!"

* * *

Professor Kaplan, widely noted among his students as a man with an exceedingly short temper, settled down in the train and was soon absorbed in his newspaper. But he was suddenly jolted out of his tranquility when an old man took the seat next to his. He was obviously a brand new immigrant, obviously Jewish and obviously bewildered. The elderly man looked at Professor Kaplan helplessly, clearly wanting to say something but unable to express himself in English. Kaplan sighed in resignation, folded his newspaper and asked in Yiddish:

"Can I help you?"

The old man brightened as though all his troubles were over.

"I have to get off in Baltimore," he said.

"This train stops in Baltimore," Professor Kaplan assured him.

"You're sure?"

"Of course."

"Must I pull the cord?"

"No, the train stops by itself."

"Should I tell the conductor?"

"No, he already has your ticket."

"Suppose the train doesn't stop in Baltimore?"

"It'll stop, it'll stop!" growled the beleaguered professor. "Quit worrying and let me read my paper."

The curt answer silenced the old man and Kaplan, with an inner prayer to the Deity that the peace and quiet continue for a while, returned to his newspaper. But a few minutes later he felt a tap on his shoulder.

"Sir," the ancient one began tentatively, "if the train stops in Baltimore, from which end should I get off?"

"Mister, you can get off from either the front or the rear," rasped the professor, completely out of patience. "Take my word for it, *both* ends stop in Baltimore!"

* * *

Grandma had just taken her first plane ride—a jet flight from New York to Los Angeles. White-faced and shaken, she disembarked and was greeted by her grandson.

"Well, *bobeh*, how was the trip?" he asked jovially.

"*Oy*, was I scared!" she exclaimed, still trembling. "I sat on the edge of the seat all the way."

"Why?"

"Why? Because I was afraid to put down my whole weight, that's why!"

* * *

Movie producer-director-author Hal Kanter recalls that he had an uncle who, Horace Greeley-style, advised him to "go West, young man." He remembers, too, where it was he received the advice: San Francisco!

* * *

Abe and Sarah grew so tired of big city life with all its frantic rushing and crowds and tumult that they moved to Kishkeh Corners, a tiny village in the wilds of Tennessee.

"It's perfectly marvelous here," they wrote to their families back in New York. "Just what we wanted—a small town. In fact, this place is so small, thank God, the tourist season is June 18th, between 2:30 and 5:00 p.m."

* * *

"My troubles as an immigrant started as soon as I got off the boat," sighed grandpa whose reputation for veracity was not too distinguished.

"I had no friends or relatives here in America and I didn't know a word of English. All I had was a reservation at the Taft Hotel. But, not knowing the language, how was I going to get there? Suddenly I had a bright idea. I showed a cab driver a picture of the hotel on a matchbook cover. He nodded and smiled—

"And he took me to the match factory!"

* * *

All the hotel rooms were taken in the town where a convention was taking place. The desk clerk was about to turn away the last traveler for the night when he remembered one empty cubicle in the basement.

"Well, I have a place for you in the cellar," he began uncertainly, "but . . ."

"I'll take it," interrupted the desperate guest.

Dutifully, the clerk led him down to the basement and opened the door to what once was probably a coal bin.

"Well," said the clerk, breaking the painful silence, "how do you like the room as a whole?"

"As a hole it will do," said the weary man, "but as a room, *feh!*"

* * *

Theodore, on the road for Threads, Inc., had just left the Jersey Turnpike heading north and was barreling his way back to his New York headquarters when he was waved to the side of the road by a motorcycle cop.

"Where's your taillight?" demanded the policeman.

"What are you talking about?" retorted Theodore. "I just put on a new taillight this morning."

"Well, it ain't there now," said the officer. "Come around back of your car and take a look for yourself."

Theodore went around to see for himself.

"Oh, my God!" he cried aloud in anguish.

"Aw c'mon, it ain't as bad as all that," protested the officer. "I ain't even gonna give you a ticket. Lotsa people lose a taillight."

"Taillight?" moaned Theodore. "Who cares about a lousy taillight? *Where's my trailer?*"

* * *

The Phoenix Chamber of Commerce was putting on its annual television show to boost the virtues of Arizona living. A roving cameraman and his companion, a TV commentator, were conducting a series of sidewalk interviews with passers-by. They stopped one likely-looking prospect.

"What is your name, sir?"

"Maurice Gross."

"And where do you come from, Mr. Gross?"

"New York."

"And will you tell our vast listening audience, please, why you settled in beautiful, sunny Arizona?"

"I came here for my health."

"Aha! And it worked?"

"Did it work? Mister, you wouldn't believe how good it worked. My doctor told me I should go to Arizona for TB, and in less than a month I got it!"

*   *   *

For a change of pace, let's tell a story about a traveling salesman and a chicken—the kind with feathers and built-in egg machinery.

The New Yorker, on the road for a hardware concern, was stranded in a small North Dakota town—not that there are any large ones up there —but he was lucky enough to find a farm family who invited him in for supper.

"That was a fine meal," said the salesman, smacking his lips. "I haven't tasted more delicious chicken in years."

"Thank ye kindly," said the pleased farmer. "An' I don't mind sayin' that you city folks miss a lot, never eatin' good ol' country poultry. None o' that city-butchered meat fer us. This chicken died a *natch'ral* death!"

*   *   *

Voice on loudspeaker at Kennedy International Airport:

"Albert Einstein the Third, will you please come to the information desk? Your grandfather is lost!"

*   *   *

In school, the teacher asked the class to write a short composition on the subject: "What I would like most to do."

Wrote imaginative little Marvin:

"First I would like to go to the moon. Then I would like to take a trip to Mars. Then I would like to travel."

*   *   *

Molly Picon tells of the woman, a newcomer to Chicago, who boarded a bus on Michigan Avenue.

"Do you stop at the Drake Hotel?" she asked the driver.

"What are you, some kind of kibitzer?" he snapped. "On my salary?"

*   *   *

Anybody can tell a joke about one measly traveling salesman. But why buy retail when you can get it wholesale? This one has *two* salesmen in the same story, offered as a special bonus for the economy-minded reader.

It was getting on toward dusk, late one August afternoon, when Alger and Alan stopped at an isolated farmhouse. They were given shelter and dinner by an attractive, lonely young lady who informed them that she had been recently widowed. Her husband, she explained, had died a year earlier.

After dinner she showed them to their separate bedrooms upstairs, and in the morning she not only served them a fine breakfast but refused to accept payment for her hospitality.

"I don't need your money," she told them. "My late husband left me a substantial bank account and the farm is very profitable."

A few months later, back in New York, Alan mentioned the incident to his friend.

"Listen, Alger, I want a straight answer from you. Remember that farmer's widow who put us up for the night and refused to charge us anything?"

"Sure, I remember her very well."

"Then tell me, did you get up in the middle of the night while I was asleep and sneak downstairs to her bedroom?"

"Well, yes, if you must know."

"And," continued Alan unrelentingly, "did you tell her you were me?"

"Well, I—I—you see . . ."

"Answer me, yes or no. Did you have the *chutzpah* to give her *my* name?"

"Yeah, I'm afraid I did," said Alger, his voice apologetic. "I'm really sorry, old buddy. Sure didn't mean to get you into any trouble. I hope you'll forgive me and we can still be friends."

"There's nothing to forgive," said Alan gently. "I just received a letter from her lawyer. The lady was killed in a car accident and left me the house and farm!"

* * *

Mark Aaronson, who had been on the road for Goodman's Sundries these past 15 years, told of the time he stopped off at a little village near Callicoon, New York.

There was no hotel or even a motel in the village. A gas station attendant directed him to a farmer's house where stragglers were sometimes fed and housed for the night. Mark hurried over to the temporary lodging, anxious now to get there for a new reason—the gas station had no rest room and the call of nature was growing urgent.

The farmer was in the front yard when Mark Aaronson arrived. They quickly made a deal, and then the salesman asked the whereabouts of the bathroom.

"We ain't got no bathrooms around here," said the farmer. "But you can use the privy around back of the house."

Mark visited the old-fashioned two-holer, and when he returned he found the farmer carrying his luggage into the house.

"Everything okay?" asked the host.

"Yes," said Mark, "except that the flies in that outhouse were something awful. They came at me in swarms—great big black ugly things."

"Yeah, I know," said the farmer. "You should've waited till suppertime, when they're all in the dinin' room!"

* * *

While in England on a business trip, Friedman the importer decided he might as well take in the sights. So he joined a tourist group and started out on the rounds. Before long they came to a naval station.

"An' 'ere, ladies an' gentlemen," announced the guide, "is Lord Nelson's ship."

Friedman edged closer to hear every word.

"An' 'ere on this very spot," the guide continued, "is where Nelson fell."

"I can believe it," said Friedman, nodding. "Almost tripped myself!"

* * *

Bluestein, on the road for Light and Tasty Dairy Products of Long Island, was marooned during a blizzard in a tiny town outside of Pocatello, Idaho. He managed to get a telegram through to his office back east:

SNOWBOUND. UNABLE TO PROCEED FURTHER.

Back came an answering wire:

START SUMMER VACATION AT ONCE.

* * *

This vignette proves one of two points: either Jewish people over-react to suspicions of anti-Semitism, or else all gall was not divided into three parts after all. In any event, the following anecdote stands in a class by itself as an example of monumental *chutzpah!*

Of the eight traveling salesmen on the payroll of Gotham Fabrics, Louie Feldman was unquestionably the best. On this particular night he was in the Pullman car, journeying to Richmond, Virginia, where he hoped to close a big deal with the city's largest department store. He had been lucky to catch this last train out of Grand Central Station, although he felt somewhat uncomfortable about having forgotten, in his haste, to pack his toiletry set.

The following morning, he arose bright and early and made his way to the lavatory at the end of the car. Inside, he walked up to a washbasin that was not in use.

"Excuse me," said Louie to a man who was bent over the basin next to his, "I forgot to pack all my stuff last night. Mind if I use your soap?"

The stranger gave him a searching look, hesitated momentarily, and then shrugged. "Okay. Help yourself."

Louie murmured his thanks, washed, and again turned to the man. "Mind if I borrow your towel?"

"N-no, I-I guess not."

Louie dried himself, dropped the wet towel to the floor and inspected his face in the mirror. "I could use a shave," he commented. "Would it be all right with you if I use your razor?"

"Certainly," agreed the man in a courteous voice.

"How you fixed for shaving cream?"

Wordlessly, the man handed Louie his tube of shaving cream.

"You got a fresh blade? I hate to use one that somebody else already used. Can't be too careful, y'know."

Louie was given a fresh blade. His shave completed, he turned to the stranger once more.

"You wouldn't happen to have a comb handy, would you?"

The man's patience had stretched dangerously near to the breaking point, but he managed a wan smile and gave Louie his comb.

Louie inspected it closely. "You should really keep this comb a little cleaner," he admonished as he proceeded to wash it. He then combed his hair and again addressed his benefactor whose mouth was now drawn in a thin, tight line.

"Now, if you don't mind, I'll have a little talcum powder, some after-shave lotion, some toothpaste and a toothbrush."

"By God, I never heard of such damn nerve in my life!" snarled the outraged stranger. "Hell *no!* Nobody in the whole world can use my toothbrush!" He slammed his belongings into their leather case and stalked to the door, muttering: "I gotta draw the line someplace!"

"Anti-Semite!" yelled Louie.

* * *

On board an *El Al* jet flight to Israel, a young mother and her two children were just getting settled when the youngsters began to clamor that they had to go to the "bafroom." Two priests, on a pilgrimage to the Holy Land, seated in front of the little family group, smiled in amusement while the embarrassed mother quickly took the children to the rest rooms on the plane. After a moment's hesitation, she put the small boy in the compartment marked "Gentlemen," while she entered the "Ladies" room with her little daughter.

The boy left quickly, and one of the two priests went in, forgetting to lock the door. A few seconds later, the mother emerged from the ladies lavatory and opened the other door a mere slit, thinking her boy was still there.

"Don't forget to slide up your zipper," she whispered.

When the priest returned to his seat, he was full of praise for the airline.

"You have to hand it to these Jewish stewardesses," he said to his fellow priest. "They think of everything!"

* * *

Not all pioneers were fortunate enough to make the trek westward in the company of a covered wagon train. Here is another folk story of a peddler who worked his way toward the Pacific Coast; a story, incidentally, which has since been found in the folk humor of other peoples. The first person narrative has been excerpted from the memoirs of Gordon Blumberg, published in 1861.

"On the Staked Plains in western Texas, life was more or less primitive when I passed through that territory in '49. I was making my way to California, a lone peddler with my horse and wagon, through that especially remote area. After several days of lonely traveling without seeing a single human being, I approached a tiny adobe house squatting in the midst of an unbroken expanse of alkali and mesquite and bunch-grass. Just as I came abreast of this forlorn little homestead, a thin and undernourished-looking woman in a faded wrapper darted out of the door, sped across the road and hid herself in the chapparal before I could either hail her or inquire into the reason for her flight. As I checked my horse, puzzled to account for this curious behavior on the woman's part, a lubberly boy of perhaps fourteen years of age came running forth from behind the hut.

"'Mister,' he called out to me, 'did y'all see a woman runnin' away jes' now?'

"'I did,' said I. 'Who is she?'

"'That's my maw.'

"'Your mother?' I repeated, feeling a sense of shock, though I did not know why. 'And what was she running away from?'

"I reckon she's runnin' away from me—doggone it!"

"'Why, you infernal scoundrel!' I exclaimed. 'I've half a mind to get down off this wagon and give you a sound thrashing. What do you mean by chasing your poor mother about over the countryside like this? What has she done to you?'

"'Plenty,' replied the youth sullenly. 'Maw's fixin' to wean me.'"

* * *

Avrum, the elder, working in the hot sun of the Negev, straightened his back and sighed. "It's hard, very hard, but we're making the desert bloom," he said proudly to his son, Zvi. "It's a thousand per cent better than the persecution your mother and I suffereed in Russia. You're lucky to be born here in Israel."

"Lucky!" snorted Zvi, his eyes sweeping the arid terrain. "You call this lucky?"

"You ungrateful pup!" stormed Avrum. "Did it ever occur to you that Moses—his name should live forever—walked for 40 years just to get here? In case you've forgotten, this is the Promised Land!"

"Did it ever occur to *you*," snapped the young fellow, "that if Moses had walked just a few more days we'd now be living on the Riviera?"

31
Magen David over Follywood

INTRODUCTION

The movies—a medium of entertainment designed to hold an audience open-mouthed, especially when everybody is yawning—began as a peep show at the turn of the century. For the trifling sum of one cent, the patron of the arts was privileged to peer into a machine, turn a crank, and watch a rather corpulent female, several buds past the first bloom of youth, in the act of disrobing. Printed dialogue was added later to give the presentations a little class, although the *artiste* continued to divest herself of her pantaloons.

Picture it in your mind. The movie is a strip-comedy "burleycue" titled, *The Shenandoah Shlepper*, starring Harlowe Anderson, born Hymie Aarons. Co-starring is the Indian maiden, Evening Blackwing, a former bubble-dancer, named Eva Schwartzfliegel, whose career blew up in her face. Hymie tenderly murmurs, "Darling, your boyish bob makes you look like a new man." So Eva coyly replies (in those days the actresses were always coy, even *sans* bloomers), "I hope I don't lose my looks when I get old." And Hymie gives it to her good: "You should be so lucky!" Well, back in those days, producers wrote their own material.

Then came the founding fathers of the motion picture industry, looking for something to found. At that time, the hub of the film business was in New York where immigrants from Dnepropetrovsk used to laugh at the funny names of such American towns as Poughkeepsie and Hackensack. Among those first entrepreneurs was Jesse Lasky, who remembered that the sun shone 365 days a year in California, if not more. Sun was all-important to filming. A cloudy day meant a day wasted; a bright one was cause for rejoicing—and work! Upon Lasky's arrival in Hollywood, the mayor declared a holiday, and the key to the city was sent out to be cleaned and pressed. At the railroad station, all the studio employees were on hand to greet him. Someone, in hopes of getting special screen credit, hollered, "Speech!" Lasky cleared his throat, cast his eyes in the customary direction of heaven, and began: "In mine heart the sun is shining." He looked up again and yelled, "*Oy vay*, the sun *is* shining! Why the hell ain't you woiking?"

Next came Samuel Goldfish, who launched a film company with a producer named Selwyn. But the name Sel-Fish Productions sounded as though it belonged on Fulton Street. What to do? Sam kept the "Gold"—natch!—and gave the "fish" to charity. It is not generally known, but he kept Charity hidden in a Westwood apartment. Anyway, as Sam Goldwyn, he is best remembered for his defiant statement: "Don't give up the ship—sell it!"

Then there was Adolph Zukor, the smartest of all the movie pioneers. He was rumored to be secretly in love with actress Zasu Pitts, but she wouldn't marry him: "Who needs a name like Zasu Zukor?" The lady first caught Adolph's attention when she came to him with an idea for a new film in which she wanted to star. "Say," he enthused, "you got the mucus of a great story!"

Carl Laemmle, the ex-clothing salesman with the imported accent, decided to do things in a big way. This was the Era of the Bathroom. They were no longer Cans, they were *Objets d'Art*—palatial affairs wherein milady bathed in a marble pool that could double for the Red Sea —and did, in several pictures.

Laemmle may not have made films better, but he made them bigger. There was the time, for instance, when he was filming *The Last Supper:* He viewed the day's rushes and storm clouds gathered on his Noble Brow. He summoned the director. "What?" he thundered. "In a gigantic, super-special extravaganza like this you want I should make a supper scene with only twelve apostles? Get me fifty!"

Another of the early producers was Louis J. Selznick, who shared Laemmle's affection for big extravaganzas. There was the time he interviewed Cecil B. DeMille, when Mr. C was still plain Cecil the *shreiber*. "You got any original ideas for a comedy?" asked Louie.

"Sure," replied Cecil, "the funniest comedy routine I ever wrote goes like this: One day I shower her with apostrophes. The next day, night-blooming asterisks. The next I carpet her path with sweetscented parentheses, and then Gorgonzolas . . ."

Louie interrupted, his voice suspicious: "Gorgonzola! That's a cheese!" His tone brooked no argument. "Stick to the flowers!"

DeMille was undaunted—although he got plenty daunted later on. "Look, why don't we film a classic drama instead of a comedy?" he persisted. "How about *The Hunchback of Notre Dame* or *The Four Horsemen of the Apocalypse?*"

"My answer to that I'll give you in two words: Im-possible!" declared Louis, his voice grim. "There ain't a dime in those Notary Dame football stories; and, as for horsemen, the public is sick of westerns!"

There were other founding fathers, of course: Men like Marcus Loew, originally a ventriloquist who was so bad his lips moved even when he wasn't saying anything. And there was Darryl Zanuck, who once asked Selznick, "What do you think of my last picture?" Selznick moaned, "Please, not while I'm eating!" There is also the memory of Harry Cohn, the man who single-handedly brought Columbia Pictures to eminence. No one seems to have had a good word for the late lamented Harry, except his former secretary, Virginia Smith, but she forgot what it was.

Other areas of show business are also represented in American Jewish humor. Eddie Cantor, for example, made the big time with his song, "Anything is Finer than to See my Carolina in the Morning." And who can forget the night Belle Baker squelched a heckler with: "If you think my act is monotonous, you should see my home life!" Yes, and Ethel Merman, who not only had a beautiful voice but a gorgeous profile—all the way down. "If I were a girl and had a profile as lovely as Ethel's," said Cantor, "I'd always walk sideways."

"But not everyone makes it to Broadway," Pitzy Katz, the vaudeville comic of yesteryear, mourned. "How can I get famous or make any money with such a peculiar agency contract? The first clause forbids me to read any of the other clauses!"

H.D.S.

Part One

Films and TV

Simson Carlebach, film critic for *The Jerusalem Post*, tells the story about film-maker David Lean's *The Bridge on the River Kwai*. A *rebbetzyn* once told Carlebach that it was her husband's favorite picture. She then revealed that the ultra-orthodox rabbi had seen exactly two movies in his life: *The Bridge* and *Exodus*.

* * *

METRO-GOLDA-MEIR
Proudly Presents
Spartacush

Kirk Douglas . . . . Spartacush
Tony Curtis . . . . Demonstratov
Leo the Lion . . . . Himself

Scene One
Kirk Douglas, Tony Curtis, Leo the Lion
Scene Two
Tony Curtis and Leo the Lion
Scene Three
Leo the Lion

* * *

In his book, *Paul Muni: His Life and His Films*, Michael B. Druxman reminds us that Paul Muni believed that to be a good actor one had to prepare well, but the style and technique that each actor develops is the result of his own intuition and instinct. Muni was fond of comparing this approach, which he believed in strongly, to the method of making apple pie used by his wife's grandmother—an excellent baker.

When asked the secret of her delicious homemade pies she would reply:

"First I comb my hair. Then I wash my hands. Then I put on my apron. Then I make a pie."

* * *

It has been said of some of the early pioneers in the film business that, on the educational and cultural scale, the average motion picture executive ranked somewhere between Key West conch fishermen and members of the Jesse James fraternity. The story of the assistant manager of one of the big Hollywood studios of yesteryear is illustrative. On the Coast this gentleman was famous. He was regarded there as a self-made man who perhaps skimped in the making.

One day Ben Hecht came to the film executive's office seeking a position as a scenario writer.

"What salary you're expecting?" demanded the great man.

"Two hundred a week."

"Two hundred *what* a week?

"Dollars."

The magnate leaped off his chair. He was accustomed to paying beautiful ingenues and glorious-looking leading men hundreds of thousands a year but the thought that a mere literary guy should even think of such money appalled him.

"Look, mister," he barked, "you ain't no writer, you're a crook. Two hundred dollars a week, yet! For what?"

"Well," said Ben, "I spent several years at college getting an education, and I have a diploma to prove it. I earned a degree in English literature. That took work and study—and I've been studying ever since. I expect to be paid for it."

The magnificent mogul lit a panatella and leaned back in his chair, a crafty look glinting in his eyes. "You're good educated, hah?"

"You might say that."

"Then say for me a big word!"

* * *

A columnist on the staff of *Variety*, the show business trade journal, was bemoaning the lack of lively news.

"If only Tuesday Weld would marry Hal March and then have a daughter," he sighed. "What a line I could write! Just imagine it in your mind: 'Tuesday March the Second!'"

* * *

In the pre-television 1930s, Phil Baker conducted a show called *The $64 Question*. A person who was selected from the studio audience would start out with two dollars and if he or she answered the question correctly, another try was made for four dollars, then eight and so forth, until the $64 jackpot was reached.

One of the more popular figures who regularly attended these programs was Mary Malkin of the Bronx. Mary, a widow with little else to occupy her mind, spent much of her time going to quiz shows in the various studios of the networks. She was always welcome and was usually called upon to answer questions because her responses were often quite amusing, and sometimes exceedingly clever.

One evening, Baker, the host, asked her what was meant by Shakespeare's line: "Good night, good night! Parting is such sweet sorrow, That I shall say good night till it be morrow."

"Now, Mary," said Baker, "tell me exactly what Juliet meant when she uttered that line to Romeo."

"Hmm, that's a hard one," replied Mary, furrowing her brow in deep thought. "Maybe you better say it again."

He repeated it. "Now, for the $64 question, what was she saying to Romeo?"

"G'night," said Mary with a certitude that brooked no denial, "seeyuh t'marruh!"

* * *

William Friedkind is known in cinema circles as a martinet who always demands the very best from his actors. Once, while directing the film, *The Exorcist*, he called out to the cast:

"Perfect, ladies and gentlemen! That scene was absolutely perfect! Now let's do it one more time—only better!"

* * *

The crew and cast of a film company specializing in TV commercials were warned by the director, a strict disciplinarian named von Eichmann, to be on location on time. They were to assemble that evening on Columbus Circle at precisely five o'clock. Von Eichmann made it clear to all concerned that he did not mean one minute before five or one minute after five; when he said five he meant *five*!

Came the appointed hour and everybody was on hand—everybody, that is, but Dave Tolar, the star. As the minutes flew by, the director was tearing his hair out in bunches, and as the clock neared six and it grew too dark for the cameras to get the required shots, von Eichmann was frothing at the mouth.

Suddenly there was a commotion at the fringe of the group of actors and technicians, and Dave burst into view. His hair was disheveled, his clothes torn and his face battered and bloody.

"Where the hell have you been?" screamed the director.

"Sorry," said Dave, out of breath, "but I started out early enough. I thought I'd take a shortcut through Central Park and on the way I got mugged."

"That's no excuse!" roared von Eichmann. "It takes a whole hour to get mugged?"

* * *

"I'm going back to Broadway," said the disgruntled actor. "Hollywood never contributed anything to either the arts or to history."

"Don't sell Hollywood short," cautioned another actor who happened to be working. "Remember, the Red Sea has only been parted three times in all history—twice by Cecil B. DeMille."

* * *

"The only way to fight type-casting," averred a Hollywood thespian, "is to sport a French haircut, London suits, Italian shoes, a Mexican divorce and a Jewish name."

* * *

The Hollywood actor, Yancey Summers, known informally to his parents as Yaacov Zimmer, was standing in line for his unemployment check. Another actor in front of him was bemoaning the Watergate scandals. Yancey nodded in agreement.

"It really scares me," he affirmed. "Just think, this administration with all its irresponsibilities and dirty tricks is my sole means of support!"

* * *

Among the founding fathers of the motion picture industry were the fun-loving Lewis J. Selznick and the irascible but brilliant Adolph Zukor.

Zukor was not only a dynamic theatrical producer but also a unique character. His own generation knew him as a shrewd and canny individual who was always ready to take a chance—and his business gambles usually paid off handsomely. He was self-educated, but in some respects, according to Selznick, his knowledge was woefully lacking.

Their continuing feud was notorious. Zukor, always the more powerful and practical, froze Selznick out of lucrative business deals whenever possible. Selznick, on the other hand, seized every opportunity to relate stories about his arch-nemesis—stories that were carefully designed to present his rival in something short of a flattering light. The following yarn about Mr. Zukor was told with great glee by the irrepressible Mr. Selznick—and you needn't believe the tale to enjoy it.

One day, at his New York office, Zukor was visited by an aspiring playwright who brought along the script of a melodrama he had written. The young man may have been gifted in other regards but, so far as his speech was concerned, he suffered a severe handicap—he stammered terribly. Being sensitive, he rarely mentioned his affliction. Indeed, he had no need to do so—as soon as he opened his mouth it advertised itself.

He came now by appointment to see the great producer. As he entered the room where Zukor sat at his desk, he was greeted with a blast from the Great One:

"Okay, skip the introductions—you know who I am and I know who you are. You say you have a play? All right, I'm a busy man. Sit right down there and open it up and read it to me."

The young dramatist shakily obeyed. He made heavy going of it but eventually he finished.

"I'll take your play and film it," said Zukor. He pressed a button and his assistant entered.

"Fix up a contract for this young man," commanded the chief. "I'm going to take his story. It's not much of a play—in fact, I think it stinks—but it's got one terrific novelty in it that ought to make an audience laugh their heads off:

"All the characters stutter!"

* * *

The late Edward G. Robinson once remarked:

"I've been in the film business so long, I can remember when actresses would bare only their souls!"

* * *

Department of Mixed Menaphores:
Fan magazine columnist Minnie Marx recently reported that actress Lauren Bacall was once married to movie tough guy Hubert Humphrey.

* * *

A tough film producer, widely known for his vulgarity, quick temper and unalloyed arrogance, finally wore himself down to a state of near exhaustion. He was an emotional and physical wreck—which, all things considered, may have been an improvement on his normal condition. At his wife's insistence, he consulted a doctor.

"Tell me," said the physician, "have you ever had an ulcer?"

"Doctor, it's pretty clear you don't know me," the old sourpuss barked. "I don't get ulcers: I *give* them!"

* * *

If you are under thirty, ask your parents—or better yet, your grandparents—for a little help on this one.

Greta Garbo went to extreme lengths to preserve her isolation from the public's prying eye. She would do anything to protect her privacy. So the storekeeper was rather surprised when she came in personally and ordered a pound of grass seed.

"Miss Garbo, pardon my curiosity," he said, "but you don't even have a garden. What are you going to do with all this seed?"

"I vill sprinkle it on my hair," she told him.

"But why?"

"Because," she answered, "I vant to be a lawn!"

* * *

Barney Glazer in *Variety:*
"Remember when a studio head used to make up his own mind instead of calling a conference? If Moses had been a committee, the Israelites would still be in Egypt."

* * *

It could only happen in Hollywood. The television star's little boy came home from school in a jubilant mood.

"Aha!" exclaimed the kid's father. "You've been promoted after all!"

"Better'n that, pop," exulted the boy. "I been held over fer another twenny-six weeks!"

* * *

Acadamy Awards Presentations, 1974:
"Will you hand me the envelope, please?"
"Thank you."
"For best editing of a tape not specifically intended for theatrical distribution, the Oscar winner is . . .
"Richard M. Nixon!"

* * *

Several years ago, when Dorothy H. Rochmis was drama editor for the *California Jewish Voice*, she wrote a well-researched column which clearly indicated much burning of the midnight schmaltz. It's a game the talented lady still enjoys playing: a sort of Revelations you won't find in the New Testament, in which she offers some unfamiliar names and then reveals their true identities.* See if you can beat her to the punch.

> Suppose I were writing my usual bits of news about the big and little stars in our town and I told you that while I lunched at the Brown Derby (does anyone who is anyone eat lunch any place else?), I saw *Benjamin Kubelsky* kibitzing with *Nathan Birnbaum, Emanuel Goldenberg* and *Melvin Allen Israel.* The talk was about *David Green*, with a little bit of *Mavis Fluck* thrown in, because, after all, the big stars aren't going to spend their lunchtime talking only politics. Actually, what they were doing was comparing *Mavis* with *Helen Gould Beck* (about whom everyone insists there is not and never was anything but friendship for *Arthur Teichman).*
> "It was a friendly, quiet lunch when suddenly the three noticed a flock of autograph hounds around *Isaiah Edwin Leopold.*
> "Well," scoffed *Kubelsky*, "just look at that old codger. You sure have to give him credit, not only for longevity and versatility, but for being one of the busiest stars in Hollywood. Not only that, but his son is busy—and now his grandson is a comer."
> "Not that I want to change the subject," grumbled *Birnbaum*, "but you remember when Mrs. Poetry-Reciter who claims she's Shakespeare's third cousin eleven times removed, used to be just plain *Mrs. Aaron Goldbogen*, may he rest in peace?"
> Just at that moment who should walk in but *David Kominski* with *Issur Danielovitch, Julius Mark*, and *Aaron Chwatt:* And right behind them, none other than *Simone Kaminker*—unescorted.
> They all called out to each other and for a while the Brown Derby was buzzing with hellos and darlings and kissing and hugging.

*From "Film Folk & Fare," by Dorothy H. Rochmis published in *The California Jewish Voice*, September 1970. (Ms. Rochmis is now editor of *Israel Today*, in Los Angeles).

But when they resumed talking, the conversation was not unified.

One group talked about that "golden boy" *Julius Garfinkle.* Another talked about their friend *Jacob Pinkus Perelmuth's* son who had just produced his first film about one potato, two potatoes; maybe he'd make a bushelful. Another group talked about that movie, *To Russia, With Love,* and the part that *Karoline Blamauer* had in it. And what is a luncheon without talk about *Frances Gumm?*

Now, how many luminaries in my little game have you been able to identify?

Kubelsky, Birnbaum, Goldenberg and *Israel* are Jack Benny, George Burns, Edward G. Robinson and Mel Allen. *David Green* is, of course, the late David Ben Gurion. *Mavis Fluck* is Diana Dors. *Helen Gould Beck,* none other than Sally Rand. And *Arthur Teichman* is that master-teacher of the dance, Arthur Murray.

Isaiah Edwin Leopold is the late Ed Wynn. *Aaron Goldbogen,* the late Michael Todd (so of course, the wife they referred to as "Mrs. Poetry-Reciter" is Elizabeth Taylor). *David Kominsky* and *Issur Danielovitch* are, as you probably know, Danny Kaye and Kirk Douglas. *Julius Mark* and *Aaron Chwatt* are Groucho Marx and Red Buttons. The lady behind them, *Miss Kaminker,* Simone Signoret.

Julius Garfinkle is the late John Garfield, and *Jacob Pinkus Perelmuth* is Jan Peerce, whose son made the movie, "One Potato, Two Potato." *Karoline Blamauer* is Lotte Lenya; and *Frances Gumm?*—surely you know she's Judy Garland.

The Brown Derby hasn't changed its spots and it's fun playing this game. Just remember, it was Mr. Berman who, when he finally agreed to let his son go into show business, admonished him not to change his name. And *Sheldon Berman* didn't, though he's known professionally as Shelley Berman.

* * *

A note from the author:

The trouble with the history books is that they never mention the role played by Jewish pioneers in the taming of the West. Either they tell about the Spanish priests who explored the Pacific Coast and set up missions, or how the Protestant adventurers crossed the Great Plains in their covered wagons, met the Indians, and squealed on the Catholics.

But Jews, too, figured largely in the settling of the land west of the Pecos.

It went something like this:

First came the orthodox in their Kohneshtoyga wagons.

Then came the conservative, in Pullmans.

Finally came the reform, in airplanes.

And their names were Metro, Goldwyn and Mayer, and together, in the neighborhood of Hollywood and Vine, they established the high-class culture of the West.

Part Two

Music and Musickers

For this offering, we journey back in time to the days when both Ziegfeld and the New York Metropolitan Opera Company were doing a big business . . . separately, to be sure.

The American Jewish Committee was holding the biggest benefit in its history. Among the top stars of the entertainment world who were scheduled to perform were Fannie Brice, of beloved memory, and Madame Ernestine Schumann-Heink, greatest contralto of her time.

As the opera star was waiting in the wings, preparing to enter onstage, Fannie tapped her on the shoulder.

"Listen, Stena," she murmured, "do me a favor, will ya? Don't sing *My Heart Belongs to Daddy*—I use it for my finale!"

* * *

Whenever and wherever Henry Silberstein is mentioned, be it in the concert halls of New York, Vienna, Paris or Tel Aviv, or in the distinguished halls of the White House, the Court of St. James or the People's Palace in Peking, the name is spoken with awe and reverence. For it was this selfsame Silberstein—this obscure little tailor—who brought peace to a war-torn world with his extraordinary musical gifts.

It all began on a cold, dreary day in February. In his dingy tailor shop, Silberstein was bent over his pressing iron and enjoying his usual daydream in which he was a great violinist. In his mind's eye he saw himself on the concert stage, bowing gracefully and with reserved dignity in response to the enthusiastic applause of a glittering audience. It was always the same fantasy, ever since he had been a boy in Russia. The little tailor sighed. What use to have such childish thoughts? He could not read a note of music and had never so much as touched a violin in his life.

All at once a Voice spoke—a mystic voice from somewhere deep within the recesses of his innermost being. And the Voice said:

"Henry Silberstein, what for art thou sitting here pressing pants for a dollar-twenty cents when thou shouldst be fiddling a fiddle on the stage? Play, Henry, play! Go forth and be a *mentsch!*"

There was no denying that imperious command. He hurriedly closed his Cherry Street shop and, as though guided by a destiny of which he knew not, took the uptown subway to 72nd Street. And, though he had never been in that neighborhood before, his feet were led unerringly to Kornblau's, violin makers for the world's most famous artists. He entered the exclusive establishment.

"Excuse me, mister," he said to the obsequious clerk, "could I see please a fiddle?"

"Would you be interested in a Stradivarius?" asked the clerk.

"A fiddle's a fiddle," observed Silberstein, nodding. "Also, I'd like to look at the stick you scrape with."

He was handed the rare violin and bow. Silberstein drew the bow across the strings and, incredibly, he began to play the Joachim cadenza of the Beethoven concerto.

The clerk listened with open-mouthed admiration. "Sir, are you a concert artist?" he asked.

"Who, me?" replied the surprised tailor. "Of course not. In my whole life I never played a single note."

"Sir, please wait right here while I make a call," pleaded the clerk. "I'll be right back."

In the rear office, the clerk telephoned the Harold Holt Concert Bureau and asked for Ian Hunter, the director. A few words of explanation and Hunter raced to the store and listened to the stranger's exquisite violin music.

"Mr. Silberstein, I don't know anything about you," the agent began, "but with artistry such as yours I don't have to. Frankly, I'm in something of a jam. Heifetz has just cancelled for this Saturday at Carnegie Hall. He was to play the Beethoven but he's got a bursitis. Could you possibly take his place?"

Silberstein shrugged. "Why not?"

The concert proved to be a sensation. The music critic for the *New York Times* called it the finest surprise since the young Menuhin. Ian Hunter booked a whole European tour for his new discovery. Again, throughout the Continent, he was wildly cheered.

Next he flew to China, just as Leonid Brezhnev was attempting to settle the main differences between that country and the Soviet Union.

"How can we disagree on anything after listening to such gorgeous music?" stated the Russian. Mao tse Tung and Chou en Lai smilingly agreed and they shook hands all around. All three leaders gave Silberstein due and public credit for their new spirit of cooperation.

In London and again in Dublin, Silberstein gave his breathtakingly beautiful music and once again it produced its magical effect of peace and brotherhood. The English and the Irish decided to abandon violence in the interests of humanity.

Now the United Nations sponsored a tour on behalf of world peace. And wherever Silberstein played his violin, war ended and nations embarked on a course of friendly cooperation where they never had before.

In Cairo, Silberstein played a concert and immediately a permanent cease-fire agreement was signed between Egypt and Israel. A few days later, he gave another of his superlative concerts in Jerusalem, and King Hussein and Golda Meir went dancing.

Then tragedy struck—that unaccountable agony that has marred or destroyed the careers of so many great men and women. The world renowned violinist had been booked into the Uganda Palace of Culture at the urgent request of the President of that country. It seems that a powerful tribal chief whose village was deep in the interior jungles, had a reprehensible habit of raiding the neighboring tribes and serving up the captives with mashed potatoes and peas. Henry Silberstein's music, the President was confident, would have a lulling effect on the cannibal chief and curb his nefarious appetite.

"Will you come with me?" urged the President, after explaining the situation in Silberstein's hotel room.

"What can it hurt?" agreed the great violinist. "Wait, I'll get my fiddle."

Using flashlights, for it was now dark, they penetrated the forbidding jungle until they came to a clearing. There, in the eerie glow of a campfire, almost surrounded by a semicircle of lions, tigers and other wild denizens of the forest, sat Bopkes, the tribal chief.

Silberstein tucked the violin under his chin and began a concerto, playing more beautifully than he had ever played before. Among the animals, the lion rubbed noses with a fawn; a cobra and a mongoose snuggled close together; a tiger tenderly nuzzled a gazelle.

Suddenly—oh horror of horrors!—Bopkes, the tribal chief, jumped up and, with a club, he gave Henry Silberstein such a hit in the head it could be heard in Nassau County. Thus, the great violinist expired in the middle of transposing *A* to *F*-sharp minor.

The President, completely taken by surprise, could only stare aghast at the lately fallen Mr. Silberstein. When he could finally speak, his voice was filled with anguish.

"Now why did you have to go and *do* that for?" he wailed. "This dear, lovely man was just giving us a concert in the interests of peace—and for *free*, too! You ought to be *ashamed* of yourself—you horrid thing! That beautiful *music*, and you had to just *ruin* everything! *Why?*"

Bopkes the tribal chief bent forward, cupped a hand to his ear, and said—

"Eh?"

* * *

Mrs. Altman persuaded Yehudi Menuhin to listen to her ten-year-old Izzy play the violin. Trapped, the illustrious artist had no alternative but to agree.

Little Izzy sawed his way through the first movement of the Mendelssohn concerto. When he was *Gott sie dank* through, Mama Altman turned questioningly to Menuhin.

"*Nu?*"

"Well-l-l," he ventured, "your son has a rather *small* tone—but *very* disagreeable!"

* * *

Jascha Heifetz, the distinguished violinist, was in London where he was scheduled to give a concert. A few hours before curtain time, he noticed that a violin string had broken, so he hurried to a music supply shop for a replacement. He was waited on by a girl who was new to the business.

"I'd like to have an *E* string for my violin," said Heifetz.

"A *what*?" asked the uncomprehending girl.

"An *E* string."

"Sorry, luv," she replied apologetically, "but ye'll 'ave ter pick it out yerself. I can't tell the 'e's from the she's!"

* * *

Fractured Follies from the Flaming Forties:

Sam and Bella, by way of celebrating their 20th wedding anniversary, were taking in a movie. Bella's eyes brimmed with romantic tears as Nelson Eddy sang the beautiful "Indian Love Call" to Jeannette MacDonald:

"When I'm calling you-hoo-hoo-hoo, ha-ha-hoo . . ."

Bella squeezed her husband's hand with a tender feeling of affection. "Oh, Sam darling, that's what happens when a man really has love in his heart," she crooned.

"No it ain't," snorted unromantic Sam. "That's what happens when a man runs out of words before he runs out of music!"

* * *

Albert Spalding, the famous violinist and an uncle five or six times removed from the present author, passed this one along for posterity.

He was doing a recital in the hinterlands of the Bronx and had in his program the Bach *Chaconne*. Standing in the wings, Spalding peeked through the curtain and gave the audience a quick appraisal. They were mostly housewives and workingmen—ordinary folks one might expect to find strolling along Intervale Avenue. So he decided that the *Chaconne* would be wasted on them and that he would be better received if he played something lighter.

When the concert was over, a native of the region came to his dressing room with a complaint.

"Mr. Spalding," he said, "I work hard for a living, and when I'm spending my few pennies I like to get my money's worth."

"Didn't you?" asked the violinist, surprised.

"No. It says on the program in black and white that you were going to fiddle the *Chaconne*."

Mr. Spalding was overcome.

"My dear man," he replied effusively, "I had no idea that anyone here would know or even care whether I played the *Chaconne* or *Yussel the Muscle*. You are a gem among stones. Please honor me by accompanying me to my hotel. You will be my guest for dinner and afterward I will give you a private concert."

The Bronxite quickly accepted the generous offer and went to the hotel with his new-found friend. After a sumptuous dinner, a liqueur and a good cigar, Spalding picked up his Stradivarius and played the *Chaconne* as he had never before played it in his life.

"Well, well, well," said the honored guest, "so that's the *Chaconne*. Would you believe, Mr. Spalding, that's the first time I ever heard it? I don't like it!"

*   *   *

It was his wife's birthday, so the man went into a pet shop to buy her a canary.

"I'll take that one," he said, pointing to one of the cages where a bird was singing beautifully. "But that sparrow, you'll have to take him out of the cage. Who needs a sparrow?"

"Sorry," said the proprietor, "but the sparrow stays with the canary."

"What for?" demanded the man. "I just want the canary."

"Look, mister, am I charging you for the sparrow? I told you he goes with the canary—free! In fact, if you don't want the sparrow you don't get the canary, and that's final!"

"But this is ridiculous! The canary sings great and I'm willing to buy it. So why do I *have* to take that scrawny little sparrow?"

"Because," explained the proprietor, "the sparrow's his arranger!"

*   *   *

Among those in the motion picture industry who are truly talented—and they are legion, whatever else you may have heard—David Raskin is among the most gifted. He is best known, perhaps, for his collaboration with Johnny Mercer on the lovely song, "Laura," but he has also written musical scores for dozens of fine films.

Out in Hollywood a few years ago, he was in the 20th Century-Fox commissary having lunch with a group of fellow writers and composers. Raskin happened to mention that his next musical assignment would probably be the scoring of Alfred Hitchcock's latest picture, *Lifeboat*.

"You're not going to get that assignment, Dave," said one of the writers. "Hitchcock is going to release the picture without any music at all."

"That's ridiculous," retorted Raskin.

"Not the way Hitchcock sees it," explained the other. "Just think about it for a minute. All the action takes place in a lifeboat, way out in the middle of the ocean. There really wouldn't *be* any musicians within a thousand miles of the boat. So where would the music come from?"

"Well, if it's a question of logic, let's follow it through to its logical end," suggested Raskin. "You go back to Hitchcock and ask him where his *cameras* come from in the middle of the ocean and I'll tell him where my music comes from!"

*   *   *

Flo, a student of classical music, and Joe, whose taste had never progressed beyond "The Celery Stalks at Midnight," were immersed in a discussion. Somehow the conversation got around to the illustriou

Norwegian composer, Grieg.

"Oh, he's my favorite!" cried Flo ecstatically. Edvard Grieg wrote such divine music!"

"Maybe," said Joe, shrugging—"for a guy who couldn't even spell his first name."

* * *

British rock 'n roll entertainer Zelig Zeligman, leader of the singing group known as "The London Derriere," arrived in America where he was booked for a huge outdoor concert on the fringes of a small town in upstate New York.

In his hotel room on that first night, he was almost asleep when an eerie hoot sounded just outside his window.

"Don't let that disturb you," said his American manager soothingly. "It's an owl."

"I know," replied Zelig in an uneasy voice, "but 'oo's 'owling?"

* * *

Shlomo Baum, the orchestra leader who attained success in Israel with his American-style music, decided to try his luck in the United States. Some members of his band were unwilling to leave Israel, however, so when Shlomo arrived in New York he found it necessary to interview American musicians to fill the vacancies.

The first man he talked with was a rather wild-eyed, slovenly-dressed saxophonist. Shlomo was not impressed with him until he played a few bars of music. The man's talent was truly remarkable. Never had he heard such gloriously beautiful notes.

"You're hired," he said enthusiastically.

"Well, man, I got a confession to make," said the saxophone player. "I got a monkey on my back."

"Dot's all right," said Shlomo, clapping the musician on the back. "In dis bend ve luff enimals!"

* * *

Part Three

The Stage-Legit and Ill-Legit

The stage is bad, so rabbis say,
And naught but evil from it springs;
But still it has what angels do
(And rabbis don't) have;
Namely, wings.

* * *

Around the turn of the century, the Yiddish Theatre was the main source of entertainment for countless thousands of immigrants. Many of these new arrivals came from obscure *shtetls* in the Pale of Settlement and, as a consequence, knew little or nothing of "quality" stage productions, including those performed in Yiddish. They were, therefore, not always appreciative of the better theatrical fare offered them—at least not in the beginning. As their familiarity with good writing and acting grew, so too, of course, did their critical reactions.

Boris Thomashevsky, actor, playwright and one of the founders of the Yiddish theatre in America won great respect among the Jewish masses after he arrived in the United States in 1881. But he, like many others of that early day, sometimes experienced the hoots and derisive howls of his untutored audiences.

But Thomashevsky, always his own man, not only expected the very best from his actors, he demanded proper respect from his audiences as well. One incident that occurred shortly after he had organized the first Yiddish theatre in New York City, illustrates his individualism.

He was appearing in a play which he himself had written, produced and directed. Months of hard work had gone into the production. But apparently it was somewhat over the heads of the very people he was trying to reach. Only eleven paying customers showed up for the first night's performance. As Thomashevsky's beautiful lines were being delivered, the puzzled spectators at first grew restless, and then came the inevitable hissing.

Thomashevsky's face turned red, but with grim resolution he kept on. The hissing grew louder. He stopped for a moment and the hissing ceased. When he started again, the audience of eleven resumed the hissing, enjoying themselves immensely.

Thomashevsky stopped once more, gathered all the members of his company onstage and, together, they out-hissed the tiny audience.

* * *

Maurice Schwartz, the legendary actor, director and producer, laid the foundation for his future fame when, in 1918, he organized his own dramatic company which became known as the Yiddish Art Theatre. He was also well known for his wit—at repartee he had no superiors and very few equals, in or out of the profession. In the autumn of 1921 he scored on another well-known actor without speaking a word. Yet, Jewish theatrical circles rocked with laughter for many months afterward.

Artistically speaking, this actor was not highly regarded by Maurice Schwartz. He belonged to the old school of ranting scene-eaters for whom Schwartz had a profound contempt. Nevertheless, his merits were valued by at least one individual—his manager, who was also a producer.

The latter was presenting *The God of Vengeance*, by Sholem Asch, with a really distinguished supporting company, featuring Schwartz's pet aversion, Ossip Leibnitz, his name before he Americanized it when he gravitated to Broadway and then to Hollywood.

On the day when the bills went up for the forthcoming production, Schwartz chanced to pass the Second Avenue theatre where the play was to be presented. In the lobby of the theatre was a large poster which, according to the usual form, read as follows:

MR. ARTHUR JACOBS

presents

The God of Vengeance

by

the brilliant playwright

SHOLEM ASCH

With the Following Notable Cast:

Yussel Nieberg....................................Mr. Carl Dymov
Nudnik..Mr. Richard Rosen
Stella Hahn..................................Mrs. Lillian Dienstock
Isaac Himmelfarb...........................Mr. Solomon Kauffman
Mrs. Vogel.......................................Miss Anna Robins

—AND—

MR. OSSIP LEIBNITZ

Schwartz read the announcement through. Then he walked to the corner, entered a hardware store, purchased an extra large carpenter's pencil and, returning to the theatre, he made one single change in the wording:

He crossed out the "AND" and for it he substituted "BUT."

* * *

Small-timers in vaudeville, even at the height of its popularity in the 1920s and early thirties, expected a certain amount of hard luck. Until they succeeded in making the grade on the main circuits with extended bookings, they counted on sporadic engagements in the four-a-day houses as their portion in life. Yet they were an optimistic lot. Only rarely did a performer or a team of performers give up the gallant struggle for "the big break" that would catapult them to main-eventers and eventual stardom.

Many years ago, about 1928 or thereabouts, a very distressing instance of hard luck and the demise of a vaudeville team occurred. A couple—George and Wilma Davidson—had a "dumb" act, as it was called in the vernacular of the profession. They owned a flock of educated ducks that did all sorts of cute tricks. "Davidson's Diabolical Ducks" was a good act, or so George and Wilma thought, but bookings were few and far. between. Finally there came a period of prolonged dullness when the two entertainers could secure no engagements whatsoever.

They were idle for almost two months, so they took refuge in a little house loaned to them by a sympathetic friend, and did their own housekeeping, such as it was. But when the fall season opened up, their New York agent sent them a wire:

GEORGE AND WILMA DAVIDSON
DAVIDSON'S DIABOLICAL DUCK ACT
SUMMIT, NEW JERSEY

HAVE BOOKED YOU FOR FULL WEEK AT FAR ROCKA-
WAY,
OPENING NEXT MONDAY
ABE SCHECHTER
SUPREME AGENCY

But this was the melancholy answer which came back:
IMPOSSIBLE TO ACCEPT. WE ATE THE ACT.

* * *

Old-timers will recall the impressario, Sid Hirschman, whose publicity stunts often stood New York's theatre-going public on its collective
ear. But there was one time when even he was unable to cope with what
he described as "an act of Divine intervention."
Sid was producing *World Without Women*, when he was forced to
cancel the play right at dress rehearsal time.
All seven women in the cast, as well as the cat, were pregnant!

* * *

For as long as he could remember, young Rueben Schiff had nur-
tured a great love for the theatre. His all-consuming ambition was to
become an actor, but his parents, extremely wealthy and acutely aware
of their position in the rarefied reaches of upper-class society, would not
hear of it. One day, shortly after his 23rd birthday, his parents were
killed in a plane crash and, as the only child, he received their legacy of
eight million dollars—give or take a few hundred thousand.
Changing his name from Rueben Schiff to Rutherford Shipstead, he
organized his own repertory company, hired actors and technicians, and
produced his own *Hamlet* with himself, of course, in the starring role.
The show was mounted with style and no expense was spared. Never was
Shakespeare's play given such an opulent first night. Rueben, or rather
Rutherford as we shall henceforth call him, even persuaded some well-
known critics to attend the first performance.
But five minutes after the curtain was raised, it became painfully
clear that this was to be a theatrical catastrophe—a caricature of Shakespeare's monumental work. Rutherford Shipstead had been unable to
engage any actors of repute, and those whom he had hired were as
hammy as he. In all the history of the theatre, never had the bard of
Stratford-on-Avon been subjected to the hamming now being given to his
Hamlet. Rutherford wasn't merely bad, he was ludicrous.
The audience not only took the farcical performance with rare good
nature, they began to get their money's worth by entering into the spirit
of the evening. Catcalls and sundry comments, none of them favorable,
reached the ears of the tyros onstage. Jeers, laughter and hissing filled
the place. Then a man's shoe was thrown from the audience. A lady's shoe
quickly followed, almost hitting Rutherford, who was hamming it up in
the leading role. Other articles of clothing, and then pennies flew through
the air in a shower around the actors. But, undaunted, they moved
relentlessly forward with their play.

Rutherford Shipstead was just getting into the soliloquy, ignoring the rain of missiles from across the footlights, when suddenly a woman's handbag, thrown from the first or second row, struck him full in the face and sent him reeling backwards.

Hamlet regained his balance and ran his hand across his face to see if any blood had been drawn. Then, his anger bubbling to the surface, he looked out into the audience and yelled at the sea of upturned faces before him:

"Are you people crazy or something? What the hell's the matter with you? You oughtta know I didn't *write* this crap!"

* * *

From the play, *Lottie Loved Latkehs*, by Milton Karp, 1932:
Cab Driver: Okay, lady, where to?
Passenger: Beth Sholom Maternity Hospital. And, please, to drive like crazy nobody needs. I work there!

* * *

Here is another of those delightful anecdotes about Harry Houdini, the ex-Hebrew teacher and son of a rabbi, whose early years as a professional magician were anything but bountiful.

One summer in 1918 or 1919, Houdini was booked into Rose's Resort Inn, a new vacation spot near Lake Placid. Rose was the breath, light and sunshine of the place; her husband, Phil, its nemesis. Rose had the good sense to keep her argumentative, grouchy old man away from the vacationing patrons and the entertainers, so all went fairly well . . . that is, until Houdini appeared on stage. Phil, it seems, was not among Houdini's more ardent admirers.

Sitting in the audience during the magician's opening night performance, Phil glowered as Houdini offered his magic feats. Houdini disentangled himself from a straight jacket within sixty seconds while handcuffed. Phil snorted, "Ridiculous!"

Annoyed, Houdini then had his hands and legs shackled. He was then locked inside a trunk and the trunk completely immersed in a glass tank of water. He would, he announced beforehand, escape from this confinement also within one minute. "That should put a stop to Phil's insulting comments," he told himself.

But when he emerged in the given time, all Phil could say was "Ridiculous!"

By this time, Harry was determined to impress the man. This time he would again be bound in handcuffs, chains and shackles, and then hanged by the neck with a rope. Once more, he told the audience, he would free himself within sixty seconds. But just as the assistants secured the knot at his neck and left him swinging in mid-air, an ear-splitting explosion sounded in the kitchen adjacent to the backstage. The stoves blew up, smoke filled the place and the panic-stricken audience raced for the exits.

Houdini found himself sprawled in the orchestra pit. Next to him was the irascible Phil, slowly rising to his knees, his face bruised. The man stared at Houdini for a long moment and then rasped:

"Whatsa matter with you? You some kinda *nut?*"

* * *

"There's one nice thing about being an actor," observed movie scripter Ralph Goodman—"he doesn't go around talking about other people!"

* * *

We have little doubt that this story was first told in ancient Phoenicia, but here is the American version, circa 1913 A.D.—After Dinner. As far as can be determined, it was related at a party by Ed Leopold, later to become nationally known as Ed Wynn.

A traveling repertory company had reached the limit of its endurance. One bad engagement had followed another. The manager was down to his last five dollars. The troupe, practically stranded in a remote corner of Arkansas, was about to disband when a ray of hope shot through the clouds of despair. Word arrived that a theatre had just been completed in an adjoining town. There had been an advance sale up to capacity for the opening night. But at the last minute the attraction booked for the gala occasion had failed to appear, and now the welcome news from the local manager was that if the embarrassed outfit could get there in time, it might give the performance and share in the guaranteed profits.

By superhuman effort, which included the hocking of his watch and fur-trimmed overcoat, the manager raised funds to provide railroad fares for his aggregation to reach the other town. Disembarking from the train, the jubilant thespians climbed into a waiting bus and started along the winding dirt road. In the front seat, alongside the driver, rode the manager.

"Beautiful country you have here," he said. "All nature seems glad. Just look yonder, ahead of us, at that glorious red sunset. I don't think I have ever seen a more magnificent spectacle."

"That ain't no sunset, mister," stated the driver. "That's our new opry house burnin' down!"

* * *

Ben Bernie, the "ol' maestro" of fond recollection, used to tell this story on himself.

The Delancey Street Dramatic Guild, a group of local denizens with theatrical aspirations, was putting on a play, *The Nymph in the Lake*, by somebody or other, in Central Park. It might well have been called the Delancey Street Theatre in the Round in the Woods. The stage was a cleared spot at the edge of the woods between 65th and 67th Streets, with the spectators sitting on camp stools in the clearing around the "stage." In those days, the area was almost a forest.

In the audience was Ben Bernie and singer Gertrude Klein, his date for the evening. Young Bernie had been quaffing beer before the proceedings. As the first act was drawing to a close, the beer began to swish around in his inner plumbing, so Bernie politely excused himself, left Gertrude, sought out an usher and asked him the whereabouts of the men's room—or a reasonable facsimile thereof.

The usher gave him careful directions. Bernie was to walk 40 paces to the left until he came to a maple tree, then go right for 32 paces until he came to a triangle of bushes, then turn left again and walk 27 paces. He hurried off and, at length, having completed his mission, finally returned to his seat.

"Has the second act started yet?" he asked Gertrude.

"You ought to know," she hissed, "You were the star!"

* * *

A group of fellow comedians were ribbing Jack Benny who had recently passed his 80th birthday.

"I always thought Jack wore a toupee," remarked George Burns between puffs on his ever-present cigar. "Then I realized that he didn't wear a toupee at all. He just had cheap-looking hair!"

* * *

"I guess I'll never understand American audiences," complained George Burns. "I tell a joke about Sammy Davis being Jewish and the people become hysterical. Yet, I've been Jewish all my life and it never once got me a laugh."

* * *

A respectable number of actors and actresses who had their beginnings in the Yiddish theatre subsequently attained fame on the English-speaking stage. Among them were Paul Muni, Vera Gordon, Edward G. Robinson, Menasha Skulnick, Stella Adler, Luther Adler, Molly Picon, Joseph Schildkraut and many others.

Our subjects for this folksy tale out of the nostalgic early 1920s are Luther Adler and the immortal tenor, Enrico Caruso. Both happened to be in England at the time, and Caruso had just concluded an engagement at the Lyric Theatre in London. Following his final concert, the *signor* gave a farewell party to the friends he had made while in England. The affair began at the theatre and culminated at a fashionable café. Adler, who had become quite fond of the temperamental and sentimental Caruso, was among those present.

He tried to escape, though, when the host insisted on kissing everyone goodbye. But luck was against him. After the singer had thus saluted his manager, his accompanist, the members of his supporting company and everyone else in sight, he insisted that Adler should accompany him in a carriage to his hotel. The hour was now three in the morning and, as a result of the excitement, affection and wine, the Italian was in a highly exhilarated state. As he reached the sidewalk, he disentangled himself from Adler's supporting hand, threw both arms around Adler's neck and implanted a resounding buss on Adler's lips; then fell into a waiting taxi and bade the driver take him to the Garrick Theatre.

The perplexed cabbie turned to Adler.

"Wot's the blinkin' idea in tykin' this cove to the theatre at this time o' the mornin', guv'nor?" he asked.

"I'm not sure, but you better take him there anyway," said Adler. "I think he just remembered that he forgot to kiss the night watchman."

* * *

This little exchange of dialogue is worth its weight in gold—as an antique. But maybe your grandchildren haven't heard it.

Si Rubin, the Tin Pan Alley agent, was drowning his sorrows in an off-Broadway pub one evening when another agent, a friend of his, joined him at the bar.

"Boy, have I got *tsuris!*" moaned Rubin.

"You look like you lost your last client," sympathized the friend. "What's the matter?"

"It's that new entertainer I just signed," explained Rubin with a sob in his throat. "Now I'm stuck with a client who sings like Frank Sinatra, looks like Ronald Reagan, has a build like Kirk Douglas and fights like John Wayne."

"You're *stuck* with a client like that?" gasped the other agent. "You must be out of your mind!! You'll make a fortune with that guy."

"That's just the trouble," wept Rubin. "It ain't a guy—it's a girl named Penelope!"

* * *

The late film star, Edward G. Robinson, was a child when he arrived in this country from Rumania. And he was still a very young man when he was bitten by the stage bug. Indeed, his love for the "live" stage continued throughout his life, despite his success in motion pictures. As is the case with so many other actors, it wasn't easy at first. This anecdote concerns his early days, long before he was lured to Hollywood and stardom in the 1933 feature, *Little Caesar.*

Young Eddie had been seeking work for many a day, trying to keep up appearances with his one carefully pressed but well-worn suit, and subsisting on little more than bread and beans. When he was down to his last few coins, somebody told him of a vacancy in a small-town stock company thirty miles away, and he borrowed the money to pay his railroad fare thither.

The resident stage manager rubbed his hands gleefully at first sight of the applicant.

"By gosh, I'm glad you turned up," he said. "You're just the man and just the type. We're going into rehearsal today for next week's bill, which is where I'll be needing you."

"Modern play, I suppose?" inquired Robinson, thinking of his one suit and mindful, of course, of the then existing rule that stock actors must furnish their own costumes.

"Sure," said the manager. "A modern society drama."

"That's good," declared the youthful actor, much cheered. "I presume, then, that an ordinary suit of clothes such as I'm wearing will be satisfactory?"

"Hmm, let's see now, just what wardrobe you'll need," said his new boss. "In the first act you will require a suit of tweeds. You are a rich mine-owner. The English syndicate calls you to London and so, in the middle of the first act you have to make a change for a suit you would wear on a train. Also, as you have an ocean trip ahead of you, there must be something characteristic in the way of clothes that're suitable for a voyage—a long overcoat should help. You could wear it and carry a lighter coat on your arm.

"The second act finds you in the smoking room of Lord Basil Metabolism's mansion. You are telling His Lordship about the mine and, as the scene takes place in the evening, you will be in full dress, naturally.

"The third act shows you talking to the Englishman aboard his yacht anchored at Ostend, and here again your dress must be precise. I would suggest white flannel trousers, a blue jacket, white shoes and something classy in the way of a cap.

"Now we come to the fourth act. This time the scene is the breakfast room of a country house. It isn't necessary for me to tell you how to dress the part for this act. It is simply a matter of looking the part—rich miner and so forth—not letting any Englishman think he can dress better than you—an American."

"Say," demanded Robinson, "who the hell wrote this show—Hart, Schaffner and Marx?"

* * *

In June, 1974, George Burns gave a one-man show at the Shubert Theatre in Los Angeles that, in show business parlance, brought the house down. At the age of 78, he displayed all of the essentials required of a top-flight comic: good timing, a quick mind, and a style of delivery that was as mellow and slow-burning as his cigar.

"At my age," he told the glittering Shubert audience, "the only thing about me that still works is my right foot—the one I dance with."

George went on to tell about the time he filled in for Karl Betts in a trained seal act called *Captain Betts and Flipper:*

"I used to bribe that seal with a fish so that he'd do his stuff. For two weeks I carried around a dead fish in each pocket, and then I had a date with a girl named Trixie Hart. But those fish didn't bother her at all—even after two weeks. Trixie had just finished a tour with Fink's Mules, and she complimented me on my shaving lotion."

Puffing his cigar, George commented wryly:

"The only thing that gets me excited is if the soup is too hot."

At the start of the show, Jack Benny came onstage to introduce his old friend, and pouted: "Nobody came out first to introduce *me!*" Then George emerged to do his opening number and several old songs which he delivered with gravelly charm—and even managed to finish a few.

"Sometimes my opening song is so great," boasted George, "people think it's my finish. (Puff.) Sometimes it is!"

Through a cloud of cigar smoke, he concluded, "I'd just as soon you found me funny. But if you don't (puff) I wouldn't disagree with you."

"Seventy-eight or not, he is the most appealing comic in the business," said one critic known for his usually scathing reviews. "He seldom tells ethnic jokes, yet, somehow, one senses a deep-down folk pathos that touches the heart."

And that is what humor—Jewish or other—is all about.

32
Lox Populi

INTRODUCTION

We are born red and die bald: what use to holler so? *Lox Populi*—may I be forgiven for coining the expression!—is the humorous Voice of the Jewish People, taking heart in the knowledge that laughter is the solace of the sad, and that happiness is largely a matter of digestion. Jewish man-in-the-street humor, analyze it as you will, is concerned mainly with the important trivia of life. It has a simplistic wisdom of its own.

"Retire?" it asks. "What for? Noah was 600 years old before he built the ark."

It is epigrammatic: The man who says "Money isn't everything" is probably in arrears to his landlord.

It possesses warmth in its nonsense: Thelma is reluctant to marry Joe because she heard that marriage is a gamble—a lottery. And Joe retorts: "If that is so, why don't they arrest the rabbi?"

It does not pontificate: Marriage *a la mode* can become boring in time, but marriage *a la carte*—ach! Goldie baby, pass the noodle soup!

What is a Jew? As if the Jewish people didn't have enough to worry about, this controversial question has been raised with increasing frequency in the past few years, with the orthodox holding one view and the conservative and reform segments of Judaism holding another. Why this should concern an American who can trace his ancestry back to the patriarch, Abraham, is unclear, but a Jew has to be miserable about something or else he's miserable. Lox Populi offers a consensus, to wit:

A modern American Jew is one who smokes Turkish tobacco in his cigarettes, orders Cuban cigars from Canada, drinks Scotch whiskey, drives a German car to an Italian movie, returns to his Mediterranean styled home where he sips Brazilian coffee while enjoying French fries, Spanish olives, English muffins, Danish pastry and Dutch chocolate—and then writes to his congressman with a Japanese ballpoint pen, indignantly demanding that he do something about the government buying all that foreign oil from the Arabs.

The jokes passed along through Lox Populi often radiate a cheery hope for the future, as though optimism was a kind of heart stimulant for failure. And when you come right down to it, it is indeed hard to lose faith in humanity, considering the fact that more than 215 million people in the United States have never played you a dirty trick. Agreed, the jokes told by the man-in-the-street aren't profound. Profundities he leaves to the cultured ones. "What is culture," he will snort, "but a matter of buttoning and unbuttoning! . . . Opera, you say? I'd go to the opera, too, if it weren't for the singing!"

Trivia, perhaps, but at least Lox Populi has cast aside its Old World hair shirt. It has abandoned its self-denigration, its subservient whine. The American Jew has long known that it is useless to scratch the back of the professional porcupine in order to secure his good will. The jokes told by your neighbor or member of your family may be a clearer indication of deeper feelings than the intentionally barbed wit of the paid comedian—proof positive that the parrot may be a showy and talkative bird, but it takes the stork to deliver the goods. So it is that your father, watching a political candidate on television, can wryly observe: "That guy's head is getting so big he'll soon need his eyeglasses stretched." And grandpa will add solemnly: "Yeah, the cemeteries are full of people the world couldn't do without." The witticisms will not cause you to fall down laughing, but they do reflect the acerbic thrusts that have characterized Jewish humor down through the ageless centuries.

The field of education is one of the more popular targets of the Jewish American public—a very strange circumstance, considering that the academic world contains a high proportion of Jews and that the Jewish people are among the most highly educated in this country. As Lox Populi sees it, however, education is the art of memorizing things read in books, and things told by college professors who got their education by memorizing things read in books and things told by college professors.

Another area of concern touches on the financial problems associated with higher education. Here is a sample college correspondence course:

Dear Dad:
Thing$ are $well here at $chool, but they could be better. $ome thing$ are needed mo$t de$perately the$e day$. I'm $uppo$ing you under$tand what I mean and will $end $ome $oon.

> Your loving $on,
> $tanley

Dear Son:
NOthing is new here. I kNOw that you are doing better NOw than you have been. Write aNOther letter soon. I want to get this off in the NOon mail, so I'll sign off NOw.

> Love,
> Dad

The traveling salesman joke may be waning in popularity but its modern counterpart is more sophisticated. It relies for its humor on astuteness rather than an escapade with a farmer's daughter. A good illustration is the office joke about Xavier and Sammy, two New York shoe salesman who were sent to Equatorial Africa to open up new markets.

On the very first day of their arrival in Zululand, Xavier sent a cable to the home office: RETURNING ON NEXT PLANE. IMPOSSIBLE SELL SHOES HERE. EVERYBODY GOES BAREFOOT.

Not a word was heard from Sammy until two weeks later when the sales manager received another cable: PILING UP ORDERS BY THE BUSHEL. PROSPECTS UNLIMITED. NOBODY HERE HAS SHOES.

Commentaries on the times in which we live need not always be modern to be current. Many years ago, a rabbinical student approached Sarah Bernhardt after she had just danced *au naturel* on the stage.

"It seems to me that we Jewish people may be in need of an Eleventh Commandment," he admonished her gently.

"The hell you say," snorted the divine Sarah. "We have ten too many now!"

Straight out of Jewish folklore comes another *haimishe* joke which, for reasons unknown, has never attained wide circulation although it is, indeed funny. Back in the 1880s, when much of the United States was still rural, the teacher in a small Hebrew school near Albany, New York, was surprised to see only one child present. She was aghast when the little pupil told her that the others were throwing cats into the river.

A few minutes later, her alarm increased when another child wandered into class. "Why are you tardy?" she asked sternly.

"I was throwin' cats in the river," he muttered.

"That's terrible—perfectly horrible!" she gasped. "How could you do such a thing!"

One by one the other students wandered into class, all with the same excuse.

Finally, the smallest pupil of all arrived.

"Well, young man," the teacher demanded coldly, "what is *your* excuse for being so late? Were you throwing cats into the river, too?"

"No, how could I?" said the little boy, wet and sniffling—I'm Katz!"

. . .

In the spirit of detente and ecumenical brotherhood, it is only fair to give credit where credit is due—in this case to the Arabs. It is said that all jokes can be traced back to six originals which were first told in Egypt during the Sixth Dynasty. If this is really the case, it is the right and duty of every Jew to improve on any old joke he may find lying around loose.

Lox Populi—the people have spoken, and this commandment doth emerge: Do not take thyself too damn serious.

H.D.S.

This one was contributed by the members of the Landover Hills, Maryland, Jewish community—all both of them.

Mike Rosen was driving along Defense Highway toward Annapolis one rainy afternoon when his car skidded on the slick pavement and slammed into a tree.

An ambulance quickly reached the scene, and when the medics saw that Rosen's nose had been cut off in the accident, they rushed him to Prince George's General Hospital.

Unfortunately for Mike Rosen, however, the doctors restored his nose upside down, and ever since then he's smelled to high heaven.

* * *

The kind, dear old lady stopped to give a beggar a coin.

"Oh, my goodness!" she cried, noticing his infirmity for the first time. "You've lost a leg!"

The beggar looked down.

"Well, how about that?" he said coolly. "Damned if I didn't!"

* * *

Pat Gold (and never mind the *traife* first name) tells us he was born in a town that was so small everybody knew whose check was good and whose wife wasn't. "If you saw a girl with a man old enough to be her father," said Pat, "he was."

"That town was so small," he continued, "there was nothing doing every minute of the day. All you had to do was use your electric razor and the street lights dimmed. Believe me, the only place that was open all night was the mailbox.

"Can you imagine a town where they have only one traffic light and it changes color once a week? Take it from me, they ring in the New Year at 8:30 P.M. and the excitement is provided by watching an Alka-Seltzer fizz."

* * *

A registered member of New York's Liberal Party was discussing former President Richard Nixon, and apparently she was not one of his more enthusiastic followers.

"I don't need a reason," she snapped. "I just don't like him, and from all the things I've said about him, I never will!"

* * *

Anna: It's true what I hear about your husband cutting down on his smoking?

Hannah: Yes, now he's smoking only after meals—his meal, my meal, the children's meal, everybody's meal!

* * *

Then there's the dog-owner who crossed a basset with a beagle—and got a bagel!

Pretty Rachel Fisher, a model with a figure that called for the once-over twice, had recently moved into the apartment building. Watching her return home from work one evening were her new neighbors, Mrs. Berman and Mrs. Lerner.

"If there's one thing I hate, it's a gossip," commented Mrs. Berman, "but do you believe all those rumors about that Rachel Fisher person?"

"Oh, yes, I certainly do!" breathed Mrs. Lerner. "What are they?"

* * *

Back in the days of "twenty-three skidoo," Al Jolson was living at the Academy Hotel in New York. In the suite across the hall lived an amiable couple, and they all soon became friends.

One evening, Al accepted an invitation to have a drink at their place. He was sipping his highball when his eyes fell on a photograph, framed in silver and displayed upon the mantle, of an exceedingly handsome and well-built boy in his early teens.

"Whose picture is that?" he inquired.

"That's our son," explained the matronly woman.

"What's his name?"

"I'll spell it for you: A-e-r-n."

"Rather unusual," said Al. "How do you pronounce it?"

"That all depends," replied the lady. "You see, I happen to be Jewish. My parents were very orthodox. But my husband is of pure Irish descent. We're both proud of our heritage. So when our son was born we decided to give him a name that would be natural for his family and mine, and still sound familiar and affectionate. After a few conferences we reached a compromise:

"My husband calls him Erin and I call him Aaron."

* * *

The traffic cop at the corner held up his hand for the flow of cars to stop, but Miss Peltz, the old maid, sailed right through the intersection.

Enraged, the cop blew his whistle and she pulled over to the curb.

"What's the matter with you, lady?" he barked. "Don't you know what I mean when I hold up my hand?"

"I certainly do," sniffed Miss Peltz in a huff. "I've been teaching school for 30 years."

* * *

The Soviet Union's Communist Party Chief, Leonid Brezhnev, following his visit to Washington, D.C. in 1973, decided to spend a day in New York to see the sights of the city. But he lost all interest in the more popular attractions when he caught his first glimpse of Macy's and then Gimbel's.

"You mean to tell me that all the merchandise in those department stores is really available to the American masses?" he gasped incredulously.

"Available!" retorted his State Department guide. "Listen, Macy's and Gimbel's and every other big store in this country has to advertise in the papers and *beg* people to buy!"

* * *

"Have you met the new boy next door?" the mother asked her daughter.

"Yes, mom," replied the girl. "His name is Myron, he's 21, and he's one of those sweet, shy, lovable types. You know—a real phony!"

* * *

Tonversation heard on a twolley tar:

1st little boy: My daddy met a Jewish man yestiddy an' he said . . .

2nd little boy: Hey, you ain't s'pose ta mention nobody's 'ligion. It's auntie-smetical!

1st little boy: Okay. My daddy met a Chinee man yestiddy . . .

2nd little boy: Yeah, that's gooder.

1st little boy: . . . an' the Chinee man said, "Izzy, where you gonna go for *Pesach?*"

* * *

It was the biggest event of the year at Yeshiva University, and Rabbi Marcus Vogel was the principal speaker at the banquet. Suddenly the appalling fact confronted him that he had forgotten to insert his false teeth. He turned to the stranger sitting next to him and asked if he would substitute as his speaker while he rushed home for his dentures.

"No need to do that," said the other genially. He reached into his pocket and brought out a dental plate. "Here, try these," he suggested.

Rabbi Vogel popped them into his mouth. "No, these won't do," he said, "They're much too small."

"All right," said the man, withdrawing another set from his pocket, "try these."

"They're too large," said the rabbi, removing them from his mouth.

"Well, here's a pair that might fit."

"Aah, that's much better," said Rabbi Vogel. "Now I'll be able to eat and then deliver my speech."

After finishing the sumptuous repast, the good rabbi was now ready to deliver his prepared talk, but first he wanted to satisfy his curiosity. He leaned over and remarked:

"Those teeth fit perfectly. But how does it happen that you carry so many dental plates around with you? Are you a dentist?"

"Oh, no," replied the stranger. "I'm an undertaker!"

* * *

"Mrs. Litvak, for two days I didn't have a bite to eat," whined Shimkus, the *schnorrer.* "Could you spare me please a slice of cake?"

"Cake!" exclaimed Mrs. Litvak indignantly. "What kind of *chutzpah* is that? Bread isn't good enough for you?"

"Today, no," replied Shimkus. "This is my birthday!"

* * *

"Mama, what happens to all the beat-up cars when they get too old to run anymore?"

"I thought you knew," replied mama. "Somebody sells them to your father!"

* * *

"Whaddyamean I'm a slave to the nicotine habit!" hubby snapped at his wife. "I'll have you know I stopped smoking cigarettes twice as much this year as I stopped last year!"

* * *

Ida Kogan entered a recipe contest and won a two-week vacation at Echo Hills in the Catskills—the heart of the Borscht Belt. She fell in love with the place at once, and above all she wanted a tape recording of the famous echo for which the hills were so aptly named. Accordingly, she set up her equipment, cupped her hands around her mouth and shouted—

"*Haloooooo* - this is Ida Kohhhgaaan!"

And sure enough, there came back a mighty echo:

"*Haloooooo* - this is also Ida Kohhhgaaan!"

* * *

The young woman was exceedingly fair to look upon. She entered the auto salesroom and an affable salesman quickly approached the modern Cleopatra.

"This looks like a nice model," she said, after having inspected several cars. "What is it called?"

"That's the Belvedere," replied the salesman.

There ensued a chilly silence. The young woman then drew herself solidly erect, fixed him with a frigid stare, and coldly asked:

"What is the price of the Belva?"

* * *

Malka and Marsha, two old maids, were strolling down Lexington Avenue when they came upon a recruiting poster: *The Marine Corps Builds Men.*

"How nice," murmured Malka.

"It sure is!" agreed Marsha enthusiastically. "Let's ask them to build us a couple!"

* * *

The fact that a horse and wagon are components of this tale of woe is a good indication of its venerable age. It is a tale that was often told with much gusto and a little water on the side by Sidney Hillman, the great labor leader.

Molly Landau was learning to drive a car. Regrettably, as it turned out, she thought she already knew how, so she dismissed her driving instructor and ventured forth upon the public highway, unaccompanied by either an experienced hand or a driver's license.

As she wobbled in an uncertain course along Southern Boulevard in the Bronx, a milkman driving a well-behaved horse turned a corner. Mrs. Landau tried simultaneously to do several things—apply the brakes, avoid a collision, turn out, turn in, veer left, veer right, speed up, slow down, and who knows what else.

The "what else" was that she banged squarely into the side of the milk-wagon, leaving it turned over on its side in the middle of the street, with the horse and driver entangled in the wreckage.

The lady, losing her head, at the same time lost control of the car. She sped away, swerved out of sight and, on squealing tires she circled the block. A minute later she reappeared at the scene of the accident, still wrestling with the steering wheel. The dairyman, who had managed to extricate himself from the mess, was cutting his struggling horse loose from the twisted harness when he heard the clatter and roar of an approaching, wide-open engine. He looked up to see the same car and the same woman again bearing down on him. Just in time to save himself, he jumped aside.

There was a second crash and once more the green motorist proceeded on her devastating way. But now the capsized wagon was a total loss. The milkman was a natural-born philosopher. As he stood in the midst of the ruins, he shrugged his shoulders and remarked to the curious citizens who had gathered around:

"About that lady's driving, I can't say she's an expert. But you have to give her credit—she's thorough!"

* * *

It was the most momentous day in the history of Man. Moses, his face aglow with spiritual fire, descended from Mt. Sinai and pointed to the tablets.

"And now," he thundered to the awe-struck multitude, "a word from the Sponsor."

* * *

Cold water from the kitchen cynic:

"You just got married? *Mazel tov!* So tell me, when your new father-in-law dies, what kind of work will you be out of?"

* * *

As long as she was in the neighborhood, Mrs. Rifkind decided that she might as well stop in at the synagogue and meet the new assistant rabbi. Inside the temple, she asked the *shammes* where she could find the new rabbi's study.

"I'm sorry," said the *shammes*, "but right now he's engaged."

"Oh, how nice!" said Mrs. Rifkind, beaming. "I hope he'll be very happy!"

* * *

When the lights in her house went out for the third time within an hour, grandma called an electrician. It took him only a minute or two to locate the trouble.

"Lady," he informed her, "you got a short circuit."

"*Nu*," said grandma, "so you'll make it a little longer!"

* * *

"This drug situation with the younger generation is getting worse and worse every day," muttered the old-timer angrily as he tossed his evening newspaper aside. "It's those doctors. The kids complain to them about a bellyache and right away they get all kinds of drugs—without a prescription, yet!"

"It's not like when I was a young girl," sighed his wife. "In those days we couldn't even buy a brassiere without a prescription!"

* * *

"The nerve of that louse!" roared Glasner the glazier. "First he runs into my car against the traffic light; next he gives me a drink it should steady my nerves; then he calls the police!"

* * *

"What are your terms for students?" asked the new college freshman.

"I got all kinds of terms for them," snapped the boardinghouse landlady: "Loafers, bums, *schnorrers, shikkers . . . !*"

* * *

From our Intelligentsia Department:
Tough Guy: Scram, before I knock your teeth in!
Linguist: You mean 'out'!

* * *

At De Witt Clinton High School, one of the struggling students may have mixed his proverbs, but he inadvertently stated a universal truth.

Mathematics teacher William Segal, writing in the *Educational Review*, stated that he returned to his classroom after a few minutes absence and beheld an announcement that a student had hurriedly chalked on the blackboard:

"You can't teach an old dog new math!"

* * *

"Your son is a very imaginative boy," wrote the teacher on the kid's report card. "He excels in initiative, group integration and responsiveness. Now," she concluded, "if he could only add and subtract . . ."

* * *

"I don't wanna scare ya or anything, Miss Galernter," said nine-year-old Joel Yingatsh to his teacher, "but my papa says if I don't get better grades next time, somebody's gonna get spanked!"

* * *

"I want to thank you for your gracious and generous offer, Marvin," said the principal, "but I seriously doubt if your resignation would help alleviate our crowded school conditions."

* * *

Some years ago, when Rabbi Milton Sontag was professor of classics at the University of Judaism in Los Angeles, a student passed him in the corridor.

"Hiya, prof," greeted the brazen youth. "What's new?"

Dr. Sontag turned a pair of steely eyes on the flippant young man. "Stand where you are," he demanded in a voice that could clip a hedge, "and I'll tell you all about what's new:

"*Nu* is the thirteenth letter of the Greek alphabet, following *mu* and preceeding *xi*. Its capital form is similar to the English upper case *N*, it's lower case form is like the English small *v*. It is sounded like the English *N*. *Nu* is also a Yiddish word connoting the interrogation 'well?' or 'so?' or 'so what?' It is further used to provoke someone into action."

The offending student was rooted to the spot, mouth agape.

"*Nu?*" roared professor Sontag as the youth fled down the hall. "You still want to know what's new?"

* * *

The Goldbergs did not know what to do with their son Jake. He refused to take school seriously. He never did his homework, and was constantly playing hookey.

The principal at the public school suggested that they send Jake to a Yeshiva. The Goldbergs took the principal's advice, but the situation did not improve. His conduct was reprehensible—and after a few weeks he was expelled. Jake was incorrigible.

Finally, in desperation, the Goldbergs were told that Catholic parochial schools were very strict with their pupils, and they might try sending Jake to one. They decided to follow the suggestion, and they enrolled him in Christ-the-King School for Boys. They warned Jake to behave and to do his lessons, because this was his last chance. If he was thrown out now, he would be sent to a school for delinquents.

After a week of parochial school, Jake came home with terrific grades. He had miraculously been converted into a well-behaved, serious student.

The Goldbergs were thrilled, and they asked their son what caused the sudden change in his attitude and behavior.

"Well," he answered, "when I got into that building and saw a man hanging on a cross in every room I knew they meant business. I wasn't going to take any chances on being a wise guy anymore.

33

Waspish Wit and Phancy Philosophy

INTRODUCTION

Thinking is a strenuous art—few practice it, and then only at rare times. We *think* it would be pleasant to inherit a million dollars; we *think* it would be helpful if those four-acre supermarkets had more than three checkout counters.

This is *thought?*

It has been said (by no less an authority than Danny, my precocious two-year-old grandson) that man represents the highest form of life because he is a reasoning creature who delights in logic—until it threatens his pet prejudices. This whole business of logic just doesn't stand up to close scrutiny. We arrive at "logic" through the study of cause and effect, which always occur in the same order. "Cause," we are told, generates "effect," which is no more sensible than it would be for one who has never seen a bagel, except when being consumed by a man, to declare that the bagel is the cause of the man. (Don't interrupt—I'm on to something hot!) If we follow this line of thought—although I'm not insisting on it—we arrive at the conclusion that unless our logic contains wisdom we are not only making a big hoo-hah about nothing, but are not necessarily improving our condition. Here is a post-Revolutionary War *bobeh myseh* that illustrates the pernt:

Schmek, a skunk abiding in a wooded area near Valley Forge, had waited many a weary day to revenge himself upon Kluger, a fox, who had made several offensive remarks about his political leanings. Kluger was a Tory whose sympathies were with the British, while Schmek was an ardent patriot who strongly advocated American independence from England; thus, the cause of the fox's contemptuous references.

One fine morning the skunk saw him coming down the path and, leaping from the bushes where he had been hiding, he presented his nether quarters to the fox and showered him with disaffection in the manner of his race.

Observing that the fox paid no attention to the unfragrant gift, the skunk, keeping carefully out of reach, said:

"Kluger, I beg leave to point out that I have presented you with an implacable odor."

"My dear Schmek," the fox replied, "you have taken needless trouble; I already knew you are no rose."

"Brother Kluger, your logic is without substance," observed Schmek. "The world cares little about the cause and effect of our confrontation. It will simply judge us both as a couple of stinkers."

Anecdotes concerning talmudic logic are a hallmark of Jewish folklore, and the tales of psuedo-talmudic logic and deduction which comprise its humorous aspect date back to antiquity. Many of these ancient tales, funny as they may be, are often quite clever and rich in wisdom. But most (though certainly not all) of the American versions are without the traditional "moral" and are told just for the sheer joy of relating a funny story. They are, clearly enough, a spoof on the older, moralistic "logic" folk tales. The first anecdote which follows this Introduction, for example, is a variant on a thousand-year-old theme.

The basis of logic, as Americans understand it, is the syllogism, consisting of a major and a minor premise—thus:

Major Premise: One hundred women can accomplish a given task 100 times as quickly as one woman.

Minor Premise: One woman can give birth to a baby in 100 seconds.

Conclusion: One hundred women can give birth to a baby in one second.

Philosophy is the rational investigation of the truths and principles of being, knowledge or conduct. It has also been described as a route of many roads leading from nowhere to nothing—an observation written by the aforementioned Danny with his fingerpainting set. To quote Nadine Nussbaum, madam of the Manhattan Mansion of Nocturnal Delight: "Philosophy-shmossophy—what we believe is all in the head! The old believe everything; the middle-aged suspect everything; the young know everything!" (We are sorry to report that Nadine, for all her wisdom, neglected to recompense the local constabulary on their next scheduled payday. For that oversight she spent 30 days in an institution so tough that bread and water was not considered as punishment—it was Sunday dinner.)

In Jewish humor, trenchant wit follows the serious statement as inexorably as a burp follows a cucumber. A son asks his father, "Dad, how do you suppose those rock groups can afford all their expensive instruments?" And dad replies, "No problem at all. Look at all the money they save on music lessons." It will be seen in this chapter that many of the jokes involve a question-and-answer dialogue between the younger and older generations, highlighting the traditional Jewish suspicion that when adults act like children they're silly, and when children act like adults, they're delinquents. But the acidity of the humor, critical though it may be, is dissolved in the affection with which the quip or story is told. As Ibn M. Ezra said so long ago, "Love without criticism is not love." In that context, a father can compare his hippie son with Santa Claus, and still sound halfway affectionate: "They both wear funny clothes, don't shave, and work only once a year."

One would think that the Jewish joke, which involves logic, deduction, the clever retort and the biting witticism, would be the natural preserve of the college professor—the intellectual. But that is not the usual case. Here, once again, Judaic tradition plays its important role. For many centuries it was the rabbi who was the scholar, the sage, the respected member of the community who sat in judgment at a *Din Torah*. His advice was sought out and followed. That tradition is still manifest in the "intellectual" jokes of modern times.

And next in the order of humorous wisdom-givers is the grandfather of the family and then the father. The difference lies in the fact that the "rabbi" stories are nearly always far more gentle than those told by others.

Consider this example:

A rabbi once asked a youngster if he had studied *Gemara*.

"I only got to page two," the boy confessed.

"Everyone does," sighed the wise rabbi.*

Or, how about this one, as another example?

As they were leaving the synagogue, a cantor confided to the rabbi that he was bothered with insomnia.

"I'm sorry to hear that," said the rabbi. "Personally, I have no trouble at all in falling asleep."

"Really?" exclaimed the cantor. "Do you count sheep?"

"No," the rabbi replied mildly, "I talk to the Shepherd."

Let us now enjoy some time with those who know so little and know it so fluently.

H.D.S.

A talmudic scholar was so fervently pious that his holier-than-thou airs became a source of numerous jokes among his fellow students at the *Yeshivah*. As a prank, and thinking to teach him the virtues of good red wine, they induced him to imbibe far more than prudence allows, under the pretext that it was "only grape juice." As they had anticipated, it wasn't long before he passed out. The students, carrying the prank a step further, brought their unconscious friend to a nearby cemetery where they gleefully left him.

The hapless victim awoke several hours later, looked around and scratched his head in perplexity.

"This situation calls for the proper application of talmudic logic," he said to himself. "First, my powers of observation tell me I am in a cemetery. Therefore, I must be dead. But, secondly, I cannot be dead if my powers of observation are still working. The only logical conclusion, then, is that I am alive. Still, if I am alive, what am I doing in a cemetery? And on the other hand, if I am dead, why do I have to go to the bathroom?"

* * *

------

*All the books of the Talmud begin with page 2. They do not have a page 1.

This is logical?

Last year we cut down 1,250,000 trees to provide paper for books warning us about our dwindling natural resources.

* * *

It has been said: "A neck is what if you don't stick it out you won't get in trouble up to."

Yet, we must remember that it was not raining when Noah built the Ark.

* * *

Little Susie, age six, had heard that her older brother, Phil, had just been jilted by the girl he had intended to marry. It was all beyond her comprehension.

"What's the difference if she marries you or somebody else?" she asked with sweet innocence.

"The main difference," sighed Phil the philosopher, "is that a husband kisses the missus, and the other guy misses the kisses."

* * *

"With woman, it's like with a car," said Theodore the thinker. "To have no car at all is uncomfortable. On the other hand, to have a car is expensive and sometimes risky. So the moral is to have a friend who has a car.

* * *

Tobias, a teenager, found some old magazines his father had saved over the years and soon he was absorbed in the "quaint ways" of the pre-World War II era.

"Y'know, pop, it must have been awful to live in those olden times," commented Tobias. He held up an old magazine. "Just look at this slogan," he added, grinning: "'Time Marches On!' What were all the people doing in those days? Marching backwards?"

His father regarded him owlishly from over his thick-lensed spectacles.

"Maybe it was a little dull at that," he said gently. "In those days we had no pollution, no nuclear submarines, no hydrogen bombs, no energy shortages. But, believe me, son, I liked it better when time was marching on instead of running out!"

* * *

Ask not what your country can do for you, or what you can do for your country, but what can you do to make a living?

* * *

Russian Proverb: Knowledge is better than riches.

Jewish translation: We should all be as knowledgeable as Rothschild.

* * *

From the Intimate Confessions File:
"I have never witnessed any indications of black anti-Semitism," declared Sammy Davis Jr., "except when I get mad at myself!"

* * *

Benny Bortnik, the pride of Bedford Avenue, looked up from his newspaper which headlined a story about the latest space launch, using the most modern nuclear rockets.

"Too many people are speculating whether intelligent life exists on other planets," he sighed, "but I'm beginning to wonder how long it will exist on earth."

* * *

"Consider yourself drunk," averred Boris the bartender, "if you feel sophisticated and are unable to pronounce it."

* * *

Did you ever stop to think that the girl who is free for the evening usually turns out to be the most expensive of all?

* * *

"A pessimist," opined Dan Sping, boy writer and busy busybody, "is one who feels bad when he feels good because he's afraid he'll feel worse when he feels better.

"He's the kind of guy who won't pick a four-leaf clover for fear he'll be bitten by a rattlesnake. He wears a belt along with his suspenders and is never happy unless he's miserable. He even keeps his fingers crossed when he says "good morning,' and complains about the noise when opportunity knocks."

* * *

Larry the ladies' man claims that the main difference between kissing your wife and kissing your sweetheart is about 60 seconds.

* * *

As Gertrude Stein might have put it: A friend is a friend is a friend until he hits you up for a loan. Then he becomes an acquaintance an acquaintance an acquaintance.

* * *

"A mosquito," observed furrier I.J. Fox, "is like a small boy. When you can't hear it, it's up to something."

* * *

Two pundits were discussing the psychological differences between Jews and gentiles.

"Have you ever noticed," asked one, "that Jewish women seem to be more emotional than Christian women?"

"Indeed I have," agreed the other. "Jewish women are like a fine watch: hard to regulate, especially when they're all wound up."

* * *

Wisdom from an Orchard Street Oracle:
If a man tells you he has never seen Grant's Tomb, the Statue of Liberty, the Museum of Art or a parking space—he's a native New Yorker.

* * *

One of the advantages of being Jewish in America is the time saved searching for pork in a can of pork and beans.

* * *

Where does humor end and pain begin? Ask the Jewish people of the Soviet Union. Through 4,000 years of bitter experience they are again learning the real difference between results and consequences. In Russia, results are what the Jews hope for, but consequences are what they usually get.

* * *

At a meeting of the Young Men's Group at the Wilshire Boulevard Temple in Los Angeles, an anonymous fellow came forth with this pearl of irony:

"My parents used to tell me of the character-building experience and moral joys I missed by not living through the Great Depression. They have since passed on to their eternal reward, but I know that somewhere in the mystic Beyond they are smiling happily upon me, their son, as I now revel in the bliss of privation."

* * *

There is a philosophy that is written in the stars and reflected on the waters: He who crosses the ocean twice without bathing is a dirty double-crosser.

* * *

From the same philosopher:
Pity the man who marries for love and then finds that his wife has no money.

* * *

In the very long-ago days when publisher Bernard MacFadden, a physical culture buff, used his New York *Graphic* as a passport to that Great Vegetarian in the Sky, there occurred a singularly dramatic incident. The body of a young woman, expensively dressed, was found in a thicket in a lonely and remote part of Long Island. She had been murdered—shot through the head and rendered *kaput.*

Harry Levine, of the *Graphic's* staff, was the first reporter to reach the scene of the crime. The body had not yet been removed, and in searching about the premises, Harry discovered something the police had overlooked—a scrap of discolored paper bearing printed and written words in Yiddish. He unobtrusively slipped the paper into his pocket and caught the first train back to the city. Harry couldn't read Yiddish himself so he took his discovery to a rabbi—a close friend of his father.

The rabbi, an old, strait-laced, orthodox adherent of the traditional school, demanded to know what it was all about. Levine told him, explaining that the identity of the murdered woman was still a mystery— that nobody could even guess who she was. He described her clothing in some detail.

"*Ach!*" snorted the ancient sage. "Such *nahrishkeit mentschen* are these American police! To the talmudic-trained mind the whole thing is simplicity itself. By a process of elimination and deduction it is possible to learn without question exactly what manner of woman this was."

"Could you do it?" asked Levine hopefully.

"It wouldn't take me more than a few minutes," said the rabbi, his voice most impressive.

"Then please do," begged Levine. "I'd be much obliged to you."

"Very well. All I ask is that you follow me closely so that I need not repeat myself. Now, this scrap of paper shows that some woman bought certain small articles in a store right here in New York. The Yiddish words indicate that she purchased a bread knife, a potato masher, some clothespins and a soup ladle. No Jewish woman would buy such things unless she was a housewife. So! That's settled!

"On the other hand, you tell me she was expensively dressed, and I see another item on the piece of paper which shows that she bought a corset for sixty-four dollars. That being the case, I must advise you that no Jewish woman would wear sixty-four dollar corsets unless she was an actress. But no actress would buy common household items. Therefore she must be a housewife. Still, no housewife would wear sixty-four dollar corsets—

"And there you are!"

* * *

The little old man with the trim, white beard went to the City College of New York to visit his son. Seeking directions to the youth's room he stepped into a sociology class to make inquiries, but immediately became engrossed in the professor's closing statement:

". . . and I say we must all remember that a wife is precious to a man in our society. Her value is unlimited, her worth immeasurable."

The professor noticed the little old stranger in the rear of the room. Wishing to emphasize his point, he called out, "Sir, what would you say your wife is worth?"

"*Nu,*" answered the old-timer promptly, "make me an offer!"

* * *

There is a morsel of good to be found in everything—even in our disappointments. Has it not been wisely said that a fly in the soup is better than no meat at all?

* * *

"What a holler would ensue if people had to pay the rabbi as much to marry them as they have to pay a lawyer for a divorce!"

* * *

It was a pleasantly warm day in June. Seated on a park bench in Chatham Square, sunning themselves and engaged in their usual mild disputes, were two old men: Leo, the *Galitzianer*, and Chaim, the *Litvak*.

"One thing you got to understand," Chaim was saying. "Us *Litvaks* are smarter than you *Galitzianers*."

"What kind of nonsense are you talking, what kind?" demanded Leo heatedly. "Read any Jewish history book and you'll see that the *Galitzianers* are ten times smarter than you *Litvaks*. It says so in *all* the books."

"What books?"

"It don't make no difference. *Any* book!"

"Well, this proposition I never heard before. If you read it in all the books, be so kind as to name me one smart *Galitzianer* who ever lived."

Leo closed his eyes, tilted his head back and began to think. He stroked his beard and hummed softly to himself. He pulled on his ear lobe, nibbled his knuckles and pursed his lips as he mentally delved into his vast book learning for the proper answer. Finally, he opened his eyes and turned to his companion.

"Chaim," he asked, "this Jew, he *has* to be a *Galitzianer*?"

* * *

From the O'Hell Corner:

"I recall the time I first met Nikita Khrushchev," reminisced multi-talented Jerry Lewis. "It was during his visit to the West Coast when he raised all that fuss about being unable to visit Disneyland. Actually, when he entered the room I said 'Hello,' but when I recognized him I reversed my salutation."

* * *

No man is old unless he can remember when the village square was a place instead of a person. Or, as the late Jack Benny so succinctly put it:

"Age is strictly a case of mind over matter. If you don't mind, it doesn't matter.

* * *

A young lady, studying at the Jewish Teachers' Seminary in New York, was discussing the subject of race with an acquaintance who happened to be a novitiate at the nearby Catholic convent.

"The trouble with you Jews is that you marry too much among yourselves. You need more outside blood. Look at me: In my blood there's French, German, English, Irish and Scot."

"Is that a fact?" replied the Jewish girl calmly. "I must say, that was very generous of your mother!"

* * *

Broadway actor Maurice Altshuler tells of the very first instructions he ever received after arriving in America from Russia. He had only been here two days when he decided to take a walk along Greene Street to see the sights of New York—hardly representative of Manhattan, but in those days Maurice thought it was the hub of the metropolis.

His older brother, Albert, who had preceeded him to this country by a few years, thought it best to instruct him in the ways of the local constabulary.

"Watch the traffic signals and do what the cops tell you," he cautioned the young immigrant. "Remember, in New York a policeman is not like a girl: When he says 'stop' he really means it!"

* * *

It is said that Rabbi Stephen Wise disliked being referred to as *Doctor*, although he had, in fact, earned his doctorate as a divinity student. "Just call me "rabbi'," he would say.

On one memorable occasion, many years ago, he was introduced to a social-climbing woman who insisted on calling him *Doctor* Wise.

"Madam," he said gently but firmly, "I am not a doctor. I am not even a nurse!"

* * *

An outstanding Jewish hero of the American Revolutionary War was Benjamin Nones. He emigrated to the New World from France in 1776, and immediately enlisted in the Colonial Army. Cited for gallant action by General Washington, Nones became a major and commanded a company of 400 men, many of whom were also Jewish.

But we are concerned here with Major Nones' piquant sense of humor. During the time of the French Revolution, when the months in France were named Thermidor, Floreal, Novise and so forth, Nones decided that it would not be a bad idea to make a few such changes in America as well. He suggested that *Chanukah* and Christmas be consolidated as *Chanukmas; Yom Kippur* and Thanksgiving Day be united as *Yomthanks;* and Passover and Waterloo be known as *Passwater*. He further proposed that America extend the French innovation to the English language with a whole new set of names for the months of the year, as follows:*

January: Freezy
February: Sneezy

---

*Rewritten from *The Baltimorean*, Vol. 9, August, 1831.

March: Breezy
April: Wheezy
May: Showery
June: Lowery
July: Flowery
August: Bowery
September: Snowy
October: Flowy
November: Blowy
December: Glowy

* * *

From the book, *My Mishpocheh: Ernest Borgstein and Franchot Kohn,* by Barbara Sandwich:

"Marriage is an institution that teaches a man regularity, frugality, temperance, forbearance and many other splendid virtues he would not need had he stayed single."

34

Naughty-Shmaughty

INTRODUCTION

We have already discussed the subject, "What is a Jew?" Now, let us address ourselves to the question, "What is sex?" Sex is the means by which reformers, censors, film producers, novelists and psychiatrists make a living. The purpose of sex is to extract a little pleasure out of life without creating a lot of problems for the sexee or sexor. Some of its more participatory aspects are frowned upon by the fastidious, which refers to the Roman, Faustidius, and his modern adherents who are known as Fastidiots.

The reason for Jewish involvement in this popular indoor sport will be found in the people's sacred writings. The Bible exhorts us: "Be fruitful and multiply, and replenish the earth." This is the first of the 613 commandments every pious Jew must observe. In the Talmud, we are admonished: "To refrain from begetting is to impair the Divine image," and it is followed by the rhetorical question, "Was not the world created only for propagation?"

And there you have it! Jews have sex because they're religious!

Not everyone will enjoy this chapter—especially the sexually-oriented type of fellow who determines how many women are at a party by counting the number of breasts and dividing by two. He will be disappointed because this is not a Jewish *Kama Sutra of Vatsametteh*, that curious and informative Eastern manual of erotica. Moreover, this chapter was not designed to meet the community standards of Sodom and Gemorrah, nor does it contain any leering double-entendres: triple, yes—double, no.

Another type who will be sorely disappointed by these pages is the "serious student" of humor. As far as I am concerned, nobody needs some goateed savant to scrutinize, hypothesize and symbolize until our jokes have been analyzed to death. Those professorial types would dress up the family dog in a cutaway suit. The socio-scientist positively slavers when he hears a funny story. ("Egad! The Oedipus complex! Anal regression! The phallic symbol!") In the first place, Jews don't have those naughty things. They just have respectable *tsuris* like decent people are supposed to have. In the second place, if it makes you all that sick you should better stick to parchesi.

An American reporter once asked General Moshe Dayan if the rumors about an increase of VD in Israel's army were true. Dayan exploded with a wrathful "That's a lot of claptrap!" The same reply may be reserved for the modern writer of fiction who weaves his spell of mysticism around "Jewish sex"—as though Jews held a patent on some esoteric monkey business unknown to gentiles. Today's children of Israel are an imaginative and resourceful people, but they have yet to invent an intimacy that wasn't at least considered by Abraham, Isaac and Joseph's brothers—and by the Pharaohs and Caesars as well. They just have a funnier way of describing it.

A word about the American-Jewish view of obscenities. Profanity, for the modern Jew, does not consist of such words as hell and damn: they are only profane when they are written h--l and d--n. The "sensitive" writer who is too respectable to use such mild expletives, and causes his character, a barroom brawler, to exclaim "Oh, shucks" instead of a healthy, heartfelt "dammit!"—is an embarrassment. Nevertheless, it is difficult to feel anything but contempt for the writer or storyteller who employs obscenities for no other purpose than their shock value, as though they were communicating with a nation of slobs. Such a wordsmith or jokester uses the oath to hide the emptiness in his head, and is often incapable of expressing himself in other terms. But there are occasions—and they are not infrequent—when a play on words—any word—is the actual point of the story rather than an intrusion. Let's say, for instance, that you owned a mare and that you bought a baby donkey for her. You could then quite legitimately and truthfully refer to the colt as a horse's ass without being accused of swearing. After all, the Bible does not hesitate to devote space to the story of Balaam's ass!

There are definite "types" in American-Jewish humor, among them the perennial *shlemiel*. Consider the young fellow who is cautioned against marrying a certain girl. "Everybody in Yonkers has slept with her," the friend warns him. The intended bridegroom thinks it over, and then shrugs. "So what?" he replies. "After all, how big is Yonkers?"

The "outraged husband" is another favorite:

Feinberg came home from a business trip and his wife coolly informed him that she had been unfaithful during his absence.

"Who was it?" shouted Feinberg, "that rotten Goldberg?"

"No," his wife replied, "it wasn't Goldberg."

"Was it that crooked partner of mine—that *goniff*, Levy!"

"No, not Levy."

"I know who it was: it was that *momzer*, Shapiro!"

"No, it wasn't Shapiro, either."

Feinberg glowered at his wife. "What's the matter?" he barked, "none of my friends are good enough for you?"

Jokes about the decline of vigor associated with old age form another large body of Jewish humor:

Grandpa and grandma, celebrating their golden wedding anniversary, decided to take a vacation at the same hotel where they had spent their honeymoon. It was a romantic idea, and they agreed to do everything they did in those first few days. Soon they were in the very same hotel and in the very same room. Grandpa undressed in the bathroom, just as he had so many years ago, and then he emerged in his long flannel underwear. Grandma, now wearing nothing but her stockings, and sitting on the edge of the bed, smiled up at him.

"Papa," she cooed, "can you wait until I'm taking off my stockings?"

"Yes, mama," he sighed. "I can even wait until you *knit* a pair!"

It is said that men do not vary much in their virtues; they differ only in their vices. On the other hand, the woman who boasts of her virtue is one who probably was tested at an inopportune time by the wrong man. But in Jewish humor, virtue and common sense play an equal role. Let us see how a Jewish girl handled one delicate situation:

Schatz, the marriage broker, called on Lorraine and happily announced that he had found the ideal husband for her.

"There's just one little problem standing in the way," said the *schadchan.* "You see, he's a businessman, and by him everything is business. So he's asking you should first give him a sample of your sexual ability."

"Well, you go right back and tell him that I know a little about business, too," snapped Lorraine. "Samples I'm not giving him. References I'll give him!"

The jokes which follow, of the above and several other types, are guaranteed to be acceptable in Boston, a city so clean that even the birds fly upside down.

H.D.S.

Two housewives were gossiping over the back fence about their neighbor's daughter, Cathy Kanter—otherwise known as Canarsie Kate.

"Oh, what a shame!" chucked the first *yenta.* "She was so sweet when she was small. Even her own family called her 'tateh's little darling.'"

The other woman nodded. "By me her heart still belongs to daddy," she agreed, "but the rest I'm afraid she's renting out!"

* * *

Louis Jourdan, the French movie star, was in the United States seeking a good literary script for his next film. He happened to run into Budd Shulberg, the American author and playwright.

"There's a new book out called *Precocious Paula,*" Shulberg suggested tentatively. "It would give you a great co-starring role."

"I nevair hear of zis book," said Jourdan.

"It's something like Nabokov's novel, *Lolita,*" explained Shulberg.

"An' what ees zis *Lolita* about?"

"Well, frankly, it's about a middle-aged man who falls in love with a twelve-year-old."

The Frenchman gave him a blank look.

"I do not undairstan'," he said. "A twelve-year-old *what*?"

* * *

Moe and Ike, aged 90 and 92 respectively, had been widowers for many many years. Both were healthy and handsome looking despite their years. The Florida climate agreed with them, and many lovely widows were still after them despite their ages.

One day Moe said to Ike:

"Ike, I'm really lonely. It's been years since I lost my Becky and I've never remarried. But I think now is the time and I'm willing to take another chance at marriage. Even at my age."

"It sounds like a good idea," said Moe. "In fact, maybe I, too, should take a new wife."

Soon thereafter, Moe and Ike both married lovely ladies (89 and 90 respectively) and they both went on honeymoons.

A few days later, Moe and Ike met on the boardwalk.

"Well," asked Moe, "how was your honeymoon?"

"To tell you the truth, Moe, I couldn't consummate our marriage."

"Well," said Moe, "to tell you the truth, I didn't even *think* of it."

* * *

In the Jurassic period, when going to Far Rockaway from the Bronx was an event similar to the departure of an astronaut for the moon, there lived a respectable young woman named Miriam Altshuler. Miss Altshuler earned her wherewithal as a piano teacher, attended *shul* regularly and minded her own business. So much for the truth of this story: Now for the *bobeh myseh:*

One summer, Miss Altshuler took leave of her students and decamped for Far Rockaway, in search of two weeks of relaxation on a farm and—O Great *Shadchan* in the Sky—perhaps a husband.

Unbeknown to her, the farmer, a recent widower, had taken a fancy to the young lady, but he happened to be one of those who deems it prudent to taste the milk before buying the dairy. So, with all the subtlety of an Internal Revenue letter, he led our sweet little Miriam Altshuler to his pasture where a herd of Guernseys were peacefully grazing on second-growth clover. With the cows was a prize Black Angus bull. The farmer, it seems, was experimenting to achieve a newer and better breed.

As the farmer and Miss Altshuler watched by the rail, the bull performed his main function in life by servicing a heifer that was in season. The farmer smiled inwardly. All was proceeding as he had planned. He had now reached the point of fail-safe.

"Miriam," he said pointedly, "I think it would be fun to do that."

"Well, who's stopping you?" she replied. "It's your cow!"

* * *

The late Ed Wynn enjoyed telling parrot stories.

"I once owned a parrot," claimed Ed, "that laid six-pointed eggs, shaped just like the Star of David. And the parrot could speak only one word—

"'Ouch!'"

* * *

Chauncey, a handsome, almost pretty young man, was speaking earnestly with his mother:

"Mumsie, the time has come—it really has—when we must have a heart-to-heart talk about my relationship with Myron. To be quite candid about it, our friendship has blossomed into—how shall I say it without sounding indelicate?—well, into something beautiful and good and even holy. The truth is, Mumsie dear, I love Myron and Myron loves me in return. We want to be married as soon as possible and we both hope you'll give us your blessing."

"But, Chauncey," the mother protested, "do you realize what you're saying? Can you honestly expect me to condone such a marriage? What will people say? What will our friends and neighbors think?"

"Oh, Mumsie, you're going to be dreary—I can feel it in my bones. And after we've been such good pals, too. I never would have believed it of you—of all people. I could just cry!"

But, son, you can't go against convention like this!"

"All right, Mumsie, let's have it right out in the open like civilized persons. Exactly and precisely what possible objection could you or anyone else have to Myron and I becoming husband and husband?"

"You know perfectly well why I object: He's Jewish!"

* * *

In his morning mail, Michael, a bachelor, was surprised to find an invitation to a wedding. His best friend, Bob, a politician, was getting married to Hannah the old maid.

"Well, whaddya know," exclaimed Michael. "The wedding of the humbug to the bum hug!"

* * *

Question of the Century Department:

Why is it that nobody ever writes elegaic poems about sex *after* marriage?

* * *

Mrs. Leibowitz went into a furniture store.

"I would like please to look at a sexual sofa," she said.

The salesman mulled the request over in his mind for a moment or two and then a smile of comprehension crossed his features.

"Oh, you mean a *sectional* sofa!"

"Sexual-sectional," she retorted impatiently. "All I'm asking is that I should have an occasional piece in the living room!"

* * *

A young woman, hardly more than a girl, went to see the local rabbi.

"You don't know me," she began with a catch in her throat, "but I just had to speak to somebody. You see, I have no mother or father and I don't know much about worldly matters."

"You don't have to say another word," said the rabbi. "I understand perfectly. It's a man, no?"

"Yes, and he's always trying to kiss me. Kiss-kiss-kiss, that's all he ever thinks of."

"You must be firm," said the rabbi sternly. "That kind of man you don't need. Just tell him you don't allow such kinds of goings-on."

As she left, the rabbi said, "Come back in a week and let me know how you're making out."

Sure enough, the girl returned a week later, but this time she was even more disturbed than before.

"What's the matter now?" asked the rabbi.

"I stopped him from all that kissing," said the unhappy young lady, but now—well, I don't know how to put it . . ."

"Put—put!" urged the rabbi. "With me you got nothing to be ashamed."

"He's trying to—er—touch me with his hands," she stammered in embarrassment.

The rabbi rose from his chair in righteous anger. "You tell that no-goodnik he should keep his dirty hands to himself!" he barked. "What kind of a way is that to treat a decent Jewish girl? Tell him to stop at once, you hear?"

But when she visited the rabbi again she was almost in tears.

"I did everything you said," she moaned, "but now he insists he wants to sleep with me."

"*What!*" yelled the outraged rabbi. "I never heard of such *chutzpah* in my whole life. You go right home and the next time you see him I want you to throw that bum out of the house. You understand? I'm *ordering* you! Throw him out!"

A few days later she visited the rabbi once more. Her eyes were red from weeping and her face was a picture of misery.

"Did you do like I ordered?" demanded the rabbi.

She nodded, and, still sobbing, she said through her tears—

"Now he wants a divorce!"

* * *

Over at Famous Fabrics, Inc., they have a gorgeous model who has everything a man could ask for—

So they're all asking.

* * *

Harvey Pincus, the passionate playboy of Prospect Park, oblivious of human limitations, speeded up when he should have slowed down. To his surprise and dismay, he awoke three days later in Bellevue Hospital where he was placed on a strict diet of raw eggs and oysters with wheat germ, garnished with ginseng and soy bean sprouts. A week later, his physical desires returned and, after having been rebuffed by Bellevue nurses of various shapes, sizes, ages and national origins, he demanded to be released forthwith so that he might resume his *al fresco* prowling in the Prospect Park perimeter.

Pincus was soon confronted by Dr. Siegel, the hospital's staff psychiatrist. "Before we release you, you'll have to take a Rorschach test," explained the medic.

"What's that?" asked Pincus, suspiciously.

"A kind of personality gauge. I'll just show you some inkblots and you tell me what each one suggests to you."

"*Nu*, so go ahead and test."

Dr. Siegel handed him the first blot. "What does this bring to mind?"

"That's easy," replied Pincus instantly, his eyes lighting with pleasure, "It's a girl's hips."

"And this?" asked the psychiatrist, handing him another inkblot.

"A woman's breast. Very nice, too."

"Hmmm—how about this one?"

"Wow, doctor—what a gorgeous pair of legs!"

Siegel had already reached an obvious conclusion about his patient's proclivities, but he continued with a half-dozen more inkblots just to make sure. When Pincus continued to respond as though all the "pictures" were sexual symbols, right up to the last blot, the doctor leaned back in his chair and rendered his diagnosis.

"My dear fellow," he began, somewhat severely, "in case nobody ever told you, you have an abnormal fixation on sex."

"What does that mean, if I may be so bold to inquire?"

"It means, sir," Siegel explained bluntly, "you have a filthy mind."

"Well, look who's talking!" Pincus yelled, outraged. "*You're* showing me all those dirty pictures and *I've* got a filthy mind?"

* * *

It was Eddie's first week in pharmacy school. Outside, the sun was shining warmly, the birds were warbling, the girls were strolling and June was busting out all over.

Eddie's head nodded drowsily and he closed his eyes. But the instructor's sharp voice soon brought him back to scholastic reality:

"Well, sir, we're waiting for your answer!"

"Please repeat the question," muttered Eddie.

"If it doesn't interfere with your slumbers too much," hissed the professor, "please enlighten the class as to the difference between amnesia and magnesia."

"Well," said Eddie uncertainly, "with amnesia you don't know where you're going."

* * *

Home cooking: The place where a man thinks his wife is.

* * *

Zelda, the Hebrew zebra, was walking down a country lane, some-place in the boondocks of Pennsylvania. Soon she came upon a flock of sheep.

"Yoo-hoo, may I speak to you please?" she called out.

One of the sheep came up to the fence.

"*Nu*, what do you want to speak about?"

"I represent the Hadassah Zebra Association of South Africa. You're Jewish?"

"Oh yes, we're all Jewish here."

"Well, I'm on a fact-finding tour. Our zebras are interested in learning how Jewish animals in America earn a living. Would you mind telling me what kind of work you do?"

"What do I do?" exclaimed the sheep. "What kind of a question is that? I give wool, what else? Every year they shear it off and next season they do the same thing. Is it any different there in South Africa?"

"Oh, no, it's just the same. Well, I must be running along. Ta-ta, and thank you most kindly."

Zelda continued on her fact-finding mission until she met a cow.

"Excuse me, madam, I'm from the Hadassah Zebra Association of South Africa. I'm interviewing Jewish-American domestic animals. Would you be so kind as to describe your work?"

"Glad to," murmured the cow. "I am employed by a strictly kosher dairy, being orthodox myself, of course. My work, you ask? Well, I'm a purebred Guernsey, and I give Grade A milk. I live up there in that pretty white barn. Sorry I can't ask you in, but we weren't expecting company and the place is a mess."

"That's perfectly all right. Thank you for your information. You've been most helpful. Toodle-oo."

A short time later, Zelda saw a stallion in a pasture, and there was no mistaking *his* Jewishness. He happened to see her at just about the same moment. He charged toward the fence, skidded to a four-footed stop and loomed over the zebra with nostrils flaring.

"And just what is it that *you* do, sir?" she asked demurely.

"Honey, you just slip out of those fancy pajamas," he said, "and I'll *show* you what I do!"

* * *

Mr. Shmendrick came home earlier than expected and found his wife in bed with a strange man.

"What are you two doing?" he bellowed.

"See what I mean?" said the wife to her lover. "A *shnook*!"

* * *

Harry was scolding his younger brother who had just dropped out of college.

"Every time I see you, you're either all *shikkered* up or running around with wild women—or both!" yelled Harry. "Don't you know what good clean fun is?"

"No," said the brother. "What good is it?"

* * *

Howard Rabinowitz, a huge, granite-fisted, super-tough young fellow, was drinking whiskey in a bar when he heard the announcement of the Six Day War on the radio. Filled with excitement and Jewish fervor, he rushed to the airport and took the first available flight to Israel where he was immediately inducted into the army.

But his reception at the military base was rather cool. He wasn't exactly avoided by the Israeli soldiers but neither did they go out of their way to welcome him.

"Listen, what's with you guys?" he complained to his sergeant. "Here I come halfway around the world to help you out and I'm practically ignored. What must an American do to get accepted in this army?"

The sergeant eyed the muscular young giant, glanced around somewhat furtively so that he might not be overheard, and then, in a voice that was almost a whisper, he said:

"Confidentially, and off the record, if you really want to be one of us, there are three things you must do."

"Name them," said Rabinowitz.

"First," explained the sergeant, "you must drink down a whole quart of our strongest Mount Carmel wine without stopping for a breath. Second, you must kill an Arab army officer. Third, you must make love to an Israeli beauty."

So Howard Rabinowtiz chug-a-lugged a whole quart of Mount Carmel wine without stopping.

"Now," he demanded, "where can I find an Arab officer?"

"Right across the Suez Canal," said the sergeant. "I'm afraid you'll have to swim both ways; that is, if you're still alive."

"I'll be alive," promised the American as he lurched off. "Hell, I was the roughest, toughest, biggest guy on the East Side. What's a little adventure like this?"

A few hours later he returned, soaking wet from his return swim, his clothes torn and his face scratched and bloody.

"Okay, I took care of that Arab officer," he roared. "Now, where's that Israeli beauty you want killed?"

* * *

There is a religious fellow who really believes in the proverb, "Love thy neighbor."

The trouble is, he can't stand her husband.

* * *

Over at Chatham Uniform and Work Clothes Manufacturing Company, during their lunch break, a cutter, a sponger and a baster were bemoaning the dilatory ways of the younger generation.

"Mein Harold is so lazy he's getting up at six every morning just so he'll have more time to loaf," moaned the cutter. "Today he told me he's putting popcorn on his pancakes so they should turn over by themselves. *Oy*, is mein Harold lazy!"

"That's lazy by you?" demanded the cutter. "Listen, mein Jerome gets into a rewolwing door and just *waits*! And does he walk in his sleep like a decent Jewish boy? No, he's sticking out his thumb he should hitch-hike!"

The baster gave a deep sigh. "I wish mein Boitram was only so lazy like your boys. Mein Boitram just married a widow with four children!"

* * *

Tired of the old fly-in-my-soup jokes? Here's a switch.

Manny sat down in his favorite restaurant and was about to taste his chicken soup when a passing waiter accidentally jostled his arm. To his chagrin, the soup spilled on his lap.

"Now look what you did," complained Manny. "I got a soup in my fly!"

* * *

In a Bronxville tavern, Lou was celebrating his one-night-out per week with his bachelor friend, George, who was declaiming on the benefits of blessed singleness.

"It's nice to be a bachelor," George was saying. "I can get in or out of bed from either side; I cook only one breakfast; I have only one set of dishes to wash; I can open my wallet without hiding in the bathroom, and I have all kinds of marvelous faults that nobody tells me about."

"How did you ever manage to avoid marriage in the first place?" asked Lou enviously.

"You have to develop the right frame of mind," counseled George. "To enjoy single bliss there are five principles to guide your steps. First, never make the same mistake once. Second, it helps to know all the ankles. Third, make up your mind that it's better to learn how to mend your socks than your ways. Fourth, you should develop a deep love for the Constitution—especially where it says all Americans are entitled to life, liberty and the happiness of pursuit. Fifth and final, you must strictly follow the Bachelor's Golden Rule—wine, women and so-long."

Lou took another drink, nodded, took still another drink, nodded some more, and let his imagination wander.

"I can see it all," he said dreamily. "A bachelor is a guy with one car, two suits, three girl friends and four all-night parking tickets."

* * *

Walt Birnbaum, of Knickerbocker Undergarments, Inc., had just finished lunch and, after two manhattans, was in an expansive mood.

"I have an idea for a new item in ladies underwear that should make us a cool million," he announced with a grin.

"What kind of an item? asked his unsuspecting partner.

"I call it space panties," explained Walt. "It's for the girl who thinks her *tuchus* is out of this world."

* * *

Fifi Flugel of Fairmont Avenue in the Bronx (not to be confused with Fifi *Fliegel* of Fair*fax* Avenue in Los Angeles) came home one evening and unleashed her tale of woe to her mother.

"Mama, I got took advantage of by my boss," she sobbed. "All he really wanted was my body, and now he's casting me aside like in the movies."

"*Himmel!*" gasped mama, "you're—you're pregnant?"

"Yes, mama, what should I do?"

"I'll tell you what you should do," said mama grimly. "You'll stay home tomorrow from work and I'm going instead to your office I should have a heart-to-heart talk with your *paskudnyak* of a boss."

The next morning, mama barged into the boss's elaborate sanctum and read him the Riot Act in several languages, among them English, Yiddish and Russian. Then, in a voice that had all the metallic resonance of a twanging bronze bedpan, she led into her demands.

"*Nu,*" she snapped as a good negotiator should, "what kind of arrangement you're intending for mine Fifi?"

"You may rest assured, Mrs. Flugel, that your daughter will lack for nothing," said the boss, applying a solid gold lighter to his expensive cigar. "I will get her the best specialist in America so that she has the finest prenatal care possible. She will go to the most exclusive hospital to be found anywhere in the United States and she will have a team of the most experienced, well-recommended doctors and nurses money can obtain. When the baby is born I will set up, in its name, a hundred-thousand-dollar trust fund and, further, I will provide Fifi with $1,000 a week for living expenses while she is bringing up my child."

"Mister," said Mama Flugel after some careful thought, "if it's a miscarriage would you be so kind you should give Fifi another chance?"

* * *

Izzie Schwartz, age six, and his little friend, Colleen McGuire, also six, were playing jacks on the sidewalk.

"I'm tired of this game," said Colleen. "Let's play something else."

"Okay, we'll play Daddy and Mommy," suggested Izzie. "I'll be the Daddy and you can be the Mommy."

"Oooh, that sounds like fun! But how do we play it?"

"Well, I'm coming home from work and you make supper and we eat."

So Colleen dutifully went through the motions of cooking and apportioning "supper" on two imaginary plates.

"What do we do now?" asked Colleen.

"Now we watch television."

So they "watched television," staring vapidly at a spot on the sidewalk.

"Now what?" demanded Colleen, impatient to get on with the game.

"Now it's time to go to bed," said Izzy.

So they stretched out on the sidewalk and pretended they were under the covers.

"What do we do now?" asked little Colleen.

"Now," explained Izzy, "we whisper in Jewish!"

* * *

Adam to Eve: "After I eat this apple I'm gonna *what?*"

* * *

A minor example of the consequences of censorship occurred in the pages of the English language weekly, *The California Jewish Voice*, a journal recently absorbed by the *B'nai Brith Messenger* in Los Angeles. The editor, it seems, was apprehensive when a music critic on his staff wrote a sentence that read:

"The oboe player spent the evening staring at his navel."

The editor apparently considered the word "navel" too risque for a nice family paper and ordered the offending word stricken from the sentence. But imagine his horror when, after the edition had been mailed out to the entire list of subscribers, he happened to read the corrected sentence:

"The oboe player spent the evening staring at his——."

* * *

Selma the secretary was about to take her annual vacation and was instructing the stunning substitute as to her duties for the next two weeks.

"It's really an easy job," Selma assured the substitute, taking note of her pretty features and curvaceous figure. "All you have to do is continue what I was doing—except with Mr. Yosselov."

* * *

"Hey, grandpa, I heard another good one today," shouted young Julius, bursting into the house. "What's the difference between a hairdresser and a sculptor?"

"*Nu*, educate me," sighed the grandfather, accustomed to the boy's riddle-of-the-day routine.

"A hairdresser curls and dyes," chortled Julius, "and a sculptor makes faces and busts."

The old man groaned. "All right, you told me your riddle. Now go out and play with your friends like a good boy."

"But I have three more," protested the youngster. "If I can't tell my riddles to you, what'll I do with them?"

"Julius," breathed the old-timer wearily, "if I weren't your very own grandpa, believe me, I'd tell you!"

* * *

Bob and Richard, two gentile brothers, fell in love with two Jewish sisters and agreed to become converts to Judaism so that they could marry the girls.

The next day, Bob, the younger brother, showed up at his doctor's office.

"I want to be castrated," he told the medic.

"You *what*! Mister, do you realize what you're saying?"

"I certainly do."

"Well, I'm not sure I want to do the operation," said the good doctor hesitantly. "Castration is a very serious, irrevocable step."

"Then if you won't do it, I'll find another doctor who will."

The doctor shrugged. "In that case, as long as you intend to go through with it anyway, I'll operate."

So he castrated the young man.

The following day, as Bob was about to leave the doctor's clinic, his brother Richard entered the reception room.

"What are you doing here?" asked Bob.

"I came to get circumcised," replied Richard.

"Damn!" exclaimed Bob. "*That's* the word I was trying to think of!"

* * *

"I come from a large family," explained Sheldon the druggist. "There were 14 of us kids. We were so crowded I never knew what it was to sleep alone until I got married."

* * *

A pregnant silence pervaded the courtroom as the judge considered the paternity suit before him. All at once he looked up from the sheaf of papers he had been studying, reached into the folds of his robe, drew out a cigar and ceremoniously handed it to the defendant.

"Congratulations!" boomed his honor. "You have just become a father!"

* * *

Then there's the story of the tightwad equestrian. He's been riding backwards ever since his horse swallowed a quarter.

* * *

The new assistant rabbi, just out of Yeshiva University, was as fervent as any newly-ordained young man of the cloth could possibly be. A real go-getter, he immediately plunged into the task of building up the congregation's membership, but was disappointed when a certain young widow in the neighborhood failed to appear for any of the services.

One *shabbes*, however, without warning, she attended the synagogue, looking radiant and quite beautiful. The young rabbi rushed over to her, smiling, and extended his hand in greeting.

"I just knew you'd come!" he exclaimed happily. "In fact, I prayed for you last night for a whole hour."

"Why, rabbi," she answered coyly, "all you had to do was give me a jingle. I'd have been over in ten minutes!"

* * *

It was a constant battle between Mrs. Levine and her twelve-year-old daughter to keep her room tidy. No matter how much the mother pleaded, cojoled, ranted and raved, the little girl kept her room in a mess.

And then came the day of miracles. Mrs. Levine went into her daughter's room and found it immaculate—everything in its place, the floor swept and the bed made.

"Now this is what I like to see!" she exclaimed. "But what changed you into such a good little girl?"

"The police changed me," replied the girl solemnly. "I heard on the radio this morning that they're gonna arrest anybody who keeps a disorderly house."

* * *

Herbie the haberdasher, after tying on a whopper the night before, woke up in a strange room the next morning, only to find a pathetically unattractive woman sleeping blissfully beside him. He leaped out of bed, dressed quickly and then furtively placed a $20 bill on top of the bureau. Stealthily, he proceeded to tiptoe out of the room.

As he neared the door, he almost tripped over the form of another female, nearly as homely as the one he'd left in bed. She gazed up at him from where she was lying on the floor and soulfully asked:

"Nothin' fo' de bridesmaid?"

* * *

Two cutters in the garment district were talking shop in a Seventh Avenue luncheonette.

"What I can't figure out," said one, "is all this interest in girls' stretch pants."

"There's lots of reasons," replied the other. "Did you ever see a girl in stretch pants?"

"Sure."

"Well, then you saw two reasons right there!"

* * *

For ten years, ever since they were first married, Michael and Tessie Weinberg were content with each other. It was an ideal, happy marriage. Then, following the birth of their third child, Tessie noticed, to her distress, that the pleasure she had always derived from her wifely intimacies had considerably waned. On the other hand, Michael's sexual appetite remained as strong as ever.

Much worried, Tessie decided to consult their family doctor.

"I still love my husband," she explained to the physician, "but I'm afraid I'm not satisfying him any more. I just don't have the same feeling like I used to. Not that Michael complains or anything—he loves me too much for that. Maybe that's why I feel so guilty. Tell me, doctor, have you got something I could take that could help me?"

"Well, as a matter of fact I do have something new that might help your condition," said the doctor. "We don't know too much about it yet, but it seems to produce the desired effect. It's a stimulator imported from Israel where it was recently developed. It is known as Jewish Fly. Unlike Spanish Fly, this is strictly kosher."

"If it will help save my marriage I'll take it."

"Very well, Mrs. Weinberg, I'll give you four tablets. Start off with just half a tablet and see what kind of reaction you get. After that, if you need it, you can take a stronger dose."

A week later, Tessie, obviously distraught, was back at the physician's office.

"Doctor, I came here for only one reason," she cried. "I want you to know that you just about ruined my marriage. That terrible drug you gave me . . . Oh, I'm so ashamed!"

"Now, now, Mrs. Weinberg," the doctor said soothingly, "just tell me what happened. Did you follow my advice?"

"Yes," she wailed.

"You followed my directions exactly?"

"Well, not exactly. I didn't take the tablets at all until last night, about an hour before dinner. I know you said I should take half a tablet, but seeing how I didn't take any all week—ever since you gave them to me—I just thought it would be all right if I caught up by taking all four at once."

"Good heavens!" exclaimed the doctor. "What kind of a reaction did you get?"

"Don't ask. We were right in the middle of dinner when all of a sudden I got this awful compulsion. Not just a normal urge, doctor, but an absolutely *crazy* impulse. I didn't want to just make love to my husband, I wanted to—you should forgive the expression—*rape* him! I jumped up and dragged him out from his chair and practically threw him on the table. Yes, doctor—on the *table*! Just thinking about it makes me so embarrassed. It was terrible. All the dishes fell to the floor and got broken. A bottle of good wine was knocked over and ruined the expensive tablecloth. *Vay iz mir*—in my whole life I never even dreamed of behaving like that! I felt so cheap—like a *kurva*."

"This is dreadful!" said the doctor, his voice shocked. "In a way I feel partly responsible, too; even though you disregarded my instructions. I really shouldn't have given you more than half a tablet to begin with. So let me make amends. You said the dishes were broken, the wine spilled and the tablecloth ruined? All right, I'll pay for the damages."

"Damages? What good will damages do?" she wept. "In a million years they'll never let us into *that* restaurant again!"

* * *

While Baron de Rothschild was visiting in New York he decided to buy a gown for his wife. The saleslady in the exclusive shoppe brought out a series of very revealing dresses.

He looked them over, frowned and shook his head.

"No, Miss, these won't do at all," he said. "The way I feel about it, my wife is like dollars in the bank. As long as I know they're there, who needs to see them all the time?"

* * *

"I think the new ladies styles are awful," complained Mrs. Shapiro.

"What's so terrible?" asked her tolerant hubby. "By me, miniskirts are very nice."

"On miniskirts I'm not talking," retorted Mrs. S. "It's those new see-through blouses. And bra-less, yet!"

"Ah, yes," hubby sighed contentedly. "It's getting so, these days, a man can't look a girl straight in the eye."

* * *

Three years ago, Jack Jacobs was struggling along with his little manufacturing concern located in a second-floor loft. Then lady luck smiled on him—he hit on a design for his dress goods and the trade went wild over it. The next season, he created another design that was a fast seller and the third year he did it again. Jack was now a wealthy man. So he decided it was time he became a real 100% American and got himself a young and pretty mistress.

His roving eye soon fell on lovely Miss Bernstein, a model who worked for one of his customers. He immediately began his campaign, plying her with food, drink and glittering promises.

"I'll rent a town house for you," he said, "and you can have your own bank account and credit at all the best shops in the city. I'll visit you a couple of nights during the week and we'll spend all our weekends together. And if we find we've made a mistake, why we can always separate."

Miss Bernstein toyed with the idea and then shook her head.

"It sounds fine, the way you put it," she replied, "but what do we do with the mistake?"

* * *

The good people of Schenectady, New York, who happen to be more truthful than the bad people of Schenectady, New York, swear and avow that the following eerie occurrence actually happened to the Memel family in that fair city. But, a word of caution: If you do not believe in reincarnation, read no further.

Sol Memel, the very selfsame gentleman who achieved a measure of local fame when he once sold 300 boxes of *yahrzeit* candles to a visiting Arab dignitary on the pretext that they were Sioux Indian mementos, suffered a heart attack a few years after that episode and was cut down in the prime of his life. He couldn't have been much more than forty or so. A pity!

Mrs. Gussie Memel, his adoring wife, was inconsolable. Long after the traditional period of mourning, she was still grief-stricken. Nothing would do but that she contact the departed spirit of her late lamented husband. So she went to a spiritualist and requested a seance. When the medium had gone into his best professional trance, and the table shook a little and a horn blew nice, a voice was heard:

"Gussie, you're there?"

"Sollie! *Oh, Sollie!*" exclaimed Gussie, It's really you! I'd know your voice anywhere. Tell me, Sollie darling, how's by you?"

"Fine, Gussie. Couldn't be better!"

"It's nice there? You're happy?"

"Take my word, Gussie, I couldn't be happier. It's absolutely gorgeous here. The sky is blue like your eyes when we got married. Everywhere is bright green grass—mine favorite color grass. And such cows, Gussie! If only you could see them! There's brown cows, white cows, black cows, white and brown, brown and black, black and white—such beautiful cows you never saw in your whole life."

"In heaven they got cows?"

"Heaven? Who said anything about heaven? I'm a bull in Argentina!"

* * *

Melvin and Miriam were so engrossed in each other as they lay upon the grass that they did not even hear the approach of the policeman.

"Hey, you two," demanded the minion of the law, "what's the idea smooching like that in broad daylight? And right here by the side of the road, too. Ya oughtta be ashamed of yerselves."

"You don't understand, officer," said the quick-thinking Melvin. "I just had a flat tire and my lady friend here is helping me fix it."

"Tire?" echoed the policeman. "What tire?"

Melvin looked around and gasped.

"My God, Miriam, somebody stole the car!"

* * *

Right out of the Old West comes the saga of Two-Gun Tannenbaum, boss of the vast Double-Bar Mitzvah spread, boasting 50,000 longhorns and 100,000 other steers. So widely known was this famous cattleman that he was acclaimed as the biggest bull-shipper west of the Pecos.

* * *

Sam and Molly Berger, who arrived in this country as impoverished immigrants, had always dreamed that someday they would have their just share of the good life America offered. Through the combination of luck, pluck and hard work, they achieved their goal. Now, many years later, they were wealthy and proud of their *kultur* and "sushel" position.

Came the long-awaited day when their only daughter, Penelope, was ready to go off to finishing school, and the Bergers selected the fashionable Hyannis Port Academy for Young Ladies where, they hoped, their daughter would acquire the grace and manners consistent with the family's station in life. She might also, they hoped, meet eligible, marriage-minded young gentlemen of proper means and background when they came to visit their sisters at the posh academy.

Penelope had not been gone two weeks when Sam and Molly Berger received a letter from their daughter requesting that they airmail a book on etiquette to her.

"Well, well," beamed Sam, "those aristocrat boys she's dating, maybe meeting their families in their fancy homes makes it important she should have good breeding." So he and Molly happily sent her a copy of Emily Post's *Etiquette*.

Six months later, the parents received another request for a book on etiquette and proper social customs. This time the overjoyed father and mother sent her a copy of Amy Vanderbilt's *Etiquette and the Social Graces*.

During her second year at the exclusive school, Penelope arrived home for her summer vacation. Enfolded in her arms was a sweet little infant.

"Penelope," stammered her father, "whose baby is this?"

"Mine, daddy dear."

"And who is the papa, if I may be so bold?"

"I don't know," acknowledged Penelope.

Sam stared at his daughter, his face livid with astonishment and mounting anger. When he finally found his voice, he cried out:

"Two expensive books on etiquette you got and you don't even know how to ask, 'With whom am I having the pleasure?'"

* * *

"Theodore, tell us, please," began the professor in the human relations class, "can you love two girls at once?"

"Yes, *sir!*" responded Theodore enthusiastically. "Immediately!"

* * *

Teenaged Izzy looked up from the magazine he was reading. "Hey, pop, it says here in *Time* that more student riots are expected next semester. Did they have all these campus protests when you were in college?"

The father shook his head. "No, son," he replied in a nostalgic voice. "In my day, student bodies were interested only in student bodies."

* * *

Elsie, in her second year at Roosevelt High School in the Bronx, wasn't exactly the world's champion speller, but her heart was in the right place. In a composition on "The Sanctity of Marriage," she wrote:

"There are millions of nice-looking, lonely women who are un-attacked and hungry for love."

Glossary

A klug tsu Columbus: "A curse to (on) Columbus." A hyperbolic term used when things go wrong in America. Also worded: *A klug oyf Columbus.*

A mazel auf Columbus: May Columbus have such luck. Opposite in connotation to the above.

Aleph-Baiz (Aleph-Bess): The first two letters of the Yiddish-Hebrew alphabet, itself called "The Aleph-Baiz" just as the English language alphabet is referred to as the "The ABC's." The Sephardic pronunciation is *Aleph-Bet.*

Alteh: Old one, when referring to a woman; *Altehr* when referring to a man.

Areyngekrokhn in frimorgen: "Crept in at dawn" or "early morning." (From a line of poetry: *Di klayneh fenster vu di zun hot areyngekrokhn in frimorgen*—"The little window where the sun came creeping in at morn."

Ashkenazi: Singular form of *Ashkenazim.*

Ashkenazim: A Hebrew word meaning "German." The name applied to the Jews of Germany and North France beginning with the 10th century. In the 16th century, *Ashkenazim* came to include Jews of Eastern Europe as well. They developed their own customs and rituals, in contradistinction to the Jews of the Spanish and Mediterranean countries, who were called *Sephardim.*

Azay: Properly *Azoi.* Just as Americans in the north and south pronounce certain words differently (fire as fahr, cement as *seement,* Chicago as Chic*awguh*), Jews in various regions of the diaspora have developed local pronunciations. *Azay* has been used in some of the anecdotes in this book to capture the authentic flavor of the local idiom exactly as told to the author. (See *Azoi,* below.)

Azay es gevayn: "It was like that," or "that's the way it was."

Azoi: This is a type of comment similar to the Japanese "Ah-so!" and its connotation is, "Really!" or "You don't say!" But it can also be used to indicate "This is how"—as in *Azoi dertzailt men a vitz?* (Yes, the word *vitz* means "joke.")

Baal ha-bais (bal ha-bos): Pl. *Baal-batim.* An efficient householder. Used in the context of some of the stories in this volume, the *baal-batim* are also those well-to-do members of a *shul* who are generous contributors, and who conduct synagogue affairs with skill and dignity.

Bagel: A hard roll shaped in the form of a ring, resembling a doughnut;

419

the dough is boiled and then baked. Usually sliced down the middle and then spread with cream cheese and lox.

Balabatish: Respectable.

Balaboosteh: See *Baal ha-bais.*

Bar Mitzvah: Literal meaning is "son of the commandment." It is a religious ceremony at which time the Jewish lad of thirteen (actually thirteen years and one day) becomes obligated to observe all religious *mitzvot* (commandments). He becomes a full-fledged member of the Jewish community.

Beblach: Beans. Also see *Bopkes*

Bissel (Bis'l): Small in amount or of quantity.

Biz a hundert un tsvantsik: "Until a hundred and twenty." (A benediction meaning you should live many years.)

Bleib: As used in these pages, it means "stay" or "remain."

Blintzes: Cheese, *kasha* (groats) or berries rolled in thin dough and fried in fat. The French would call them *crèpes suzettes*. There is no singular form for the word *blintzes* because who eats just one?

Bobeh: Grandmother.

Bobeh myseh: Literally, a grandmother's tale. Actually, it refers to a story that is a complete fabrication; a fairy tale or a lie.

Bopkes: Beans.

Borscht: A soup made of beets or cabbage. The beet *borscht* may be eaten hot or cold, with or without sour cream. The cabbage *borscht* is served piping hot and is especially good with pumpernickel bread.

Bris (B'rit): Covenant (of Abraham): the act and ceremony of circumcision, performed on the eighth day after the birth of the boy, unless it has to be postponed for health reasons.

Broyges: Angry.

Challeh: Rich white bread usually associated with Sabbath or holy day feasts. In our "affluent society" however, *challeh* may be eaten at any time.

Chanukah: Holiday commemorating the victory of the Maccabees in the year 165 B.C.E. It is celebrated for eight days beginning on the 25th day of the month of *Kislev.* One of its traditions is the lighting of candles for eight days as a reminder of the miracle of the cruse of oil which burned for eight days instead of one. It is a festival most popular with children who enjoy lighting the candles, receiving traditional gifts of money *(Chanukah gelt)* and playing appropriate games, especially the *dreidel* which is a top with four Hebrew letters: *Nun, Gimmel, Hay* and *Shin.* These letters stand for *Nes Galol Hayah Sham,* or "A great miracle happened there." *Chanukah* marks what was probably the first struggle for religious freedom in history.

Chasseneh: Wedding.

Chassid (pl. *Chassidim;* adj. *Chassidic*): The word itself means "pious." In actual reference it is a follower or member of the *Chassidic* movement which was founded by Israel Baal Shem Tov in the 18th century. While *Chassidism* has lost its significance as a mass movement, it is still practiced by numerous small groups—some as close as the Williamsburg section of Brooklyn, New York.

Chazan: A cantor.

Cheder (Heder): Jewish parochial school for the teaching of the Bible, Hebrew, history, prayers, etc.

Chochem: A wise man or sage. In the vernacular it is also used sarcastically as a "wise guy." Paradoxically, *chochem* can also denote a simpleton who will believe anything; as in the jeering expression, "Tell that *bobeh myseh* to your *chochem fun Chelm!*"

Cholerya: Cholera; also pronounced *Cholyera.*

Chozzer: Pig; glutton. *Chazir* is the Hebrew word for pig.

Chozzerei: Piggish, piglike, slop.

Chupah, Chupeh: The canopy under which the bride and groom stand during the wedding ceremony.

Chutzpah: Impudence; unmitigated nerve.

Daven: From the Hebrew expression *davnen,* meaning "to pray." The origin of the word is not definitely established, though some say it is connected with the Latin *divino.*

Diaspora: Exile; dispersion of Jews after the conquest of Palestine by the Romans in 70 C.E. Also called *Galuth,* or in Yiddish, *Golos,* referring to the collective lands of Jewish dispersion.

Di hoyz vu ich bin gevayn geboyrn: "The house where I was born."

Dinchazzan: "To study" or "to learn" by heart. One may learn by the process of *dinchazzan,* memorizing or absorbing by rote. The word may also be used as a noun: one who learns (He is a real *dinchazzan.*)

Din Torah: A Hebrew term applied to a trial held in accordance with the principles of Jewish law. A rabbi nearly always presided over the *din torah.*

Dort or *Dorten:* There.

Dreidel: A top which is spun with the fingers. (See *Chanukah.*)

Dumkopf (Dumkup): Literally a "stupid head," a dumb-bell.

Dus: This.

Echot: Also. Often pronounced *oichet.*

Efsher: Maybe, perhaps.

Eppes: Something.

Eretz Yisrael (Eretz Yisroel): The land of origin of the Jewish people: "The land of Israel." The State itself is called *Medinat Israel.*

Ess: Eat. *Ess a bis'l eppes*—"Eat a little something."

Fahrshtunkene: stinking

Feeselach: Feet (dim.) The mother who kisses her baby's toes (Jewish mothers are notorious infant-toe kissers) will exclaim, "What pretty little *feeselach,*" rather than *feese* (feet).

Feh: An exclamation of disgust or distaste.

Fenaigler: A con man; a conniver.

Folkskeit: That which pertains to the nature or traditions of the masses—the *folk.*

Forvertz: Forward, progress. The anglicized name of the Yiddish daily newspaper in New York, *The Forward.*

Fress: To gobble up one's food; to eat to excess. The difference between *ess* and *fress* is that in the former, one eats in a civilized manner; in the latter, like a *chozzer* at the trough.

Froy: A housewife; wife. Originally the German *Frau.*

Frume Yid: An ultra-religious or extemely pious Jew.

Galernter: A learned one; a scholar. (He's a regular *galernter!*")

Galitzianer: A Jew from Galicia.

Gan Eden: Heaven.

Gantseh: Whole.

Gedenk: Remember.

Gefilte fish: A variety of fish (usually carp, pike and white fish) fileted, and chopped up fine with spices added. It is shaped in round servable portions and dropped into broth to simmer until cooked. Originally, a Sabbath and holiday delicacy.

Gegent: Neighborhood, district.

Gehakhta leber: Chopped liver.

Gehakhta tsuris: While *gehakhta* means "chopped" and *tsuris* means "trouble," in this case the expression means "utter misery."

Gehenna: Hell.

Gelacht: Laughed. Sometimes pronounced *gelachen.*

Gelt: Money.

Gemara: That part of the Talmud which is an elaboration of the Mishna.

Genz: Geese.

Genzineh gribben: Goose fat, rendered and spiced. Gribben is also referred to as *gribbenes.*

Gevald (Gevaldt): Help!

Gezenge, marshe mit tentze: Songs, marches and dances. The *Gezenge, Marshe mit Tentze:* A social club that flourished on New York's lower east side in the early 1920's.

Goldeneh Medina: "The Golden Land," referring specifically to America.

Golem: A term used in Jewish folklore to describe a robot made of clay or wood and given artificial life with the aid of magic, or the use of the Divine name. The express purpose of these living automatons was to protect the Jews from menacing dangers, and were usually under the spell and control of their creators. They could, however, become destructive if not checked. The *Golem* is mentioned in the Talmud, in medieval folk literature, and in modern stories.

Goniff (Ganeff, Ganev): A thief. The correct pronounciation of this word, which is basically Hebrew, is *Ganav* (pl. *Ganavim*).

Gornisht (Gornit): Nothing.

Gornisht mit leber: An ironic expression, literally meaning "nothing with liver," but actually denoting little or no recompense or reaction. ("For my efforts I received *gornisht mit leber.*")

Gottenyu: The diminutive form for God. (For a further description of the Russian-Polish suffix *nyu,* see listing for *Mamenyu.*)

Gott sie dank: Thank God! Also pronounced *Gott zai dank.*

Gott zol oftn. God forbid!

Goy (pl. *Goyim*): Gentile.

Goyishe: That which pertains to gentiles; un-Jewish.

Gribben, Gribbenes: Fat of a fowl that has been rendered and spiced. More precisely, well-browned roasted bits of goose skin.

Griener: A greenhorn; a new arrival to this country, especially one who lacks the most basic knowledge of American ways and customs.

Griven: See *Gribben.*

Haimish, Haimisheh: Homey, friendly.

Hamantashen: A pastry designed specifically for *Purim*, and shaped into a triangle like Haman's three-cornered hat. The dough is filled with either a prune paste, a cheese filling, or poppy seeds.

Helzel: Neck of a fowl. In Jewish cookery, *helzel* refers to the neck-skin of a turkey, goose, chicken or duck, and it is stuffed with meal, egg, spices, etc., to make a tasty dish.

Himmel: Heaven.

Hockflaish: Hock means "chop and *"flaish"* means "meat." Together they spell "chopped meat" or (you should pardon the expression) "hamburger."

Hoyz: House.

Ich (Ikh): The personal pronoun, "I."

Ingeleh: Little boy. A boy is an *ingel* (and a girl is a *maidel*), but when the suffix "eh" is added, it is so much more tender and diminutive. Also pronounced *yingel* or *yingeleh.*

Irisher Yontif: An expression attributed to James J. (Jimmy) Walker, Mayor of New York City from 1925 to 1932, to describe an Irish holiday-gathering where "the water flowed like wine and the wine flowed like whiskey." While *Irisher Yontif* is a Yiddish expression for "Irish holiday," it was apparently originated by Irish-American Walker and later picked up by the fun-loving Jewish community.

Kaftan: Long black coat worn by East European Jews.

Kalah, Kaleh: A bride.

Katchkeh: Duck

Kaynmol gevayn: "Never happened," or "never was," or, "at no time did a specific thing occur."

Kibitzer: A spectator at a card (or other) game who gives uninvited advice; one who jokes and chitchats while others are trying to work or play.

Kimmel (Kiml, Kim'l): Caraway seeds, used in the baking of bread and rolls, and in the distilling of liquor.

Kinderlach: The plural of *kind* (child) is *kinder,* and the affectionate or diminutive form of *kinder* is *kinderlach.*

Kishkeh: Stuffed intestine. On some menus this is listed as "derma."

Klayneh: Small; little. As in *klayneh maidel* (little girl), or *klayneh hoyz* (small house). *Klayneh* refers to small in size; *bissel* refers to small in quantity.

Knaidlach (sing. *Knaidel*) Matzoh-balls.

Knish: A fried or baked turnover or roll of dough with a filling, as of meat, cheese or potato. Usually used in its plural form: *Knishes.*

Kosher: Food prepared according to Jewish ritual law. Relates to the slaughter of animals, preparation of food and dietary regulations. The Jewish dietary laws are based on biblical law and were elaborated upon in the Talmud. These laws distinguish between foods which are *kosher* (permissable) and *traif* (forbidden).

Kreplach: Dough filled with meat and boiled. The Chinese call them *won ton* and the Italians have a version which they call *ravioli.*

Kugel: Noodle or bread pudding usually cooked with raisins.

Kurva: A prostitute.

Lach (Lakh): Laugh.

Landsman (pl. *Landsleit):* Countryman; someone who comes from your hometown.

Latkes: (sing. *Latkeh):* *Chanukah* is the time for this delicious pancake. It is made of grated raw potatoes, onion, egg, and seasoning, all mixed thoroughly and fried. The singular form, *latkeh*, is seldom used, although it is a perfectly permissable word, because eating just one is as impossible as eating one potato chip or peanut.

Le'chayim: A drinking toast. Figuratively, "To your health," "Here's mud in your eye," "Bottoms up," etc...*Chayim*, literally means "life."

Lekach: A brown honeycake.

Litvak: Lithuanian Jew.

Lokshn: Noodles.

Lox: Smoked salmon.

Luftmentsch: A dreamer, an idealist. A builder of castles in the air.

Maggid: A preacher; usually an itinerant preacher.

Malach: Angel.

Malach-Hamoves: Angel of death; a ghost.

Mamenyu: In that inimitable manner of the Jews, the diminutive for mama has the Russian-Polish *nyu* added as a suffix to become the very endearing *mamenyu*. Similarly, *tateh* (father) becomes *tatenyu*. And when *mamenyu* raises her eyes to the ceiling and moans *Tatenyu* (note the capitalized "T"), she is of course, addressing God whom she frequently refers to affectionately as *Gottenyu*.

Mashiach: See *Mosheeach*

Mazel: Luck.

Mazel tov: Good luck!

Megillah: A scroll. Although, technically, there are five scrolls, or *Megillot*, in the Bible, only the Book of Esther is known as **the** *Megillah*. It is read on *Purim* eve and *Purim* morning. In the vernacular, a *megillah* is used freely to indicate a long and complicated story. *Megillah* is a common word, especially around show-biz people.

Mentsch: Man, person. Often used admiringly to denote a gentleman or a decent person. ("He's a real *mentsch*!"). Also used to describe strength of character ("Be a *mentsch* and stand up for your rights!" or, "If you were any kind of *mentsch* you'd marry the girl!").

Mezuzah (pl. Mezuzoth): A small metal or wooden case containing a handwritten piece of parchment on which are inscribed 22 lines from Deuteronomy (6:4-9 and 11:13-21) dealing with the Jew's obligation to love God and to obey His commandments. The reverse side of the parchment bears the name *Shaddai* (Almighty), plus three additional words meaning "God, our Lord, is God." This case is attached to the right doorpost of the house as one enters, and also on the doorpost of each room used for living purposes. Actually, the word *mezuzah* means "doorpost."

Minyon (Minyan): Quorum of 10 adult males required before public religious services may be held. Women are now demanding the right to participate in the *minyon*, but don't hold your breath until it happens.

Mishnah (Mishna): The earliest section of the Talmud consisting of the collection of oral laws edited by Rabbi Judah ha-Nasi, circa 200 C.E. The *Gemara* is an elaboration of the *Mishnah*.

Mishpocheh: Family, relatives.

Mohel: Circumciser.

Momzer: Bastard.

Mosheeach: Messiah.

Nacht: Night.

Nahr: A fool; an ignorant person.

Nahrishkeit: Foolish, foolishness.

Nash: See Nosh.

Noch: As used in some of the anecdotes in this book, it means, loosely, "yet!" as in, "I should have twins, *noch*!" The word has several other meanings, such as "more," "again," etc.

Noch amol: One more time; once more.

Nosh (Nash): There are several variations of this word. Used as a verb, it means to eat something that tastes good. Moreover, it can also mean to "nibble" goodies between meals or at bedtime. To snack. Such a person is a *nosher*, or *nasher*. Used as a noun, a *nosh* is something that appeals to your sweet tooth.

Nu: This is a most versatile non-word. It can be used to urge someone to take action. It is also used to mean "well?" or "so?" or "so what?" and "what about it?" and so on.

Nudgeh: Nagged; goaded.

Nudnik: A bore; a pest. Best illustrated thusly: A *nudnik* is a person who, when asked how he is, really tells you how he is—from his headache to his ingrown toenails.

Oy: An exclamation denoting either pain or surprise, and sometimes even rapture. It all depends on the inflection—and, of course, on how many *oy's* you say, sigh or scream: *oy, oy!* or *oy, oy, oy!*, and occasionally, even five or six *oy, oy's*.

Oysgematert: Tired out. ("How do you feel?" *Oysgematert!*")

Oy vay: You already know what *oy* means (see above). When you add *vay* to it, you are adding "woe." And if you hear an overprotective mother exclaim: *"Oy vay iz mir!"* she is saying "Oh, woe unto me!" and is probably rushing her mischievous young one to the sink to stop his nose-bleed.

Paskudnyak: A nauseating individual. In plain English, a louse.

Passover: The spring festival which commemorates the deliverance of the Jews from their bondage in Egypt. It lasts eight days, beginning on the 15th day of the Hebrew month *Nisan* (March-April). It is a time when only Passover foods are eaten (matzoh and such), and only on special Passover dishes.

Peltz: A lined, fur coat worn by men.

Pesach: The Hebrew word for Passover. (See above.)

Peyess: Side curls or earlocks, worn by very orthodox Jewish males, particularly Chassidic Jews.

Peygern zol ehr: The word *peyger (payger)* means "perish" or "die." Loosely, as quoted in these pages, the term means, "He should drop dead!"

Pogrom: Organized compaigns of persecution, usually accompanied by robbery, physical injury and sometimes death. *Pogroms* were often instigated or supported by the State, the church, or both. The worst culprits in modern times were Russia and Poland, and of course Nazi Germany.

Pogromchiks: Ruffians who were part of the gangs that pillaged, beat and murdered Jews in Russia, usually under Czarist command or tolerance.

Ponem (Punem): Face. (A pretty girl would have a *shayneh ponem.)*

Poopik (Pippik): Technically, this means a belly-button or navel. But it is used freely in Yiddish to denote something small and insignificant. It is even personalized when the individual referred to is called "Moishe Pippik" and, as such, it means "Mr. Nobody."

Pootehr (Pittehr): Butter.

Potch: A slap or smack.

Purim: Festival of Lots, marking the deliverance of the Jews from Haman's plot to exterminate them as described in the Book of Esther. It is celebrated on the 14th day of the Hebrew month *Adar* (March). Children enjoy Purim carnivals when they can dress up like Ahasuerus or Mordecai, Esther, and even like the villain, Haman. Children and adults participate in "beauty contests" in which the lovely Queen Esther is selected. *Hamantashen* are the traditional delicacy of the holiday.

Pushkes (sing. *Pushke):* Small tin boxes with coin-slots on top. These charity boxes were nailed up on the wall (often whether the apartment or house-dweller liked it or not) by a little old man with a black bag, who emptied the boxes every week. A number of groups and organizations vied with each other for the coins, and many homes were lined with several *pushkes.* The money was collected for Jewish orphans, widows and the desperately poor who had even less than the poverty-stricken Jews who contributed the coins.

Raycher: A rich man. Also spelled *Reicher.*

Rebbe: Teacher; title given to a learned or respected man. It is also used as the equivalent of "mister."

Rebbetzyn: Wife of a rabbi. Also spelled *Rebbetzn.*

Saichel: Good common sense; good judgment. That common sense is multiplied when it is referred to as *Yiddishe saichel.*

Schmaltz: Usually chicken or goose fat which has been rendered. It has been freely adapted into the English language, particularly in show business, to denote anything well larded with corny sentiment. Schmaltz is delicious when spread on a piece of pumpernickel bread and lightly salted.

Schnapps: Any strong alcoholic beverage. The "aperitif" was very popular among Jewish families who could afford it—but it was called a *schnapps.*

Schvartze: Derived from the German *schwartz,* meaning "black." As used in this book, the word refers to a Negro. There is nothing pejorative in the term, any more than the use of *goy,* which simply means "gentile."

Sephardim: A Hebrew term denoting Jews of Spanish and Portuguese origin. Expelled from Spain by the Inquisition of 1492, the Sephardi Jews were dispersed throughout the Turkish Empire as well as Europe and, later, in North and South America. The customs, language, rituals, traditions and synagogue services of the Sephardim differ markedly from the *Ashkenazim.* The Sephardi pronunciation of Hebrew is basically that which is used today in Israel.

Shabbes: Sabbath.

Shadchan: A marriage broker; professional matchmaker.

Shaigetz: A male gentile; a *goy;* sometimes applied to a Jew who is ignorant of Jewish customs or Judaism in general.

Shalom: Literally "peace." It is also used to denote hello or goodbye.

Shammes: The sexton of a synagogue.

Shandeh: A shame.

Shayneh: A good-looking girl or woman. A handsome man is called a *shayner.*

Shifskart: Ship's passenger ticket. *Shifskart gelt* refers to the passage money for the voyage.

Shikker: A drunkard.

Shikse: The feminine of *shaigetz* (see above).

Shlemiel: One who is clumsy, inept and a dolt.

Shlepper: This is the noun taken from the verb *shlep,* which means "to pull or drag." When used as a noun it is quite unflattering, and means someone who just drags along without ever achieving anything. When used about a woman, it conjures up a total picture of someone whose slip is showing, whose hair is bedraggled, and whose nose is running.

Shmatteh: Rag. The complaining wife will often weep that's all she has to wear. If she steps all over her husband, he becomes a *shmatteh*.

Shnook: In the English vernacular, "a jerk." Somewhere between a *shlemiel* (see above) and a *shlimazl* (the perennial "hard-luck Harry") —except that the *shnook* has most of the problems of both. Sometimes, it simply means "an ordinary guy."

Schnorrer: A beggar.

Shoichet: Ritual slaughterer.

Shtetl: Small town, village or hamlet.

Shul: Synagogue.

Shund: Trash.

Streimel (Shtreimel): A fur hat worn by *Chassidim*.

Talmud: A Hebrew word meaning "study" or "teaching." It is also the name for a library of books (63 volumes) which contain a record of rabbinical comments on the teachings of the Bible. Although dealing primarily with law, the *Talmud* also contains a rich store of historic facts and traditions. In its pages are found scientific discussions, ethical teachings, legends, and profound observations on all phases of human experience.

Tanteh: Aunt.

Tateh: Father; papa; daddy.

Torah: Term variously applied to the first five books of the Bible and the Pentateuch. Also an overall term for Jewish learning and law.

Traif: Food which, according to dietary law, is ritually impure and unfit for consumption. Not *kosher*. Also pronounced *traifa*.

Tsailt mir eppes: "Tell me something." Also expressed as *Der tzailt mir eppes*.

Tsibileh: Onion. Plural: *Tsibiles*.

Tsimmis: A sweet dish in which carrots and prunes are mixed with honey and several other ingredients. It is eaten as a side dish.

Tsuris (Tsouris, Tsorres): Troubles, miseries.

Tuchus: A person's rear end.

Tzaddik: A righteous man. In *Chassidism*, the title given to the leader of a sect.

Umglik: Tragic.

Ver Fahrblunjet: Get lost.

Yahrzeit: The memorial anniversary of the date of death.

Yarmulke: Skull cap worn by religious Jews.

Yenta (Yenteh): Someone who sticks her nose into everyone else's business; a busybody; a gossip and tattle-tale. And Jews, being the wits they are, sometimes give the one they are calling "*Yenteh*" a surname: *Yenteh Tellabendeh*. The surname does little else than rhyme with *yenteh*.

Yeshivah: Rabbinical academy; talmudic college.

Yiddishe saichel: Native Jewish sense (See listing for *saichel.)*

Yiddishkeit: That which pertains to the nature or traditions of the Jewish people; Jewishness.

Yidden (Yid'n): Jews.

Yingatsh: A young smart-alec; a fresh kid; or, to put it bluntly, a snotnose.

Yom Kippur: Day of Atonement. The most solemn of all Jewish holidays during which time one abstains from all food and drink for twenty four hours.

Zaftik: Buxom, pleasingly plump.

Zin: Son.

Zun: Sun.